the elvis films

Jon Abbott

for my Uncle Ivor and my mother-in-law Jean,

the other two Elvis admirers in the family

ISBN 13 978-1500509972

ISBN 10 1500509973

© Jon Abbott, 2006, 2014

Also by Jon Abbott

Irwin Allen Television Productions, 1964-1970: A Critical History of
Voyage to the Bottom of the Sea, Lost in Space, The Time Tunnel, and Land of the Giants

McFarland, 2006

Stephen J. Cannell Television Productions: A History of All Series and Pilots

McFarland, 2009

"When I was a child, ladies and gentlemen, I was a dreamer. I read comic books and I was the hero of the comic book. I saw movies, and I was the hero in the movie. So every dream that I ever dreamed has come true a hundred times".

Elvis Presley, accepting an award in January, 1971

"The mistake which most critics make is to persist in trying to evaluate pop culture as if it were something else: the equivalent of insisting on considering a bicycle as if it were a horse. And this fallacy is by no means confined to the opponents of pop culture. Many sympathetic critics have subscribed to it with equal conviction"

--George Melly, writing in December 1966, for his 1970 publication *Revolt into Style--The Pop Arts in Britain,* Penguin Books.

contents of book

introduction--a personal note   9

part one: the early films   17

Love Me Tender; Loving You; Jailhouse Rock; King Creole; G.I. Blues; Flaming Star; Wild in the Country

part two: the sunny '60s   55

Blue Hawaii; Follow That Dream; Kid Galahad; Girls! Girls! Girls!; It Happened at the World's Fair; Fun in Acapulco; Kissin' Cousins; Viva Las Vegas; Roustabout; Girl Happy; Tickle Me; Harum Scarum; Frankie and Johnny; Paradise, Hawaiian Style; Spinout; Easy Come, Easy Go; Double Trouble; Clambake; Speedway

part three: the dreadful mistakes   197

Stay Away Joe; Live a Little, Love a Little; Charro; The Trouble with Girls; Change of Habit appendix 1--the documentaries   224

Elvis--That's the Way it Is; Elvis on Tour

appendix 2--the Elvis impersonators; Elvis on TV   231

appendix 3--chronology   243

appendix 4--closure   247

appendix 5--sources and bibliography   260

index   265

introduction--a personal note

I must admit to being something of an unusual Elvis fan, in as much as I love his movies. Many Elvis fans didn't, and neither did Elvis himself, very much. As a result, his films have never received much critical attention other than knee-jerk put-downs from film snobs who have pre-judged them, derogatory remarks from the uninitiated, and throwaway footnotes from admirers who understandably would rather concentrate on his magnificent music. When a man single-handedly changes the course of popular music with one of the most pure, passionate, and original sounds of the 20th century, it's tough to care about his sideline occupations. However, Elvis Presley wanted to be an actor as much--if not more--as he wanted to be a singer. In fact, he was a singer. That was the reality. The Hollywood film star was the fantasy.

Often, commentators are uninterested in these films' place in pop culture, oblivious to their merits, and all too eager to announce their failings, perceived and real. This seems to be true of the best and the worst of Elvis reference sources, all of them primarily interested in other aspects of Elvis Presley. Fair enough. But my cussedness in actually enjoying the Presley movies doesn't stop there; I prefer the fluffy, sunny vapid romances of the 1960s to such semi-serious fare as *Love Me Tender* and *Jailhouse Rock*. Again, most Elvis fans don't.

However, there are several factors to explain this radical position. Firstly, born in 1956, I'm just that little bit too young to have been influenced by Elvis in my teens. I was completely oblivious to the Elvis hysteria sweeping the United States as I entered the world in Britain in June, 1956! I was a child in the '60s and a teenager in the '70s, so I was merely aware of Elvis Presley rather than passionate about him.

This in no way diminished my admiration or respect for Elvis, which has actually grown over the years, partly through recognition of his importance and his charisma, and partly, I admit, through nostalgia; he represents an era that never was, or perhaps partly was, idealised youth in a summer that never ends in a country where the pursuit of happiness is enshrined in its birth. Despite the fashionable credibility of Carnaby Street, the Oxbridge satirists, and the Mersey beat, most kids in stuffy, shabby, austere, WWII-obsessed Britain in the 1960s drooled over the sunny skies, huge finned cars, wide freeways, towering buildings and bustling cities we knew as America. I was raised on a heady diet of Tamla Motown, Hanna-Barbera, *The Man from UNCLE,* pulp sci-fi, *Batman,* and Marvel Comics. I could not have cared less about wartime nostalgia or the 1966 Football World Cup, although many others cared more.

I knew Elvis Presley's place in rock and roll history, and acknowledged it, and was as saddened as anyone when he died suddenly in 1977, shortly after I turned twenty-one. But my memories of Elvis are not those of '50s Elvis, the grainy Elvis of *The Ed Sullivan Show,* the rebellious Elvis, the Elvis brought to heel by the authorities who sent him into the army to break him and succeeded only in breaking his mother. In the long hot summers of my youth in the '60s, that Elvis and those concerns were already old news.

My memories of Elvis Presley are of Saturday evening or Sunday afternoon films set in a sunny, sexy America English kids could only dream of. I was in love with American pop culture--the wacky sit-coms like *The Beverly Hillbillies, The Flintstones,* and *The Munsters,* the giant bug movies, the glossy sci-fi series, the cop shows, the New York city of the Universal backlot and the Marvel super-heroes, the picket-fence suburbs of the feel-good movies, the walk and talk of the comic-book gangsters in the James Cagney films and *The Untouchables*. I was a naive, well-spoken, good-natured, shy, stand-up, lower middle class English boy in his own little world that I could neither leave, nor wanted to.

From this perspective, rather than that of a hip-swivelin', fist-throwin' rock and roll rebel, I had sucked up the Elvis movies. We may have had the Beatles and the Rolling Stones (I was too young for swingin' London too), but America had wide roads and bright red sports cars, and in the Britain outside the London hot spots it looked pretty damn good--bigger and better, sunnier and shinier--no serial killer TV shows or moronic Presidents just yet. Hollywood told us that in the U.S.A. the men were taller and tougher, the girls were prettier and friendlier, and the cars and buildings a fabulous backdrop that looked better than any of them. I knew nothing of the Cold War or Vietnam until both were history, and when America became immersed in the disillusion of post-Vietnam, post-Woodstock, post-Watergate despondency, that, too, was more interesting to a long-haired 1970s teenager than the problems of poor old Blighty and the endless rain and strikes.

And while Britain suffered through Thatcherism, I was lapping up slick American comedies and the fantasies of Steven Bochco and Stephen J. Cannell. My musical tastes through these decades ranged from the Beatles and Motown (how lonely I was among my schoolfriends in my appreciation of Marvin Gaye, Diana Ross, Al Green, and Curtis Mayfield) to Bob Dylan and Patti Smith. I didn't really begin to listen to 1950s sounds until the deadly duo of punk and disco drove me to it in the late '70s and vile 1980s. As films became grimmer and more derivative, and music became sleazier and crummier, I found myself re-evaluating and rediscovering the pop culture of my past. Or perhaps I was just getting old.

Elvis films, of course, had never gone away. I had moved on from them, and now I was sidling back. The plots of the Elvis films were simple, because they were supposed to be. I didn't want drama from Elvis films, then or now, and when things went wrong for him, I wanted the situation resolved as quickly as possible so that we could get to the next musical set piece. There had to be misunderstandings and disappointments for his characters or there would have been even less plot than there was, but I wanted them sorted out, not dragged out. I wanted happy, carefree, easygoing films, and in the early '60s, that's what Elvis was delivering--the best feel good mind candy in the sweetshop of '60s cinema, and a little lighter on the sugar than Disney, a little less patronising and more sophisticated than Jerry Lewis, a lot less feminine and fluffy than Doris Day movies.

Back then, these films and all others took five years to reach television from the cinemas, and so that version of America was already the stuff of nostalgia by the time they started to filter onto TV in the late '60s. By the time Elvis was doing the hula-hula in Hawaii or diving off rocks in Acapulco, flower power was wilting and American cinema had ditched beach parties for biker movies and druggie dramas. But Britain needed Elvis movies more in the '70s than it did in the '60s anyway. To me, the perfect Elvis film is *Viva Las Vegas, Blue Hawaii, Girl Happy, Spinout, Clambake,* or *Speedway.*

Others, like *Double Trouble* and *Harum Scarum* were fun, but a little weird. They were caper movies, and I liked to see Elvis winning and confident, and in the environment I expected. Nevertheless, there were plenty of Elvis beach movies and sports car movies, and the capers made a pleasant second choice.

And then there were the earlier films, with the troubled Elvis, the ones the fans love, and the ones that gave him a chance to do some real acting. The wildly overrated *Jailhouse Rock* shows Elvis acting, and more importantly, it has Elvis at his peak, so it's not so bad. *Loving You* has Elvis in his prime, lots of him, and in color. *King Creole* has perhaps the best musical performances by Elvis ever committed to film. The westerns are just plain old westerns with the added plus of Elvis.

What were bad were the last few films he made. Painfully bad, dreadful mistakes, embarrassments to rank alongside Lee Marvin in *Paint Your Wagon* or Laurel and Hardy in *Atoll K*. Films like *Live a Little, Love a*

Little, *Stay Away Joe*, and *The Trouble with Girls* are bad in the way that so many late '60s films are bad, and the worse for deceptively sounding like the fluffy fantasies of the early '60s; *Charro* is all wrong and *Change of Habit* is an absolute disaster of the what-were-they-thinking? variety, a ludicrous travesty.

Consequently, for this book, I have divided the Elvis films into three categories--the early films (which I respect), the sunny '60s (which I love), and the dreadful mistakes (which are fascinating in their own awful way!). I am certainly indebted to Peter Guralnick's massive and comprehensive two volume biography of Elvis, *Last Train to Memphis* and *Careless Love*, which, although typically moving quickly through the Elvis films, provided a useful chronology, perspective, and several anecdotes, as well as a healthy and much-needed revision of the slimy Albert Goldman book.

I should also mention *The Elvis Presley Scrapbook* by James Robert Parish, which provided the most comprehensive cast lists for the Elvis movies, more detailed certainly than the spartan onscreen credits of the '60s, or most Elvis reference books, which think they're doing you a favor by listing the first five names in the cast.

Other facts, information and incidents related here come from various published interviews over the years with actors and actresses who worked with Elvis, the numerous books on Presley in the marketplace, and most significantly, and dominating this fresh and original work, my own extensive knowledge of 1960s TV and film.

I say most significantly, because Elvis films are usually written about as a footnote to his personal life or music career, by those whose expertise lies in those two areas, and rarely in relation with other films or TV of the time. However, my own particular expertise lies in the area of 20th century film and TV.

I have not sat down to write a book about the life of Elvis Presley, or the music of Elvis Presley. It's been done. In this book, I have considered the Elvis films not as an aberration of, or unwelcome intrusion into the insular Presley universe, even though this is how Presley and his associates usually and understandably viewed them, but as a significant part of the late 1950s and primarily 1960s pop culture they represented. It might be argued that I digress too much, that I bring in films and TV series that were "not Elvis", that I discuss actors and aspects not directly related to Presley's life. But that's the point.

The Elvis films did not exist in a Graceland-like vacuum, they co-existed not just alongside the Beatles, Tamla Motown, Dean Martin, and Woodstock, but Jerry Lewis, Peter Sellers, Brigitte Bardot, Doris Day, and

John Wayne... Batman, beach movies, Bond, Lucy, the Monkees, UNCLE, and the Beverly Hillbillies. They were very much a part of the 1960s that has been remembered and survived for us to enjoy today.

Importantly, and unusually, this book discusses how the Elvis Presley films related to--or, in some cases (*Frankie and Johnny, Easy Come, Easy Go*), did not relate to--the popular culture of the period (Elvis, in fact, loved film and TV). At the same time, at appropriate and relevant points, it considers 1960s attitudes in the media toward race, sex, the arts, the counter culture, and Elvis Presley himself.

Those commentators who malign Elvis Presley's '60s films and mourn the end of the *Jailhouse Rock* era are perhaps not thinking things through. Regardless of the Colonel's well-documented machinations and vetoes, the 1950s were over. Beach movies, biker movies, and spy films were on the way. Could Elvis Presley act? Yes. Would the material have been there? Nope. With hindsight, Elvis was better off chasing girls in Hawaii and Acapulco than trying to be an imitation James Bond, which would almost certainly have otherwise been his fate in the decade to follow. 1960s cinema and TV was not about serious dramatic acting, it was about escapism. Such escapism may have been into a shiny outer space, a cleaned up not-too-wild west, globetrotting secret agent fantasies, or a beach-front property stuffed with wild bikinis, but it was Austin Powers, not Tennesee Williams.

"Colonel" Parker, Hal Wallis, and Elvis Presley for that matter, worked with what they had got in terms of talent, material, and opportunities... not what might have been. There were certainly mistakes made, and these will be discussed... but there was much to be amused by and admire. And, as the more perceptive Elvis admirers and pop culture commentators have noted, sometimes reluctantly, sometimes not, Elvis was probably exactly where he should have been in the 1960s--in Hollywood, making family entertainment.

Elvis Presley made his mistakes, but he was an impressive guy. He was not cowed or assimilated by the American mainstream due to his time in the army (although it is ironic that instrument of the establishment was responsible for his introduction to drugs). Any of the rock stars who followed in Elvis Presley's footsteps would have raged and frothed at the mouth at the vicious injustice of being drafted out of malice, and then run for the hills, snapped like a twig, or employed a battalion of lawyers and PR people to get themselves out of it. Elvis fought back in a way most men, including myself, wouldn't have. He went reluctantly and in good spirits and he came back the same person, no better, no worse, just a little older, two valuable years of his life lost to him and rock and roll. He showed he was bigger and better than the small people and narrow minds who stalled him for two years. He beat them.

It's true he came out of the army with a different act, but he was not a different man. He was simply no longer a teenage child. In fact, Elvis was never a teen rebel, like James Dean, or a symbol of anti-authority like Marlon Brando, or a fugitive from conformity like Jack Kerouac, however much some of his admirers--and detractors--might have wanted him to be. He was a shy, respectful, church-going ordinary youth from an ordinary, dirt-poor part of America, who rather unfashionably believed in God and the flag, something most of my generation, including myself, didn't, and something many of his admirers--and detractors--could never accept. It wasn't Elvis who scared the powers-that-be, it was his music, and most of all, its ties to the rhythms and sexuality of the Negro race, what we call today the African-Americans. That's what scared the small minds of America and the rest of the world that Elvis touched and changed forever.

At first glance, the Elvis films may seem to be a curious, almost insignificant subject for serious study. There are, certainly, no secret meanings, intellectual messages, or hidden agendas in the Elvis Presley movies. The middle-aged, cigar-chewing, Hollywood writers involved with these films simply weren't that smart, and--certainly with no admonishment on my part--had no goal in mind other than a salary. Elvis had no say at all in his choice of films and was in no way an auteur, or even in charge of his own material. He literally quite simply turned up on the set. Therefore, we cannot over-intellectualise about these movies.

Elvis Presley is probably the most heavily documented person of the 20th century, and there is no known record of him choosing scripts, rewriting, wanting to direct, changing dialogue on the set, or objecting to anything enough to refuse to do it--even the puppet show in *G.I. Blues*, or "dragging up" briefly for *Girl Happy,* both of which he hated doing. The few times he did show an interest in the movie-making process, his entourage dragged him away. Time and again we are told by those who were there that he spent his time on the set breaking bricks and playing football. No-one, all available reference sources make quite clear categorically, was trying to send any messages other than those specifically on the screen.

However, popular culture tells us much, if not the most, about the society and times in which it was produced--moreso than the films and documentaries that attempt to record the times, because they tend to arrive with predetermined agendas. Certainly, the Elvis movies, James Bond, *Batman* and Woodstock reveal more about the 1960s than such films as, say,

Austin Powers--International Man of Mystery, The Dreamers, Taking Woodstock, or *Born in '68,* as entertaining as those films are.

One last thing. Readers of my first two books may have noticed that while those titles were published by McFarland (and to my great satisfaction), this latest book is self-published.

There are several reasons for this, not the least being that print-on-demand and tablets are the face of the future, and much more profitable than mainstream publishing, as well as being cheaper for you to buy and offering complete creative freedom to me, but I'll be upfront with you. The main reason is quite simply that this book has been completed since 2006 and trying to get into print since 2007. It is now 2014! It's not a bad book, as I hope you will agree. But this is how long it takes to submit, and re-submit, a book idea to a publisher and then wait for a reply in the 21st century. Literally, months.

When I submitted the idea to my previous publisher, confident in the knowledge that a book about Elvis was a commercial certainty, it turned out they had come to the same conclusion, and already committed to a different book on the Elvis films by another author. And while the months rolled by, and alternate publishers either admired or ignored my work, and for one reason or another, didn't reply, or couldn't commit, I worked on other projects. When another publisher passed on the Elvis project for exactly the same reason as McFarland a whole five years later, and then another interested in my work couldn't proceed because I hadn't mastered the computer technology to send it to him in the format he required, I realised I was in the same position I had been twenty years earlier when I forced myself to move on from the typewriter ribbon and learn word processing.

During the months I learned Word Perfect, publishers went from not wanting my work on disc to insisting on it. I saved myself from being left behind then, and now I had some more learning to do. It was at this point I became aware of the self-publishing phenomenon, and having initially dismissed it as vanity publishing for losers, I spent the next six months reading about it and the next few months trying to achieve it. As a wise person has pointed out, self-publishing is not for people who can't get published (bad books don't sell any more copies on the internet than they do in bookshops), it's for the people who could. I'd already proved I could — twice.

The Elvis Films was the obvious guinea-pig, and here it is. Finally! If you're reading further than *Look Inside,* or better still, holding an actual printed copy of *The Elvis Films* in your hands, then all gods willing, you can hope to see more of my work sooner, rather than much, much later.

Concluding chapters discuss the Elvis documentary films made for cinema release (although only those made during his lifetime, with his participation), and Elvis on TV. There is also a chronology of when the films went into production and when they were released, plus an alternate 'what if...?' timeline based on where Elvis' Hollywood career might plausibly have gone had he lived.

As we discuss and review the 33 Elvis Presley features made for the cinema, I hope readers will discover new nuggets of information and insights, rediscover old memories, and consider new opinions and perspectives. Although this book takes Elvis Presley and his movies seriously, the films themselves were most certainly not intended to be taken seriously, but made purely for the audience's pleasure and the participants' profit. They provided much of both. With that in mind, enjoy this book!

The Early Films

Love Me Tender (1956)

(formerly The Reno Brothers); wr. Robert Buckner, from Maurice Geraghty, dir. Robert Webb, pr. David Weisbart (Fox)

with Elvis Presley (Clint Reno), Richard Egan (Vance Reno), Debra Paget (Cathy), William Campbell (Brett Reno), Mildred Dunnock (Mrs. Reno), Neville Brand (Mike Gavin), Robert Middleton (Siringo), Bruce Bennett (Major Kincaid), James Drury (Ray Reno), Russ Conway (Ed Galt), Ken Clark (Kelso), Barry Coe (Davis), L.Q. Jones (Fleming), Paul Burns (Jethro), Jay Jostyn (Major Harris), Jerry Sheldon (train conductor), James Stone (storekeeper), Ed Mundy (auctioneer), Joe Di Reda (soldier), Bobby Rose (stationmaster), Tom Greenway (paymaster), Steve Darrell (second train conductor), and the Ken Darby Trio

Elvis sings: "We're Gonna Move" (impromptu dance on porch); "Love Me Tender" (ballad on porch); "Let Me" (at summer fair); "Poor Boy" (at summer fair)

Bizarrely, and as a sign of Presley's amazing sudden success during 1955 and '56, no-one involved in this film was initially aware they were making the first Elvis movie. All the actors involved, including leading man Richard Egan, an all-purpose upstanding tough guy type, and leading lady Debra Paget, who had met Elvis a few months earlier on *The Milton Berle Show,* had signed on to make a routine western titled *The Reno Brothers,* directed by the anonymous former cameraman Robert Webb (the potboiler story concerns a romantic triangle and some stolen money). For his part (although the Colonel had other ideas), Elvis had told audiences and interviewers that he would not be singing in his movies, but acting. In fact, Presley--like many young men--had never been keen on musicals of any kind when accompanying girls to the movies, disliking the way performers would suddenly break out of character and into song. It was an unfortunate and unusual trait for a professional singer to possess!

As it is, the songs in *Love Me Tender* fit into the film naturally--even the ghostly reprise of the title song at the film's end filmed a few weeks after the film wrapped to placate Elvis and his audience... not to mention Gladys Presley and Colonel Parker, both equally upset that Elvis' character died at the film's end for entirely different reasons! Music performed live (there was no other way to hear it in the Old West) was part of everyday life, although the scenes at the school fund-raising are hilariously anachronistic as Elvis wows a predominantly female audience squealing on cue! Up on a stage, he's at home and in charge, but in the other musical sequence in the film we see evidence of how green he still was, and how other more experienced actors could exploit his innocence. Watch how William Campbell shadows Elvis as he moves around the porch, trying to turn a scene in which Elvis performs into a scene about how much his character is enjoying the music!

Presley, not without cause, saw himself as the heir to James Dean, and perhaps less realistically, fancied himself as another Brando. He certainly possessed the looks and charisma, as well as the ambition and enthusiasm. As a teen idol, if not a performer, he might have carried it off.

The Colonel, and the other middle-aged men who managed his career, saw things somewhat differently. They demanded--as did Elvis' followers-- to hear the man sing. Also seeing things differently were the critics, to whom Presley was always remarkably diplomatic and tolerant given the prejudice and unpleasantness demonstrated by most of them. The exact opposite of blinkered fans who would hear no wrong, many of them were unreasonably hostile, and plainly motivated by malice, spite and envy. They lost all objectivity when reviewing anything by Presley, as any cuttings library or newspaper morgue will attest, writing the ugliest copy they could conjure up (the prestigious Life magazine called him a "howling hillbilly"; Presley never howled in his life).

Some were racist, resenting his popularisation and integration of black music with country, some were uptight prudes, infuriated by the sexuality of his performance, and others were intellectual bigots, snobs who looked down on rural America and saw in Elvis nothing more than a God-fearing hick. One only has to see Elvis' first scene in the movie to see the boy can act--and the one thing that immediately stands out is just how young he was at this point in time.

In a scene requiring him to run through every difficult emotion in the actor's repertoire, Presley acquits

Trading card for Love Me Tender showing the iconic image of cowboy Elvis

himself magnificently. First he must show surprise and joy when he sees his brother alive and well, then discomfort and pain when he realises his brother's hurt. It's a bravura performance that, to an unbiased observer, is a powerful confirmation that, had others wanted it as much as Presley, he might have been a fine dramatic actor. However, the world has plenty of fine, dramatic actors. It needed the one Elvis Presley much more. Paradoxically, had his music career not existed at that time, those same critics would surely have hailed this fresh young find.

Presley was eager to learn and to please, but the mean-spirited, small-minded minions of journalism outside the music press wanted only to mock and tear down. To read quotes from the reviews of his films and music in the mainstream press of the day is to see small men embarrassing themselves. In the years to follow, they would ridicule his lightweight movies, but had he attempted anything tougher, they would have put away their needles and stickpins and brought out the steak knives to tear into him.

Recent television exposure had moved Presley away from the security and passion of paying fans and into the homes of all and sundry, exposing his performances to people who hadn't sought them out. The prudes and the puritans didn't like what they saw or heard--black music reworked for white kids, spawned by hillbillies and country and western types, packaged and delivered with raw, unbridled sexuality. Racists, tightasses and pseudo-intellectuals were united in their dismay and the page-fillers of the press scented blood. Presley, like comic books, j.d. flicks, and monster movies, had been safe as teen culture for a teenage audience, but exposed to the outside world he was an easy and obvious target for the miserable and the mighty. He was the first pop performer to discover that when television presents an act to the wider public gaze and exposes that material to a larger, less appreciative audience that was previously in blissful ignorance... Well, teen culture has been taking a kicking ever since.

Presley was hardly the first popular performer to fall victim to the vultures of the press, of course. Sinatra had suffered resentment, envy and vilification from hostile small minds, but he was an arrogant bully offstage, who had courted disaster and bought some of it down on himself, and would continue to do so. Presley was a well-meaning, ambitious eager-to-please kid who had done nothing to deserve the opportunist abuse that was thrown at him when his act reached the masses, and it genuinely upset and shocked both him and his family. In fact, one of the factors that defused the initial hysteria so promptly was the uncomfortable reality for the fire and brimstone brigade that Elvis was a Church-going boy with a clean slate and a background in gospel singing. They would have loved him to be a sulky, leather-jacketed delinquent, but he wasn't. He was, in these early days, humble, courteous and polite. When Elvis responded to the antics of one bigoted churchman he professed genuine dismay that a man of the church could be so hurtful and intolerant to a fellow church-goer--after all, hadn't God given him his voice and talent? Unlike the more provocative acts of the '60s, '70s, '80s and on, which deliberately baited the bluenoses and Bible-thumpers for publicity and promotion (the Rolling Stones, the Sex Pistols, Madonna, the Spice Girls, and ever onward), Elvis had not set out to irritate or inflame the gullible or the impressionable. Time and again Elvis saw off prejudice and intolerance simply through his honest naivete and humility--it wasn't an act. He didn't accept that he'd done anything wrong, he would say, he had nothing to apologise for and couldn't understand what all the fuss was about. He was a young man who loved girls, music, and his family.

It was no carefully crafted act, there was nothing to expose or unravel. By never descending to the level of his critics, he confounded them and made them look like fools. And the louder the voice, the more hysterical the accusations, the more ignorant the assumptions, the bigger the fool they came out as. Today, it's all a carefully orchestrated game, but Presley had inadvertently attracted this attention, and for a short period during the summer of 1956, it was perceived by everybody except the cunning old Colonel as an obstacle to his career, and the injustice of it angered and upset him.

The mean-spirited response to his acting endeavors left him feeling much the same way. While the vast majority of the hostility generated by his TV appearances blew over within a few furious weeks, the films of Elvis would, for a variety of reasons to be discussed, invite lazy commentators into a new arena of effortless outrage and irrelevant controversy. The Colonel and the film producers, of course, bore Elvis no malice, and simply saw dollar signs. They worked for the good of their star, and despite the random factors that conspired to create *Love Me Tender,* they had a gameplan.

Meanwhile, in Hollywood, Elvis attracted the attention of ambitious young actor Nick Adams, an anxious, attention-seeking wannabe and hanger-on who had latched onto James Dean and Natalie Wood while in the supporting cast of *Rebel Without a Cause* (released posthumously after Dean's death in a road crash). Adams saw in Elvis a suitable replacement to idolise, and Elvis saw in Adams a guide to Hollywood. Over the next few months, Elvis would spend a fair amount of time with Adams and, briefly, a mostly unimpressed Natalie Wood, but Adams never secured a role in an Elvis movie.

He did secure roles in two unsuccessful TV series during the early '60s, the western series *The Rebel* (1959-'61) and the journalism drama *Saints and Sinners* (1962). After that, it was downhill into pulp sci-fi, each title a little less respectable than the one before, until he was found dead from a drugs overdose in 1968.

Richard Egan had made about a dozen films before *Love Me Tender* and would make another dozen afterwards, none of them particularly notable. His one TV series--*Empire,* reformatted as *Redigo*--struggled and died. "Elvis had a dramatic part, and he showed extraordinary ability to catch on" said Egan. "I liked him. When Elvis came to the set he was very modest. He realized he hadn't had any experience as an actor, and he wasn't afraid to ask for help. And he remained very direct, very straightforward".

Debra Paget (real name, Debralee Griffin) was the daughter of a stage mother who made careers for all her daughters (Paget's actress sisters are Teala Loring and Lisa Gaye). She too made a bundle of nondescript films before and after *Love Me Tender,* and it was only the film's promotion from routine western to Elvis Presley vehicle that made this one any different. Paget was conservative and religious (she had just attracted attention in the special effects blockbuster *The Ten Commandments*), and one of the few actresses who worked with Presley who did not succumb to his charms, either in the bedroom or as a friend. "He wasn't really my cup of tea--too much backwoods, if you know what I mean" she said, haughtily, many years later. "Besides, at that time, I wasn't dating anyone. Mother was chaperoning me wherever I went."

William Campbell spent most of his career in exploitation films of all genres, doing quite a few movies for Roger Corman and/or AIP. He's probably best known for portraying "The Squire of Gothos" in the legendary *Star Trek* episode of the same name. He also portrayed a Klingon bad guy in another famous *Star Trek,* "The Trouble with Tribbles", and recreated the role for 1990s spin-off series *Star Trek--Deep Space Nine* in an episode called "Blood Oath". By the time Presley was making his film debut, Campbell--like almost all the other leads in the film--had been acting in Hollywood for around a decade, and knew everybody. His comments on working with Presley would be echoed repeatedly for the next decade.

"He was one of the nicest guys" he told one interviewer, "but I did not socialise with him outside of work, because he couldn't have a social life. He invited me up (to his hotel room) several times but I never went because I didn't want to just go up to a hotel room and sit around. He was totally insulated. He had his guys around him that were his bodyguards".

Nevertheless, he claimed, they drove down to the ocean for burgers a couple of times, with Elvis saying he preferred the little seaside greasy spoon joint to more fashionable places because the owner didn't recognise him. This was not a luxury he would long hold on to.

Neville Brand was best known for his war films and gangster movies, and portrayed Al Capone in *The Scarface Mob,* the TV film that became *The Untouchables.* He was also behind bars in *Riot in Cell Block 11* and *The Birdman of Alcatraz* and starred in the TV western series *Laredo* (1965-'67). Mildred Dunnock, an elderly character actress, would have extensive credits ranging from *Baby Doll* to *The Nun's Story.* Robert Middleton was a burly character actor who usually played villains or officials. Stand-out roles included episodes of *The Untouchables, Target: the Corruptors,* and *Burke's Law.*

Bruce Bennett was a former Tarzan in the 1930s while acting under his true name of Herman Brix. He also starred in the excellent Republic serial *The Fighting Devil Dogs.* With a more mundane name, more mundane roles followed. James Drury later found fame on TV as the star of the long-running western series *The Virginian* (1962-'70). Russ Conway was a middle-aged character actor who usually played silver-haired figures of authority. Ken Clark was a B-movie tough guy. Barry Coe was an ambitious young actor who never made it to the top of the cast list, but worked again alongside Egan in *The 300 Spartans.* He starred in a short-lived TV series called *Follow the Sun.* L.Q. Jones, frequently in westerns (he would be back for *Flaming Star* and *Stay Away Joe*), worked regularly with Sam Peckinpah.

Love Me Tender was filmed between August and October 1956, the shooting time spread out over those months largely because of Elvis' recording commitments and the last-minute decision to add the footage of a ghostly Elvis reprising "Love Me Tender" after his demise. Presley, and to a lesser extent, Parker, had both been uncertain about the wisdom of having Elvis' character die at the end of the movie, although one of Presley's girlfriends assured him that a tragic death always made a memorable impact. She was right--women wept openly in cinemas across the country.

Either way, there was little to be done--Elvis had been offered a part already prepared, it had not been written with him in mind (B-movie dependable Cameron Mitchell had originally been cast). Indeed, Elvis doesn't make his first appearance until nearly twenty minutes into the film, and this was the only occasion Elvis wasn't top-billed--Richard Egan and Debra Paget were billed above him. Parker had actually turned down an offer of top billing for Elvis--name above the title--while holding out for extra money instead. Despite Parker's haggling, the deal was take it or leave it, and neither Presley or Parker would be dumb enough to leave it.

Elvis wasn't satisfied with his performance in the movie, but carping critics aside, he was the only one. *Love Me Tender* was a huge box office success (although despite featuring hundreds of cheap B-movies, the *Aurum Encyclopedia of Western Films* deems it too insignificant to include), and might even have made a few more bucks had, reports Peter Guralnick in his book *Last Train to Memphis,* truant officers not been combing the queues outside the cinema, where they made quite a catch!

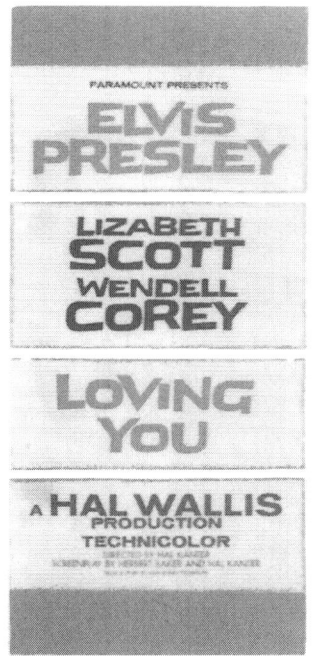

Dolores Hart and Elvis Presley

Loving You (1957)

wr. Herbert Baker, Hal Kanter, from Mary Agnes Thompson, dir. Hal Kanter, pr. Hal Wallis (Paramount)

with Elvis Presley (Deke Rivers), Lizabeth Scott (Glenda Markle), Wendell Corey (Tex Warner), Dolores Hart (Susan Jessup), James Gleason (Carl Meade), Ralph Dumke (James Tallman), Paul Smith (Skeeter), Ken Becker (Wayne), Jana Lund (Daisy), Yvonne Lime (Sally), Madge Blake, Almira Sessions (elderly women), Irene Tedrow (Mrs. Jessup), William Forrest (Mr. Jessup), Skip Young (Teddy), Vernon Rich (Harry Taylor), David Cameron (Castle), Grace Hayle (Mrs. Gunderson), Dick Ryan (Mac), Steve Pendleton (O'Shea), Sydney Chatton (Grew), Hal K. Dawson (police lieutenant), Harry Cheshire (Mayor), Joe Forte (editor), Karen Scott (waitress), Beach Dickerson (Glenn), Gail Lund (Candy), Timothy Butler (Buzz), Myrna Fahey, Sue England, Barbara Hearn, Elaine Du Pont (the girls), Jack Latham (TV announcer), Bill Black, Scotty Moore, D.J. Fontana (musicians), and the Jordanaires

Elvis sings: "Got a Lot of Living to Do" (on stage outdoors--daytime); "Let's Have a Party" (on stage outdoors--nighttime); medley ("Let's Have a Party"; "Teddy Bear"; "Got a Lot of Living to Do"; "Hot Dog" over montage); "Lonesome Cowboy" (on stage); "Hot Dog" (on stage at county fair); "Mean Woman Blues" (in teenagers' hangout); "Teddy Bear" (on stage); "Loving You" (at the Jessup farm); "Loving You" (reprise; on stage); "Got a Lot of Living to Do" (reprise; on stage for broadcast).

Quite the very opposite of *The Reno Brothers*, aka *Love Me Tender*, Hal Wallis' first picture for the King was intended as an Elvis vehicle from the off. A thinly-veiled, watered-down retelling of how Presley's career and influence on the music scene had occurred, *Loving You* is a difficult film to dislike, but boy, is it corny. It doesn't exactly play fast and loose with the facts, it just shoehorns them into a 1930s melodrama with 1940s dialogue and 1950s rock and roll movie characteristics. You will cringe, rather than cry, at the Hollywood heartache and teen angst served up here, but the film doesn't go completely off the rails until the wildly demented wrap-up, and by that time you will have been drawn into the film on its own terms and also seen some great footage of the young Elvis that more than compensates.

Loving You is generous with Elvis' music and features some great turns including "Got a Lot of Living to Do", "Mean Woman Blues", "Hot Dog", and the wonderful "Teddy Bear" and "Party", although the brand new ballad that provides the title of the film is a dreadful, turgid dirge a million miles from the gorgeous and soulful "Love Me Tender", and took Elvis a record number of over thirty attempts before they had a version he was satisfied with.

Even though *Loving You* is squarely and fairly aimed at the teenage market, writer and director Hal Kanter--who went on to write *Move Over Darling* for Doris Day and *Dear Brigitte* for Brigitte Bardot--can't help but tell the tale from the point of view of a bemused middle-aged man. The hilarious teenager dialogue is straight out of the 1940s, and the plot is even older, pure crowd-stirrin', rabble-rousing, over-enthusiastic 1930s musical material. Although, as with the MGM and Warners musicals, one never escapes the feeling that the cast are reciting a script or that the viewer is watching a movie, it's a good script, full of witty remarks, comebacks, and zingers, and the paint-by-numbers storyline is professionally performed and presented and never takes a wrong foot, even during the frantic, hilariously over-the-top ending.

Writer and director Kanter, amused by Elvis' insistence that all the best actors were never caught smiling on camera, was impressed by the young Presley, who, he said, quickly formed a mutual admiration society with Wendell Corey. "On set, Elvis was not cocky at all. Once he was told what to do, he did it, and did it very well. He was very playful between set-ups (but) he came on set knowing his lines. If anyone had a suggestion, he would always entertain it. He was a delight to work with--very intuitive and prompt. He showed up. That's a big step in anybody's movie career--just showing up on time".

For the hardcore Elvis fans, there is much to enjoy from the sugar-coated retelling of the origin of Elvis as they sort the half-fact (discovery, national uproar, flashy cars, special girls) from the total fantasy (the reluctant Elvis dodging fame, the ludicrous runaway from the orphanage contrivance). For the uninitiated, *Loving You* is quality cornball schmaltz, professionally served up with lashings of American apple pie.

One wonders also if the carny con-man James Tallman was the writers' way of getting a dig in at the Colonel. The similarities are quite scary, but having Lizabeth Scott as the hungry promoter gets them off the hook and provides the fictional romantic triangle. However, while Ralph Dumke's Tallman is the cheeky decoy, many Colonel Parker traits are there in the scenes with Glenda, such as the blind unquestioning trust Elvis' Deke Rivers puts in his promoter and publicist, the brazen manipulation of the gullible and/or hypocritical media, and the marginalising and quiet disposal of Elvis' supporting band (Bill Black, Scotty Moore, and D.J. Fontana), the edging out of which was being put into process by Parker and Wallis at precisely the same time *Loving You* was in production. Never much admired by the Colonel, they were to be replaced onscreen in later films by the Jordanaires.

Both Wallis and Parker saw Elvis as a long-term project and a family entertainer, not a teenage fad to be exploited, and as his career progressed, they were keen to keep him away from the juvenile delinquent roles like *Jailhouse Rock* and *King Creole*. It has been suggested, with some credibility, that Parker was even instrumental in getting Elvis drafted.

At the same time Elvis was making his first movies, exploitation kings like schlockmeister Sam Katzman were making waves with quick cash-ins like *Rock Around the Clock* and *Don't Knock the Rock*. When this rock thing was over (no-one knew, in 1957, that "rock and roll will never die"), they and the teens would move on to something else, and neither Parker or Wallis wanted to see Elvis turn into a one week wonder. Nevertheless, for all its traditional Hollywood content, Kanter had put plenty of rock and roll movie must-haves into *Loving You,* like the defiant, misunderstood kids loudly proclaiming the decent virtues of their equally misunderstood rock and roll, and the classic swingin' oldsters insert, showing the mean old killjoys having undergone a cautious conversion to the music of the kids (this involved the classic rock and roll movie cliche of the old misery who previously put down the hipsters being caught clicking fingers and bopping around to the music with everyone else, pausing with embarrassment, and then carrying on regardless; here, it's the city hall grannies, three fuddy-duddies on the road to Damascus, inexplicably in the TV studio audience!). Lizabeth Scott's speech at City Hall is classic "weren't you old coots kids once?" rhetoric from every rock and roll film ever made--and plenty had been made by the time *Loving You* hit the screens in July 1957.

Also, it's revealing that Deke never makes a record or goes into a recording studio in *Loving You*--he goes straight from the stage to the TV broadcast. Parker at this time was smugly basking in the afterglow of the complete u-turn Ed Sullivan and Steve Allen had done in booking Elvis on their influential shows after banning or mocking him, and was focusing solidly on TV and film. RCA were already having to squeeze in studio time for the actual record releases around the schedules of the Hollywood movies.

Lizabeth Scott (real name, Emma Matzo) was in her mid-thirties when she portrayed Glenda, and had been making movies for the previous ten years (she had worked for Wallis earlier, in the 1953 Martin and Lewis film *Scared Stiff*). Although she didn't know it at the time, this was the end of her career. Dogged by unpleasant and pointless rumors of lesbianism in the Hollywood gossip mags (which she sued), she found little work until an unsuccessful comeback attempt in the less bigoted '70s. It has been said that Wallis made no secret of the fact that had he not faced re-shooting most of her scenes, he would have fired her (despite being well aware of the rumors all along), and David Bret, author of *Elvis--the Hollywood Years*, and a writer eager to find homosexual sub-texts in the Elvis movies, suggests that several coded references to the gay lifestyle were slipped into the dialogue by sympathisers (although how this might be achieved is not explained). It has also been said that Presley wanted her off the film, but this seems a little ruthless and out of character for Presley, certainly at this early stage; Parker, maybe--but Elvis was just glad to be on the way, and Wallis had previously backed Scott's career, so all these inferences should be taken with the huge pinch of salt kept by for any stories involving gossip mag revelations.

Wendell Corey (Tex), whose voice and stature were reminiscent of a second string Gig Young, had been working steadily and anonymously in mostly routine movies for the previous ten years as a bland, dependable everyman type, and was also coming to the end of the road. He made a couple of undistinguished and long-forgotten TV series before ending his days (he died in 1968) in low-budget pulp sci-fi like the luckless Nick Adams. And even though eager beaver Adams was hanging around Elvis at this time trying to grab a role, it would have been just too cruel to cast him as the unintentionally parodic Teddy, the typical second banana comedy relief who appears in the opening scenes as his admiring hanger-on!

Eighteen year old Dolores Hart (formerly Dolores Hicks) was at her most attractive ever here, and probably the only person in Hollywood even greener than Elvis. A new discovery of Wallis, this was her first film role, and after working with George Cukor in *Wild is the Wind,* she made another Elvis film for Paramount, *King Creole.* She enjoyed a steady if unspectacular career in film and TV for the next six years until suddenly finding religion and joining a convent in 1963, where she became--and still is at time of writing--Sister Judith. It was the most bizarre fate of all the 1960s starlets.

Whatever the reason for her retreat from one unreal world to another, no-one who ever worked with Hart, including Wallis and Presley, had a bad word to say about her. The cliche became that she was just too sweet and nice for the Hollywood life. Here, she is the impossibly pure idealised fantasy version of the two or three steady girlfriends Elvis had at this point in his career, while poor doofus Tex and his hillbilly buddies represent all the baffled and bitter country and western traditionalists whose noses were put out of joint when Elvis first started performing around the South

(Elvis really did have a truck driving delivery job while he was starting out, but unlike the reluctant Deke Rivers, the real Presley was hungry for success). For his part, despite his stated desire to stretch, Elvis looks infinitely more comfortable playing a sanitised version of himself and portraying emotions he was familiar with (Elvis had been hypocritically possessive with his girlfriends, but had yet to demonstrate the jealous rage of a Clint Reno).

Jana Lund, who plays the teenager who lures Elvis into his photo opportunity for the gutter press, also appeared in *Frankenstein 1970, Hot Car Girl,* and *Married too Young* during this period (the 1970 date on the first is deceiving). Bit player Myrna Fahey would shortly get her big break in Roger Corman's *Fall of the House of Usher* with Vincent Price. Later she would guest in *Batman* and *Time Tunnel* (the latter alongside Debra Paget's sister Lisa Gaye).

Also in the bit players, William Forrest (here Susan's father), next up in *Jailhouse Rock* (as the studio chief), Ken Becker (Wayne), back for *G.I. Blues,* and then *Girls! Girls! Girls!* in a minor role as a drunk, Corman regular Beach Dickerson, also later in *G.I. Blues,* and Sue England, later in *Clambake.* Elaine Du Pont, another bit player, was the wife of stunt man Ray 'Crash' Corrigan, star of Republic's wonderful *Undersea Kingdom* serial and owner of the Corrigan Ranch, a frequently employed film location facility. She was a dancer and minor player in B-movies, flitting back and forth between uncredited bits in rock and roll films (*Rock Around the Clock, Don't Knock the Rock, No Time To Be Young*) and horror movies (*I Was a Teenage Werewolf, The Ghost of Dragstrip Hollow, The Beach Girls and the Monster*). She would also appear in *Jailhouse Rock.*

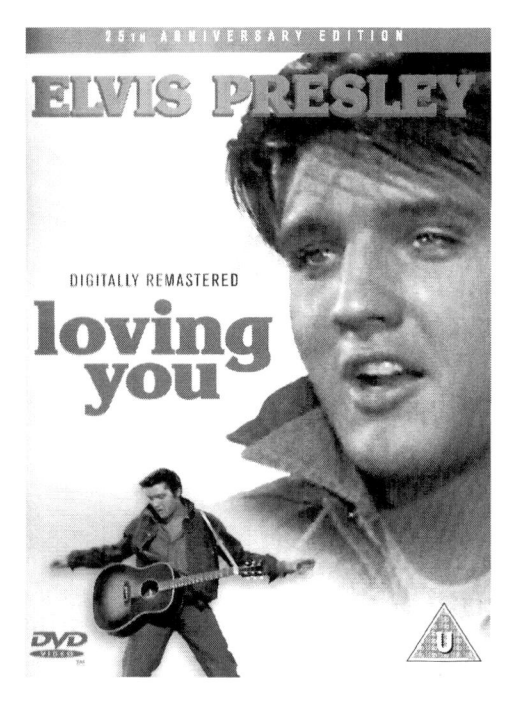

Trivia buffs will note a curious coincidence for fans of super-hero adventures--two elderly ladies with comic-book connections have uncredited bit parts. One of the bribed old biddies coerced into provoking a squabble for the press is Madge Blake, later Aunt Harriet in the *Batman*

TV show, while the mother of Susan at the farm is portrayed by Irene Tedrow, who was Aunt May in the *Amazing Spider-Man* TV series. More significantly for Elvis buffs, Gladys and Vernon Presley can be seen in the audience for Deke's TV special, making even more of a mockery of the silly dimestore novel orphan boy plotline. Sitting at the end of a middle row next to the aisle, Elvis' mother is seen first from the back in a dark blue dress, clapping away enthusiastically as Elvis leaves the stage to sing to the audience, and in the middle of the screen to the right with Vernon in the master shot of the audience.

Producer Hal Wallis began his highly profitable run of quality fluff for the Presley films after a similar string of hits with the comedy team of Dean Martin and Jerry Lewis, who were in the process of acrimoniously breaking up. In fact, he was preparing *Loving You* while his final Martin and Lewis film was being prised from them. He was the archetypal Hollywood movie producer stereotype--a balding lech with a cigar and a casting couch--and like Sam Katzman and Sam Arkoff, two similar figures commercially in tune with the times (they had pulled the old coots banning rock and roll bit in *Don't Knock the Rock* and *Shake, Rattle and Rock* respectively the previous year), he cut corners until squares were circles and tore pages out of scripts to solve problems.

However, he had been a film producer since the 1920s, and his (nearly four hundred) movie credits included *Little Caesar, Adventures of Robin Hood, Casablanca,* and *Gunfight at the O.K. Corral.* Furthermore, his lowbrow Martin and Lewis comedies frequently made more money than the prestigious films of the day, as well as outselling the 1950s Presley films by other producers. But Presley (who idolised Dean Martin) was in good company--also beneath Martin and Lewis at the box office at the time of *Loving You* were films by Brando, Bogart, Gene Kelly and Sinatra. Wallis was later married to the beautiful actress Martha Hyer, and after his stint with Presley, his career marched on, and included several vehicles for John Wayne that revitalised Wayne's career at a time when other actors of his era were moving into television. He was shrewdly commercial and frequently successful.

Wallis had been the first movie producer Parker had taken a meeting with, but much to his disappointment, the Colonel had been wise and greedy enough not to sign away exclusivity, and while Wallis would keep Presley gainfully employed, he could not obtain sole film rights to Presley for Paramount. When *Love Me Tender* beat his own projects into the movie houses it must have been both galling and rewarding at the same time. On the one hand, he had failed to be first into theaters with a Presley film, despite having made the first overtures (the wife of a friend had tipped him off after seeing Elvis on TV with the Dorsey Brothers in New York), but on the other, the success of *Love Me Tender* had proven him right and assured him of money in the bank. Someone else had taken what little risk there was (Elvis singing the 'phone book in a duet with Betty Boop would have been a hit at this point), and all he had to do was gather up his share of the kudos and cash. He had Elvis in his pocket, but Colonel Parker's incessant deal-making would soon demonstrate that it was far from sewn up...

Jailhouse Rock (1957)

wr. Guy Trosper, from Ned Young, dir. Richard Thorpe, pr. Pandro Berman (MGM)

with Elvis Presley (Vince Everett), Judy Tyler (Peggy Van Alden), Mickey Shaughnessy (Hank Houghton), Vaughn Taylor (Mr. Shores), Jennifer Holden (Sherry Wilson), Dean Jones (Teddy Talbot), Anne Neyland (Laurie Jackson), Hugh Sanders (Warden), Grandon Rhodes (Professor Alden), Katherine Warren (Mrs. Van Alden), Don Burnett (Mickey Alba), George Cisar (bartender), Percy Helton (Mr. Brewster), Glenn Strange, John Indrisano (convicts), Robert Bice (Bardeman), Peter Adams (Jack Lease), William Forrest (studio chief), Dan White (paymaster), Robin Raymond (Dottie), John Day (Ken), S. John Launer (Judge), Dick Rich (guard), Elizabeth Slifer (cleaning woman), Gloria Paul (stripper), Fred Coby (second bartender), Walter Johnson (Shorty), Frank Kreig (drunk), William Tannen (record distributor), Wilson Wood (recording engineer), Tom McKee (TV director), Donald Kerr (photographer), Carl Milletaire (Drummond), Francis De Sales (surgeon), Harry Hines (hotel clerk), Dorothy Abbott (girl in cafe), Bill Black, Scotty Moore, D.J. Fontana (musicians)

Elvis sings: "Young and Beautiful" (in jail cell); "I Want to be Free" (at prison concert); "Young and Beautiful" (reprise; interrupted in bar); "Don't Leave Me Now" (in recording studio); "Treat Me Nice" (in recording studio); "Jailhouse Rock" (on stage for television); "Baby, I Don't Care" (on movie set); "Young and Beautiful" (second reprise; sung to Judy Tyler)

The three-picture deal Parker had secured from Fox would result in three unusual and ambitious efforts that probably owed their courage and originality more to indecision and lack of forethought than any actual desire to push the envelope (*Love Me Tender* would be followed by another western, *Flaming Star*, and the melodrama *Wild in the Country*). Other producers took a more obvious and appealing path to get to Presley's panting, perspiration-soaked fans.

Rather than trying to put Elvis into other worlds, Wallis and the others recreated a cinematic Hollywood version of Presley's life and environment, and that of his fans. With *Loving You* we had seen the sanitised and sugar-coated version of Good Elvis, the shy, humble, thoughtful, God-fearing Deke Rivers. With *Jailhouse Rock,* filmed in a month during May and June of 1957 by MGM, we received the lurid, pulp novel Hollywood version of the media's Bad Elvis, Vince Everett.

The real Elvis was both and neither, of course, but the myth-making machine was revved up for another alternate Elvis, and interestingly *Jailhouse Rock* remains one of the most popular Elvis movies, certainly better remembered than the more lavish and better-looking *Loving You*. Many fans consider it his best. Originally titled *The Rock,* and then briefly *Jailhouse Kid,* this was in the grand tradition of the Warner Bros. Cagney/Bogart prison melodrama, and all the usual scenes are wheeled out--the sadistic guards, the cynical convicts, the sympathetic, suffering central character, the weak, indifferent warden, the mess hall food fight, the lurid punishments.

The plot was very similar to that of *Loving You,* with Elvis misunderstood and manipulated until redemption and surrounded by another set of cliche characters. Again, the emphasis on the erzatz Elvis' career is on TV and movies, once more reflecting Parker's long term plans for his boy (one can't help wondering whether the defrosted starlet character in the film was a dig at such unimpressed co-workers as Debra Paget or Natalie Wood, both of whom successfully resisted Elvis' charms in real life!). Once again, there is a female guiding his career rather than the unphotogenic carny Colonel, and once again there is an absurd, overkill climax (ironically mirrored in real life as Elvis was briefly and career-worryingly hospitalised after swallowing a tooth cap during the film's major dance number). The closing scenes of everybody expectantly waiting to see if Vince has kept his voice intact are a clever conceit--it forces the audience, including those who overrate him purely for his sexuality or popularity, and those who underrate him because of their prejudices, to listen closely and carefully to the Presley voice when Everett nervously sings his ballad.

However, the difference between *Loving You* and *Jailhouse Rock* was that this was the anti-matter Elvis, a thoroughly unpleasant and churlish lout without any redeeming qualities--Vince Everett is a cold, careless creep and if it wasn't for Elvis playing his part, he would be unwatchable. We never get the feeling that Vince is behaving the way he is out of bitterness or any other justification--he's horrible when he's at rock bottom, and horrible when he's at the top. He's mean to every single person he meets in the movie, arrogant and selfish from the film's first scene. It's an unpleasant, negative film with a bland, plastic love interest in Judy Tyler, and dull direction and photography. The script is sharper than *Loving You,* but it's a curiously uninvolving movie; some monochrome films benefit from being in black and white (director Thorpe's son Jerry's TV work on *The Untouchables* being a perfect example), but *Jailhouse Rock* just looks drab. Color wouldn't have made it a good movie, but it wouldn't have hurt.

The director was sixty-one years old and not much good. The dance scenes, however, choreographed by Alex Romero, who had handled some of the best Fred Astaire musicals, were pure MGM. With the exception of the title number, choreographed by Romero, the staging is flat and uninspired, bordering on the incompetent. Several times, actors aren't even blocked properly. For an MGM film, the production values are astonishingly low. One can only wonder what teenage audiences saw in *Jailhouse Rock* that was attractive, apart from Elvis. Perhaps the unfairness, selfishness, frustration and anger in the film hit a nerve. Its only strength is Elvis, and if Vince Everett was played by anyone other than him, it would be less than nothing.

Songwriters Jerry Leiber and Mike Stoller hadn't much respect for Presley, and the songs are a dull bunch, the exception being "Jailhouse Rock", which the duo condescendingly announced as a parody that Presley "wouldn't get". A closer look at Presley's act would have revealed to the smug songwriters that Elvis' entire routine was a provocative send-up of sorts, and that Elvis knew exactly what he was doing when he got up on stage, but they fancied themselves far more sophisticated than he.

The Colonel, however, had even less respect for Leiber and Stoller. Without the slightest intention of humor, as the duo finalised their work on follow-up movie *King Creole,* Parker sent them as a contract for further work a blank sheet of paper with his signature and a space for theirs. He'd fill in the rest when they'd signed it, he said, straight-faced. Leiber and Stoller knew that Elvis was a safe bet with any deal, and that they stood to make a lot of money regardless, but were smart enough to run like their pants were on fire. During their time working with Elvis they had been pleasantly surprised by his attitude, work ethic, and blues knowledge, and ended up frustrated that some of their ideas had been stamped on by the suits. Forseeing disaster, and almost certainly rightly assuming a relationship with Presley/Parker would end in tears, they declined to work on further films. They did, however, submit songs in the '60s that had already been recorded by other artists.

Judy Tyler (real name, Judith Hess) had just completed the now forgotten teen exploitation quickie *Bop Girl Goes Calypso* with Bobby Troup when she signed on for *Jailhouse Rock*. Mickey Shaughnessy had made his debut in the 1952 western *Last of the Comanches*, followed by roles in *From Here to Eternity* and *Conquest of Space*. He worked with several big name stars, but never in their best work. Dean Jones spent most of his career in Walt Disney films, including *That Darn Cat*, *Blackbeard's Ghost*, *The Love Bug*, and *Million Dollar Duck*. Both he and Shaugnessy appeared in the short-lived and unfunny early '70s TV comedy *The Chicago Teddy Bears*.

Trading cards for Jailhouse Rock

Elderly character actor Percy Helton's strange, high-pitched sing-song voice caused him to frequently be cast either as a loveable or sinister eccentric. As a grasping informant, he famously had his fingers crushed by Mike Hammer in the classic 1956 version of Mickey Spillane's *Kiss Me Deadly*. At around the same time he was appearing in *Jailhouse Rock*, he had a larger role as a harassed hen-pecked husband in *Shake, Rattle and Rock*. He had memorable roles on TV in *The Untouchables* and *Land of the Giants* among many others, including episodes of *The Twilight Zone*, *The Beverly Hillbillies*, *The Fugitive*, *Honey West*, *The Green Hornet*, *The Girl from UNCLE*, *Batman*, *Get Smart*, *Mission: Impossible*, and *The Wild Wild West*.

Former boxer, rodeo rider and western bad guy Glenn Strange portrayed Universal's Frankenstein monster in *House of Frankenstein* and *House of Dracula* among others, and went on to several year's employment as bartender Sam in the long-running western series *Gunsmoke*. Donald Kerr, seen briefly as a photographer, was the comic relief stowaway in *Flash Gordon's Trip to Mars*. Studio chief William Forrest, who played Mr. Jessup in *Loving You,* had been top of the cast list in the Republic serial *The Masked Marvel*.

Shortly after the film was completed, and just a week before the premiere of *Loving You,* leading lady Judy Tyler died alongside her husband in a car crash. Elvis was devastated, and even moreso when he realised he couldn't attend her funeral without turning it into a media circus. He reluctantly settled for sending flowers.

King Creole (1958)

wr. Herbert Baker, Michael V. Gazzo, from Harold Robbins, dir. Michael Curtiz, pr. Hal Wallis (Paramount)

with Elvis Presley (Danny Fisher), Carolyn Jones (Bonnie), Walter Matthau (Maxie Fields), Dolores Hart (Nellie), Dean Jagger (Mr. Fisher), Jan Shepard (Mimi Fisher), Vic Morrow (Shark), Paul Stewart (Charlie Le Grand), Lillian Montevecchi (Nina), Brian Hutton (Sal), Jack Grinnage (Dummy), Dick Winslow (Eddie), Raymond Bailey (school principal), Ziva Rodann (chorus girl), Ned Glass (desk clerk), Candy Candido (doorman), Lilyan Chauvin (woman), Franklyn Farnum (elderly man), Minta Durfee, Hazel Boyne (elderly women), and the Jordanaires

Elvis sings: "Crawfish" (from window); "Steadfast, Loyal and True" (trial in club); "Lover Doll" (in store); "Trouble"; "Dixieland Rock"; "Young Dreams"; "New Orleans"; "Hard Headed Woman"; "King Creole"; "Don't Ask Me Why"; "Take a Day Out of Your Life"; "As Long as I Have You" (all on stage in clubs)

By mid-1957, it was evident that Elvis Aron Presley seriously faced the draft (it's astonishing to think that but for timing, Elvis could have served--and died--in Korea or Vietnam). Many people felt that the government would never call up Elvis simply because of the thousands upon thousands of dollars in taxes they would be losing out on, but they hadn't figured on the short-sightedness or vindictiveness of the authorities, or the likely machinations of the devious old "Colonel" (who wanted to tame his rock and roll rebel and charm the general public in a damage limitation strategy) and Elvis duly got his papers. This humble boy would be humbled by experts.

In public, Elvis confounded the tightasses and the bluenoses by announcing that he wasn't keen on the idea, but he would serve his country faithfully that had done so much for him, blah blah blah. In private, he was hurt, nervous, and confused, as well as being seriously concerned about his future in show business. He was, many of his friends told interviewers much later, convinced that this was the end of his career, and that by the time he got out, he would be washed-up, forgotten, old news.

This was, undoubtedly, what the powers-that-be hoped, although the Colonel confidently believed otherwise. Elvis hysteria was at its peak, and entire auditoriums were being trashed by over-enthusiastic teens. Critics were still gnashing their teeth impotently in the press. Take away the kids' toys and they'll cry a little, get over it, and move onto something else. The army would straighten him out, they thought. And even if it doesn't, who's going to remember Elvis Presley in two years?

The Colonel was going to make sure everybody did. He had informed the authorities outright, loudly and publicly, that his prodigy did not want any special treatment. He too hoped that the army would settle him, but was more interested in slowing down the gravy train, concerned that the speed it was moving at would derail it. Had the authorities not been so keen to break him, Elvis may well have spent the next two years self-destructing or burning out. Family Elvis and Vegas Elvis may never have existed.

Say what you like about "Colonel" Tom Parker, and everyone has, but he kept Presley's career on the boil for two long years, pushing his completed movies, promoting the soundtrack albums, placing Elvis-related nuggets of news and gossip in the press, and most bravely and brilliantly of all, defying the pleas and protestations of public, record company, and even Presley to record any new material, or even to perform in public. They want Presley out of circulation for two years? Fine--let them serve the sentence. Let the authorities take the rap. He knew about teenage angst, fury, and contrariness. They had walked right into his hands. He'd force the prudes, petty power-mongers, and politicians to take the consequences of their actions, and then give Elvis the most powerful and profitable comeback ever, to spite the spiteful.

Parker was sharp enough to know that if Elvis hadn't actually been away there could be no comeback, just a subdued anti-climax. The public had to be deprived. It wasn't necessarily the way he would have played it, but the situation had been forced on him and he was going to make the best of it.

But as cynical and downright crooked as he could be, it should be noted that Parker never had a back-up plan for himself alone. He demonstrated genuine faith in his personal project by taking on not a single new client in his absence. As ever, Parker devoted one hundred percent of his time and energies to Elvis Presley, and he would stand or fall with him. If Elvis came out of the armed forces a forgotten and broken man, then Parker would be right behind him in the unemployment line--for about five minutes, at least. And "the Colonel" was no damn fool. If he had shared the doubts of RCA or the film studios that the Presley star might fade for even a minute, he would have had no qualms about organising a back-up plan and prowling around for potential replacements. But he didn't. Elvis was right to trust him.

For his part, Elvis was genuinely baffled by all the hostility that had been leveled against him. Both the single of "Jailhouse Rock", and a 1957 Christmas album had reached number one in the charts, and yet he was surrounded by the chattering din of moralistic critics--he was even accused of demeaning Christmas! Raised with gospel, it drove him to seek religious counsel and he retained an interest in spiritual matters right up until his death.

That same Christmas had come the news--Elvis was being called up into the army. The Colonel would do what had to be done--if his client was an anti-Christ who couldn't even touch Christmas without tainting it, it was time to start planning the resurrection...

The Colonel, typically, had three movie deals lined up when the news came through, but the only one well into pre-production was the adaptation of the Harold Robbins novel *A Stone for Danny Fisher*, working title *Sing, You Sinners*, and eventually known as *King Creole*. After much wrangling and special pleading, Elvis was given a couple of months extra freedom to get *King Creole* in the can before 1950s hardhat America climbed onto its high horse and took its two year revenge on the Presley clan. Even the wily old Colonel couldn't know how this would impact on his meal ticket, but he certainly covered all the angles.

Most people regard *King Creole* as Elvis Presley's finest performance. Intentionally or not, Danny Fisher occupied the middle ground between Deke Rivers and Vince Everett. A young ne'er-do-well, he was Deke Rivers if he hadn't had the breaks and lived in a bad part of town, or Vince Everett with good intentions and a conscience.

Again, we were given the good girl (Dolores Hart from *Loving You*) and the bad girl (off-the-rails Carolyn Jones, giving depth and substance to the tart with a heart cliche). Despite the literary source, it was a good script, and it gave Elvis the chance to act, even if it was yet another thinly-veiled alternate universe version of his own life. Once again, Presley was playing a boy who was trying to do the best for his family. Once again, he was getting involved with chicanery. Once again, he was pursuing a music career. Once again, uptight adults just didn't understand him. Once again, a mentor was giving him a chance to better his lot. All of this was mixed in with teen-friendly lashings of self-pity, temptation, anxiety, mistakes, and young love, playing mercilessly on the hard-done-by, whole-world's-against-me sympathies of the teen market. If only dad and the school principal would just understand... While it wears a little thin when it comes from today's prating, over-privileged kids, back in the '50s, the teens had a point. They were maligned and misunderstood, and nobody more than Elvis Presley...

King Creole was shot, in monochrome, at the Paramount lot and then later New Orleans locations, during the first three months of 1958. Michael Curtiz, although another elder statesman of cinema (his dozens of films from the 1920s to the early '60s included *The Adventures of Robin Hood, Angels with Dirty Faces, Yankee Doodle Dandy,* and *Casablanca*), was a vastly more talented and imaginative director than the tired Richard Thorpe, and although no one particular scene stands out, the entire film sparkles with busy sets, strong compositions, and a general polished sheen of professionalism about it (the director of photography, Russell Harlan, had photographed *Red River*).

Also, although the story is thoroughly routine and rarely involving, poor old Danny Fisher--unlike the mean and surly Vince Everett--is at least sympathetic, and the cast is uniformly excellent. Charles O'Curran, who staged the choreography for Presley's previous Paramount film, returned to stage the musical sequences here, and would remain with Wallis and Presley for the rest of their Paramount productions.

Greeted with a torrent of intimidating foul language from the notoriously bullying Curtiz, Presley apparently walked calmly onto the set and offered his handshake, alongside the traditional courteous Presley greeting, thus making the unfortunate Curtiz look an even smaller man than he already was. However, Presley came to admire Curtiz' ability, regarding him to be the best director he ever worked with. Location work in New Orleans was inevitably fraught, as Wallis and Parker schemed to keep the fans away, but the shoot was a happy one--the supporting cast respected Elvis, including old timer Walter Matthau, and there were endless parties and set visits with Hollywood names. Partying with Elvis during the making of the film were TV stars Nick Adams, Ty Hardin, and Vince Edwards. The still starstruck Elvis even got to shake hands with Marlon Brando.

Musically, the film is one of Elvis' strongest, possibly the strongest, although most of the good stuff (with the exception of the one-of-a-kind "Trouble") doesn't appear until well into the second half of the film, when we are treated to fairly frequent chunks of 1950s Elvis rock n' roll--"Dixieland Rock"; "Young Dreams"; "New Orleans"; "Hard Headed Woman"; "King Creole"; "Don't Ask Me Why"; "Take a Day Out of Your Life"; "As Long as I Have You"--in succession. This is what the kids were paying to see in 1958, and it was a satisfying going away present--a poignant one too, as when Presley returned two years later it was with easy going musical numbers, the cloying showbiz stroking of the Frank Sinatra TV special, the militaristic marching band childishness of *G.I. Blues* and the cutesy family feelgood sound of *Blue Hawaii*.

Walter Matthau (who wisely changed his name from Matasschanskayasky to a somewhat shorter sneeze) had a career already well in progress, but he was the first big name in an Elvis film to still have a way to go, and many major performances were still in the future. Dean Jagger was an old timer on the way down, but still had a fair number of working years ahead of him. Paul Stewart, who had appeared in *Citizen Kane,* was also mid-career.

Carolyn Jones went on to star in *The Addams Family* TV show as Morticia and appear in several episodes of the 1960s cult TV show *Batman* as Marsha, Queen of Diamonds, a sort of faux man-seducing Poison Ivy type. Her film career had already included *Road to Bali* with Bob Hope and Bing Crosby, plus *House of Wax, The Big Heat,* and *Invasion of the Body Snatchers,* and she appeared alongside Elvis' buddy Nick Adams in the pilot film for *Burke's Law* in *Dick Powell Theater.* She was accompanied to New Orleans by her later husband and future schlock TV mogul Aaron Spelling (*Starsky and Hutch, Charlie's Angels, Vegas, Fantasy Island, Love Boat, Hotel, Dynasty,* etc.), and producer of *Burke's Law* (his first big hit); Spelling would give her a plum part in the series when he cast her as four odd sisters in the episode "Who Killed Sweet Betsy?", a showcase role that included both victim and murderer!

King Creole co-writer Michael Gazzo would write numerous TV show episodes during the 1970s, including many for Spelling. Gazzo was also an actor, usually typecast as a gangster. Jan Shepard would take a minor role in *Paradise, Hawaiian Style*. TV roles included *Wanted--Dead or Alive, Land of the Giants* and *Ironside.* Cast as Shark was a young Vic Morrow, fresh from *The Blackboard Jungle* and later to star in the 1960s TV series *Combat.*

Playing one of Shark's thugs was Jack Grinnage, later to co-star in *Kolchak--the Night Stalker* as a prissy straw man. Busy character actor Ned Glass, often a shopkeeper or a stoolie, would be back in *Kid Galahad.* In a minor role as the school principal was Raymond Bailey, who made numerous bald-pated bit player appearances in the 1950s as doctors and authority figures before donning a salt-and-pepper toupee and finding fame in the long-running sit-com *The Beverly Hillbillies* as greedy banker Mr. Drysdale. He also played the college Dean in the *Many Loves of Dobie Gillis* sit-com.

Despite all the glowing publicity that the army enjoyed regarding Elvis Presley, the only significant long-term contribution the military made (besides getting him interested in karate) was to introduce him to amphetamines, which Elvis was rapidly depending on from the early '60s on. Elvis' ultimate dependency on drugs was doubly tragic due to his absolute hatred of the 1960s recreational drugs culture. When Elvis naively popped pills he had been slipped by not-so-helpful friends to give him energy and keep him going day and night, he never once acquainted or related it for a second with the deliberate drugs-taking of pot, or later, cocaine that was rife in the rest of the entertainment industry. Like many people vehemently anti-drugs, Presley's ignorance was as dangerous as other people's casual acceptance or outright enthusiasm for them.

G.I. Blues (1960)

wr. Edmund Beloin, Henry Carson, dir. Norman Taurog, pr. Hal Wallis (Paramount)

with Elvis Presley (Tulsa McLain), Juliet Prowse (Lili), Robert Ivers (Cookie), James Douglas (Rick), Leticia Roman (Tina), Sigrid Maier (Marla), Arch Johnson (Sergeant McGraw), John Hudson (Captain Hobart), Mickey Knox (Jeeter), Ken Becker (Mac), Jeremy Slate (Turk), Beach Dickerson (Warren), Trent Dolan (Mickey), Carl Crow (Walt), Edward Stroll (Dynamite), Fred Essler (Papa Mueller), Ronald Starr (Harvey), Erika Peters (Trudy), Ludvig Stossel (puppeteer), Edith Angold (Mrs. Hagermann), Dick Winslow (orchestra leader), Edward Coch (band leader), Robert Boon (guitarist), Ed Faulkner (Red), Fred Kruger (Herr Klugmann), Torben Mayer (head waiter), Gene Roth, Roy C. Wright (businessmen), Harper Carter, Tip McClure (military police), Walter Conrad (chaplain), William Kaufman (coffee house manager), Hannah Melcher (female singer), E.M. "Bitsy" Mott (sergeant), Judith Rawlins (Fritzie), Blaine Turner (bartender), Marianne Gaba (barmaid), Britta Ekman, Tom Creel (customers), and the Jordanaires

Elvis sings: "G.I. Blues" (in bar); "Doin' the Best I Can" (in bar); "Frankfurt Special" (on train); "Shoppin' Around" (in nightclub); "Tonight Is So Right for Love" (in restaurant); "Wooden Heart" (to kids); "Pocket Full of Rainbows" (on cable car with Juliet Prowse); "Big Boots" (to baby); "Didja Ever" (at army show)

In his superb Presley biography *Last Train to Memphis,* Peter Guralnick opens the chapter "Walking in a Dream" with an often told anecdote whereby a newspaper reporter thrust a quote from Frank Sinatra under Presley's nose. Sinatra, a skinny teen idol in the 1940s who had twenty years later returned from the wilderness to become middle-aged America's premiere nightclub entertainer, was quoted as saying that "rock and roll smells phoney and false! It is sung, played and written for the most part by cretinous goons... imbecilic... sly, lewd, dirty... the martial music of every sideburned delinquent on the face of the earth... the most brutal, ugly, desperate, vicious form of expression it has ever been my misfortune to hear...". And so on.

Sinatra would also go on to make some specific, unpleasant, and equally absurd remarks about Presley himself. It was, of course, the transparently jealous mewling of the middle-aged man who suddenly finds he has been usurped by another, younger cock of the walk and can't deal with it. Ironically, Sinatra at the time was at the pinnacle of his success, although he was soon to be an anachronism, and certainly right to be worried.

It was a pitiful display, and Elvis dealt with it in the same calm, polite, banal and disarming manner that he employed to render the prudes, the pastors, and the draft board impotent. He, Sinatra, was a proven successful entertainer, he said, who was entitled to his own opinions, even if he, Elvis, didn't agree with them, and he had a right to express them, but with respect, he was mistaken, and here's why, etc. etc. Nevertheless, Presley's performance was very potently putting a lot of middle-aged men's noses out of joint, and they retaliated the only way they could--with power. Elvis had been drafted and to hell with the lost taxes.

Two years later, Elvis--still huge, much missed, widely anticipated--was coming out of the army, and Sinatra paid through the nose to boost his flagging popularity by securing the first performance by Presley when he returned to civilian life... one hundred thousand dollars (1960s money) for ten minutes of Elvis in a banal TV variety format brazenly titled *Welcome Home, Elvis!* Presley played the game, and duetted with Sinatra, mauling each others' signature songs, but neither he or Parker forgot those earlier remarks.

Sinatra's Rat Pack buddy Dean Martin, however, who held more quietly the same opinion of rock and roll as Sinatra and was no hypocrite about it, was much admired--idolised, even--by Elvis, who loved his sly, easy going, couldn't-give-a-shit onstage irreverence and drew from it. Martin was one of many celebrities who sent a telegram of condolence when Presley's mother died, and Presley made a point of meeting Martin's three awestruck daughters when they visited the Paramount lot.

Presley's next movie was what today would be called a no-brainer by every definition of the phrase. *G.I. Blues* told of the exploits of the improbably named Tulsa McLean, an American G.I. who, by an amazing coincidence, is stationed in Germany. The film was, announced the opening credits in very large letters, "produced with the full co-operation of the U.S. Army and the Department of Defense". Well, no kidding! Every ghastly cliche of the American military movie is here in all its glory, all lit up by Joseph Lilley's thumping "army life" score as heard in every film that a tank trundled through from the 1930s through the 1960s.

G.I. Blues is so wretched, it's difficult to decide what to complain about first--the film's unquestioning celebration of the military service Elvis dreaded as some sort of government sponsored adventure holiday with tanks and girls (even though, for the real Elvis, that's exactly what it was; not so lucky, the poor devils just back from Korea, or the saps who enlisted after seeing this ninety minute promo, just in time for Vietnam), the cheerful Hollywood war movie banter between Elvis and buddies Cookie and Rick (Ivers and Douglas), the straight-from-central-casting comedy sergeant played by character actor Arch Johnson (who specialised in such bluff blowhards), the (even then) antediluvian attitude to women, or the fact that Elvis and teenage America were expected to go merrily marching into cinemas to see this laughable watered down recreation of Presley and his life, when nobody, including Elvis, had wanted the world robbed of Elvis Presley for two valuable years in the first place.

In a just, sane world, *G.I. Blues* would have bombed unreservedly and audiences would have sent a firm, rigid finger skyward to all the beaming Establishment figures who thought they could have their cake and eat it. In the unfair, real world, *G.I. Blues* was a huge success, and massively profitable. Audiences streamed into cinemas to see this dreck, and the album of the film's limp, stupid score made a mint too. The American public lapped it all up, as did the rest of the world, and the powers-that-be not only kept their cake and ate it, they bought the whole bakery and burned it down.

Why did this happen? As ever, the answer is timing. America was between wars and the country was feeling pretty good about itself, tough and exuberant (Vietnam would change everything). The American teens who had been to see *Jailhouse Rock* in 1957 were three years older, a mere quantum leap in their lives but just long enough to settle down, have babies or face the draft themselves (*Jailhouse Rock,* already nostalgia, would be re-released some months after Elvis left the army). This is exactly what happens to the three cardboard G.I.s in the film--they each find a wife for life and one has become a father. In a few years time, these crewcut cavemen would be hating hippies, resenting women, and slapping down their dollars for copies of *Playboy* and lurid pulp fiction mags glorifying warfare. And although *G.I. Blues* could, in terms of attitude and dialogue, quite easily have been made anytime twenty years earlier (including a good two thirds of the crappy songs), it was, in 1960, very much the last gasp of the consensus.

Shawn Levy, writing in his book *Ratpack Confidential* about the early Sixties and Sinatra, Martin and co. summed it up perfectly. "For the first sixty years of the (20th) century, save a couple of dozen months after Elvis made the scene, everybody in every house in America found pleasure in the same type of comedy, music, movies. And (then) nobody seemed to agree about anything ever again". For irrefutable evidence of this blanket generalisation, the American record charts, cinema box office, and television schedules up until 1964 back this up with cold, hard commercial reality. Or, as Nick Tosches wrote in *Dino,* his Dean Martin biography,

"Those days were the beginning of the end of timelessness. Homer's *Odyssey* spoke throughout the ages; Kerouac's American odyssey, *On the Road,* would have a shelf life, and would prove, after a handful of years, more outdated and stale than Homer's after thousands. But like the detergent on the shelf in that other supermarket aisle, it was for the moment, new and improved...".

Specifics. The title *G.I. Blues* may well have been appropriate from Elvis Presley's point of view (he spent two years mourning his mother and wondering if he had a career to come back to), but there were no "G.I. blues" in the film, either in music or mood. It was a romp, a romantic adventure, with all the soldiers portrayed as interchangeable loveable goofballs (in a war drama, we would have found the merriment peppered with occasional minor tragedies, an accident here, a suicide there, a skirmish with the enemy... but this was a musical, set in peacetime, but as gung ho as any of the war effort propaganda films).

In fact, *G.I. Blues* is pretty bad even by the paint-by-numbers standards it sets itself. It can't be called a mistake or a misfire because the film was a huge success, but equally undeniable is what's on the screen-- the guys are all loutish creeps, the women unappealing drips. The storyline concerns a three hundred dollar bet between Elvis' buddies and those of the repugnant Turk (Jeremy Slate, later the bad guy in *Girls! Girls! Girls!*) that Elvis can spend the night in the apartment of ice queen Lili, a lithe but unfriendly exotic dancer who Turk has only got as far as the doorstep. The only time sex looks like fun is when an alluring barmaid (*Playboy* model Marianne Gaba, whose credits also include pulp fear-of-women sci-fi cheapie *Missile to the Moon,* a guest spot in *The Beverly Hillbillies,* the beach movie *How to Stuff a Wild Bikini,* and *Austin Powers* predecessor *Doctor Goldfoot and the Bikini Machine*) comes on to a cautious Tulsa and tells him her car is available (he tells her to "keep her motor running"). And unlike Ann-Margret in the later and vastly superior *Viva Las Vegas,* who was consistently and persistently sexy both in the plot and the dance sequences, Juliet Prowse's dance pieces are less about ability and personality and more about marching around while athletically and robotically showing off her body.

Even if you accept the unlikely existence of a shy and retiring cabaret dancer, the hot-and-cold running Lili, who has a reputation for resisting the advances of all men while strutting around in next to nothing on the dance floor, inadvertently comes across like a cold-hearted, jaded, matter-of-fact prostitute, rather than an entertainer. Prowse spends half the film as an overcoat-clad, headscarf-wearing wide-eyed Cold War peasant and the other half as a near-naked methodical man-teasing vamp. As the bamboozled bulldog in the Warner Brothers cartoon would say, "It don't add up!".

Characterisation, or even motive, is completely absent from any of the film's characters, but for Lili it is not just non-existent but a necessity to make sense of events. Just what is she doing, and why is she doing it? Why do any of the men in the film fall for the women they do, or are they just grabbing the first girl who responds positively?

Things were very different off-set, as Elvis and his entourage (shortly to be nicknamed the Memphis Mafia after a celebratory trip to Vegas on the film's completion) worked their way through a constant procession of admirers, innocents, and starlets. One young actress who found her way into the King's court was Kathy Kersh, the later wife of Vince Edwards, TV's super-medic Ben Casey, and then Burt Ward, TV's Robin on the *Batman* show. At the front of the hedonistic parade were Presley (as ever, distastefully dividing his female companions into the categories whore or madonna, albeit through experience) and Prowse (formerly involved in an on-again, off-again engagement to good ol' blue eyes himself, Frank Sinatra, her previous Hollywood co-star in 1959's *Can-Can*). According to several accounts, while acting out this ludicrously chaste parody of sex in the movie, they were energetically rockin' and rollin' in Prowse's trailer virtually every afternoon after filming wrapped!

But if Elvis was enjoying himself between takes in early 1960, his low opinion of the movie was common knowledge then as well as now. As Tulsa McLean, Elvis is Bilko Junior as the movie opens (conning money repeatedly from his gullible sergeant for a planned nightclub back home in a plotline conveniently mislaid as the story moves on), but even this would have been preferable to the embarrassments that followed. Of the generous number of songs on offer in *G.I. Blues,* most of them are childish rubbish, more infantile than almost anything in the 1950s or 1960s hit parade by anyone--one almost expects Elvis to start singing "My Boy Lollipop" or "How Much is That Doggie in the Window".

There is, for a start, an almost total lack of irony (almost, because when a soldier starts the obligatory Elvis movie punch-up by drowning out Tulsa's ballad with a clearly marked Elvis Presley classic on the juke box, he says he'd rather listen to "the original"). Absurdly, this--"Doin' the Best That I Can"--is the movie's only halfway decent track, spoiled and ended abruptly by, ironically, the troublemaker playing "Blue Suede Shoes" on the jukebox. Even this momentary wink at the audience--actually, more a case of the movie shooting itself in the foot with a bit of "friendly fire"--could not have saved the film's lowpoint, a horrible comedy bit that Elvis hated performing (and not just because his entourage taunted him over it) in which he is obliged to show what a great guy he is by saving an old man's puppet show and singing to a hand-operated marionette for a bunch of appreciative kids (the interlude with sweet little kiddies would be a regular recurring feature throughout the Elvis movies).

Just when it seems that the film can't sink any lower, Presley and Prowse mime a dreary duet to each other--badly--on a cable car. Only one item--the aforementioned "Doin' the Best I Can"--is of any merit; of the rest, Elvis is obliged to perform a sort of patriotic circa 1942 Hollywood marching dance to two of them, gyrates to none of them, mimes appallingly on several occasions, and produces at least four gimmicky monstrosities that are among the worst he ever performed. Indeed, while virtually every Elvis film features at least one song or situation to make discerning audiences cringe, *G.I. Blues* surely holds the record for the most. As well as the above, a supposedly hilarious scene with a crying baby (Elvis as Dagwood Bumstead said Albert Goldman) is quite simply distressing, not least for using at length an actual upset child.

For film buffs, delights are few. Veteran serials villain Gene Roth, reduced in the '60s to bit parts, appears briefly as a businessman, and two Roger Corman regulars, Jeremy Slate and Beach Dickerson, are among the faceless recruits in an otherwise uninteresting cast. The only real entertainment to be had comes from noting the interminable use of long-shot doubles in the location shots (filmed in the little town of Idstein on the Rhine, south of Frankfurt) and phoney rear-projection for everything else. With the exception of sequences involving military hardware (which the movie makers had no problems accessing, for obvious reasons), every single scene with the named actors is shot on a soundstage (the set for the already abysmal puppet show sequence is particularly phoney). Even a scene featuring Presley accompanying Prowse down a neon-lit nighttime street is produced by having the actors bob up and down in front of a backdrop projection, which obligingly bobs along with them until a perfectly timed abrupt stop. Ironically, Elvis was still in the army, and still in Germany, when Wallis and his second unit had been filming doubles in duplicate wardrobes flitting round German tourist spots for establishing shots. Everything involving the film's cast was shot in Hollywood, giving every bit-player of German or Austrian descent a chance to make a few dollars as barkeeps or frauleins (although the German orchestra leader in Lili's nightclub is Dick Winslow, last seen in *King Creole* as Eddie Burton).

This paint-by-numbers preparation obviously offered no leeway to either director Norman Taurog or Presley himself (who described himself miserably in a letter to a girlfriend as "locked into it"). All studio shots filmed six months later had to match the material previously filmed. And, one has to say, they did, perfectly. However, the technique was used so laboriously throughout the film (including some nondescript outdoor scenes that could easily have been filmed anywhere) that it becomes unavoidably and glaringly apparent. Had, say, the boat trip or the city street scenes been filmed outside the soundstage, the expedient use of rear-projection and location long-shots elsewhere would not have been so obvious.

This was the third of nine Elvis films produced by Hal Wallis for Paramount, and some of the later ones, untainted by the shadow of Elvis' spell in the army, would be quite good fun. Certainly, the Wallis formula is firmly in place--he has had the foresight to include the token fight scene and the token misunderstanding from previous Elvis vehicles, although the absence of the romantic triangle or competitor for true love makes *G.I. Blues* even more torpid, the only challenge for Elvis being the unsavory business of the financial betting to see if Tulsa can melt ice-maiden Lili, an obnoxious premise that had previously been employed by Wallis and his writers in the Martin and Lewis film *Sailor Beware* ten years earlier.

It was also the first of nine Elvis films to be directed by the old-timer Taurog, who had worked for Wallis during the Martin and Lewis days and previously helmed vehicles for the likes of Bing Crosby, Deanna Durbin, Bob Hope, Mickey Rooney, Judy Garland, Mario Lanza, and Debbie Reynolds (David Bret, in his book *Elvis--the Hollywood Years,* suggests that Taurog included two of Lanza's favorite classical pieces in the film score in tribute of the singer, who had recently died; Lanza was the opera world's Elvis, a performer who had found a second career making fluffy feelgood movies that damaged his reputation with the snobs).

Taurog did not produce art, he produced commercial entertainments, and as such, he was perfect for the Elvis films. A former child actor in the silents, born in 1899, he was virtually blind by the 1960s and could barely walk without assistance. Presley did not need an ambitious or artistic director with a personal career agenda, as his following film, the pointless *Flaming Star,* was about to prove.

However, the point of *G.I. Blues* was blindingly obvious, and advertising for the film made no secret of the direction Elvis was being steered by Wallis and Parker. "The idol of teenagers yesterday is the idol of the family today!" screamed the front-of-house poster. "It's a `U' for you!". In one corner is comedy Elvis pulling a face at the unfortunate baby ("Every audience will go for the New Elvis... as the world's most famous baby-sitter!"). In another is a picture from the wretched puppet show ("Every audience will go for the New Elvis in the wonderful puppet sequence!"). And so they did. Elvis had been accepted into the mainstream--at a price.

Elvis made new male acquaintances at this time, as well as female friends. Joe Esposito had joined the entourage, as had Sonny West, the younger cousin of Red West, Elvis' old college buddy who had now left the Marines and was working steadily in Hollywood, at first with Nick Adams on *The Rebel*. West invariably had a role in the Elvis movies, often in fight scenes (as in *G.I. Blues, Wild in the Country,* and *It Happened at the World's Fair,* to name but three), and would later work frequently with Nick Adams' buddy, Robert Conrad, a feisty former boxer who would cast West regularly in his '60s *Wild Wild West* TV spy show and in virtually every project he made after that.

Presley also went to see dancer and future Elvis stand-in Lance Le Gault perform his rhythm and blues act at around this time (in fact, it was while he was filming *Wild in the Country*--Tuesday Weld accompanied him). Le Gault too became an Elvis film regular (that's him just behind Elvis in the "Return to Sender" sequence in *Girls! Girls! Girls!*) and would also enjoy an extensive career in Hollywood later in life, working regularly as an actor for producers Stephen J. Cannell and Donald Bellisario, and enjoying recurring roles throughout the 1980s on *The A-Team* (as their pursuer Commander Decker), *Magnum p.i.* (as another hard-nosed military man), and *Werewolf* (as bounty hunter Alamo Joe). For Elvis, he was an extra, stand-in, musician, dancer, and choreographer.

As for Sinatra, the previous recipient of Juliet Prowse's affections, his hypocrisy did not end with the *Welcome Home Elvis* special. When Presley died in 1977, ol' two-face announced "There have been many accolades uttered about Elvis' talent and performances through the years, all of which I agree with wholeheartedly. I shall miss him dearly as a friend. He was a warm, considerate and generous man"! And so he was, but those attributes were not apparently extended toward Sinatra himself--Presley's late afternoon visits to Prowse's trailer were a delightfully relished open secret to (almost) everyone. In fact, Red West's favorite gag at the time was to stand outside the trailer and stage-whisper "Frank's coming!!".

Flaming Star (1960)

wr. Clair Huffaker, Nunnally Johnson, dir. Don Siegel, pr. David Weisbart (Fox)

with Elvis Presley (Pacer Burton), Steve Forrest (Clint Burton), Dolores Del Rio (Mrs. Burton), John McIntire (Mr. Burton), Barbara Eden (Roslyn Pierce), Rodolfo Acosta (Buffalo Horn), Karl Swenson (Mr. Pierce), Richard Jaeckel (Angus Pierce), Ford Rainey (Doc Phillips), L.Q. Jones (Tom Howard), Anne Benton (Dorothy Howard), Douglas Dick (Will Howard), Marian Goldina (Ph'Sha Nay), Monte Burkhart (Ben Ford), Ted Jacques (Hornsby), Roy Jenson (Matt Holcomb), Barbara Beaird (Dottie Phillips), Virginia Christine (Mrs. Phillips), Tom Reese (Jute), Sharon Bercutt (Bird's Wing), Perry Lopez, Rodd Redwing, Red West (braves), Tom Fadden, Red West (townspeople)

Elvis sings: "Flaming Star" (over titles); "A Cane and a High Starched Collar" (impromptu dance at ranch)

While Paramount and MGM sensibly but unimaginatively followed the tried and tested Elvis formula, Twentieth Century Fox persisted--and failed miserably--at trying to be adventurous with Elvis. With an unwanted project and star thrust upon them (Nunnally Johnson, writer of *The Grapes of Wrath* and *The Three Faces of Eve* among others, had already departed in despair), writer Huffaker and director Siegel immediately conspired to dispose of the musical interludes, arguing quite justly that there were no places for them as the melodramatic tragedy unfolded. Indeed, producer David Weisbart also didn't want any musical interludes in the film at all, but was swiftly overruled by Parker and the front office, who wanted to cover all bases.

Weisbart, who would ultimately produce four Presley films (*Love Me Tender* and *Flaming Star* for Fox, and *Follow That Dream* and *Kid Galahad* for United Artists), was one of the few non-actors who shared Presley's high opinion of his acting potential, although Siegel had still to be convinced he wasn't presiding over a miscast disaster, and had already fought--rightly-- to replace tall, British, and dark-haired Barbara Steele in the girlfriend role that ultimately went to short, American, and blonde Barbara Eden. As always with situations where everyone is compromising and struggling to make the least rubbish film possible, the result, both here and with *Wild in the Country,* was to make mediocre films that pleased nobody, least of all Elvis Presley.

Equally frustrated with *Flaming Star* was director Don Siegel, who had already scored critical kudos with films such as *Riot in Cell Block Eleven* and

Invasion of the Body Snatchers, and would later achieve his greatest artistic and commercial successes in the 1970s with rising star Clint Eastwood, and films such as the beautiful and stunning *The Beguiled* and the groundbreaking (and rule-breaking) *Dirty Harry*. Unlike workhorses like Norman Taurog, who could dutifully and efficiently film sequences to fit six month old second unit work, or old-timers like Richard Thorpe and Hal Kanter, who were non-committal and happy just to be working, Siegel was ambitious and creative, and viewed film as an art form. In his self-aggrandising, score-settling autobiography, *A Siegel Film*, full of recalled conversations in which he's always right and always wins, except when he doesn't and is then proven right, he was full of praise for Presley's efforts, even though at this early stage in his career, Siegel didn't want or need an Elvis film--and while he never said so directly, he made little effort to hide his antipathy from Presley and his entourage.

The feeling was mutual, and Presley didn't need, or gain from, the attention of prestigious or ambitious directors. In interviews during his career, Siegel had little to say about *Flaming Star,* other than how he had managed to keep the musical interludes down from ten to four to a bare minimum (what remained were the title track and a dosey-doh-style period number). Clearly, he saw Presley's presence as an obstacle to overcome rather than an asset.

Flaming Star, originally titled *Black Star* until after completion, was not a bad film or a bad western, it was just an ordinary film, and a typical western of the period just like any of the others, preaching a message of peace and tolerance while delivering the requisite lurid action. The flaming star of the title was a sort of mystical portent of death that the Native Americans--or Indians as they were then still known--were supposed to experience before expiring, and the film ends with Presley's character witnessing it and riding off into the sunset to his fate (the Colonel apparently not so worried about negative public response this time). Siegel was a slightly more creative director than some at this point in his career, but again there was no shortage of competent western directors; for his part, in a role originally intended for Brando, Presley delivered an adequate performance that any other young actor could have matched. Siegel turned in a perfectly ordinary western which, had his name not been on it, would have attracted no more attention or analysis from film students than any other.

Dolores Del Rio, here playing the Kiowa-born mother of half-breed Elvis, was a fiery leading lady of the twenties and thirties who was on the comeback trail as a character actress, but for the rest of the cast it was business as usual--Steve Forrest was an adequate male lead in the sort of square-jawed cipher role that any athletic young man in Hollywood could have played, John McIntire was in his usual role as rancher/homesteader, Rodolfo Hoyos and Perry Lopez were the ethnic actors playing Red Indians, and Barbara Eden--later the lead in television's *I Dream of Jeannie*--played a pair of blue jeans. Rodd Redwing, also playing an Indian brave, would be back for *Charro* in 1969. Richard Jaeckel was surprisingly good in a minor role, Ford Rainey, Roy Jenson, and L.Q. Jones were among the dependable familiar faces making the show interesting. For Red West, it was a little more than interesting--he almost got strangled by Elvis while they were horsing around with a lasso, injured his elbow while stunt-doubling for an Indian brave, and then had to play a fight scene as a bad guy.

Wild in the Country (1961)

wr. Clifford Odets, from J.R. Salamance, dir. Philip Dunne, pr. Jerry Wald (Fox)

with Elvis Presley (Glenn Tyler), Tuesday Weld (Noreen), Hope Lange (Irene Sperry), Millie Perkins (Betty Lee Parsons), Rafer Johnson (Davis), John Ireland (Phil Macy), Gary Lockwood (John Macy), William Mims (Uncle Rolf), Christina Crawford (Monica George), Raymond Greenleaf (Doctor Underwood), Doreen Lang (Mrs. Parsons), Charles Arnt (Mr. Parsons), Alan Napier (Professor Larson), Will Corry (Willie Dace), Jason Robards Snr. (Judge Parker), Robin Raymond (Flossie), Ruby Goodwin (Sarah), Harry Sherman (Sam Tyler), Red West (Hank Tyler), Walter Baldwin (Spangler), Harry Carter (bartender), E.M. "Bitsy" Mott (trooper), Pat Buttram (yokel), Mike Lally (huckster), Joe Butham (Mr. Dace), Hans Moebus (conductor), Linden Chiles (doctor), Jack Orrison (coroner), and the Jordanaires

Elvis sings: "Wild in the Country" (over titles); "I Slipped, I Stumbled, I Fell" (melting Millie Perkins); "In My Way" (to Tuesday Weld); "Husky Dusky Day" (with Hope Lange in truck)

Filmed quickly and efficiently just before Christmas 1960, partially on location in Napa Valley, this soapy and slightly absurd melodrama was another perfectly ordinary film that could have been filmed with any combination of actors and any young man in the leading role taken by Elvis, once again cast as a troubled and undeservedly luckless young man. The rather pointless story is overwritten, but there are a few good lines, and in an era when most modern day films are formulaic and no-one seems to be able to write dialogue of substance any more, films like *Wild in the Country* seem better today than they probably did at the time.

Apart from the singing sequences, in which Elvis sings dreary ballads as if someone has his balls in a vise, it is a perfectly watchable film, but like *Flaming Star*, it is nothing special--and Elvis was something special. He had better things to do than make mediocre films, particularly those in which the musical interludes were a liability. Director Philip Dunne claimed the preview audience laughed when the characters broke into song (who wouldn't, at the pathetic ditty sung by Presley and Lange in the truck?), and said "I shot them so that they could be dropped out, and I wish they would drop them out of the prints now. They'd see a good movie". Screenwriter and playwright Clifford Odets felt the same way, and indeed, repeating the *Flaming Star* compromise, Fox did drop two of the six songs from the film. What remained were the title ballad "Wild in the Country", the jolly "I Slipped, I Stumbled, I Fell", the romantic ballad "In My Way" and the appalling kiddie folk song "Husky Dusky Day".

Considering her own apathy toward the project, Millie Perkins gives an excellent performance in the most thankless female role. An adventurous actress rather than the usual happy-go-lucky starlet of Presley pictures, her films include Monte Hellman's *Ride in the Whirlwind, The Shooting,* and *Cockfighter,* as well as *Wild in the Streets, The Witch Who Came from the Sea, Wall Street,* and *Slamdance.* Weirdly, she would portray Elvis' mother Gladys in the 1990 television drama series *Elvis,* an ambitious, short-lived interesting failure.

Tuesday Weld (real name Susan), although she graduated to more prestigious fare in later life despite her silly stage name (*The Flintstones* called her Tuesday Wednesday), had begun her career in such films as *Rock, Rock, Rock, Rally Round the Flag Boys* and *Sex Kittens Go to College.* She had an extraordinary aptitude for turning down sure things, and passed up *Bonnie and Clyde, Bob and Carol and Ted and Alice,* and *True Grit* (any of which would have both suited her and made her), all in the space of three years, while lending her considerable talents to undeserving rubbish. She'd have been perfect in all three of the above.

She was luckier with her earlier TV credits, turning up in *Dick Powell Theater, 77, Sunset Strip, The Naked City, Route 66,* and *The Fugitive.* She finally secured quality film credits in the late '70s/early '80s with *Who'll Stop the Rain, Thief,* and *Once Upon a Time in America.* Here, Weld offers an interesting take on an unusually three-dimensional jailbait role (she was always undeniably sexy, even in her poorest films), but it is the bland Hope Lange who has the most screen time and the most preposterous role. To add insult to injury, her character originally committed suicide at the end of the film, but some cast members were called back after Christmas to reshoot the ending, which was now considered too downbeat, and Lange's character was miraculously reprieved!

Lange--married to the inspired but unlucky director Alan Pakula--was a dowdy, uncharismatic actress with a hard face and shrill voice, and whenever she had to show warmth she usually looked as though she was sucking lemons. She had her greatest success on film in *Peyton Place* and *The Young Lions,* later settling for the long-running supernatural sit-com *The Ghost and Mrs. Muir,* but while *Bewitched* and *I Dream of Jeannie* are re-run in perpetuity, this similar show is now virtually forgotten. She was equally cold and charmless in the 1970s incarnation of *The New Dick Van Dyke Show* as the effervescent comic's screen wife, and did not have much of a career in film, but despite everything, the motel scenes with Presley are quite sexy.

John Ireland plays a stiff bore stiffly, while Gary Lockwood--in his first of two Presley films--is somewhat more animated as his stupid son. Once again, best buddy Red West rough and tumbles with Elvis, this time in the opening scenes as Elvis' brother Hank. West was given his first line ever in a movie during the courtroom scene, rehearsed all weekend, and then muffed it ("I couldn't even remember my name. Elvis laughed like hell"). Minor roles were taken by Christina Crawford, the daughter of actress Joan Crawford (who famously stuck a metaphorical knife in her mother and twisted it with the infamous book, later filmed, *Mommie Dearest*), Olympic decathlon athlete Rafer Johnson, and Alan Napier, the English actor best recalled for playing Alfred, the butler in *Batman*. Crawford and Presley had a run-in off-set when some horseplay got out of hand and Presley unceremoniously dragged her to the door and apparently booted her up the rear on the way out. In uncredited bit parts were character actor Pat Buttram as a gossiping yokel in the same vein as his *Green Acres* character and preppy young Fox contract player Linden Chiles as the last minute miracle doctor. Buttram--formerly comic relief in many Gene Autry films--would later play a major role, and one of his best, in *Roustabout*. Robin Raymond (Flossie) had been in *Jailhouse Rock* (as Dottie).

As soapy and fraught as it was, and saddled with dull direction by the apparently unfriendly Philip Dunne, *Wild in the Country* was not nearly as deep as it pretended to be, and was widely mocked for its pretensions at the time by cast and critics alike. However, although the characters were formulaic, the script and the actors managed to make them seem fresh and original. The three Fox films were not disasters; indeed, from a balance sheet point of view the inclusion of Elvis in them has given them a financial life and a historical status they would otherwise not have enjoyed. The distinction between Fox's movies and Paramount's is that *Love Me Tender, Flaming Star* and *Wild in the Country* were films with Elvis in them, rather than Elvis films. All were profitable, and all are worth watching. *Wild in the Country* was and is still no classic, and should not be overrated, but it is worth a look on a rainy afternoon.

2. The sunny '60s

Blue Hawaii (1961)

wr. Allan Weiss, Hal Kanter, dir. Norman Taurog, pr. Hal Wallis (Paramount)

with Elvis Presley (Chad Gates), Joan Blackman (Maile Duval), Angela Lansbury (Mrs. Gates), Roland Winters (Mr. Gates), Nancy Walters (Abigail Prentiss), John Archer (Jack Kelman), Howard McNear (Mr. Chapman), Jenny Maxwell (Ellie Corbett), Darlene Tompkins (Patsy), Pamela Kirk/Austin (Sandy), Christian Kay (Beverly), Steve Brodie (Mr. Garvey), Iris Adrian (Mrs. Garvey), Flora Hayes (Mrs. Manaka), Gregory Gay (Mr. Duval), Hilo Hattie (Waihila), Lani Kai (Carl), Jose De Vega (Ernie), Frank Atienza (Ito), Tiki Hanalei (Wes), Richard Reeves (drunk in jail), Michael Ross (police lieutenant), Red West (fight victim)

Elvis sings: "Blue Hawaii" (over titles); "Almost Always True" (to Joan Blackman in car); "Aloha Oe" (at beach); "No More" (at beach); "Can't Help Falling in Love" (at Duval party); "Rock-a-Hula Baby" (at Gates party); "Moonlight Swim" (in car with girls); "Ku-U-I-Po" (at beach party); "Ito Eats" (at beach party); "Slicin' Sand" (at beach party); "Hawaiian Sunset" (in nightclub); "Beach Boy Blues" (in jail cell); "Island of Love" (with girls); "Hawaiian Wedding Song" (at wedding to Joan Blackman)

After the disappointment of the latter two Fox efforts at the box office (although subsequently profitable), Wallis and the Colonel knew what worked and what didn't, and it hadn't cost them a penny to find out. Back came Hal Kanter, just as the writer this time, back came the workmanlike and competent Norman Taurog, and back came Elvis from the army--again. Beginning a profitable and prolific career with Presley was writer Allan Weiss, who would be involved with the nominal plots of many of the bright and breezy '60s storylines.

By now, the box office was dictating the direction of Elvis' movie career, and the trial-and-error period was over. Of all the producers and studios to work with Presley and Parker, it was Wallis and Paramount who stuck most rigidly to What Worked, and who subsequently enjoyed the most consistent success with their seemingly infallible formula. Wallis knew it too--*Blue Hawaii* was trailered as Elvis' "first big musical since the song-sational *G.I. Blues!*"--neatly rubbing salt in the wounds of the far less successful Fox duo of *Flaming Star* and *Wild in the Country*, which had shied away from musical numbers. This, Wallis was clearly implying, was Elvis as the audiences of the day wanted to see him--and as much as it might grieve purists to face up to it, it was true.

Usually, Elvis films could be expected to be slighted sarcastically by the snobs--but the 1960s movies found detractors among Elvis aficionados too. And yet, someone was buying the tickets and the vinyl, and they were coming back for more of the same in far greater numbers than the distressed and disenfranchised were supposedly staying away.

It's too easy, and plainly wrong, to suggest that audiences were paying up in spite of the material just to see Elvis. Although that's true of a select few, and Presley's earliest fans were furiously loyal and faithful to his death and beyond, the numbers were just too big, the audiences too wide to be made up solely of disappointed but defensive blue suede-shoed hound dogs. *Blue Hawaii* grossed over four million dollars--a huge amount for 1961--and the soundtrack album beat that figure, coming in at over five million in sales, the fastest selling album of 1961, the longest stayer for 1962. The songs were not unpleasant (the memorable "Can't Help Falling in Love" was among them), but most were Hawaiian themed and blend into each other effortlessly--sometimes literally, as with the touristy "Ku-U-I-Po", the awful "Ito Eats" and the pleasant period pop piece "Slicin' Sand", which are all performed back-to-back at a beach party. It's a delightful film, but certainly not rock and roll. Elvis was making family movies, and they were successful because by 1961 his 1950s fans had matured and begun their own families.

This was the first of no fewer than three Elvis movies to be started and completed that year, and during the filming of *Blue Hawaii,* in March 1961, the dire *G.I. Blues* album was still at the top of the charts. As much as the Elvis fans still stuck in the '50s may have disliked the post-Army film period, or even the fact that Elvis aged a year every year just like everybody else, as much as rock critics and pop culture historians may complain--with some justification--that the quality of the musical material had declined, and as much as film buffs and reviewers may agree retrospectively that Presley was at his best as an actor in *Jailhouse Rock* and *King Creole,* the facts are that the bright and breezy Elvis films--and film score albums--that began with the loathsome *G.I. Blues* and the fun and fluffy *Blue Hawaii* were vastly more popular than anything Elvis did before or later. By far. And he was sleepwalking through the work, partly due to indifference and partly due to a constant intake of the uppers and downers he had discovered in the army. He was also partying constantly--so much so that teenage girls were literally risking their lives trying to jump down to Presley's balcony from the hotel roof, and the female cast members were moved by the rattled Wallis to a different location than the males. But he had earned it. In film and vinyl form, the early '60s Elvis product--and my goodness, it was product--roared to the top of the movie and album charts.

However, Minnie Pearl, a country and western singer who had accompanied the entourage to Hawaii to participate in the high-profile U.S.S. Arizona concert to honor the memory of those lost at Pearl Harbor, saw Elvis on one of his quieter days. "We did the show on a Saturday" she told writer Alanna Nash for her book *The Colonel,* "and Sunday afternoon, a bunch of us were down on Waikiki Beach, cavorting and kidding and having a big time. We got to talking about how we wished Elvis would come down and be with us, and we turned and looked up at his penthouse, which was facing the ocean. He was standing on the balcony, looking down at us, this solitary figure, lonely looking, watching us have such a good time. He was just getting ready to start making the film, and he literally was a prisoner because of the fans. We sat there on the beach and talked about how it would be--what a price you pay for that sort of fame".

Onscreen, however, Elvis was a happy-go-lucky everyman paradoxically loved by all. The standard Hal Wallis ingredients for an Elvis film would now consist of songs, sun, sea, sand, romance, mild conflict, sports cars, and speed boats. And when he made movies in color, he made them in color--the scenery, both natural and mortal, was beautiful.

There would usually be a bluff idiot to be taken down a peg or two, and at least one comedy relief oldster in the cynical Sam Katzman tradition, but these would be outnumbered by friendly ordinary guys who liked or even admired Elvis (in this one a friendly cop waives a speeding ticket and replaces it with a motorcycle escort when Joan Blackman tells him Elvis' character is at the airport), and other representatives of the older generation who would be treated with respect and courtesy; Elvis, somewhat absurdly, sings his most romantic song in this film, the beautiful "Can't Help Falling in Love" ("Wise men say...") to a grateful granny, a family friendly ploy repeated in the follow-up *Girls!, Girls!, Girls!*

Elvis might also have a goofy buddy, a jealous rival, a combination of the two, or both (this film is an exception). There would be a punch-up in a bar at some point, a romantic misunderstanding (an inevitability given that there would usually be about three women involved with Elvis, one blissful winner, one pragmatic loser with the second male lead as consolation prize, and one plainly unsuitable from the off), a harmless brush with the law and perhaps brief incarceration (accompanying Elvis in the cells, a drunken doofus on harmonica who likes his singing so much that he hopes Elvis will get life--it's all a long way from the lurid whippings of *Jailhouse Rock*), light innuendo and chaste dating, the mandatory family-friendly cute kid/s, and an animal or two.

Elvis would be a rebel, but only against insular, personal conformity, not society; usually, the story would be about Elvis compromising, rebelling against other people's expectations or prejudices to join society on his own terms. Presley was perpetually cast as that curious oxymoron, the hard-working beach bum, and all his future roles would be an odd mix of respectable, decent guy and hedonistic but moralistic layabout.

Like Laurel and Hardy he played the same character every time, but in a different world, perpetually doomed in each film to begin life from scratch and end it with death by marriage--the outcome was always the same, and only the cast and circumstances would change (and often, not

This gloriously camp publicity shot of Elvis and the girls from Blue Hawaii shows Darlene Tompkins and Joan Blackman (l) and Jenny Maxwell and Christian Kay (r), presumably competing for the silliest pose

much). And if Laurel and Hardy, to continue the analogy, were the same guys living a string of separate lives with different wives in each appearance, never straying from their pre-ordained fate, Presley was an eternal teenager doing the same. As with Laurel and Hardy, each film seemed to pick up where the previous one left off, but in a parallel world, with a new premise, identity, and life. The Wallis Presley was like the later TV characters of the aforementioned and prolific Stephen J. Cannell in the 1980s--they were not adventure-seekers; they never sought trouble, it came to them. They were white knights by default, seeking a playfully energetic quiet life. Perhaps it was no coincidence that so many of the Presley entourage and beach movie players of the early '60s would later join the Cannell caravan, including Red West, Lance Le Gault, Joan Freeman, James Darren, and John Ashley, or that the Cannell productions in L.A. would be the 1980s playground for fun-seeking starlets inbetween B-movies.

As with *G.I. Blues,* this second Wallis/Taurog production would open with Elvis completing a two year stint in the army, and in a bizarre way was picking up from where *G.I. Blues* left off, only now Elvis has metamorphosed into Chad Gates, heir to a massive pineapple farming and distribution business, and the 'plane is touching down in Hawaii. Here, the urge to conform he is railing against is represented by his stuffy but fair father (Roland Winters, particularly good in his early confrontation with Joan Blackman's Maile) and his scatty, silly, snobbish mother (Angela Lansbury--Dolores Del Rio very wisely declined to play Elvis' mother a second time).

Lansbury, the actress sister of TV producer Bruce Lansbury (*Wild Wild West, Wonder Woman, Buck Rogers in the 25th Century, Streethawk*), and later the star of the long-running television series *Murder She Wrote,* was, like most of the more experienced professionals who worked with Presley (including co-star John Archer), impressed by his behavior and attitude. Lansbury was only ten years older than Presley, but her offbeat looks and broad acting style had already assigned her to a career of mumsy character roles, and she was regularly cast much older than she really was. She responded not so much by chewing the scenery, as flitting around delicately nibbling at it.

The film opens with Chad's girlfriend Maile whizzing through the wide and pristine highways of Hawaii to meet him at the airport in a bright red sports car, while typical early '60s movie music trickles around in the background--everything is bright, breezy, and sexy, full of the promise of the future; the '50s are officially over. When the door of the 'plane opens for the passengers to disembark--this was that wonderful era of air travel when you just stepped out of the 'plane into fresh air and down steps onto tarmac--Elvis is sucking the face of an appreciative air hostess (not "flight attendant"). It's all a gag, and when Maile's finished acting the huffy girlfriend for a bit they set off for the beach to try on swimsuits at an idyllic beach hut--paradise Hawaiian style indeed, although that title was yet to come.

Blue Hawaii gets its cringe-making scenes out of the way early--Elvis croons a reasonably amusing song ("Almost Always True") about "almost always being faithful" but mugs horribly (Elvis was charming and had comic timing but he couldn't do wacky), and there's some cheesy local color from the natives during an otherwise splendid set-piece on the beach--with token kids and animal, of course. (Did he have a swingin' time in Europe? The swingin'-est, man!). When Elvis defies his parents and sets out to work for himself, he joins the tourist agency of comedy relief boss Howard McNear where Maile works, and much to her consternation, his first task is to escort a young teacher and her four teenage girl charges around the island.

The expected complications ensue, enlivened by the punchy dialogue of Hal Kanter--there's the dust-up, a brief spell in the clink, the small misunderstanding (that results in Maile and Chad starting up their own tourist guide company and pilfering the teacher and her girls from McNear), and it all ends in a happy compromise (Chad and Maile will run tours for daddy's sales reps among other clients) and multiple marriages.

Despite the occasional awkward moment or brief misfire, it's a wonderful, charming slice of early '60s escapism, and the general holiday ambience of the film means that the musical numbers don't seem to be shoehorned in as in some of the earlier films; they are an integral part of events because there is no heavy-going plot to be slowed down by them. Elvis bounces through a lively rendition of "Rock-a-Hula Baby" at his parents' party (the atmosphere ruined by the awful admonishment from Chad's father to his silly wife "That's something you're going to have to get used to, my dear--the sound of youth!") and there are a string of entertaining set pieces at the beach party. A personal favorite--which must be seen widescreen--is the kitschy, cornball harmony about taking a moonlight swim as Elvis and the girls (including the lovely Jenny Maxwell as troublemaking sulk-pot Ellie) drive out to the pineapple farm for free samples. "What were you expecting--bananas?" snaps surly Ellie.

Despite a litany of familiar excuses and hard luck stories which rightly hold no water with a smirking Elvis, but which today would secure her a small army of hand-wringing trauma counselors, she gets her outdated and inappropriate just desserts in a hilarious--and sexy--scene, as Chad tames his shrew by smacking her butt *McLintock*-style, the inevitable sexist '60s spanking from a male authority to set her straight.

As already established in earlier Elvis films, including Wallis' *G.I. Blues,* the leading ladies are invariably bland, pretty-plain good girl types. With only a few exceptions (Juliet Prowse and Ann-Margret being the most obvious), this would remain the pattern for most of the Elvis fictions. Possibly this was so as not to distract from Presley (as Ann-Margret most certainly did in the later *Viva Las Vegas,* much to the Colonel's consternation), or possibly it was the intention to offer up bland ciphers for Presley's huge female following to identify with rather than be threatened by. Had Elvis been seduced by great beauties, his young female admirers may well have felt hopelessly outmatched in their fantasies. Also, any young man identifying with the Elvis persona wouldn't want to be too intimidated--men could be threatened by female beauty too. The illusion for both sexes had to be protected.

Then again, maybe Wallis really was working with the best he had on offer (the stunningly beautiful Pamela Tiffin had declined the role of Maile, despite appearing in numerous similar films of the non-Elvis variety, and Juliet Prowse had been sacked or walked off the film, depending on whose account of creative differences one chose to listen to). Whatever the rationale, the part went to the pretty, competent, but ordinary Joan Blackman, who would be back again with Presley the same year in *Kid Galahad,* where she would be virtually invisible onscreen (*Blue Hawaii* may be her best film).

Cast as the teacher Abigail Prentiss was the plastic Nancy Walters, mouthing clumsily along to the moonlight swim sequence like a broken ventriloquist's dummy. Saving the day are the four schoolgirls, Christian Kay, Pamela Kirk (actually Pamela Austin, later to reappear in *Kissin' Cousins*), scene-stealing Darlene Tompkins (back for some *Fun in Acapulco*) and pouting Jenny Maxwell as the malevolent elf Ellie Corbett.

None of the four "schoolgirls" in *Blue Hawaii* went much further in their careers. However, they kept busy in the '60s (Walters turned up in *Gunsmoke, Get Smart,* and *The Monkees;* Joan Blackman turns up in a *Peyton Place* storyline and episodes of *Perry Mason, Bonanza, Gunsmoke,* and *I Spy*). Pamela Austin's TV credits included a memorable *Twilight Zone* ("Number Twelve Looks Just Like You", truer today than it ever was back then) and the inevitable *77, Sunset Strip, Hawaiian Eye* and *Surfside Six* for Warners. Later she would appear in *It Takes a Thief, The Virginian, My Three Sons, The Wild Wild West, Rowan and Martin's Laugh-In* and *Columbo.*

Jenny Maxwell had made her debut in the dreary melodrama *Blue Denim* in 1959, directed by *Wild in the Country* director Phillip Dunne. She made only two other films after *Blue Hawaii,* both in 1963--teen movie *Take Her, She's Mine* (with Sandra Dee and *Kissin' Cousins'* Cynthia Pepper), and *Shotgun Wedding,* as more teenage jailbait (the gloriously named Honey Bee Heller) in a script by the infamous Ed Wood. However, she appeared in numerous classic and/or cult TV shows of the period, including *Father Knows Best, Bachelor Father, Bonanza, Route 66, The Twilight Zone, Doctor Kildare, Wagon Train, Hawaiian Eye, 77, Sunset Strip, The FBI, My Three Sons,* and T*he Wild Wild West,* usually as teenage trouble. Cruelly, Maxwell and her second husband were shot and killed during an assumed botched robbery in 1981.

Darlene Tompkins was undeservedly less fortunate work-wise, with several disappointments and bad luck stories despite a smattering of TV spots and good reviews for her debut in the sci-fi cheapie *Beyond the Time Barrier* and the Debbie Reynolds comedy *My Six Loves.* She later worked as stand-in and stunt double for Cheryl Ladd on *Charlie's Angels.* "The movie's success really, really surprised me" she said some years later, "because it was done so light-hearted. We had so much fun filming it, nobody expected it to be as big as it was. You'd think if a movie was going to be such a hit you'd put your blood, sweat and tears into it, but on *Blue Hawaii* we just had fun". So did the audience.

Although there was some rear projection where necessary, *Blue Hawaii* did not have the cheap, second-rate look of *G.I. Blues,* and Presley, cast and entourage had all travelled to Hawaii for location filming. Elvis had toured Hawaii with his act in November 1957 with the draft looming over him, and it was the dream holiday of choice for 1960s America. *Blue Hawaii* is a delightful time capsule that is still entertaining today.

Follow That Dream

Follow That Dream (1962)

wr. Charles Lederer, from Richard Powell, dir. Gordon Douglas, pr. David Weisbart (UA)

with Elvis Presley (Toby Kwimper), Anne Helm (Holly Jones), Arthur O'Connell (Mr. Kwimper), Alan Hewitt (Arthur King), Joanna Moore (Alicia Claypoole), Simon Oakland (Nick), Jack Kruschen (Carmine), Herbert Rudley (Mr. Endicott), Roland Winters (Judge), Howard McNear (George), Harry Holcomb (Governor), Frank De Kova, Robert Carricart, John Duke (hoods), Red West (bank guard), Pam Ogles (Ariadne), Robin and Gavin Koon (Teddy and Eddy)

Elvis sings: "What a Wonderful Life" (in car, over credits); "I'm Not the Marryin' Kind" (on beach to Anne Helm); "Sound Advice" (with Kwimper family in cabin); "Follow That Dream" (to Joanna Moore); "Angel" (to Anne Helm on porch)

In July 1961, Elvis' buddy and Hollywood bit player Red West married Presley's secretary Pat Boyd, and after a brief pause in Nashville for recording, the entourage headed for Crystal River, Florida for the filming of the next Elvis movie. Everyone wanted a piece of Elvis, and Tom Parker was openly boastful of it.

United Artists were next in line. David Weisbart had produced *Love Me Tender* at Fox back in 1956 (and later, *Flaming Star*), but six years on Elvis was no longer an unknown quantity, and a formula was beginning to develop. Weisbart took the elements from *Blue Hawaii* that Wallis would later run into the ground--the idyllic beach life, the cute kids, the comedy oldsters, the clumsy misunderstandings and jealousies, the plain-but-pretty romantic interest, the rejected vampish rival, Elvis as good-hearted rascal--and added comedy gangsters (the highlight of the film), a genuinely witty script full of simple country folks wisdom of the *Beverly Hillbillies* variety ("I wonder where that road leads?"/"It's hard to tell just from lookin' at one end"), conservative values (the girl just wants to set up house with Elvis, but he's wary of getting hooked, and rather than playing around recites mathematical tables every time he's aroused from his virginity) and a dash of last-minute melodrama in the form of a typically Capra-esque trial sequence of the sort already indulged in during *Loving You* and *Wild in the Country*. As ever, Elvis is the misjudged rebel, the misunderstood teen, but this time he has an entire family to defend from detractors.

Elvis, looking decidedly chubby in this outing, and delivering dialogue that could have been written for *South Park's* Butters Stotch, is Toby Kwimper, one of a small family of freeloaders under the paternal eye of elderly Pa Kwimper (Arthur O'Connell of the first *Gidget* movie in one of his more rewarding and substantial roles here). Described in *Halliwell's Filmgoer's Companion* as "usually mildly bewildered", that pretty much sums up his requirements here, and gifted with marvelous comic timing, he was always seen to best effect in lighter fare. TV work included *Dick Powell Theater, Burke's Law, Voyage to the Bottom of the Sea, The Wild Wild West, The Name of the Game,* and plenty of westerns and sit-coms.

Pa and Toby have acquired an extended family in the form of two abandoned twin boys (Eddie and Teddy, played by Gavin and Robert Koon), a female toddler, and young Holly Jones (Anne Helm), a young girl orphaned in her teens and now grown to alluring womanhood ("*1 x 1 = 1...*").

In *Follow That Dream,* people who in reality would have the paying audience spitting feathers (they exist entirely on government handouts, and Pa Kwimper expects it) are here written up not only to expect our sympathies, but to reduce us to giggly merriment as they frustrate the pompous stuffed shirts and comedy bureaucrats, represented here by Alan Hewitt (also the Aunt Sally figure in the *My Favorite Martian* TV series).

At the same time, scriptwriter Lederer (working from the book *Pioneer Go Home* by Richard Powell) sends up the Kwimpers, *Beverly Hillbillies*-style, notably with a bit of business about the family's first real toilet, which provides several childishly hilarious slapstick moments in the film. However, like the much-maligned *Beverly Hillbillies,* the dialogue is much cleverer and funnier than it is often given credit for, particularly with a talent like Lederer at the helm.

"I like girls, except when they start to bother me" explains the virginal Toby to Alicia. "A young, virile man like you, I'd think you'd love to be bothered!" she exclaims. "Well, the botherin' part's alright, but I ain't goin' to marry no girl and build no house so I can be bothered regular!" he replies, earnestly.

Needless to say, he has a lifetime of botherin' ahead of him at picture's end. Holly connives--with Elvis' Toby--to make honest men of the Kwimpers by rejecting the welfare money and running a tourist fishing business on the beach they stumble onto, exploiting the homesteading laws to defy Hewitt's fuming highways officer Arthur King, who falls at every fence as he tries to send the Kwimpers packing. Hewitt was a regular in Disney films and TV sit-coms during the 1960s, appearing in *The Absent-*

Minded Professor, The Misadventures of Merlin Jones, and *The Computer Wore Tennis Shoes* for Disney, and sit-coms such as *Bewitched, The Lucy Show,* and *I Dream of Jeannie.*

Assisting him is evil intellectual and condescending social worker and psychologist Alicia Claypoole (Joanna Moore), who gets a double drenching from a) angry Holly after a doomed attempt at seducing Toby ("*1 x 1 = 1...*") and b) the impartial toilet facilities, and is soundly outwitted in the courtroom by country folk cunning.

Moore was one of about two dozen Elvis movie starlets who also appeared in an episode of the phenomenally successful 1960s spy series *The Man from UNCLE.* If you were an ambitious young actress in the 1960s and you didn't do either *UNCLE, Batman,* or an Elvis film, you hadn't really made the grade. Moore also had 1960s credentials from *Dick Powell Theater, The Untouchables, 77, Sunset Strip, Hawaiian Eye, Bourbon Street Beat, Route 66, Bewitched, The Wild Wild West,* and *The Fugitive.*

Character actor Herbert Rudley, often cast as stand-up conservatives in 1960s comedies such as *The Beverly Hillbillies, My Favorite Martian, The Munsters,* and *Mothers-in-Law,* the latter of which he co-starred in, plays Mr. Drysdale to O'Connell's Jed Clampett (*The Beverly Hillbillies* was in pre-production during 1961, with the pilot filming in December), and Howard McNear and Roland Winters both return from *Blue Hawaii.* Winters, once an improbable Charlie Chan in the movie series, does a nice turn as the affable judge, and comic actor McNear, a regular throughout the 1960s on the long-running hick-com *The Andy Griffiths Show,* does his usual schtick as a flustered suit and tie by-the-book guy, a routine of tics and double-takes he would not only perform to perfection in two Elvis movies that year, but a third time in the unusual venue of the opening scenes of the *Voyage to the Bottom of the Sea* feature film.

Although O'Connell and his brood are presented as struggling good-natured survivors rather than con-men, any film with protagonists on the fringes of respectable society needs real heavies added to the mix to provide the audience with genuine villains. Enter the Disney-esque gangsters, genuinely funny, with character actor Simon Oakland doing a blatant Edward G. Robinson impression, and Jack Kruschen as his pragmatic, calmer, but equally baffled lieutenant.

While Winters, Hewitt, O'Connell, Oakland and Kruschen all played straight roles during their careers, they were all in their element playing comedy. Simon Oakland's numerous TV credits include *The Untouchables, The Twilight Zone, The Outer Limits, The Detectives, My Favorite Martian, Get Smart, Combat, Tarzan, It Takes a Thief, Hawaii Five-O, The Name of the Game,*

Kojak, The Rockford Files, Police Story, Charlie's Angels, and *Lou Grant.* He was a regular cast member on *Kolchak--the Night Stalker, Toma,* and *Black Sheep Squadron,* and his films included such diverse projects as *Psycho, West Side Story,* and *Bullitt.* Jack Kruschen's usually jolly demeanor enlivened a variety of feature films for the general audience, and dozens of TV shows across five decades, some of the more memorable including *The Untouchables, The Naked City, Batman, I Spy, Bonanza, Ironside, Hawaii Five-O, Columbo,* and *The Rockford Files.* Frank de Kova appeared as gangsters and heavies on *The Untouchables* and others, but found regular work as Chief Wild Eagle of the Hekawi tribe ("where the heck are we?") on the sit-com *F Troop.* Robert Carricart, back for some *Fun in Acapulco,* was another veteran of *The Untouchables,* for which he played a delightfully sleazy Lucky Luciano. John Duke, the third hood, had also inevitably done time on that show.

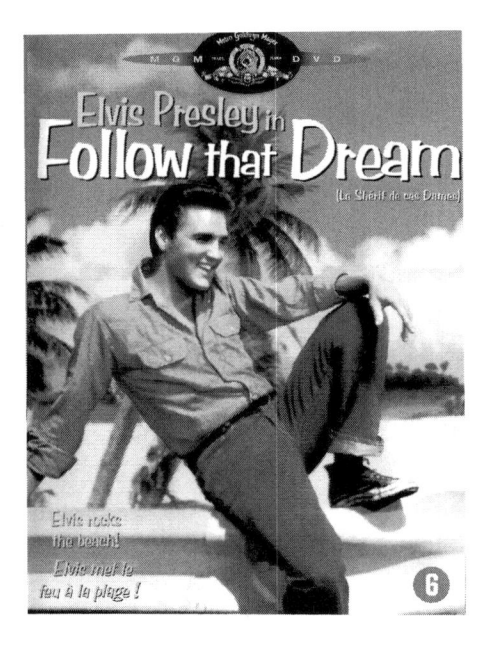

As a director, Gordon Douglas was competent, efficient, and totally without a personal signature of any kind. Consequently, filming went so smoothly as to verge on the boring, with no Siegel-style conflicts or Dunne-like pretensions to get in the way of what results in a perfectly pleasant addition to the Presley canon (the only upset involved Lamar Fike, one of the Memphis Mafia, driving a white limo onto the beach and having the wheels sink into the sand; Douglas bawled out Fike, Presley bawled out Douglas).

Screenwriter Charles Lederer had made his name working with Howard Hawks, for whom he wrote *The Front Page, His Girl Friday,* and perhaps more surprisingly, *The Thing from Another World.* He also wrote Juliet Prowse's *Can Can,* and Sinatra's *Ocean Eleven.* Even in *The Thing,* sometimes improvised by the actors, Lederer's talent for writing sing-song clever dialogue is plainly apparent, and *Follow That Dream* may be Presley's most professionally conceived script--the accidental bank robbery sequence, an old chestnut, is wonderful.

There were only two drawbacks to the film becoming a classic. Firstly, the five songs were utterly banal and uncharacteristic of the Presley style, with two of them so badly mimed they become parodic. Crying out for the cutting room floor is the excruciating sequence where Elvis supposedly sings along with the radio to Joanna Moore; it's difficult to ascertain who is the most uncomfortable--Moore, Presley, or the audience watching through their fingers. Fortunately, of the five, one song opens the film, accompanying the credits, and another, the reasonable ballad "Angel", closes it, so the pain is fleeting and mostly unobtrusive.

Slightly more discomfiting is that the character of Toby Kwimper recreates, accentuates and parallels far too effectively some of the less appealing qualities of Elvis Presley--his naivete, his sheltered environment, and most of all his sexual immaturity. His unfortunate ability to divide women into just two categories--up-for-anything starlet or untouched princess on a pedestal--ensured that Elvis Presley, unlike Toby Kwimper, had no need for $1 \times 1 = 1$, but Toby's reticence to allow himself to succumb to Holly's charms in the film uncomfortably echoes his attitude toward Priscilla and his other wives-in-waiting at this time in his life, while the wonderfully funny scenes of him as sheriff prompt recollections of his later similarly guileless and simple-minded infatuation with blindly upholding a sort of *Hawaii Five-O* version of the law.

These similarities with the otherwise charming Presley's dumber side play to his critics and the Hollywood sophisticates Presley feared were laughing at him, and with hindsight bring the film perilously close to unintentional satire. Fortunately, Presley's private life was not the open book then that it is today. Needless to say, such subtleties were lost on the critics of the day, some of whom overrated it, having suddenly found Presley "harmless" after the castrating *G.I. Blues* and conformist *Blue Hawaii,* and some of whom underrated it, missing the movie's many charms due to their disdain for Presley, who shows considerable comic ability in the bank and the gangster scenes.

As for his latest leading lady, Anne Helm's film career was brief and undistinguished. She came to Elvis films from a Bert Gordon movie, *The Magic Sword* (co-starring two-time Elvis co-star Gary Lockwood), and swiftly returned to schlock straight afterwards (*The Couch, Mother Goose-a-Go-Go, Nightmare in Wax,* the titles tell it all), even falling so far as to make a film in England (*The Swingin' Maiden,* directed by the *Carry On* man, Gerald Thomas). When your best film is an Elvis movie, even this one, you're in trouble.

Her TV work, guest-starring in many of the better known series of the early '60s, was, like that of many Elvis girls, actually more impressive and prestigious than her movies, and included parts in *Bilko, Alfred Hitchcock Presents, The Untouchables, Wagon Train, Gunsmoke, Rawhide, The Detectives,*

Route 66 (with O'Connell, the same year as *Follow That Dream*), *Hawaiian Eye, Perry Mason, Laramie, Doctor Kildare, Burke's Law, Twelve O'Clock High, The Big Valley, The Virginian, The Fugitive, Hawaii Five-O,* and *Streets of San Francisco*, many times in more than one episode.

One of many, many young starlets doing films and TV in the early '60s, she never amounted to anything career-wise, but may very well not have tried to or cared to. Many young former models and dancers were in Hollywood for fun and adventure, and Helm undoubtedly had plenty of both, so she has nothing to be ashamed of--the turkeys she appeared in were improved, but not saved, by her presence. She dated Elvis while they were in Florida, citing boredom rather than passion ("There was really nothing to do down there except play cards and go out on the boat" she told Peter Guralnick), and had no illusions that this was anything serious; she found the situation with his ever-present entourage slightly disconcerting, and when they returned to Hollywood to complete the interiors they drifted apart amicably. She continued to appear in various cop shows and medical dramas during the '70s, and made appearances in *Hart to Hart, Airwolf,* and *Amazing Stories* in the '80s.

Kid Galahad (1962)

wr. William Fay, from Francis Wallace, dir. Phil Karlson, pr. David Weisbart (UA)

with Elvis Presley (Walter Gulick), Gig Young (Willy Grogan), Lola Albright (Dolly Fletcher), Joan Blackman (Rose Grogan), Charles Bronson (Lew Nyack/trainer), David Lewis (Otto Danzig/gangster), Robert Emhardt (Maynard the cook), Michael Dante (Joey Shakes), Judson Pratt (Mr. Zimmerman), Ned Glass (Max Lieberman), George Mitchell (Harry Sperling), Roy Roberts (Jerry/ promoter), Liam Redmond (Father Higgins), Richard Devon (Marvin), Jeffrey Morris (Ralphie), Ed Asner (Frank Grissom/Asst. D.A.), Chris Alcaide (hood), Ralph Moody (Pete), Ramon De La Fuente (Sugar Boy Romero), Frank Gerstle (Romero's manager), George J. Lewis (Romero's trainer), Tommy Hart, Mushy Callahan (referees)

Elvis sings: "King of the Whole Wide World" (on truck); "This is Living" (on porch with the guys); "Riding the Rainbow" (in jalopy); "Home is Where the Heart Is" (to Joan Blackman); "I Got Lucky" (at picnic); "A Whistling Tune" (to Joan Blackman)

Kid Galahad started filming in October 1961 and was finished in time for Christmas. Elvis is Walter Gulick, a mechanic looking for work who finds interim employment as a sparring partner and later prizefighter whose technique consists of taking innumerable punches in the face before throwing a knockout punch. He acquires the Galahad nickname during the traditional Elvis film moment of standing up to a bully (Galahad having been one of the legendary noble and heroic knights of King Arthur).

As the film opens, he has just left the army--again--and is first seen sitting on the back of a truck looking for work while miming badly to the first of a series of forgettable but acceptable songs. Elvis preferred a nod to logic if he was going to suddenly start singing, and scriptwriters obliged as often as possible by putting the musical interludes into moments when a young man just might conceivably burst into song--we see him switch on a radio and sing along, start whistling and sing along, and so on. The songs are so bland that *Kid Galahad* isn't so much a musical as a drama with musical interludes. More than that, it's an ensemble drama with a huge cast and multiple storylines, half of which have nothing to do with Elvis-- one frequently finds oneself drawn into the melodrama and almost surprised when Elvis suddenly walks into a scene. Only Hal Wallis would ever figure out that what the public primarily wanted from an Elvis movie was Elvis.

Fortunately for *Kid Galahad,* the ensemble cast is excellent, and the film is surprisingly upbeat and watchable, particularly considering it's a boxing movie, a genre more notable for being grim and depressing (Francis Wallace's novel had already been made into a 1937 melodrama at Warners, with Edward G. Robinson, Humphrey Bogart, Wayne Morris, and Bette Davis). Perhaps this is because the boxing ring is as much a sideline for the movie as it is for Walter.

Gig Young (real name, Byron Barr) had taken his stage name from a 1941 film role and kept relatively busy in the twenty years since. He was perfect for one of the finest ever *Twilight Zones,* the heartbreaking and gut-wrenching "Walking Distance", would shortly co-star in the smarmy Aaron Spelling series *The Rogues* (1964-'65), and later win an Academy Award for his role in 1969's *They Shoot Horses, Don't They?*, but he was an alcoholic and his career was on the slide. In the early 1970s he would be superb in two of Sam Peckinpah's most cynical and brutal films, *Bring Me the Head of Alfredo Garcia* and *The Killer Elite,* before returning to TV for the magnificently camp drama series *Gibbsville* (1976) and the failed Gene Roddenberry pilot *Spectre* in 1978. That same year he made the mistake of marrying a woman too young for him, and she made the mistake of teasing him about it. He shot her dead, and then himself. Here he saunters amiably through one of his sad-eyed, jaunty, All-American loser roles, Lola Albright gives a nothing female role three dimensions, and Joan Blackman--looking and performing very differently from her *Blue Hawaii* role--reduces her two dimensional girlfriend role to one dimension. The following year, Blackman appeared alongside Elvis' buddy Nick Adams in the courtroom melodrama *Twilight of Honor.*

Lola Albright, a B-movie peroxide blonde, ended up in television, notably a two-part *Man from UNCLE* titled "The Prince of Darkness Affair" released to cinemas as *The Helicopter Spies* and a two-part series highlight for *The Incredible Hulk* titled "The First" alongside Elvis sidekick and series lead Bill Bixby in the 1980s. Other TV included a recurring role in *Peter Gunn* in the early '60s, and episodes of *The Detectives, The Beverly Hillbillies, Burke's Law, Branded, Kojak, Police Story,* and *Airwolf.*

A wonderful supporting cast of character actors includes Ned Glass, Ed Asner, Richard Devon, and Roy Roberts doing what they usually do, and David Lewis and Robert Emhardt playing against type. Lewis, as the gangster, went on to play the hapless prison reformer Warden Crichton in several episodes of cult '60s TV show *Batman,* and usually plays conformist stiffs, while Robert Emhardt, cast here as the cook in a far-from-gourmet kitchen, usually played corrupt or sinister stuffed shirts in positions of authority. George Mitchell, on the other hand, was one of those chameleon actors who played a wide range of character bit parts and consequently, was neither stereotyped nor noticed. In my research on other projects, I've found him as Scotsman, redneck, and Red Indian chief!

Charles Bronson, then a minor league actor doing mostly television and B-movies (he was Roger Corman's *Machine Gun Kelly*), was cast as his trainer. TV included *The Twilight Zone, The Untouchables,* and *Combat.* It has been said that Presley and Charles Bronson did not get on; if this is true, they are both better actors than they are given credit for and hide it well on camera. In reality, Elvis was coached by a former boxer with the wonderful name of Mushy Callahan, and who appears in the movie as a referee. Callahan had trained Wayne Morris in the 1937 version, which Elvis was a big fan of, and also trained James Dean for his fight scenes in *East of Eden* and *Rebel Without a Cause*--more than adequate credentials for Elvis to employ him as his own trainer here.

Kid Galahad was filmed at Idlewild, near Los Angeles; one visitor to the set was Gig Young's then-wife, Elizabeth Montgomery, later to star in the TV series *Bewitched,* produced by her next husband, beach movie producer William Asher. Presley was besotted with her, but she was unattainable and he was dating singer Connie Stevens at the time. Ironically, Gig Young had worked with James Dean a couple of weeks before his fateful motor-cycle crash in the even more ironic cornball road safety commercial he made; this infamous, blackly comic slab of 1950s insincerity has to be the phoniest piece of film ever committed to celluloid.

Phil Karlson had been efficiently directing undistinguished low-budget movies for twenty years, and his direction is fine, but the silver cup goes to cinematographer Burnett Guffey, who shoots the film beautifully in rich but realistic colors. The sets and costumes are just right, and the songs are okay, although Jeff Alexander's music is the sort that, although employed sparingly, tells you what's going on through various over-literal musical cliches even if you're facing the opposite direction of the screen--for example, every time an Irish character or name appears, Irish jigs folk-dance across the soundtrack like demented leprechauns. Nevertheless, the plusses far outweigh the minuses, making this the boxing film for people who don't like boxing films (and for those who do like boxing films, all your favorite cliches are there!). Why, there's even a montage.

Girls! Girls! Girls! (1962)

wr. Allan Weiss, Edward Anholt, dir. Norman Taurog, pr. Hal Wallis (Paramount)

with Elvis Presley (Ross Carpenter), Laurel Goodwin (Laurel Dodge), Jeremy Slate (Wes Johnson), Stella Stevens (Robin Gantner), Robert Strauss (Sam), Frank Puglia (Mr. Stavros), Lili Valenty (Mrs. Stavros), Guy Lee (Chen Yung), Benson Fong (father), Beulah Quo (mother), Nestor Paiva (tourist fisherman), Ann McCrea (bored wife), Mary Treen, Marjorie Bennett (hat store customers), Gavin Gordon (hat store manager), Barbara Beall, Betty Beall (Stavros girls), Ginny Tiu, Elizabeth Tiu, Alexander Tiu (Yung children), Red West (bongo player), Ken Becker (drunk), Richard Collier (clerk)

Elvis sings: "Girls! Girls! Girls!" (over titles); "Mama, Never Let Me Go" (Stella Stevens only, in nightclub); "I Don't Wanna Be Tied" (at nightclub); "We'll Be Together" (at Stavros party); "A Boy Like Me, A Girl Like You" (on boat); "Earth Boy" (with kids and Laurel Goodwin); "The Nearness of You" (Stella Stevens only, in nightclub); "Return to Sender" (in nightclub); "Because of Love" (in nightclub); "Thanks to the Rolling Sea" (on fishing boat); "Song of the Shrimp" (on fishing boat); "The Walls Have Ears" (in Laurel Goodwin's apartment); "We're Coming in Loaded" (on fishing boat); "Dainty Little Moonbeams" (with kids); "Girls! Girls! Girls!" (reprise; finale dance number)

For the official follow-up to *Blue Hawaii*, filmed in the Spring of 1962, Hal Wallis didn't miss a trick. With Edward Anholt providing the banter this time, he and storyman Allan Weiss went through *Blue Hawaii* with a fine toothcomb to pick out, shuffle around, and recreate all the elements that had produced Presley's most successful film to date.

And it works. What isn't swiped from *Blue Hawaii*, is swiped from *Loving You, G.I. Blues*, and *Follow That Dream*, and this would be the procedure from now on, each film feeding off the DNA of the previous ones. Despite the cheesy title--which looks even cheesier in the cheap-looking animated titles--this was one of the better examples of sunny, fluffy Elvis, beautifully photographed by Loyal Griggs to take full advantage of the stunning scenery. As Charles Lang's efforts in *Blue Hawaii* had proven, it was almost impossible to point the camera at Hawaii and get a bad shot, but Griggs was either exceptionally lucky, or went that extra mile; an insert shot of Laurel Goodwin turning up at Presley's boat at the Ala Wai Harbor to find him absent lasts only a few seconds, but looks fantastic, the early evening sun sparkling on the water.

Elvis plays Ross Carpenter, an easy-going fisherman, whose life is disrupted when his kindly, elderly employers, a Greek couple named Stavros, are forced to sell up for health reasons. The only buyer on the horizon is the sleazy Wesley Johnson, who Elvis takes an instant dislike to, and treats to a wild ride on the waves during a test run in the Kingfisher, a motor boat, an indulgence he will come to regret (Presley was known, on those frequent occasions when he rented entire amusement parks after hours, to deliberately leave people on the funfair rides for an overlong time to purposely make them queasy--particularly if they were guys making eyes at girls he fancied for himself).

Johnson's real prize is the Stavros fishing business, but thrown in with it is the West Wind, a sailboat with a strong personal connection to Carpenter. It was a personal project built by him and his father, who died the day it was completed. Now he lives on board, but Stavros must sell, and Ross hasn't got the ten thousand dollars to buy it. To the conniving Johnson, Carpenter's sentimental attachment to the boat is simply an added plus to get Carpenter to work for him at the lowest rates possible to buy the boat. Johnson figures that as long as Carpenter wants it, he'll not only stick around to buy it with his wages, but maintain it too. And he's right.

Ross first meets his latest romantic interest (Laurel Goodwin) at the club, where in tried and true Elvis movie fashion, he dispatches her drunken boyfriend. Grateful and immediately intrigued, the girl--the perky but mysterious Laurel (Goodwin's character shares her name)--pursues him with the usual 1960s hot and cold playfulness.

A Doris Day-style light comedy of constant minor misunderstandings and complications ensues, with one of the best selections of music in an Elvis movie, including the classic "Return to Sender"... and the music is almost continuous, yet unobtrusive. Light drama and light music gel to perfection (although Elvis was less happy with such inoffensive non-classics as "Song of the Shrimp", actually a plus in the mix rather than a minus!). The only thing unusually absent from the entire movie, oddly enough, are the girls, girls, girls, until a final number to close the film attempts to justify the film's sappy title in a musical set piece. Bizarrely, though, until those final few minutes, this film probably has the least amount of female flesh frugging about than any other similar Elvis film of the period. "You're Sir Galahad, Don Juan and Casanova all rolled into one" snaps Stella Stevens' character, while meandering through an on-again, off-again relationship with him. "If it isn't this boat, it's girls, girls, girls!". And yet, the very ordinary Laurel nabs him effortlessly.

Although Elvis apparently didn't think much of this movie, and wouldn't think much of any of those that followed, it's better than it's given credit for, avoiding the obvious resolution of having Ross get the boat, and instead ending with Ross and Laurel promising to build a new boat to inaugurate their new life together.

Like so many of Elvis' leading ladies, Laurel Goodwin was no great beauty by Hollywood's narrow standards. She was pretty, likeable, lanky, a good actress, and good at comedy--the sequence in her apartment, in which she first attempts to cook Elvis a meal and they end up doing a tango while the neighbors knock on the walls, floor and ceiling is a highlight of the film. She carries the sequence off not with good looks or sexiness, as *G.I. Blues'* Juliet Prowse or *Viva Las Vegas'* Ann-Margret might, but sheer chutzpah and comedy talent. The other leading lady, the talented Stella Stevens, has made it abundantly clear over the years that she didn't want to be in Hawaii, and didn't want to be in an Elvis picture, two opinions even the camera can't hide. Fortunately, she was playing a sulky sourpuss, so what Laurel Goodwin called sour grapes passes as a good performance as Stevens' one-dimensional and completely emotionless Robin Gantner loses Elvis scene by scene.

Laurel Goodwin was a child model who got lucky--she was one of the last contract players to be taken on by Paramount, and her picture was fortuitously seen by producer Hal Wallis after both Dolores Hart and Pamela Tiffin had proven unavailable (Tiffin also turned down *Blue Hawaii* and *Fun in Acapulco,* and later decided she regretted it; ironically, one of those who "poisoned her mind", as she put it, was two-times Presley co-star Dolores Hart, who promptly went off to join the convent!). The Presley film remains Goodwin's finest moment. She followed it with a little-known Jackie Gleason comedy film, *Papa's Delicate Condition,* and three westerns (one of which she was cut out of, but another of which was *The Glory Guys,* written by Sam Peckinpah). On TV, she guested in *The Virginian, Run, Buddy, Run,* the original *Star Trek* pilot "The Cage" (later shown in the series as flashbacks in the two-part "The Menagerie"), *Get Smart,* and bit parts in two consecutive episodes of *The Beverly Hillbillies* as a flower child, in which she has little to do but stand around.

By the end of the '60s, Laurel Goodwin's movie career was over, although she was happily married and not too sad about it. There were, she accurately points out, too few roles and too many actresses going for them, and all she was offered was "Beth the preacher's daughter, Beth the preacher's daughter, and Beth the preacher's daughter!". Today, she jokes about her cult status, as the proud owner of two iconic accolades--leading lady in an Elvis film and a significant role in the genesis and mythology of

Star Trek. Add to this the names of Jackie Gleason and Sam Peckinpah, and it's a short but classy resume.

Considering that her career has always been motivated by the need to earn (she was a single mother with a young son, future actor and producer Andrew Stevens), Stella Stevens, the former Estelle Eggleston, has had quite a few jewels in her crown. She appeared memorably alongside Jerry Lewis in what many consider to be his best film, *The Nutty Professor,* she excels alongside Lewis' former partner Dean Martin in the *Matt Helm* spy caper *The Silencers,* in which she plays the archetypal mid-'60s kooky bimbo with such comic flair and sexuality that she set the standard for those who followed, and was outstanding in Sam Peckinpah's end-of-the-west western *The Ballad of Cable Hogue.*

After this though, it was downhill into mediocre television and exploitation fare (often of the straight-to-video variety). Even some of these weren't too bad; *Slaughter* and *Cleopatra Jones and the City of Gold* are superior black exploitation features, even if Stevens is under-used. She appeared in the pilots for *Wonder Woman* and *Hart to Hart,* numerous TV movies and mini-series, and TV series episodes of varying quality and longevity. A regular role in a 1980s soap based on the book and subsequent movie *Flamingo Road* was short-lived--the series lasted only a few weeks, and from thereon her career descended into cheap tat and sleaze, some of it made in collaboration with her son to help his career along.

All in all, it seems there was little love lost on the production between happy-go-lucky newcomer Laurel Goodwin and jaded and badly treated Stella Stevens, appearing in the Elvis movie under duress. "Little acting talent--or vamping ability--was required for 1962's *Girls! Girls! Girls!*" wrote Kim Holston in the book *Starlet,* and little was proffered by Stevens. Stevens didn't want to be there, had asked for, and been refused Goodwin's role, claimed Elvis "disappointed" her, was stand-offish with cast and crew, performed her torch songs rigidly, and was plainly going through the motions in her few stiff dramatic scenes. Laurel Goodwin, who, many decades later, was quite prepared to be frank, told journalist Tom Lisanti, "Everyone was getting along wonderfully. Then Stella Stevens arrived in Hawaii...!".

The story is told in full in Lisanti's interview book *Drive-In Dream Girls,* but to put it bluntly and briefly, Stevens didn't want to be there and made sure everybody knew it. However, it must be said that had she wanted to use her scenes as a showcase, as she later would so brilliantly with Dean Martin in *The Silencers,* the opportunity was there. Instead, her rage against Hal Wallis practically burns through the screen. She is, without exaggeration, the only actress in interviews who ever worked with Elvis and didn't exude admiration.

Considering that dozens of other actresses have all made complimentary remarks about Elvis, bearing in mind that Goodwin has been quite bluntly honest when discussing Jackie Gleason and *Star Trek*, and factoring in the circumstances under which Stevens was present, it seems fair to say that Stevens' derogatory remarks can be taken with more than a pinch of salt. Indeed, Goodwin has stated that Stevens made herself quite unpopular, and Elvis may have got his own back. He particularly requested Goodwin's presence during the shooting of the nightclub scenes, even though she wasn't on camera, claiming that he didn't "feel comfortable".

"Previously I had taught Elvis how to do `the Twist'" she explained to Lisanti. "Anyway, I showed up and watched Elvis while he was lip-synching the songs and dancing. He was singing and dancing to me, and I was behind the camera going crazy, encouraging him to do things. He was not that comfortable with public performance. This happened a number of times. That's why I worked that day". Or perhaps Elvis, who had practically invented the dance moves of '60s pop music and performed in public hundreds of times, just wanted to irritate someone!

Jeremy Slate had previously appeared as the vile Turk in *G.I. Blues*, but was here deservedly elevated to second male lead, where he makes a meal of a great role as Presley's token antagonist. He has several lively exchanges with both Elvis Presley and Laurel Goodwin, and is excellent as the opportunist employer of Elvis and clumsy, would-be seducer of Goodwin. On TV, he had starred in the troubled beach-based adventure series *The Aquanauts,* which had changed first co-star, and then title (to *Malibu Run*) during it's short, single season life. He worked again for Wallis in the 1963 Anhalt-scripted comedy *Wives and Lovers,* and the 1965 Weiss co-scripted John Wayne western *The Sons of Katie Elder*. Also in 1965, he appeared with Bob Hope and Tuesday Weld in the comedy *I'll Take Sweden*. Alongside Elvis babes Diane McBain and Jocelyn Lane, he appeared in campy biker flicks *The Mini-Skirt Mob* and *Hell's Belles* respectively. TV guest shots included episodes of *One Step Beyond, The Untouchables, Route 66, The Man from UNCLE, Combat, Bewitched, Mission: Impossible, Ghost Story, Police Story, Wonder Woman,* and *Starman*.

Playing the owner of The Pirate's Den, the nightclub employing Presley and Stevens was Robert Strauss, whose swarthy, shifty looks had condemned him to a busy career playing gangsters or con-men--usually of the not-to-be-taken-seriously variety in light comedy. His best known movie was *The Seven Year Itch* with Marilyn Monroe, while a typical gangster role was *I, Mobster* with Steve Cochran. TV spots included *Wanted--Dead or Alive, The Man from UNCLE, Honey West,* and *The Green Hornet,* and inevitably numerous sit-coms, including *Bewitched, The Munsters, Get Smart, The Beverly Hillbillies, The Monkees,* and *Mr. Terrific,* almost always as a shady character. He would return to the Presley fold to appear in *Frankie and Johnny* three years later.

Mary Treen appears in three Elvis films in bit parts, and here has her best scene of the three alongside Marjorie Bennett, a fine character actress who brought a special glow to a variety of mad old women (and a few wise ones) in film and TV, as they fight over hideous hats.

Portraying the Stavros couple were veteran supporting players Frank Puglia and Lili Valenty. Puglia played several different ethnic types during his career, including roles in *The Mark of Zorro, Blood on the Sun,* and *Twenty Million Miles to Earth*. Guy Lee was Chen Yung, Elvis' shipmate. Ordinarily a bit player cast as nameless cabbies and bellboys, this was one of his bigger roles. Busy character actors Benson Fong and Beulah Quo played his traditional Chinese parents, with the Tiu children as their offspring. Another Tiu, Vicky Tiu, plays a significant role in Presley's next production, *It Happened at the World's Fair*.

Not only were the Elvis movies very white, but when ethnic types were included, it was always in a condescending way, often as supporting players well down the cast. As the arrival of political correctness has inadvertently caused a fair amount of knee-jerk stupidity and anxious foolishness over the last half of the 20th century and looks set to do the same for the first half of the 21st, this issue is worth examining in depth, and in no better place than under the Elvis title which features both a Chinese family and a Greek family to add some exotic color. The nature and purpose of the Elvis films must be considered, and as ever, it's all about context.

It's absolutely true that the Elvis films were glaringly short on African-Americans and other brown skins, and there is every possibility that money men at the studios considered the presence of black people in Presley's movies to be commercial suicide. They were not social engineers. Presley, while carrying no racialist baggage himself (he did, after all, adore blues and gospel, and as a youth hung out in black parts of town), came from the South, where he had his greatest concentration of admirers. As late as 1965, some Southern states were refusing to air the classy espionage series *I Spy* because it gave fair billing to co-star Bill Cosby (an attribute the series' star, Robert Culp, was exceptionally proud of, and supported). As late as 1968, there was a media furore when science-fiction series *Star Trek* featured what was believed to be television's first inter-racial kiss (albeit an unwilling one, forced by hedonistic aliens). As late as 1970, Elvis was told by promoters not to bring "those black girls", his backing group, Sweet Inspiration, with him to a performance in Houston. "Elvis had laid down the law that if we didn't come, he wasn't coming either" said Myrna Smith, one of the group. "So when we did the show, I wondered why everyone was so nice to us. None of the guys told us, because they didn't want to hurt our feelings. I found out years later that Elvis had stood up for us". Later, when Smith set up home with Jerry Schilling, one of Elvis' buddies, Schilling offered to be discreet, nervous that Presley might be concerned about the reaction of some of the fans and even certain members of the entourage. Elvis dismissed such concerns out of hand, saying "Look, you're my friend, Myrna's my friend, you're welcome in my house. Screw what anybody else thinks". In the 21st century, this might not seem such a big deal, and most intelligent people would expect nothing less, but this was the time when the fight for Civil Rights was at its peak, and many performers were not so brave, some not even so clear-minded. Throughout the 1970s, virtually every television series would have a black person in the regular cast (referred to by some critics, with some justification, as the "token black"). Throughout the 1980s, most series had a varied ethnic mix (*I Spy*'s Bill Cosby returned with the first aspirational black family on TV in *The Cosby Show,* a series where color didn't matter and which didn't focus earnestly on race). By the 1990s, hardly anybody was treading on eggshells any more, and the racial mix was more random, less cautious. A few pressure groups aside, audiences hardly noticed whether casts were black, white, gay, or extraterrestrial.

It may also be true that no-one involved with the Presley pictures even gave race a second thought, especially as most of these films were set in locales either naturally dominated by whites, or other ethnic groups. As shocking as it might read today, not too many black people could afford holidays in Hawaii in the early 1960s (one solitary black actor walks on to deliver a telegram in *Paradise, Hawaiian Style;* black actors also appear briefly in *Roustabout* and *Frankie and Johnny,* the latter of which is set in New Orleans).

Whatever the reason for these movies' whiteness, it did have the knock-on effect of putting other ethnic groups in the frame. In the case of *Girls! Girls! Girls!,* this was the Greek Stavros family and the Chinese Yung family. The manner in which these people were presented was, not uncommonly for the period, patronising but not prejudiced, high spirited rather than mean-spirited, and condescending rather than demeaning. In short, they were innocent, interested portraits presented without hate, and it must be remembered that jet travel and global holidays were only just then becoming a reality for the average citizen of the world. Marshall McLuhan's "global village" was finally (mostly) at peace after two world wars, and ordinary, semi-affluent people were for the first time able to explore it. For some, Hawaii was exotic enough. But it is no coincidence that so many of the Elvis films are set in vacation hot spots where Americans could enjoy local color just different enough not to make them feel out of place.

We do know, because Elvis Presley is one of the most well-documented and heavily studied human beings of the 20th century, that-- although he was not immune to the temptations of a tactless joke--there wasn't an ounce of racial hatred in his body. With his assimilation of the black sound into white music, it would have been absurd even to assume so. However, despite America being a country built by immigrants, it has become through its largeness and greatness, an insular country, with often only a vague and confused notion of Eastern, Asian and European countries. Consequently, when the outside world and its inhabitants are portrayed in American films and TV series, writers often resort to cliche and stereotypes in their efforts to portray the culture (see, for a shining example, the Europe-set Elvis film *Double Trouble*).

This is as true of other countries, including my own, as it is of America, and it is also true that many of those stereotypes become so because they are true ones, supported by collective experience. Anyone who has ever seen an Englishman's dental work, asked for ketchup on their steak in Paris, drunk the water in Mexico, or driven through Rome, must admit that stereotypes do not materialise out of thin air. The Stavros and Yung households in *Girls! Girls! Girls!* may be portrayed in a stereotypical fashion, but they are truthful portraits for the 1960s, painted with affection and genuine fascination for the cultural differences of the Greeks and the Chinese. And this is true of all the ethnic characters in the Elvis movies. Yes, they were subservient and deferential to the characters Elvis played, but that was true of anyone in an Elvis film who was not antagonistic, from the best buddies to the drooling women. In an Elvis film, the world revolves around Elvis.

This was also the film in which Lance Le Gault was officially brought aboard the gravy train. He supervised the nightclub performances, and plays bass and sings back up on "Return to Sender". In future movies, all the way up to *Speedway*, Le Gault would be there somewhere, as stunt man, bit player, choreographer, or stand-in, although he was no hanger-on. When the Elvis pictures wound down, he went straight into TV bit parts and guest shots, finding work in episodes of *Land of the Giants, Barbary Coast, How the West Was Won, The Rockford Files, Black Sheep Squadron, Police Woman, Logan's Run, The Incredible Hulk, Wonder Woman, Battlestar Galactica, Buck Rogers in the 25th Century, Simon and Simon, T.J. Hooker, Murder She Wrote, Knight Rider, Voyagers, Automan, MacGyver, Call to Glory,*

Airwolf, Star Trek: The Next Generation, Quantum Leap, and *Renegade,* among others. He also appears in the improvisational circle in the 1968 Elvis "comeback special" banging away on a tambourine. One of the fishermen on the tuna boat is a brown-haired Red West, playing the bongos.

Laurel Goodwin and Elvis

It Happened at the World's Fair (1963)

wr. Si Rose, Seaman Jacobs, dir. Norman Taurog, pr. Ted Richmond (MGM)

with Elvis Presley (Mike Edwards), Gary Lockwood (Danny Burke), Joan O'Brien (Diane), Vicky Tui (Sue-Lin), H.M. Wynant (Vince Bradley), Guy Raymond (Barney Thatcher), Dorothy Green (Miss Ettinger), Edith Atwater (Miss Steuben), Kam Tong (Mr. Ling), Yvonne Craig (Dorothy), Russell Thorson (Sheriff), Olan Soule (Dorothy's father), Jacqueline De Witt (Dorothy's mother), Robert B. Williams (foreman), Wilson Wood (mechanic), Red West, John Day (gamblers), Kurt Russell (young boy), Sandra Giles, Evelyn Dutton, Linda Humble (girls), the Jordanaires, and the Mello Men

Elvis sings: "Beyond the Bend" (in cropduster 'plane, over opening titles); "Relax" (during attempted seduction of Yvonne Craig); "Take Me to the Fair" (to Vicky Tui, in truck); "They Remind Me Too Much of You" (on monorail); "One Broken Heart for Sale" (in trailer park--hilarious); "I'm Falling in Love Tonight" (to Joan O'Brien, in Space Needles' revolving restaurant); "Cotton Candy Land" (to Vicky Tui); "A World of Our Own" (to Joan O'Brien); "How Would You Like to Be...?" (with Vicky Tiu); "Happy Ending" (grand finale, with Joan O'Brien)

If it hadn't been for the dazzling performance of Ann-Margret in *Viva Las Vegas* and the sizzling chemistry between herself and Presley, then MGM's first Elvis film of the '60s (and second after *Jailhouse Rock* six years earlier) might be better remembered and have gained more respect and attention. A single released from the soundtrack, "One Broken Heart for Sale", written by Otis Blackwell of "Return to Sender" fame, sold over a million copies (the scene in the film, Elvis strolling through the trailer park, singing and strumming guitar with posse of rapt middle-aged men, is a camp classic hoot). But overall, it's a genuinely witty script, with some excellent comedy, strong dialogue, and all the usual Elvis ingredients.

If *It Happened at the World's Fair* proves anything, it's that the 1960s Elvis persona and formula could be dropped into a quality product and work beautifully--it didn't have to be a recipe for inexpensive throwaway fluff. Before the first fifteen minutes are up we've enjoyed witty banter between Presley and best buddy Gary Lockwood, feelgood scenes with their employer and a couple of "sweet potatoes" whose car is buzzed by the boys' bi-plane, a choreographed cat and mouse game between Elvis and the ever-welcome Yvonne Craig, some comedy with familiar face Olan Soule as a furious father, and a splendid dynamic punch-up between the boys and some card sharks (one of whom, inevitably, is Red West!).

Presley and Lockwood play Mike Edwards and Danny Burke, two carefree but ambitious young men (the usual contradictory Presley film formula of charming layabout and decent hard worker) with a crop-dusting 'plane. They're supposed to be saving up to expand the business, but Mike spends all his money winning over women and Danny spends all his losing at cards ("You know, there's so many things you could've been... a drunk, an arsonist..." fumes Elvis after bailing him out of trouble). These were the days, if they ever truly existed outside of Hollywood, when you could pick up a couple of male hitch-hikers on the road (as Kam Tong's Walter Ling does), and not only let your infant daughter ride in the back of the pick-up truck with them, but entrust her to one of them for a day at the Seattle World's Fair! Luckily for Mr. Ling, he's in an Elvis film and not an episode of *NYPD Blue,* and Mike only has eyes on some shapely women, ultimately falling for Joan O'Brien's Liz Warren, the medical office's nurse, who defies his charms; "Some doll gives you the brush and right away it's a challenge" complains Danny.

The songs, while undistinguished, are romantic and at least mostly grown up, although Elvis is required to perform one of his many ballads to a baby. Apart from this tiresome and overlong song involving clowns, the rapidly standardised scenes with the cute kid (in this case young Vicky Tui) aren't too intolerable. As in most Elvis films, there is a swiftly patched-up romantic understanding and a valiant rout of hard-nosed authority which, echoing *Follow That Dream,* wants to take the kid away when her father temporarily disappears due to a motor accident and hospitalisation.

Providing support was lanky character actor Guy Raymond as the henpecked gambling-addicted patsy Barney Thatcher, manager of the trailer park where Mike and Danny are residing until better times, and hard-faced H.M. Wynant as the token bad guy Vince Bradley. Wynant often played heavies, turning up in episodes of shows like *Bat Masterson* (alongside Joan O'Brien), *Hawaiian Eye, Cheyenne, The Untouchables, Combat, Branded, Get Smart, The Man from UNCLE, Garrison's Gorillas, Mission: Impossible, I Spy, The Wild Wild West, The Name of the Game, Hawaii Five-O, The Six Million Dollar Man, Police Story, Airwolf,* and *Simon and Simon* (although he played the terrified man who releases the devil from a monastery in the legendary *Twilight Zone* episode "The Howling Man"), while Raymond was one of those invaluable, anonymous, yet instantly recognisable character actors of the sort they just don't make any more in today's more synthetic Hollywood. He was usually cast as a country hick or small town trader, and always gave a broad, almost vaudevillian performance (he's the bartender in the corny "Trouble with Tribbles" episode of *Star Trek,* which--like this role--displays his talent for well-worn "bits of business", and had a recurring role in the small-town sit-com *The Ghost and Mrs. Muir*). Other guest shots include *The Twilight Zone, The*

Naked City, Route 66, and numerous westerns and sit-coms. This is also the film in which young child performer Kurt Russell, later to grow up into an impressive adult actor after a teenage career in Disney films, famously kicks Presley on the shin to get him access to the nurse in the first aid area, and then gives the game away in front of her later by offering to do it again!

Gary Lockwood, who had worked with Elvis before, as the adversarial lout in *Wild in the Country,* is fine in the best buddy role, a part with a fraction more depth than was usual. Other than his two appearances with Elvis, his main claim to pop culture immortality is in the SF arena, memorably appearing in the second *Star Trek* pilot "Where No Man Has Gone Before", but somewhat overshadowed by the visuals as one of the two astronauts in *2001: A Space Odyssey.* His numerous TV credits include guest shots on *Twelve O'Clock High, Combat, Mission: Impossible, Ironside, Banacek, The Six Million Dollar Man, The Bionic Woman, Starsky and Hutch, Charlie's Angels, Police Story, Vegas, T.J. Hooker, Simon and Simon, Murder She Wrote, Hotel, Matt Houston,* and *MacGyver.*

Vicky Tui and Kam Tong are okay as the Lings (the choice of ethnic identity may well have been an attempt to recall the environment of the super-successful *Blue Hawaii*) and Joan O'Brien does her best with a plot-driven rather than character-driven girlfriend role. A favorite of John Wayne, she appeared in his pet project *The Alamo,* and a year later, *The Comancheros,* but *World's Fair* was at least her third appearance as a nurse; she had romanced Cary Grant in *Operation: Petticoat* and played opposite Jerry Lewis in *It's Only Money.*

Having entered the business as a singer, O'Brien was a little disappointed not to get an opportunity here, but also smart enough to realise that not only did it go against her character's frosty persona, but that the Colonel would have considered it a distraction from his golden boy. "I like the fact the film was relatively uncluttered" she said. "It didn't have all these women falling out of the sky and dancing to bongo drums!".

Her first sight of Elvis was on location in Seattle, being mobbed by excited crowds. She made several TV guest appearances in various quality shows of the early '60s, including, inevitably, many westerns, but by 1964, her ambition sated, and finding herself playing second fiddle to younger starlets Mary Ann Mobley and Nancy Sinatra in a Sam Katzman quickie (*Get Yourself a College Girl*), had retired into domesticity. Both Katzman and his two young starlets would work with Elvis in the months to follow, but O'Brien was happy with her contribution to the Elvis canon. "I think *It Happened at the World's Fair* was a better than average Elvis film" she said, "but as far as Elvis' acting ability, *Love Me Tender* and *King Creole* were better showcases for him. I think Elvis had dramatic talent that if developed, would have made him an extremely fine actor... but he really just wanted to play his guitar and face those live audiences".

Fun in Acapulco (1963)

wr. Allan Weiss, dir. Richard Thorpe, pr. Hal Wallis (Paramount)

with Elvis Presley (Mike Windgren), Ursula Andress (Marguerite), Elsa Cardenas (Dolores Gomez), Alejandro Rey (Moreno), Larry Domasin (Raul), Paul Lukas (Maximillian), Robert Carricart (Jose), Teri Hope (Janie Harkins), Charles Evans (Mr. Harkins), Alberto Morin (hotel manager), Howard McNear, Mary Treen (tourists), Francisco Ortega (desk clerk), Robert de Anda (bellboy), Linda Rivera (telegraph clerk), Darlene Tompkins, Linda Rand (Janie's friends), Adele Palacios (secretary), Eddie Cano, Leon Cardenas, Red West, Carlos Mejia, Fred Aguirre, Tom Hernandez, the Jordanaires, the Four Amigos, the Mariachi Los Vaqueros, the Mariachi Aguila

Elvis sings: "Fun in Acapulco" (over titles); "Vino, Dinero Y Amor" (sung by the Four Amigos only, in boat); "Vino, Dinero Y Amor" (sung with the Four Amigos in bar); "I Think I'm Gonna Like It Here" (in bar); "Mexico" (on bike, with Larry Domasin); "El Toro" (at nightclub); "Marguerita" (at open air cliffside restaurant); "The Bullfighter was a Lady" (in nightclub); "There's No Room to Rhumba in a Sports Car" (in car on date with Elsa Cardenas); "Bossa Nova Baby" (in nightclub); "You Can't Say No in Acapulco" (at poolside restaurant); "Guadalajara" (finale at open air cliffside restaurant)

Elvis and the boys were looking forward to some r&r in Acapulco, but this was a Hal Wallis production and it didn't take long for them to figure out this would be another backlot and stock footage job like *G.I. Blues*. This, in fact, is the most disappointing thing about *Fun in Acapulco*--that one is constantly distracted from the story by the realisation that half the time his character of Mike Windgren is on the screen, we are not watching Elvis at all. Consequently, there are numerous long-distance shots of stand-in Elvis clumsily matched with close-ups of real Elvis against a back projection, and endless shots of Mike Windgren's back, as he walks through the beautiful, bustling Mexican locations not toward the camera, but away from it. The film is saved by it's color (director of photography Daniel Fapp and art directors Hal Pereira and Walter Tyler work wonders), but one is left wondering just how much better this picture might have been had Wallis sprung for some air fare and hotel rooms.

As with *G.I. Blues,* extensive and very precise location shooting has been done for the movie (there are very few, if any, clips from the library) to be matched with what must have been a mind-numbingly boring studio shoot, with at least half the performers in front of process screens. For an audience in blissful ignorance about film-making tricks, the illusion just about comes off, although the benefits of 21st century viewing technology

COME WITH ELVIS TO FABULOUS ACAPULCO!
Hear "Fun In Acapulco" "Bosa Nova Baby" And Other Tuneful And Terrific Songs In RCA's "FUN IN ACAPULCO" Album.
Elvis is a free-swinging sailor out of funds—but never out of fun or girls—in the most dazzling playground in the world!
ELVIS PRESLEY
FUN IN ACAPULCO
A HAL WALLIS PRODUCTION
TECHNICOLOR®
CO-STARRING
URSULA ANDRESS · ELSA CARDENAS · PAUL LUKAS
DIRECTED BY RICHARD THORPE · WRITTEN BY ALLAN WEISS
A PARAMOUNT RELEASE

betray at least one instance of an obvious Presley double when Mike and Dolores drive to a lovers' lane-style clifftop.

Although Richard Thorpe and/or his editor appear less skilled than Norman Taurog at matching the location footage with the close-ups, *Fun in Acapulco* still looks less forced and phoney than *G.I. Blues,* and the studio sets are better. The cantina set is particularly good, and some obvious thought and attention has even gone into the kitchen and hotel manager's office. The nightclub sets put MGM to shame. Thorpe's direction is still utterly conventional, but we are spared the clumsiness of his work on the spartan *Jailhouse Rock.*

On its own level, *Fun in Acapulco* is a competent and efficient piece of work, an enjoyable entertainment, and probably Elvis' most colorful film. It just seems a shame that Elvis, so easily bored, didn't demand outright a few extra thousand for a week on location. So often Elvis was culpable in his own career shortcomings, and this seems such a minor thing to provide a major jump in quality. After all, if Elvis didn't care about his movies, he certainly cared about his playtime... but then at this particular moment in his life playtime was almost completely consumed by the visiting Priscilla Beaulieu, which may explain his reticence to travel.

There were also stories that Elvis was *persona non grata* in Mexico after making some uncharacteristic disparaging remarks about the country and been denied entry, surely the maddest example of bureaucrats cutting off the nose to spite the face--or was this face-saving spin from Wallis and/or Parker? It was revealed, many years later, that Parker was an illegal immigrant to the U.S., who had no passport, or way of getting one. Perhaps it was all a smokescreen to obscure the fact that Parker couldn't cross the border. Either way, the end result is that *Fun in Acapulco* suffers from all the technical failings of the reprehensible *G.I. Blues,* but is a far more satisfying fantasy.

Plotwise, we are on very familiar ground. Elvis is the subject of catty romantic competition between an obvious winner and an obvious second placer (as in *Girls! Girls! Girls!*), he has a swarthy, pushy romantic rival for the woman he wants (as he would in *Viva Las Vegas*), there is a cute kid sticking his nose in and keeping the sex action down to a censor-friendly minimum (as in almost every Presley film from *Blue Hawaii* on), and the film even opens with a seafaring Elvis (surely in the same sailor's cap as *Girls! Girls! Girls!*) replaying the Jenny Maxwell/Ellie routine from *Blue Hawaii,* but with Teri Hope as the curvy lookalike (same hairstyle, same jailbait seduction technique, same pouty, rich girl defiance and deceit as she drops Elvis in the ordure--even Darlene Tompkins, one of the other *Blue Hawaii* girls, as one of her companions).

Just as *Blue Hawaii* seemed to almost pick up from where *G.I. Blues* left off, but with Presley in a reformatted, revised role to clear away the awkward inconsistencies from the previous film and provide a clean slate, so *Fun in Acapulco* almost seems to do the same with *Girls! Girls! Girls!* Here, Presley's nemesis is not the ghost of his father, but the ghost of his brother, who died during a mishap during the Flying Windgrens' trapeze act and left Mike with a fear of heights. With phobias and traumas not apparently recognised in 1960s Latino culture, Moreno considers lifeguard Elvis to be "a coward" for not using the high diving board, as does Latino love interest Dolores Gomez (Elsa Cardenas), an early feminist and female bullfighter! Larry Domasin plays the little street-smart wiseguy scheming to get Mike alternative work as a nightclub singer, a pint-sized Colonel Parker.

Ursula Andress, hot from the James Bond franchise, was a poor match with Elvis both onscreen and off, although somewhat more glamorous than the usual pairing. Despite inevitable rumors, Elvis reassured Priscilla, visiting from Germany for the first time, that there was nothing going on by joking that Andress' shoulders were broader than his were (Elvis liked his girls skinny). If the young Miss Beaulieu had any real doubts, she had only to see the movie. Although Andress gives a competent performance and is stunningly beautiful, any kind of sexual chemistry between her and Presley is completely and utterly non-existent, making the supposed conflict between Elvis and Alejandro Rey's Moreno equally unconvincing and redundant. Moreno seems more obsessed with baiting and exposing Windgren than romancing Marguerite, and one cannot believe that the characters of Mike and Marguerite spent more than a minute or two together after the movie fades!

Argentinian-born Alejandro Rey had worked with Andress the previous year when they made "La Strega", an episode of the superior anthology series *Boris Karloff's Thriller* together. Andress then went on to her most famous role in the Bond film *Dr. No,* but after *Fun in Acapulco* her career slipped downward with each successive film--'60s time capsule sex comedy *What's New, Pussycat?,* Hammer's *She,* the Bond send-up *Casino Royale*... until by the end of the '70s Italian-made efforts with titles such as *Slaves of the Cannibal God* and *The Sensuous Nurse* were turning up in a filmography mired in sleaze. By the 1980s she was reduced to the pilot of short-lived sci-fi show *Manimal* and a recurring role in the soap opera *Falcon Crest*. With the writing on the wall, she returned to Italy, and more TV.

Poor Alejandro Rey managed to prove that there was a worse fate than anything Presley or Andress may have thought they were enduring-- after a few more TV guest shots, including several *Dick Powell Theater*, and a notable *Voyage to the Bottom of the Sea,* he spent the remainder of the 1960s co-starring in a notoriously stupid sit-com titled *The Flying Nun*. Like Andress, in the 1970s he appeared in bad films, and ended up in soap. In the 1980s, shortly before his death, he had a recurring role in *Dallas*. They

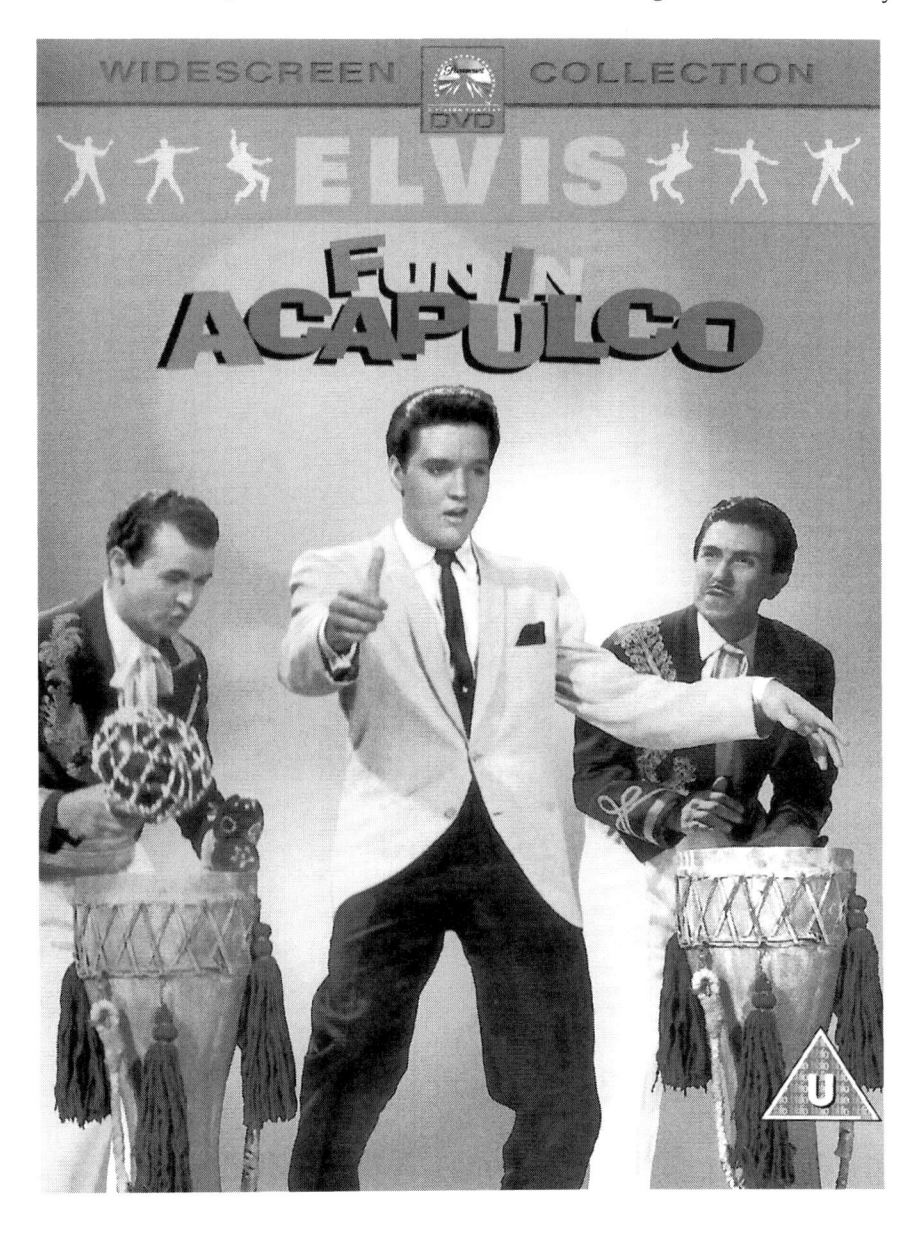

were in interesting company, at least; from 1983 to 1988, Priscilla Presley herself played a regular role in *Dallas*.

Back in the swinging '60s, in studio-bound downtown Acapulco, there were few new faces behind the scenes. Allan Weiss had been co-writer on *Girls! Girls! Girls!*, and was now deemed competent enough to provide a paint-by-numbers script solo; the script notably lacks the witty polish of *Blue Hawaii* or *Girls! Girls! Girls!* Richard Thorpe had directed *Jailhouse Rock*; Michael Moore was back on second unit, a position he held on all the Paramount Presley movies until he got a shot at directing with *Paradise, Hawaiian Style*.

Darlene Tompkins, who had struck up a friendship with Elvis while portraying one of the vacationing schoolgirls in *Blue Hawaii*, returned in a bit part (sitting with the erzatz Ellie in the cantina, she only has one line, but is sharp enough to turn her head to the camera at the start of her scene), and fluttery, flustering Howard McNear makes his third and briefest appearance in an Elvis film (following *Blue Hawaii* and *Follow That Dream*) as a twittering tourist (although this time he does not appear with Elvis, but with Elsa Cardenas). Playing his wife is another Elvis film standby, Mary Treen, also in *Girls! Girls! Girls!* as the hat lady and *Paradise, Hawaiian Style* as the FAA man's wife.

Robert Carricart had previously appeared in *Follow That Dream*, and TV work included *One Step Beyond, Cheyenne, The Untouchables, The Detectives, Combat, Branded, Honey West, The Time Tunnel, Mission: Impossible, Get Smart, The Man from UNCLE, The Girl from UNCLE, I Spy*, and *Kojak*. Whether Presley's stand-in for the Acapulco scenes is Lance Le Gault is not clear (he started working for Elvis as of *Girls! Girls! Girls!*), but the bogus Mike's recoil on the diving board in the first hotel pool scene looks so much like a lithe dance move that it is a distinct possibility.

Viva Las Vegas (1964)

wr. Sally Benson, dir. George Sidney, pr. Jack Cummings, George Sidney (MGM)

with Elvis Presley (Lucky Jackson), Ann-Margret (Rusty Martin), Cesare Danova (Count Elmo Mancini), William Demarest (Mr. Martin), Nicky Blair (Shorty), Robert B. Williams (Swanson), Bob Nash (Big Gus), Roy Engel (Baker), Jack Carter (host), Ivan Treisault (head waiter), Eddie Quillan (M.C.), Barnaby Hale (mechanic), Ford Dunhill (driver), Francis Raval (Francois), Lance Le Gault (musician/stunt double), Red West (gambler), Lori Williams, Teri Garr (among the dancers), Rick Murray (delivery boy), Larry Kent (race official), Howard Curtis (starter), Alan Fordney (race announcer), the Forte Four

Elvis sings: "Viva Las Vegas" (over titles); "The Yellow Rose of Texas" (at club); "The Eyes of Texas are Upon You" (at club); "The Lady Loves Me" (around pool with Ann-Margret); "C'mon Everybody" (on stage at university); "Today, Tomorrow and Forever" (on houseboat to Ann Margret); "The Climb" (Forte Four only, at disco); "What'd I Say?" (at disco); "Santa Lucia" (to Ann Margret during the Count's date); "If You Think I Don't Need You" (to Ann Margret during the Count's date); "Appreciation" (Ann-Margret only, on stage); "Viva Las Vegas" (reprise; on stage); "I Need Somebody to Lean On" (melancholy solo); "Does He Love Me Or Does He Love My Rival?" (Ann-Margret only, on houseboat); "Viva Las Vegas" (reprise; on stage)

The short time Elvis spent making *Viva Las Vegas* in the summer of 1963 was one of the happiest and most fulfilling periods of his life. He was being challenged, admired, and evenly matched by a woman who could not be treated like a childlike fragile flower, and he'd found a soul-mate. Everyone who knew Elvis couldn't help but notice that he loved her and she loved him; and they loved them together. It wasn't even necessarily about sex, although they both oozed it--more than a few people referred to her as a female Elvis. By her own admission, music lit a fire under both of them--and their passion, professional and otherwise, kept it burning.

Ann-Margret Olsson was a Swedish-born nightclub performer who was as ambitious and as talented in her way as Elvis was. Stage struck even as a plain and ordinary young girl, she blossomed into a stunning beauty and--by now living in America--sought fame and fortune in a three-man, four-person singing group first in Las Vegas, where things fell through, and then, ultimately solo, in Hollywood. Her first film was a role way down the cast list in the Frank Capra swan song *Pocket Full of Miracles* in 1961 (co-scripted by Hal Kanter), followed by a pointless remake in 1962 of the already twice-filmed *State Fair* for the teenage audience, co-starring alongside Pat Boone, Pamela Tiffin, and Bobby Darin. Much more significant was her third film. She came to *Viva Las Vegas* direct from an amusing and enjoyable movie version of the stage play *Bye Bye Birdie*, the theme of which was the hysteria that greeted the induction of pop sensation Conrad Birdie into the army! Not only was this a fun film (Dick Van Dyke starred, with Bobby Darin again, and the hilarious Paul Lynde) and a blatant parody of the Presley scenario (he didn't seem to hold it against her), but it introduced a smitten middle-aged director named George Sidney to the bundle of superhuman energy that was Ann-Margret.

Much to the irritation of the Colonel, Elvis and Ann-Margret were very much equals in *Viva Las Vegas*, on screen as well as off. Throughout the film, more often than not, if Elvis sang, Ann-Margret sang with him, before him, or after him. Elvis didn't mind. Like Sidney, he was besotted. "But Parker was threatened by an actress who both competed with his star and engaged Elvis' attention offscreen" wrote Alanna Nash perceptively in her book *The Colonel*. She was "pretty, vivacious, a gifted singer and dancer whose personal magnetism and bubbling energy overwhelmed even her substantial talents", wrote Peter Guralnick in *Careless Love*.

"Instead of playing up their natural chemistry", wrote Nash of Parker, "he grumbled that Ann-Margret got more close-ups and flattering camera angles, and fought to cut their duets to just one song. Parker... was clueless as to how the movie rejuvenated his client's spirits and musical dynamism... It's success should have shown Parker that spending money for more alluring co-stars, creative directors, and imaginative scripts would go a long way to assure his client of longevity. However... all he saw was that *Viva Las Vegas* had soared over budget".

Unusually and uniquely--perhaps even incredibly--there isn't one bad scene or misjudged moment in the entire film, quite an accomplishment for a Presley vehicle, given the dazzling vulgarity and tastelessness of Tom Parker, Hal Wallis, Sam Katzman, and the others. Indeed, the expense, quality, and sexuality of the film would be considered an unnecessary indulgence by the marketeers and money men that was best not repeated-- so much so that MGM and Parker back-pedalled so furiously that they shot off the graph at the other end for future MGM efforts, to the point where even Parker had to concede they'd been too cheap. But in the meantime, their so-called mistake had given cinema it's one flawless Elvis Presley musical.

Unlike the mechanical and cynical gyrations of Juliet Prowse in *G.I. Blues,* Ann-Margret felt the sexuality in the music in the same way Elvis did, and if her performance and talents weren't as unique as his, they were certainly as finely-honed, and she matched him equally in energy, commitment, confidence, and charisma. Affectations that no other would-be glamour-puss could get away with, Ann-Margret Olssen could carry off--a breathy gasp, a flirty pout, an earthy yelp (the Nevada University dance number), a husky, parodic come-hither ("Appreciation"), she brazenly unleashed them all.

Was it parody? It teetered on the edge of mockery, and yet her performance was sexy. Was she making fun of sex, of men, or of herself? It was too honest and affectionate to be satire. It was too genuinely sexy to be camp. Somehow, she could carry it off, where other women would have attracted only contemptuous laughter. Her performance oozed love of life, the joy of being a woman. More than a female Elvis, she was perhaps the new Monroe... although unlike Marilyn, there was an air of knowing self-confidence about her, a haughty independence; unlike Monroe, willing and compliant, she was nobody's bimbo, even Presley's. She gave an air of being in control, but not in charge, the perfect female fantasy for the '60s. She could come across as loving and open to offers without looking like a sucker... a dream girl for the sort of men who didn't need to dream. And unlike the Ursula Andress debacle in *Fun in Acapulco,* the atmosphere between Elvis and Ann-Margret is so sexually charged it sizzles.

Elvis' penniless and clumsy race car driver Lucky Jackson and Cesare Danova's smooth and mature rival Count Mancini are in competition not just for a racing trophy, but for the beautiful redhead who stops off at their garage showing off such a shapely pair of legs and derriere that they are accompanied by their own theme tune (Ann-Margret's wiggly, compact little ass has almost as many close-ups as her stunning, camera-confident face, while Presley's sleepy-eyed close-ups are almost erotic). In *Viva Las*

Vegas, Danova's corny Count Elmo Mancini is just sophisticated and charming enough to pose a credible threat as competition to the not-so-Lucky Jackson, and so Danova is consequently entirely plausible as a potential rival, if never actually a serious consideration.

Danova had made a career out of pandering to middle-America's stereotype of the charming Italian seducer (he was the sophisticated charmer in *Gidget Goes to Rome*), and played the role everywhere from *The Man from UNCLE* and *The Girl from UNCLE* to *Honey West* and *The Lucy Show* either side of co-starring in the short-lived war series *Garrison's Gorillas* (1967-'68). In middle age in the 1970s he played two memorable roles superbly, as the suavely corrupt, thoroughly unpleasant and chillingly pragmatic Little Italy mobster in Martin Scorsese's magnificent *Mean Streets,* and the equally corrupt but seething comedy mayor in the hilarious *National Lampoon's Animal House.* TV roles were more mundane, but included *The Green Hornet, Mission: Impossible, The Name of the Game, McMillan and Wife, McCloud, Night Gallery, Police Story, Charlie's Angels, Fantasy Island, Vegas, Magnum p.i., Murder She Wrote, Simon and Simon, Airwolf, Hunter, Hotel,* and *Matt Houston.* The relationship between Lucky Jackson and the sophisticated, worldly Count is expertly defined in just three lines of dialogue when Ann-Margret makes her first appearance. "I'd like you to check my motor--it whistles" she announces to the two overall-clad mechanics. "I don't blame it!" quips Elvis. "Forgive my friend," smarms Danova confidently, "He's very young!".

While Presley pulls the old trick of pretending her vehicle is in worse shape than it is to keep her and the car within reach, Danova steals a march on him by earning kudos for fixing it behind his back. When she drives off into the distance, they realise they have no idea how to find her again, and--deciding that her devastating beauty, poise, and confidence means she must be a showgirl--catch each other scouring the Vegas nightclubs that evening after both pretending they wouldn't. They come up empty handed, only to find that she's been at their hotel all the time, where she works as a swimming instructor for the kiddies (note the delightful xylophone sound when the little ones topple into the pool--this attention to the smallest detail permeates the entire film).

When Elvis loses his roll of money in the swimming pool after a fully-clothed tumble off the diving board courtesy of Ann-Margret (we now know her name is Rusty Martin), his race car fund is endangered, but he gains some sympathy from her. Unable to pay his hotel bill or make the payment on his car, Lucky and best pal Shorty (Nicky Blair) take on jobs as waiters to pay their way (every time Elvis dons the red jacket he seems to be thoroughly enjoying himself in these frantic, comedic scenes).

Rusty, genuinely touched by his plight, and having been pursued to her satisfaction, stops playing hard-to-get and agrees to a date, telling him to meet her at the Nevada University, where each demonstrate their skills to the students--he rocking and rolling, she whirling and twirling like a dervish--before embarking on an exhausting whirlwind tour of daylight Vegas. Having impressed each other with their versatility, they cram a week into a day, clay shooting, motor-bike riding (she stands, arms wide to balance, on the traveling bike seat), role-playing at a western town, water-skiing, and helicopter sight-seeing, each understandably smitten at the day's end, when Rusty's father, running a tourist boat trip business, inadvertently lets slip that Rusty is more interested than she has let on.

Elvis serenades her with a beautifully realised romantic ballad (swiped from Lizst), and they extend the day into an evening at a nightclub for two further excellent musical numbers. A black group, the Forte Four, deliver a dreamy, Inkspots-style backing for a dance sequence that segues into Ray Charles' "What'd I Say?" which then erupts into frenzied acrobatics in the court of King Lucky and Queen Rusty. At last, the songs in an Elvis movie are not only memorable, but appropriate as well, perfectly paced and placed throughout, and properly integrated into the movie (sometimes too well--Elvis' gorgeous and faithful interpretation of "Santa Lucia" is mere background to Danova's doomed seduction).

The conflict and inevitable romantic misunderstanding comes, rather absurdly, when--despite her daring love of life so far demonstrated--Rusty falls out with Lucky over his risky racecar hobby, having been rattled by the ghoulish story-spinning of the opportunist Count, who she stubbornly and impetuously agrees to join for dinner (again absurdly, given that the Count has exactly the same career in motor racing!). This gives Elvis the opportunity to indulge in some childish but effective slapstick comedy as he finagles his way into becoming the waiter for the romantic meal he subsequently ruins (again, Elvis actually seems to be enjoying the comedy for once, as in *Follow That Dream* but no other Presley vehicles, in which he usually seems uncomfortable or embarrassed). In the meantime, the torn Rusty has been delivering broken heart dialogue that would embarrass a 1950s romance comic ("I've wronged him so!") with her astonishing ability to once again transcend parody.

Still quarrelling, they compete against each other in a talent contest which Lucky erroneously assumes will grant the winner a cash prize to finally finish the race car, but after further stops and starts the entire cast are finally on the same page, the race is on, and there is more comedy mayhem as Rusty relents and clumsily tries to assist the guys in preparing for the big event. A standout scene has a furious Rusty angrily preparing sandwiches and otherwise flouncing about the galleon-style interiors of her father's houseboat jealously singing about how her rival is "a baby-blue racing car"! The melody follows her into the garage where she finally dons overalls and becomes swept up in the excitement. The subsequent success of the motor racing climax resulted in two further Presley films involving road racing, *Spinout* and *Speedway,* and another--*Clambake*--with a motorboat race.

The costumes and sets are gorgeous, the colors are stunning, the lead performances perfectly judged, and the final motor race genuinely gripping... and the supporting cast--surprisingly but efficiently small--was also touched with fairy dust. Nicky Blair gives color and panache to the best friend and eunuch role, creating a likeable one-man fan club and foil for Presley as the insultingly named Shorty. Sidekick characters like this were a frequent addition to films from the 1930s to the 1960s working on the assumption that audiences needed to project themselves into movies by identifying with the characters, and that any young man too insecure or grounded in reality to fantasise himself into the hero role, could identify with the best buddy instead, a fascinating insight into the presumed psychological status of the general public (comedian Phil Silvers, who had played a few in his youth, called them "the Blinky role, 'cause the character's always named something like Blinky").

Blair would later earn his '60s stripes playing a fashion photographer in a superior *Man from UNCLE* episode, "The Sort-of-Do-It-Yourself Dreadful Affair", and a stooge for Mr. Freeze in the *Batman* episode "Green Ice/Deep Freeze". Coincidentally or not, he had also worked alongside Presley's pal Nick Adams, as a recurring character at the bottom of the cast list of his short-lived series *Saints and Sinners* the previous year. He returned to Vegas two decades later as a bit player in *The Godfather, Part II,* where he also ran a restaurant.

Old timer William Demarest was more likeable here as Ann-Margret's father than as the stereotypical Uncle Charlie on the sit-com *My Three Sons* throughout the '60s, where he had the unenviable task of following William Frawley of *I Love Lucy* fame. He had been working in films since the first talkie, *The Jazz Singer,* in 1927, becoming a regular fixture in films about Al Jolson (he turns up in *The Jolson Story* and *Jolson Sings Again* in the '40s), but quickly carved out a niche for himself as a loveable but sharp-tongued old grouch in literally dozens of films throughout the '30s, '40s and '50s. Director George Sidney was himself a veteran of the stylish Hollywood musical, with--among others--*Anchors Aweigh, Annie Get Your Gun,* and *Showboat* to his name.

Viva Las Vegas was filmed on location in Vegas. Filming would start at six in the morning, with production closing down at around two thirty because of the heat. Then filming would resume at six in the evening. Lance Le Gault worked as extra, musician, and stunt player on the film, including taking the backwards dive off the diving board into the pool, clothes, guitar, and all, during one of the movie's major highlights, the duet "The Lady Loves Me". "That's not Elvis, that's me" he said, many years later. "The insurance companies would not let Elvis do a fall like that. That was about a twenty foot fall with a suit on and a guitar round your neck, going off backwards. That's a good way to lose your face. It had nothing to do with whether he could, would, or wanted to do it. If Elvis had done the fall and gotten hurt, he could have shut production down on a picture for two or three weeks...". Le Gault is onscreen playing guitar between Elvis and Ann-Margret in the second disco number. It was also a memorable time for Red West, who got one of his own compositions into the movie-- the raucous "If You Think I Don't Need You" that interrupts Mancini's dinner plans. Among the dancers is future film and TV actress Teri Garr, a regular dancer in Elvis films, today best known as the hapless secretary in *Star Trek's* "Assignment: Earth" and later as Phoebe's mother in *Friends*.

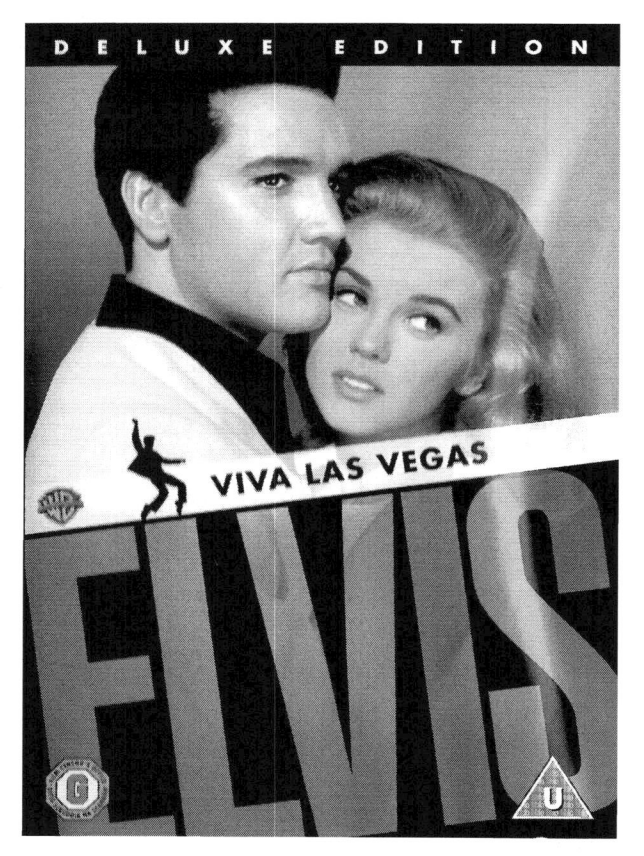

Elvis and Ann-Margret are so plainly kindred spirits made for each other that one suffers soap-like angst that they never got together permanently in reality. Apart from, even then, some inevitable unpleasantness with the fantasies of the British press, it was a problem-free relationship. Had Presley's sexual maturity not been so stunted by his fame, his hypocritical hang-ups from his religious background, and his all-male support staff and hangers-on, one feels the end result would have been both inevitable and successful. Instead, Elvis went back to his virgin future child-bride, his starlets, entourage, and a new arrival and playmate, living toy Scatter, the self-abusing chimp...!

Absurdly, Ann-Margret's film career never really went anywhere, although she has always kept working--even making a comeback after a serious near-fatal accident during one of her cabaret shows in 1972. By then, she was happily married, to actor Roger Smith, star of early '60s cult TV series *77, Sunset Strip*. Elvis frequently attended her opening nights in Vegas, and she his.

An entertainer in the traditional show-biz sense (she was discovered for Vegas by the even then middle-aged raconteur George Burns), she bypassed the counter-culture phase of Hollywood completely. She never again made a movie that was as good or as successful as *Viva Las Vegas*, and although she made a film almost every year throughout the 1960s and '70s, and despite receiving rave notices for the adult drama *Carnal Knowledge* in 1971 and the pretentious rock musical *Tommy* in 1975, her filmography is a string of dated and forgotten obscurities that failed to do her talents any justice at all, a catalogue of disasters, misjudgements and misfires.

In many cases, one has to question her wisdom in accepting the roles-- her first film after career high *Viva Las Vegas* was the sleazy *Kitten With a Whip*. Hindsight is 20/20, but she would have maintained a higher profile by going the usual small screen route of Elvis movie girls and doing *Burke's Law, Batman,* and *The Man from UNCLE* rather than disappearing wraith-like into bad, dead films. No-one could have guessed it at the time, but 1960s TV has turned out to have had a more prominent afterlife than most movies of the 1960s, but she by-passed the TV drama and sit-com guest-shot circuit entirely, bizarrely doing only a perversely enjoyable edition of *The Flintstones,* in which she provided a voice for animated show-biz sensation Ann-Margrock!

Then again, her glitzy, stage show form of singing and dancing was already drifting out of vogue when *Viva Las Vegas* was made, and was itself almost prehistoric. While other female entertainers of her age were trying to look five years younger and go the dippy hippie route, she was dripping in furs and jewelry and often seen on variety bills alongside popular big name middle-aged entertainers (including Dean Martin, in whose second *Matt Helm* spy film, *Murderers' Row,* she co-starred), the last of the good girl bad girls. Most recently she has played a mom role in the Christmas film *Santa Clause 3,* in which she looks wonderful for her age. Perhaps she was simply born at the wrong time, although happily not too late to collide with Elvis so fortuitously for posterity. But it seems very wrong that *Viva Las Vegas* remains her sole great claim to fame.

Contrary to the protestations of Hal Wallis and Tom Parker (to be discussed as we move on), *Viva Las Vegas* is that rare specimen, a flawless Elvis film.

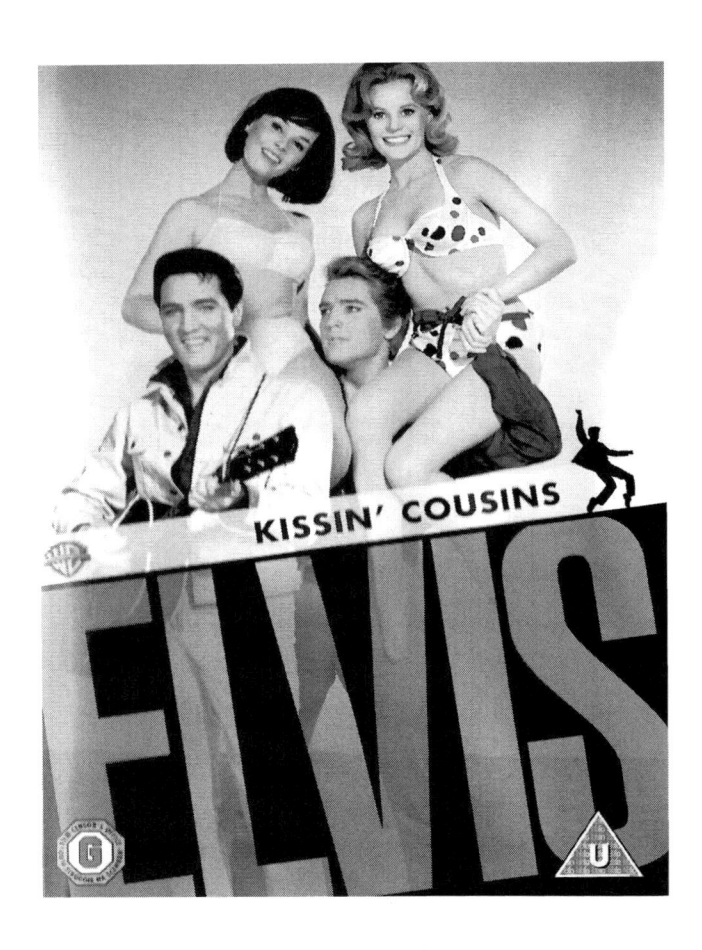

Kissin' Cousins (1964)

wr. Gerald Drayson Adams, Gene Nelson, dir. Gene Nelson, pr. Sam Katzman (MGM)

with Elvis Presley (Josh Morgan/Jodie Tatum), Yvonne Craig (Azalea Tatum), Pamela Austin (Selena Tatum), Jack Albertson (Captain Salbo), Arthur O'Connell (Pa Tatum), Glenda Farrell (Ma Tatum), Cynthia Pepper (Midge), Tommy Farrell (Master Sergeant Bailey), Donald Woods (General Danford), Hortense Petra (Dixie), Beverly Powers (Trudy), Robert Stone (General's aide), Robert Carson (General Kruger), Maureen Reagan, Joan Staley, Lori Williams (girls), Joe Esposito (soldier), Lance Le Gault (dancer/stunt double)

Elvis sings: "Kissin' Cousins" (over titles); "There's Gold in the Mountains" (in haystack with Pam Austin and Yvonne Craig); "One Boy, Two Little Girls" (in hills with Pam Austin and Yvonne Craig); "Catchin' on Fast" (to Yvonne Craig); "Tender Feelings" (to Cynthia Pepper); "Pappy, Won't You Please Come Home?" (Glenda Farrell only); "Barefoot Ballad" (at dance, with ensemble); "Once is Enough" (at party with ensemble, to Yvonne Craig); "Kissin' Cousins" (grand finale; Elvis and Elvis to Cynthia Pepper and Yvonne Craig, with ensemble)

Viva Las Vegas was considered a rousing success by almost everybody except one person--Colonel Tom Parker. For Parker, the Elvis films were solely about the three P's--Presley, profit, and publicity. Nothing else mattered. He was not impressed by the vivacious Ann-Margret, not because he found her lacking, but because for the first time Elvis had been featured with a leading lady of seriously significant beauty and talent, and she had come close to blowing him off the screen. He was not impressed by the showmanship of director George Sidney, because every lavish number cost money that had to be subtracted from the profits, and the Colonel knew that an Elvis film would make money regardless of the number of sets or dancing girls in the background. And he knew that Ann-Margret had not only stolen half the movie, but half the column inches as well. The fact that *Viva Las Vegas* had been a quality film meant nothing to him unless it had been a plus without the minuses. Certain bean-counters at MGM had come to the same conclusion, because the next Elvis project was turned over to the cheapest producer on the lot, and was put into production and completed so quickly that it actually beat *Viva Las Vegas* into the cinemas!

It is ironic that the storyline of *Kissin' Cousins* concerned a double of Elvis (tactless, too, as Presley was still touchy over the death of his own baby twin, Jesse Garon), as *Kissin' Cousins* introduced Parker to his own

Hollywood duplicate, the cigar-chewing schlockmeister Sam Katzman. The Colonel could've been looking in a mirror.

Almost everybody has seen something of a production by the Katzman family. The Katzmans were never involved with anything earth-shakingly ground-breaking, but there's been a Katzman beavering away in the low-budget or offbeat corner of Hollywood since the 1930s.

The Katzmans aren't that well known, because most of their programming has been fairly insignificant, a collection of footnotes throughout the reference libraries of film and TV... but put them all together and their efforts become a body of work worthy of... well, a bigger footnote, a collection of diverse and fascinating productions ranging from Sam Katzman's Superman and Batman serials, bargain basement sci-fi, and teen exploitation drive-in movie fare, to nephew Leonard Katzman's failed 1970s SF TV series *Fantastic Journey* and *Logan's Run* to grandson Omri Katz's straight-to-video films and TV series *Eerie, Indiana* in the '90s, all of them linked by two intriguing factors--their anonymity and their low budgets.

Sam Katzman was one of the first movie producers to belong to that canny breed who spot a trend just as it's starting and then jump on the bandwagon as cheaply and quickly as possible to exploit it to maximum profitability at minimum expense. In this respect, he preceded such later masters of the tactic as Roger Corman and Glen Larson, and he has had a hand in the careers of some of American pop culture's greatest icons, both living and fictional. Despite this, many film books mention him only in passing, or not at all.

Like his nephew Leonard, whose father was a prop man and electrician, and Leonard's son Frank, Sam Katzman started out in the movies as an assistant director, swiftly and briefly graduating to director before becoming a producer of B-features with such wonderful titles as *Fighting Renegade* and *Texas Wildcats*. One of Katzman's earliest production credits was *A Face in the Fog*, a mad hunchback story made in 1936. It was a mixture of *The Phantom of the Opera* and *The Hunchback of Notre Dame* and was primarily notable for featuring no fog!

Throughout the 1940s, Katzman made many super-cheap stinkers with the post-Dracula Bela Lugosi, including *The Invisible Ghost* (1941), *Black Dragons* (1942), *Bowery at Midnight* (1942; this plot--mad doctor experimenting on vagrants--is still frequently in use today), *The Corpse Vanishes* (1942; the old killing to keep youth chestnut), *The Ape Man* (1943), *Return of the Ape Man* (1944), and *The Voodoo Man* (1944), after which Lugosi continued on the same route with other producers. Katzman also had a hand in the popular *East Side Kids* films of the '40s (a series of lowbrow running around comedies starring a bunch of Brooklyn toughies), many of which had the boys being pursued by ghosts and weirdies in old dark houses in titles like *Ghost Crazy* (1944) and *Spook Busters* (1946).

By 1947, Katzman had predictably entered the serial arena on behalf of Columbia, with *Brenda Starr, Reporter* (1945), *Tex Granger* (1947), time-traveling *Brick Bradford* (1947), battling *Jack Armstrong* (1947), *Congo Bill* (1948), and saucer fighting *Bruce Gentry* (1949). *Superman* (1948) introduced athlete and dancer Kirk Alyn to the world as the first live-action Man of Steel. The following year, Katzman was the obvious choice to safeguard *Batman and Robin,* the 1949 sequel to Columbia's 1943 *Batman.* Katzman recast the roles, with Robert Lowery as Batman, Johnny Duncan as Robin, and Lyle Talbot as the evil adversary the Wizard. The following year, in 1950, Talbot would play Lex Luthor in Katzman's *Superman* sequel, *Atom Man Vs. Superman* (oddly, evil Atom Man Luthor gets top billing in the title!). Once again, Alyn was Superman, but only after a wrangle over money, for a film which was being made on an even smaller budget than the first. When Katzman threatened to make "Son of Superman" instead (this was before the comics had dreamed up Superboy), Alyn replied "Okay, you tell the kids where he came from!".

At around this time, Katzman earned the nickname that would stay with him for the rest of his career--Jungle Sam! In sixteen shorts made between 1948 and 1955, which the late film buff, buyer, and critic Leslie Halliwell suggested were "shot in Sam Katzman's back garden", the now ageing screen Tarzan Johnny Weismuller, too out of condition and overweight to play lord of the jungle any more (he had dominated the role between 1932 and 1948), appeared as *Flash Gordon* creator Alex Raymond's *Jungle Jim.* One of the lions they used was so old they had to photograph him quickly before he fell over, but unsung hero was bartender Steve Calvert, who bought a gorilla suit from Ray 'Crash' Corrigan of *Undersea Kingdom* fame and spent the best part of the 1950s playing gorillas for Katzman.

During the 1950s, Sam Katzman's unit at Columbia turned out an astonishing number of cheapo adventure films in every genre, including sword-and-sandal, westerns, jungle mayhem (*King of the Congo, Valley of the Headhunters, Adventures of Captain Africa*), pirate adventures on the high seas (*Prince of Pirates, Pirates of Tripoli, The Great Adventures of Captain Kidd*) and all manner of historical adventure (*Serpent of the Nile, Charge of the Lancers, Drums of Tahiti,* and *Saracen Blade*). He also produced the first film of a TV show--a *Captain Video* serial in 1951. In amidst this hive of activity sit a number of SF films, including one worthy of Ed Wood (*Creature With the Atom Brain,* 1955), one genuine classic (*Earth vs. the Flying Saucers,* 1956), and another that became a legend for all the wrong reasons (the mind-numbingly hilarious *The Giant Claw*, 1957)!

It Came from Beneath the Sea (also 1955) marked the start of Katzman's brief association with the godfather of special effects Ray Harryhausen and his producer Charles Schneer. It was one of the giant-creature-terrorises-civilisation movies so popular of the period, and although it deserves to be remembered for more, critical comments are always dominated by the octopus that possessed only six tentacles, a Katzman budget-crunching classic. Refused permission to film in San Francisco (where the creature memorably attacks the Golden Gate bridge), the director shot location footage secretly from the back of a bread truck.

In 1956, Katzman discovered rock and roll and made the notorious *Rock Around the Clock,* which--although laughably tame by today's standards--had '50s juvenile delinquents dancing in the aisles. No fool, he followed it with the likes of *Don't Knock the Rock* (1957), *Calypso Heat Wave* (1957), *Twist Around the Clock* (1961) and *Don't Knock the Twist* (1962) among countless others, and it was these credentials that dared the Colonel to hope he'd found the man to make the next Elvis film. Infamously, when the script was sent to the Colonel, he sent it straight back, saying that he'd charge 25,000 dollars for his opinion. Making the movie was their job, he explained; he just needed to get an album out of it. The budget was a mere 1.3 million dollars, of which only 650,000 of that money went on the actual movie--750,000 dollars went straight to the bank accounts of Elvis and the Colonel.

The story the Colonel declined to peruse concerns the military's ham-fisted attempts to secure the Tatum-owned mountain for a missile base, something considered a good thing in those days, and naively presumes that any government wouldn't just march in and take it. Seeking a co-conspirator who understands mountain folk, Jack Albertson's Captain Salbo, himself bullied by Donald Woods' General Donfield, pressgangs Presley's Lt. Josh Morgan into service, unaware that the family connection is even tighter than he supposed and that Presley has an identical blond cousin living in the hills with Ma and Pa Tatum and their two lovely daughters Selina and Azalea.

Also running through the hills like water are a stream of teenage girls from the nearby town, where no young men have been born for twenty years, creating a drought of potential suitors for the man-crazed Kittyhawks, a pubescent fantasy of Daisy-Mae-type Amazons led like sheep by the bouncy Beverly Powers as Trudy (fortunately, the mountains don't seem to be short of hair-stylists). When the Sad Sacks of Salbo's military platoon roll in, Christmas has come early for boys and girls alike...

although it has to be said that these lucky goofs should be grateful the girls have had so little exposure to the male species!

There is little more substance to the storyline than this, and little more required. Suspense is attempted, but not generated, by the question of whether Pa will allow the military in, and the only jeopardy comes from Pa's misfortune when he is chased off a cliff-edge and onto a precarious tree branch by an offscreen bear (which is presumably a kissin' cousin of Yogi Bear, as it has somehow managed to hook him onto a branch!). As if acknowledging the entire exercise as a good-natured sham, the cast even pose with a sign reading `the end' when the final dance number finishes.

The film was, of course, a rush job (even the nine songs were recorded in eight hours flat), leaving Elvis and his performance high and dry, the situation exacerbated by the fact that Presley was playing two roles, army Lt. Josh Morgan and hillbilly hog chaser Jodie Tatum, his old buddy Lance Le Gault playing his stand-in again.

Although the busy dance sequences are excellent, Elvis is clearly confused and harassed by the shooting schedule, and is given no possibility of developing characters for either of his two roles. Worse still, the hurried solo songs are not only mundane, but barely even sound like the distinct and special Presley voice, the only occasion this occurs in any of the Elvis movies. It was all a long way from Las Vegas and the lavish Sahara hotel, where the director had actually been adding scenes, much to the intense irritation of the Colonel, who knew only too well that every extra flourish was coming out of his profits! For this movie, he pocketed the fee well before shooting.

Some relief came with the casting of several performers with whom Presley had worked before. As well as the usual Memphis Mafia to hand (Joe Esposito has a minor role), and Le Gault as his stand-in, Yvonne Craig returned from *It Happened at the World's Fair* to enjoy more substantial screentime as Azalea, Pamela Austin of *Blue Hawaii* was back for a bigger and better showcase as Selina, and best of all from Elvis' point of view, he had the chance to work again with Arthur O'Connell, Pop Kwimper from *Follow That Dream,* who, although playing a similar part, manages to create a completely different character as the cartoonish Pa Tatum.

Former *Playboy* pin-up Joan Staley, and Jack Albertson, an old vaudevillian who had previously appeared in *Miracle on 34th Street* and *The Shaggy Dog,* would prove amiable enough to be invited back to feature in small roles in *Roustabout.*

Other new arrivals included former Hollywood femme fatale Glenda Farrell as Ma Tatum, now getting on in years, but famous in her day for dozens of brassy floozie roles in the 1930s, usually as gangsters' molls or dancing girls, starting with *Little Caesar* (a rare victim part) and culminating in the *Torchy Blane* series of B-movie comedy crime thrillers. The '50s were quiet for her, but she appeared in *Bewitched* and the Jerry Lewis film *The Disorderly Orderly* in 1964 before making *Kissin' Cousins*.

Also in *Kissin' Cousins* was her son Tommy Farrell, who would play minor roles in broad comedy sequences in *The Beverly Hillbillies, The Munsters, The Addams Family, Lost in Space, Get Smart, Captain Nice*, and several *Lucy Shows*. He plays an unconvincing consolation prize for poor Pam Austin, who deserves an Oscar for looking so thrilled and satisfied with his pop-eyed Sgt. Bailey when Elvis plumps for Yvonne Craig's Azalia (the lovely Craig slightly plumper herself in this film than in many of her other roles, including her later guise as TV's Batgirl). While sparkle-eyed Austin pours herself all over this grateful gargoyle like gravy, the dapper Jack Albertson--on the receiving end of several cruel barbs--is deemed too undesirable even for the none-too-fussy Kittyhawks! Even tribal leader Trudy is seen seducing the baffled General Donfield (Donald Woods smartly turned out, but way past his leading man days with Lupe Velez!).

Despite the film being one of Presley's cheapest, Craig and Austin are among his most attractive female co-stars, and one wishes they had done more than two Elvis films each. Craig was the highlight of *It Happened at the Worlds Fair* and should have had the female lead; Austin was unfairly overshadowed by Darlene Tompkins and Jenny Maxwell in *Blue Hawaii*. Here, they both get a fair crack of the whip--Presley serenades them no less than three times during the picture, and one barely looks at Elvis when they are onscreen, which is high praise indeed. If one can overlook the production flaws, it's a fun hour-and-a-bit.

Yvonne Craig had already made her scene-stealing single scene appearance in *It Happened at the World's Fair,* and would sparkle in every 1960s film or TV series she appeared in. She had started her career in vamp/bad girl roles before enjoying more success cast as innocent cute and perky types. Her early films included teen movies such as *Eighteen and Anxious* and *Gidget,* alongside smaller roles in melodramas *The Gene Krupa Story* (with Sal Mineo and *Gidget's* James Darren) and *By Love Possessed* (with Lana Turner), and family fare *High Time* (with Bing Crosby, Fabian, and *Wild in the Country's* Tuesday Weld), *Advance to the Rear* (with Glenn Ford and *Girls!, Girls!, Girls!'* Stella Stevens) and (with George Maharis and *Clambake's* James Gregory).

However, it is for her cult sci-fi and spy roles she is best remembered today, having appeared in memorable episodes of *My Favorite Martian, Voyage to the Bottom of the Sea, The Man from UNCLE, The Wild Wild West,*

Star Trek, Land of the Giants and *The Six Million Dollar Man,* spy movies *In Like Flint, One Spy too Many,* and *One of Our Spies is Missing,* and brightened up the turgid pulp sci-fi film *Mars Needs Women* and the weak third season of *Batman* as the dazzling Batgirl.

Other TV included *Mr. Lucky, Bronco, Dobie Gillis, 77, Sunset Strip, The Detectives, Wagon Train, Doctor Kildare, The Aquanauts, McHale's Navy, Mr. Roberts, Ben Casey, The Big Valley, My Three Sons, The Ghost and Mrs. Muir, The Mod Squad, It Takes a Thief, Mannix, Love American Style, The Courtship of Eddie's Father* (with Bill Bixby, who she was then dating), *Emergency, The Magician* (again with Bixby), *Kojak, Starsky and Hutch,* and *Fantasy Island.* She's wonderful in the snowbound 1964 beach movie-like *Ski Party,* with Deborah Walley of *Spinout* and Lesley Gore (of "It's My Party" fame, which Gore sings in the movie).

Cynthia Pepper was another wide-eyed innocent specialist from a show-biz family who played a recurring role on the sit-com *My Three Sons* for a year before securing a starring title role in her own one season wonder *Margie.* Out of work for a while after a supporting role in *Take Her, She's Mine,* a teen comedy starring Sandra Dee and *Blue Hawaii's* Jenny Maxwell, she suddenly received a message from her agent saying she had a role in *Kissin' Cousins* "if she could get to MGM in 45 minutes and fit in the costume"! She became friends with Yvonne Craig and like most Elvis co-stars, could only find compliments for him.

"He couldn't have been sweeter" she told Tom Lisanti for his book *Drive-In Dream Girls.* "He kept the set on an even keel. Usually on a set, the main star's demeanor sets the tone for the working environment. With Elvis, it was always fun. He didn't hang around much, but he would stand there behind the cameras if you had to do a take for a close-up. He wouldn't leave--unlike some other stars. He was also very gentlemanly". Echoing Mary Ann Mobley later on *Harum Scarum,* she said "A number of times he offered me his chair if he saw me standing".

Following *Kissin' Cousins,* she made two unsold pilots with *Loving You's* Hal Kanter (one with two-time Elvis co-star Gary Lockwood, the other with Elvis co-stars Joanna Moore and Yvonne Craig), but motherhood interrupted any further ambitions. Other TV roles included *77, Sunset Strip, Surfside Six, Bourbon Street Beat, Boris Karloff's Thriller, Wagon Train, Perry Mason, Dobie Gillis, The Addams Family, The Flying Nun,* and *Lassie.*

Leader of the intimidating Kittyhawks in *Kissin' Cousins* was busty dancer Beverly Powers, who would also appear in *Speedway.* One of the few advantages of no-retakes shooting is on display, along with Trudy, when Powers wrestles with Elvis in the foliage and her breast is briefly exposed. The bouncing babes frequently appear as if they are going to bounce right out of their skimpy costumes and the equally well-endowed Yvonne Craig very nearly tips out of an army jeep when it breaks suddenly, another moment comically left in the finished film. Powers is naively exuberant in all her under-rehearsed scenes with the girls, a typically 1960s legion of squealing automatons, a dozen women apparently controlled by one shared brain, as if a science-fiction alien was giving the orders.

Also among the Kittyhawks is Lori Williams, who also appeared in *Get Yourself a College Girl* (with two time Elvis co-star Mary Ann Mobley), *The Disorderly Orderly* (with Jerry Lewis and Glenda Farrell), *Viva Las Vegas* (the discotheque dance scene), *Roustabout, Pajama Party, Girl Happy, Swingin' Summer, Tickle Me, Our Man Flint, It's a Bikini World*, and, her big claim to fame, Russ Meyer's ridiculous *Faster, Pussycat! Kill! Kill!* TV included episodes of *Honey West* and *Love, American Style,* as well as dancing in several editions of legendary American pop shows *Hullabaloo* and *Shindig.*

Shooting took place at the Big Bear ski resort in the San Bernadino mountains, swiftly moving onto a studio set which shrunk a little bit smaller each day as Katzman gradually dismissed crew and technicians to skimp and scrimp. The to-ing and fro-ing from sunny location shots to indoor studio shots is fairly conspicuous (although nowhere near as distracting as on the far more expensive and prestigious musical *Carousel* during its beach scenes some years earlier), and the film writes out the duplicate Elvis in several scenes simply to avoid the special effects headache (even split screen is barely used when a cut and back-of-head shot can be used instead), giving Cynthia Pepper few scenes alongside Craig and Austin.

One of these shortcuts cost Glenda Farrell dearly, when she had to judo-throw Jodie and send him away from the dinner table scene, which could easily have incorporated Presley's double and some two-shots; she wrenched her neck and had to wear a neck-brace when not filming. When the optical effects are attempted, even the primitive techniques then being frequently employed on TV series like *Bewitched* and *I Dream of Jeannie* were superior.

In the plus column, the bustling dance sequences at the end of the film actually benefit from the rapid shooting schedule, the rushed rehearsal giving the film a more realistic, spontaneous, chaotic look than the more ritualistic, often mechanically performed show scenes in other, more lavish Hollywood musicals (witness the stagey, phoney, over-rehearsed beach party number in *Girl Happy* or the horrors of the *Comeback Special*), but the special effects to create the two Presleys are pitiful, and overwhelm everything. Lance Le Gault is plainly on view next to Elvis in part of the final dance scene, and even when his face is clumsily obscured or his back to the camera, his build is different and the hairpieces don't even match. Bearing in mind that blond Elvis is wearing a wig himself, this is intolerable! Several sources comment on Presley's discomfort and unhappiness with the blond wig, even though--or perhaps because--it was remarkably close to his natural hair color.

Worst of all, in the final dance number when the two brothers dance next to each other, each taking turns to spin around with their back to the audience, Katzman and Nelson cut back and forth between two dance routines instead of using split screen. Although the editing is efficient, a child of five could see through it. It would have been so easy, and so effective, to have Josh and Jodie standing and dancing next to each other. A fight scene after the boys' first meeting has some of the worst doubling ever seen on film, and the stunt man portraying the second Elvis (not looking much like Lance Le Gault either, but surely a third stand-in) has a plainly older face and bone structure.

The critics were not kind to *Kissin' Cousins,* but it was quickly, and perhaps unfairly overshadowed by the premiere of *Viva Las Vegas* the following month. Some complaints centered around the film's broad portrayal of the South, which was a bit rich given that the same people had picked on Elvis as an easy target for snobbish superiority because of his Southern origins.

In fact, it's not a bad film, although some of its defenders have been a little too exuberant in their praise. David Bret , in his book *Elvis – the Hollywood Years,* calls it "an unadulterated exercise in unexpurgated high camp and deliberate homo-eroticism", which is extremely doubtful, and even cites the names of Russ Meyer and John Waters. However, Bret's book seems obsessed with finding a homosexual slant in the Elvis movies, and frankly, as with Batman and Robin, it's often only there if you really want it to be; *Kissin' Cousins* is actually a resoundingly heterosexual movie overflowing with masculine, if juvenile fantasies--Elvis sings no less than three songs to two of his most stunningly desirable co-stars ever (Craig and Austin have never looked more beautiful, and only look awful when they return from town smeared in cosmetics) and the soldiers are there solely to be mobbed by a bunch of giggling bimbos on auto-pilot who make the *Playboy* mansion look like Harvard (true, the dancing G.I.s in the final dance numbers are a *little* gay...!).

However, this is a red-blooded guy's film, full of tanks, jeeps, and female flesh, the one commercial error perhaps being that there is nothing for the girls in this one, other than an off-form Elvis. Perhaps this is why, subliminally, *Kissin' Cousins* is not rated very highly by many Elvis admirers. Katzman's films frequently were camp, but only incidentally and after the fact--his super-hero, sword-and-sandal, sci-fi and rock and roll movies have become camp retroactively, they were not deliberately made so (Kirk Alyn's stockroom change of identities in Katzman's *Superman* serials is priceless).

The truth is that comedy hillbillies had been a staple of lowbrow entertainment for years previously (Katzman himself had just completed *Hootenanny Hoot,* with Johnny Cash and *Kissin' Cousins'* Pam Austin), from the *Lil' Abner* comic strips, movie, and stage plays, to *Ma and Pa Kettle* comedies, Warner Brothers cartoons, and TV series such as *The Real McCoys* and *The Beverly Hillbillies* on one side of it, to post-*Kissin' Cousins* entries like *Hillbillies in a Haunted House* and *Las Vegas Hillbillies, The Lucy Show's* hoedown with Tennesee Ernie Ford, *The Munsters'* (very funny) encounter with hillbillies in "All-Star Munster" (*Roustabout's* dog-faced Pat Buttram hilarious), the *Burke's Law* episode "Who Killed Lenore Wingfield?", which features Elvis babe Anne Helm as an Elly May Clampett clone, a *Lost in Space* episode with Daisy Mae and Jethro-like teens who transform into monster makers in "The Space Croppers", a *Flintstones* satire on the Hatfield and McCoy feud, Hanna-Barbera's *Hillbilly Bears,* and *The Man from UNCLE's* hillbilly outings "The Bat Cave Affair" (with *Roustabout's* Joan Freeman) and "The Apple-a-Day Affair" on the other.

All of these featured one or more of the standard hillbilly cliches such as barn dances, shotgun marriages, pot shots at tax collectors, moonshine stills, rifle-toting grannies, barefoot husband-hunting adolescent nymphs, hulking young morons, wise fools, and hideous foodstuffs (one very funny scene in *Kissin' Cousins* has Jack Albertson literally turn green when informed he's eating possums and grits and catfish eyes, a difficult but not impossible optical effect at that time, here performed simply with a green spotlight).

It was grossly corny, and possibly even offensive to the terminally indignant, but it was a comedy staple of the mid-20th century, and far less heavy-handed here than in some of the above. Played out and old hat by the early 1970s, these cliches would be replaced by the new stereotype of the corrupt small town Southern sheriff and the sinister farmboy redneck until paired off together in the inexplicably popular late-'70s TV series *The Dukes of Hazzard...*

Kissin' Cousins, with its gaggle of giggling girls and Disney-esque comedy military (right in the middle of Vietnam, no less) is a film that could only have been made in the '60s. Stumbling around in his two different roles, a hurried and harried Elvis is plainly clueless as to who and what and where he is during the shots with both his characters in, visibly lost onscreen, and glancing at cue cards (he had come to *Love Me Tender* with everyone's lines memorised), and certain actors can be seen mouthing their fellow performers' lines, although old-timers O'Connell, Albertson, and Farrell acquit themselves well and the alluring Yvonne Craig and Pamela Austin pout and pose and twirl and whirl with admirable confidence and style given the rushed shooting. In the event, because *Kissin' Cousins* was actually released first, *Viva Las Vegas* and Paramount's *Roustabout* gave the erroneous impression of looking like comeback films, a step up from cornball comedy--a small blessing that would soon be wasted by more cheap and cheerful quickies like *Harum Scarum, Tickle Me,* and *Double Trouble...*

Cynthia Pepper (l) and Yvonne Craig (r) can't quite believe Lance Le Gault's Elvis face transplant in this publicity pic from *Kissin' Cousins*

Roustabout (1964)

wr. Allan Weiss, Anthony Lawrence, dir. John Rich, pr. Hal Wallis (Paramount)

with Elvis Presley (Charlie Rogers), Joan Freeman (Cathy), Barbara Stanwyck (Maggie Moran), Leif Erickson (Joe), Sue Ane Langdon (Mme. Mijanou), Pat Buttram (Harry Carver), Joan Staley (Marge), Dabbs Greer (bank official), Steve Brodie (bully), Norman Grabowski (college boy), Jack Albertson (Lou), Joel Fluellen (Cody), Jane Dulo (bully's wife), Wilda Taylor (Little Egypt), Marianna Hill (Viola), Beverly Adams (Cora), Lance Le Gault (announcer for Little Egypt), Arthur Levy, Toby Reed, Ray Kellogg, Lester Miller, Lori Williams, Raquel Welch, Richard Kiel, Billy Barty, Red West

Elvis sings: "Roustabout" (over titles); "Poison Ivy League" (at club); "Wheels on My Heels" (on bike); "It's a Wonderful World" (on ferris wheel to Joan Freeman); "It's Carnival Time" (at carnival); "Carny Town" (at carnival); "One Track Heart" (in tent show); "Hard Knocks" (in tent show); "Little Egypt" (at stage show); "Big Love, Big Heartache" (at stage show); "There's A Brand New Day on the Horizon" (finale at carnival)

There was one other person who hadn't liked *Viva Las Vegas,* and that was Hal Wallis. Whether he was being genuinely critical, or just understandably irritated that MGM had duplicated the successful ingredients of his Paramount films so effortlessly and successfully with *It Happened at the World's Fair* and *Viva Las Vegas* (and done it with more style), he found a willing and receptive Colonel Parker happy to listen. Together, they agreed that Elvis had to look meaner and leaner for this next movie, Parker's long-imagined carny-based adventure. Usually not remotely interested in anything not pertaining to profit or publicity, Parker was keenly concerned that *Roustabout* represented carnival life accurately, and for the first and only time tinkered with the script, making alterations and suggestions to stress reality and avoid cliche. He was, you might say, acting as a "technical advisor", a credit he helped himself to on all Presley's films.

This was the last time Elvis played a character to be taken seriously (if *Viva Las Vegas* had provoked Wallis to raise the bar for himself with *Roustabout,* it didn't take long for him to limbo underneath it again). In an effort to return just half-way to his *Jailhouse Rock* tortured tough guy persona, Elvis was Charlie Rogers, a lonely and cynical motorcycle vagabond paying his way with his guitar and vocal chords.

Charlie carried no physical baggage, but mentally he had a huge chip on his shoulder. As the story opens, he's taking out his frustrations on a group of underage drinking college kids, who subsequently take out their own frustrations on him outside after the show. Elvis flattens two of them with karate and spends the night in jail, bailed out by shapely Joan Staley, whose reward is to be left on the sidewalk pleading with him to keep in touch after he's lost his job. This is the last we see of her.

Run off the road by surly middle-aged drunk Joe Lean (Leif Erickson) after making a mobile pass at his daughter Cathy (Joan Freeman) from his bike--much to the wry amusement of tough-as-nails silver-haired carny owner Maggie Moran (Barbara Stanwyck)--he's given a job as a roustabout while they get his bike fixed and guitar replaced. When Charlie gets his guitar back, Moran is thrilled to find that Rogers' musical talents are pulling in the rubes... and while Cathy's fuming father makes every effort to save both his dignity and his daughter and send lustful Charlie packing, the manipulative Maggie makes as valiant a try at persuading Charlie to put down roots, save the struggling carny, and declare his true feelings...

The role of Maggie Moran was originally intended for human cartoon and legendary Hollywood super-slut Mae West, a camp joke who was a sort of grotesque amalgam of Marilyn Monroe and W.C. Fields. Elvis was apparently looking forward to working with her, but once again, as so many times before, Parker was looking out for him and astutely realised that West and the attendant publicity would blow Elvis off the center stage. Still smarting from the Ann-Margret scenario, he swiftly vetoed West. Although this was, as always with Parker, an entirely self-motivated move, West's casting was a horrible idea that would have reduced what would be one of Presley's better films to a bad joke.

Barbara Stanwyck's film career (over 80 films in all genres between 1927 and 1964) was on a downward slide, and the outspoken and opinionated actress was only a few months away from doing a TV series--*The Big Valley,* a sort of distaff *Bonanza*--five years before it became pragmatically fashionable and acceptable for other movie stars of her generation to jump or be pushed into their own small screen retirement homes.

Known for being rather frosty and speaking her mind, Stanwyck surprised everybody by being thoroughly pleasant to cast and crew. However, it has been said that Stanwyck and Presley did not get on, and that there had been words. If so, such animosity could only have been good for the film and the performances, as there were several scenes in which their characters were required to participate in venomous exchanges of dialogue. It's revealing that Elvis is intimidated in every single one of them.

Director John Rich was already a veteran of TV westerns *Gunsmoke* and *Bonanza,* and had just completed a lengthy stint on the classy TV sitcom *The Dick Van Dyke Show.* He was looking for new directions, and had signed on with Paramount to make movies. What he felt about being handed an Elvis script we don't know, but like his predecessors, Rich was impressed by Presley, who was eager and helpful. He was not as impressed with the Memphis Mafia, particularly when they disdainfully talked him out of learning about the editing process.

Rich was planning to move up in the world, but unlike Siegel and Dunne, he had no personal agenda other than to move from TV to film. Nothing in his background other than his obvious versatility suggested he was the man for *Roustabout,* but his ambition made *Roustabout* a slightly classier affair than those directed by the old warhorses working their way to retirement, and several song sequences that might usually have been done lazily as mattes were done on location on the massive outdoor funfair set constructed especially for the movie and peopled with over a thousand extras.

When Rich does resort to the usual Wallis short cut of back projection and a double in long-shot for a bike ride near the end of the film, it's quite jarring ("Elvis always rode a Harley, yet in the film they put him on a 350 Honda" sneered Lance Le Gault with amusement to Jerry Hopkins. "And this is a guy who's playing the part of a drifter... this guy supposedly goes across country on a machine that's about right for the driveway!").

The band-aid on Elvis' forehead in the opening scenes is real--Rich had unwisely been cajoled by Elvis into letting him do his own fight scene after reassurances about Presley's "black belt in karate". As anyone who has ever seen Presley going through his karate moves will know, his various awards were almost certainly generous and honorary. You don't refuse Elvis, as the unhappy FBI man who denied Presley a badge discovered when he was over-ruled by Nixon. With Presley injured in a mishap that required several stitches at the hospital, Rich realised with gratitude that the band-aid was in character, and an apologetic Presley returned to a set that everyone was relieved would not have to be shut down for a few days--especially as the penny-pinching Colonel, despite his personal interest in the quality of the project, had cut the shooting schedule down from eight weeks to six. It was not the first time Presley had committed the cardinal sin of getting himself injured during shooting--he had cut his face around the eye badly while playing football with Gary Lockwood and the Memphis Mafia during the filming of *It Happened at the World's Fair*, after which he reluctantly conceded to wear a helmet.

The musical sequences are better for being mostly performed on stage, and again the exception--Elvis looking particularly foolish serenading Freeman on a ferris wheel with the usual atrocious miming--is jarring in a film of such quality, despite the adventurous directorial choices. The inevitable punch-ups with belligerent oafs are there, but above average; unusually, Red West is left holding a broom in the background while Elvis sorts out Leif Erickson, Norm Grabowski, and Steve Brodie. And amazingly, there are no cute kids center stage, and no comedy old timers or patronised minorities.

Leif Erickson (real name, William Anderson--he inexplicably swiped the name of a famous Norwegian explorer) was a B-movie tough guy who had never quite made his mark, and he too would be heading for TV ranch retirement from the big screen in yet another *Bonanza* clone, *The High Chaparral*.

Joan Freeman, despite looking good in blue jeans, strongly resisted overtures to market her as a glamour girl, which was probably wise. Like fellow Elvis co-stars Anne Helm and Laurel Goodwin, she had that sweet and innocent farm girl look, and survived the disappearing act fate of most beach movie types to become a character actress as she got older. From juvenile bit parts in big films to larger roles in B-movies, Freeman moved into television quickly, appearing in such titles as *Gunsmoke, The Virginian, Doctor Kildare, Perry Mason, Hawaiian Eye, Wagon Train, The Outer Limits, Laramie, Lassie, The Man from UNCLE,* and *Land of the Giants*. She lost the female lead in the Don Knotts comedy *The Ghost and Mr. Chicken* to fellow *Roustabout* co-star Joan Staley, but secured his follow-up film *The Reluctant Astronaut,* and worked with Elvis movies assistant director Michael Moore when he filmed *The Fastest Guitar Alive,* a vehicle for Roy Orbison (Orbison was one of the few performers who followed in Presley's footsteps who impressed Elvis). More TV followed in the 1970s, and in 1984 she accepted the inevitable, and the role of a mother in *Friday the 13th--the Final Chapter,* followed by several guest spots in Stephen J. Cannell productions such as *Riptide, Hardcastle and McCormick,* and *Renegade*.

"Miss Purity I've never been" Sue-Ane Langdon laughed to an interviewer. "I'm usually playing some dizzy blonde broad out after someone else's husband!". Broad is a fairly good description of her acting style, which ain't subtle, but as she's usually cast as a floozy or a showgirl in light-hearted romps, it hasn't much mattered. In *Roustabout,* she enjoys the novelty of having dark hair and pursuing unmarried Elvis/Charlie... although as usual, not very seriously, and stealing from the more high-minded, long-suffering Freeman.

"The parts I played in the '60s were fun, and there is just not that kind of humor around any more" she told interviewer Tom Lisanti. "The innocence is gone from films today. The humor is harsh and it's not funny. Most of my roles were innocent, daffy women. These roles don't exist today, but I don't miss acting an awful lot. I've done television, films, and theater so I guess I got it all out of my system!".

Langdon appeared in about a dozen films during the 1960s, usually in up-for-it bimbo roles, including a second Elvis film, *Frankie and Johnny,* and the Peter Noone Sam Katzman musical *Hold On* with Shelley Fabares, before ending up playing a housewife in the banal blue-collar 1970s sit-com *Arnie.* TV work included numerous variety shows in the '50s, a recurring role on *Bachelor Father,* and parts in fashionable and/or cult shows *Bourbon Street Beat, Surfside Six, 77, Sunset Strip, Boris Karloff's Thriller, The Dick Van Dyke Show, The Man from UNCLE, The Wild Wild West,* and *The Name of the Game,* as well as numerous other guest shots in more mundane fare including *The Detectives, Ironside, Police Story,* and several episodes of *Perry Mason* and *Bonanza.* In the early 1980s she appeared in teen comedy *Zapped* alongside an assortment of '80s starlets.

"I thought Elvis Presley was sweet and very nice" said Langdon, "but I almost didn't do *Roustabout* because doing an Elvis Presley movie was not really much of a stepping stone. I'm glad I did it, because it is one of the main things I'm remembered for today. I enjoyed working with Elvis and can't say one bad thing about him, but I don't think he was that comfortable making movies. He was much more relaxed on stage". With no further qualms, she returned to the Presley fold once more for a similar role in *Frankie and Johnny* two years later.

Former *Playboy* model Joan Staley (real name, Joan McConchie) also had a lengthy string of TV credits, including *Perry Mason, Bonanza, Maverick, The Tab Hunter Show, 77, Sunset Strip, Hawaiian Eye, Surfside Six, Wagon Train, The Naked City, The Untouchables, The Dick Van Dyke Show, Ozzie and Harriet, Burke's Law, Laredo, The Virginian, Amos Burke--Secret Agent, Batman, The Munsters, Mission: Impossible,* and *Ironside.* Various bit parts in movies (including *Oceans Eleven* and *Cape Fear*) eventually resulted in a larger role as a curvy cavegirl in sci-fi B-movie *Valley of the Dragons* alongside Cesare Danova, but then it was back to mostly minor parts, including her Presley movie. She had met Elvis many years earlier, at Sun Records, where she worked as a back-up singer for record producer Sam Phillips.

While the likes of Billy Barty and Richard Kiel were inevitably cast to type as carny novelty acts (Kiel, later Jaws in the *Bond* franchise, has no lines and is glimpsed only twice), character actors Jack Albertson, Pat Buttram, and Dabbs Greer all played different roles than they were used to. Jack Albertson, as the owner of the saloon bar Elvis is fired from, is virtually unrecognisable without his trademark dust-brush moustache (also missing in *Kissin' Cousins*) and only identified by his distinctive voice, while Pat Buttram, usually cast as a hayseed, laps up the role of scheming showman Harry Carver, Maggie's rival. Dabbs Greer, often cast as a farmer or preacher, has little to do as the bank representative pursuing Maggie for a loan that, if unpaid, will close the business down. Greer's numerous roles include a recurring role in the small-town sit-com *The Ghost and Mrs. Muir* and the distinction of being the very first person rescued by Superman in the premiere episode of *Adventures of Superman*.

Norm Grabowski, the lead troublemaker from the Poison Ivy League sequence, was a broad, hulking fellow usually cast in second banana and doofus roles, and turns up in this capacity in episodes of *The Munsters, The Lucy Show, The Beverly Hillbillies, The Monkees,* and *Batman*. He had also schooled in the infamous Mamie Van Doren exploiters *College Confidential* and *Sex Kittens Go to College* for Z-movie producer Albert Zugsmith, having previously appeared in *Girl's Town,* again with Van Doren for Zugsmith. He would go straight from *Roustabout* to a similar, larger role in the next Presley film, *Girl Happy,* already in pre-production as the cameras rolled here. Presley's other punching bag, Steve Brodie, here playing the obnoxious creep who keeps ducking Cathy in the cold water tank in an overblown and overlong scene, had previously taken a thumping in *Blue Hawaii's* bar scene.

Wilda Taylor would return to the Presley fold as one of the three dancing girls in *Harum Scarum* and a saloon girl in *Frankie and Johnny;* Beverly Adams would be back in *Girl Happy* and fellow bit player Marianna Hill would secure a much larger role in *Paradise, Hawaiian Style*. Joel Fluellen's TV credits during this period included *The Invaders* and *I Spy*. Elvis buddies Lance Le Gault and Red West put in brief appearances, Le Gault as an on-stage huckster for Carver's Little Egypt show, West as background in Presley's dust-up with Erickson. Raquel Welch, soon to be a major movie star in just a couple of years, was still doing bit parts in 1964, and appears briefly as one of two girls coyly seen in a shower stall.

Writer Alan Weiss, who had already co-written *Blue Hawaii* and *Girls! Girls! Girls!* and turned out *Fun in Acapulco* to order on his own, would be paired with TV workhorse Anthony Lawrence, a veteran of westerns and cop shows, for his next three Elvis assignments, this one, *Paradise, Hawaiian Style,* and *Easy Come, Easy Go* (also directed by Rich), which--three years later--would mark the end of both Weiss' and Wallis' association with Elvis movies. *Roustabout* is not as much fun as the bright and breezy Hawaiian-set Elvis movies, but it might well be Wallis' best Elvis film.

Girl Happy (1965)

wr. Harvey Bullock, R.S. Allen, dir. Boris Sagal, pr. Joe Pasternak (MGM)

with Elvis Presley (Rusty Wells), Shelley Fabares (Valerie), Harold J. Stone (Big Frank), Gary Crosby (Andy), Mary Ann Mobley (Deena), Fabrizio Mioni (Romano), Joby Baker (Wilbur), Jimmy Hawkins (Doc), Jackie Coogan (Sergeant Benson), Peter Brooks (Brentwood Von Durgenfeld), Nita Talbot (Sunny Daze), John Fiedler (hotel manager), Chris Noel (Betsy), Lyn Edgington (Laurie), Gail Gilmore (Nancy), Pamela Curran (Bobbie), Rusty Allen (Linda), Norm Grabowski ("Wolf Call"), Milton Frome (Police Chief), Richard Reeves (motorcycle cop), Ralph Lee (station cop), Lori Williams, Nancy Czar, Beverly Adams (the girls), Mike De Anda (bartender), Olan Soule (waiter), Don Haggerty, Jim Dawson, Ted Fish, Red West, the Jordanaires

Elvis sings: "Girl Happy" (over titles); "Spring Fever" (in cars, with supporting players); "Fort Lauderdale Chamber of Commerce" (poolside to Shelley Fabares); "Wolf Call" (in nightclub with Mary Ann Mobley); "Do Not Disturb" (to Mary Ann Mobley); "Cross My Heart" (to Mary Ann Mobley); "The Meanest Girl in Town" (on stage with Shelley Fabares); "I Got News for You" (Nita Talbot only); "Do the Clam" (on the beach); "I Got News for You" (reprise; Shelley Fabares only); "Puppet on a String" (poolside to Shelley Fabares); "I've Got to Find My Baby" (in nightclub); "Girl Happy" (reprise; on stage with Shelley Fabares)

Joe Pasternak was another old timer (born 1901) who had spent his career at MGM making musicals with most of their leading lights, and specialised in light, fluffy entertainments. His career had begun at Universal in the 1930s with Deanna Durbin, a sort of female Elvis in a different way to Ann-Margret, a talented young singer whose fluffy, feelgood films were an enormous success, but who had grown bored and frustrated by her onscreen persona of "the girl who fixes everything for everyone and then bursts into song".

Leaving Universal for MGM, where he stayed as a producer for the best part of his career, Pasternak had worked with all the greats at one time or another, but his career was now on the wane. He had also been a player in MGM's dirty war for the Dean Martin and Jerry Lewis team that had put the duo's otherwise tough agent in the hospital with a nervous breakdown... a war which Wallis and Paramount had won (Pasternak finally secured Martin solo for the hollow victory that was the 1957 flop *Ten Thousand Bedrooms*, directed by *Jailhouse Rock's* tired and jaded Richard Thorpe). A natural for Parker's vision of a Presley film producer, he had recently enjoyed some success with Hollywood teen movies like *Where the Boys Are* with future nun Dolores Hart and pop singer Connie Francis--in short, Elvis films without Elvis.

Unfortunately, *Where the Boys Are* was a dreary period piece that was depressing enough to make anybody join a convent, with four bright young things trying to find a husband while retaining their virginity--easily done given the standard of salivating incompetents and smooth louts portrayed by the male leads, who all knew their place in the film's pecking order. It tried hard to be a bright and breezy teen film in the Corman/Katzman manner, but found itself weighed down by the finger-wagging morality that studios smaller than MGM could ignore.

An uneasy mix of comedy and drama in which the drama bogged down the comedy and the comedy belittled the drama, it was ponderously directed by the tedious Henry Levin, who had been turning his heavy hand to any genre that came his way since the 1940s and had just finished transforming Jules Verne's high concept fantasy *Journey to the Center of the Earth* into an overlong snorefest. Some scenes (particularly the mermaid sequence with blowsy Noo Yoik party goil Barbara Nichols in full flow) were genuinely funny, others unintentionally so, but in general, far from creating the '60s nostalgia buzz for innocent times that the Elvis films provoke, Pasternak's *Where the Boys Are* leaves contemporary audiences longing for the lowbrow idiocy and vulgar excesses of the 1980s post-*Animal House* Spring Break-style films. As *Girl Happy* pursued the same theme, audience, and locale, things did not bode well for the next Presley vehicle.

However, while *Girl Happy* is as infantile as *Roustabout* was more grown-up, it is a pleasure to discover just how much fun *Girl Happy* is--and what a difference just five years could make in the swingin' '60s (even if a potential night of passion for Gary Crosby's character might result in "pickin' out the furniture" the next day).

Despite being set, like *Where the Boys Are,* in Fort Lauderdale, Florida, home of the Spring Break, there was little location work, even in that relatively attainable locale. Although he had worked regularly with directors Norman Taurog, George Sidney, and Richard Thorpe, all of whom had made successful Presley pictures, Pasternak chose as his director Boris Sagal, a competent but undistinguished journeyman who flitted between TV and film, and generally turned his hand to any genre. Sagal did an excellent job.

Filmed in June and July of 1964, *Girl Happy* is corny, heavy-handed, moderately offensive by contemporary standards, and dated, but also very funny. Elvis, curiously named Rusty Wells (Rusty was the name of Ann-Margret's character in *Viva Las Vegas*), is looking forward to leaving snowbound Chicago for sunny Spring Break at Fort Lauderdale, where he and his band have a commitment to the Seacrest Hotel and their sexual libidos. Unfortunately, Big Frank, the cartoon gangster who employs their combo in Chicago, has other ideas and intends to hold them to their contract.

When Frank's precious daughter Val calls to say that she's spending Spring Break in Florida, Elvis sees his chance, and--in a good comedy sequence--spins scary stories about all the predatory young men out there. Taking the bait, her devoted dad sends Elvis and the band on their way to keep a watchful eye on his unsuspecting offspring... the foxes are guarding the hen house. Rusty and the boys and Val and the girls simultaneously head for Florida in a blatant recreation of the opening scenes and "Moonlight Swim" sequence of *Blue Hawaii* as Elvis and Shelley Fabares sing "Spring Fever" together via split screen. When they do eventually meet, writers Allen and Bullock pull the time-honored cornball trick of having Elvis see her at her worst, figure hidden, face behind reading glasses, nose in book. Convinced that his job as secret chaperone will be quite unnecessary, Presley pursues his own interests, the shapely Deena (Mary Ann Mobley), while the guys ambitiously pursue all the other female cast members.

The ensuing series of events are a thoroughly enjoyable debacle of misunderstandings and juggling acts, a bedroom farce that has escaped the stage for a larger playground, as Elvis protects and pursues Val (now revealed as a beauty), tries to have his cake and eat it with Deena, and stumbles around trying to fend off other suitors for both while keeping his buddies in the dark. For once, Jeff Alexander's sledgehammer wit musical cues are appropriate, and even funny--the cavalry reveille call whenever Top Cat Elvis summons his cool cats to ditch their pouty babes and head back to the throne for instruction captures the spirit of the moment, and the three blind mice melody when Elvis is snowing his buddies almost borders on satire.

Certain attitudes towards some of the characters are uncomfortably lowbrow (a bookish wimp unkindly predates the *Revenge of the Nerds* movies by twenty years, announcing at the end of the film--in front of all the women--that he's giving up on girls with brains), but the film's sheer likability, and that of its strong cast, overpower any niggling reservations and ultimately win over all but the most easily offended of the audience. However, the unhappy assumption that books are bad, brains equal nerds, and intelligence in both men and women is not only downright undesirable but hinders sexual attraction and signifies virginal naivete is persistent and unfortunate. It's a theme that still prevails today in even more lowbrow fare.

However, the set pieces compensate. Like the later *Spinout, Speedway,* and *Easy Come, Easy Go,* the film also looks good as only 1960s films can-- the large indoor studio set for the Seacrest Hotel exteriors is delightfully retro today, and the furnishings and costumes are a delight. When the Italian lothario Romano (Fabrizio Mioni), a younger, crasser Count Mancini, lures a tipsy Val onto his boat, the vessel is hauled through the streets of Fort Lauderdale with the would-be seducer and his victim rolling around inside, getting increasingly smothered in food and drink. The vessel and it's baffled captain end up in the Seacrest swimming pool, as happy, sappy Val, more than a little worse for wear, stumbles back onto dry land and thanks him for a lovely evening.

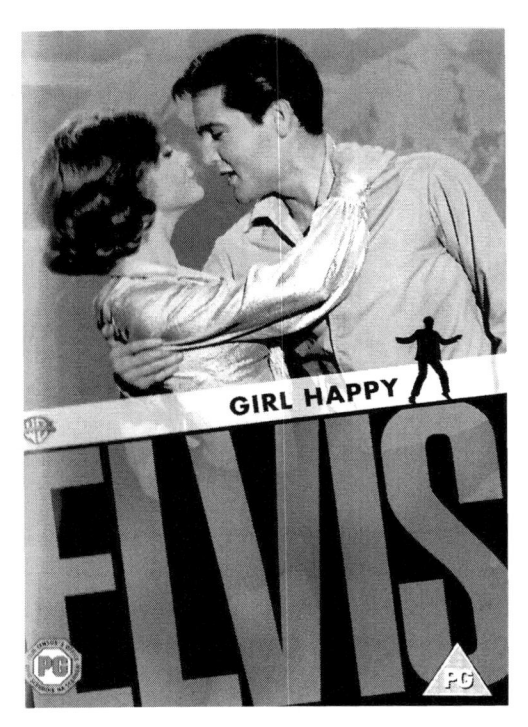

When the guys complain that they're missing all their opportunities while guarding Big Frank's daughter, Elvis loyally offers to sacrifice his own pleasures by protecting Val by himself, leaving his buddies consumed with guilt that they are partying while he grimly chaperones the gangster's little darling. Shots of the guys moping around with their girls alternate with clips of Elvis having the time of his life with Val! It's infantile stuff aiming for easy laughs, but it works.

Of course Elvis fouls everything up, ending up in a storming prison break-in sequence after an over-zealous police chief locks up practically every girl in Fort Lauderdale, at which point an army of guys organise the demolition of the police cells (some commentators will tell you that Elvis is in drag, conjuring up some appalling mental images of the sexiest man of the 20th century, but putting a headscarf on doesn't really qualify; Elvis did, however, hate the scene, and didn't like the film much either). Later, a vengeful Val, discovering that lover boy has been sent by dad, puts on a hilarious strip tease at the nightclub where the guys are working, just as--of course--father turns up.

Choreographer David Winters and his regular troupe of dancers were back, and having previously devised The Climb for *Viva Las Vegas,* now offered The Clam for *Girl Happy,* and Shelley Fabares, in particular, has just the right attitude to give a perfect performance as Val. Winters' gruesome dance sequence on the beach mechanically hauls out every teen dance troupe cliche of the '60s in a time capsule for posterity. The fight scene at the strip club, on the other hand, is a genuine original, with some great moments worth watching for, including the sozzled Val blithely dispensing with female adversaries with the offhand efficiency that comes with the confidence of alcohol.

Fabares went on to make two more films with Elvis, *Spinout* and *Clambake* (for career details, see *Spinout*). She was perfect in all three, and although she couldn't pull off the sort of performance Ann-Margret could deliver, she could produce a superb self-parodic impression of that style, giving all three of the films she graced a sly, knowing ambience that was perfect for the material. Elvis loved her. Ann-Margret could vamp it up like no other, but she couldn't have pulled off virginal Val's incompetent comedy burlesque show. If Fabares couldn't duplicate Ann-Margret's *Viva Las Vegas* persona, she could certainly manage the next best thing--perhaps the better option--and send it up. Both Fabares and Mobley get to wiggle their butts furiously onstage in a mad orgy of only-in-the-'60s kitsch.

For Mary Ann Mobley, a former Miss America, it was her first big break, after a debut in *Get Yourself a College Girl* the previous year with fellow Elvis movie babes Joan O'Brien, Nancy Sinatra, and Lori Williams. She had also just made gangster nonsense *Young Dillinger* with--wait for it--Nick Adams, John Ashley, and Robert Conrad! "Elvis had a great sense of humor, a good attitude, and he was a perfect gentleman" she told *Filmfax* magazine. "When I entered, he stood up and said `Where's Mary Ann's chair?'. I never dated him, but I did two movies with him, and we became friends. Elvis and Shelley Fabares got along well too. She didn't have any hidden agendas with Elvis either".

Mobley went on to make *Harum Scarum* with Elvis, as did co-star Gail Gilmore. Mobley, later a regular visitor to Aaron Spelling's *Fantasy Island* (one of her earliest TV breaks was in Spelling's *Burke's Law,* an essential 1960s starlet credit), never made it any further in the movies and was unlucky in TV--she was second choice for Batgirl (losing to another two-times Elvis babe, Yvonne Craig), replaced for *The Girl from UNCLE,* and second choice for the sole female regular in *The Time Tunnel,* and despite guest-starring in the premiere episodes of *Mission: Impossible* and *Legend of*

Custer, only appeared briefly in other series as a singer or hostess. However, she kept busy in guest roles during the 1970s and '80s, turning up in *Ironside, Police Story, Fantastic Journey, Vegas, Matt Houston, Hotel,* and others.

Character actress Nita Talbot, playing the slightly over-the-hill stripper (like prostitutes, all Hollywood movie strippers had to look like they'd had a hard life too soon), had co-starred in the Debbie Reynolds/Eddie Fisher musical *Bundle of Joy* (directed by Norman Taurog), and the Dean Martin comedy *Who's Got the Action?*, and would later join the casts of Richard Thorpe's *That Funny Feeling* with Sandra Dee and Bobby Darin, and Gene Nelson's jaw-dropping contrivance *The Cool Ones*, with Roddy McDowall and Debbie Watson. A regular face on TV, she was also a supporting character in several short-run TV series, and took numerous guest roles in such shows as *The Untouchables, The Fugitive, The Monkees, Bewitched, Kolchak--the Night Stalker, McCloud, Columbo, The Rockford Files, Police Story, Charlie's Angels, Lou Grant, Fantasy Island, Matt Houston,* and *Remington Steele.*

Big and blustering Harold J. Stone was always cast as overpowering loudmouths, but was never to be taken seriously, and frequently played bombastic military men and comedy mobsters. He enjoyed his role in *Girl Happy*, despite the usual typecasting, and liked Elvis. "It was great" he told interviewer Harvey Chartrand. "I loved him, and he loved me! We didn't talk much, because he had his bunch around him, but we got along great. Years later, I went to see Elvis when he was playing in Vegas. I sat right in the front row. I knew the comic who opened the show, talked to him, kidded around, and left. He told Elvis I'd been there. Elvis got upset, asked the comic why I didn't come backstage and see him. I figured if I went backstage I'd be a pain in the ass, but then I found out Elvis was kind of teed-off I didn't go back there. He wanted to see me. Anyway, Elvis and I worked together beautifully on *Girl Happy*. He was a helluva guy and Big Frank was a very strong part".

Stone's TV roles include at least five episodes of *The Untouchables,* plus episodes of *The Twilight Zone, Target: The Corruptors, Cheyenne, Wanted--Dead or Alive, Rawhide, The Naked City, 77, Sunset Strip, Surfside Six, Route 66, The Detectives, Voyage to the Bottom of the Sea, Get Smart, I Spy, Mission: Impossible, It Takes a Thief, The Felony Squad, The Man from UNCLE, Ironside, Hawaii Five-O, Kojak, Police Woman, The Rockford Files, Lou Grant, Charlie's Angels, Vegas,* and *Simon and Simon,* with recurring roles in the now forgotten sit-coms *My World and Welcome to It* and *Bridget Loves Bernie.*

Jackie Coogan, cast as the over-zealous comedy cop, was a Hollywood old timer who had started out as a child actor and enjoyed a healthy career as an adult afterwards, although as he got older his roles took a very pronounced dive into B-movies and even Z-movies (*Outlaw Women, Mesa of Lost Women, The Space Children, High School Confidential, Sex Kittens Go to College*) before he found renewed fame as Uncle Fester on *The Addams Family* in his twilight years. He was still playing Fester in Hanna-Barbera cartoons and reunion specials throughout the 1970s and lending his name to low-budget efforts right up until his death in 1980.

Cast as the comic foil hotel manager was balding and bespectacled John Fiedler, who specialised in snippy, humorless and ineffectual authority figures. He seems to be having a great time, playing difficult lines effortlessly with perfect timing. Over thirty film roles included *Twelve Angry Men, That Touch of Mink, The Odd Couple, True Grit, The Shaggy D.A., Sharkey's Machine,* and *The Cannonball Run.* TV roles included *Tom Corbett--Space Cadet, The Twilight Zone, Boris Karloff's Thriller, The Fugitive, My Favorite Martian, The Munsters, Bewitched, Get Smart, The Felony Squad, Star Trek, I Spy, Kolchak--the Night Stalker, Columbo, Police Story, The Bob Newhart Show,* and *Fantasy Island.*

Gary Crosby had played a similar role to that of his girl happy sap a couple of years earlier in *The Bill Dana Show,* but later became more associated with drama shows, guesting in *Emergency, The Rockford Files, The Bionic Woman, Wonder Woman, Project UFO, Vegas,* and *Simon and Simon,* and appearing in recurring roles on *Adam 12, Chase,* and *Hunter.* At 31, he's already ten years too old to be leching in Fort Lauderdale during Spring Break, but somehow, it works. Young people were still growing up slower back then, but unlike the other cast members, he looks his age--a drink problem in the footsteps of his famous father, about whom, more later, had taken its toll. In *Girl Happy,* he gets the jarring and unfortunate line "The King is dead!".

Fabrizio Mioni was a young Italian actor trying to make it in Hollywood, but typecast due to his strong accent. He appeared three times in the *UNCLE* series, cast--of course--as Italian agents or adversaries and inevitably in *I Spy* and the wartime adventure series *Garrison's Gorillas.*

Joby Baker starred in the short-lived 1967 sit-com *Good Morning World* alongside future Elvis co-star Julie Parrish and then disappeared. He had previously co-starred in all three *Gidget* films, *Gidget, Gidget Goes Hawaiian,* and *Gidget Goes to Rome,* a distinction shared only with James Darren. Jimmy Hawkins returned with Presley and Fabares for *Spinout.*

Peter Brooks appeared in episodes of *My Favorite Martian, My Three Sons, The Addams Family*, and *Batman* at around this time, and alongside Joby Baker in *Gidget Goes to Rome,* the cast of which seems to be composed entirely of people from Elvis films or *Man from UNCLE* episodes. The same year as *Girl Happy* he was reunited with *Gidget Goes to Rome* co-star Noreen Corcoran for *The Girls on the Beach*.

Chris Noel (real name, Sandra Noel) appeared in several light musicals during the '60s including *Get Yourself a College Girl* (with Mary Ann Mobley), *Beach Ball* (with Edd Byrnes of *77, Sunset Strip* and Elvis girls Brenda Benet and Gail Gilmore), *Wild Wild Winter*, and *For Singles Only* (with Mary Ann Mobley and Lana Wood), but was sidelined by events during the Vietnam war when she started working with Armed Forces radio and making morale-boosting trips over there. This--and the suicide of her Vietnam vet husband--resulted in her involvement with sympathetic productions such as the Vietnam vet movie *Cease Fire* and the late-'80s television drama *China Beach,* on which she appeared as herself, reminiscing. She also appeared in the 1987 beach movie reunion film *Back to the Beach,* with Frankie Avalon and Annette Funicello. Early TV work included *The Lieutenant* (with Gary Lockwood), *Perry Mason, Doctor Kildare, Burke's Law, Bewitched, My Three Sons,* and several unsold pilots.

Pamela Curran's TV work included *The Detectives, Branded, The Man from UNCLE, The Green Hornet, The Invaders,* and *I Dream of Jeannie.* Nancy Czar had begun her career appearing in the films of infamous minor league B-movie producer Arch Hall Snr. (including the loony *Wild Guitar*) before a brief scene as a bikini-clad distraction in *Girl Happy* resulted in a more substantial role in snowbound beach movie *Winter-a-Go-Go*. She appears briefly in the opening scenes of *Spinout*.

Beverly Adams, seen briefly in both *Roustabout* and *Girl Happy,* also appeared in *Winter-a-Go-Go* and the similarly-themed *How to Stuff a Wild Bikini*. She played bit parts on *Ozzie and Harriet, Burke's Law, My Three Sons,* and *Doctor Kildare,* but didn't obtain more substantial supporting roles until after the Elvis films, when she joined Columbia and was cast as Dean Martin's loyal assistant in the *Matt Helm* series of spy spoofs in the late '60s, where her duties inevitably called for service above and beyond, although her most substantial spy movie role was in the obscure *Hammerhead*. She also secured guest spots on *Bewitched* and *Gidget,* before marrying celebrity hairdresser Vidal Sassoon.

Playing the Chief of Police was comic actor Milton Frome who specialised in blustering or bumbling authority figures and had worked extensively with Jerry Lewis, Milton Berle, Bob Hope, and many other big names. He appeared in several episodes of *The Beverly Hillbillies* as the owner of a movie studio and was memorably chided by Batman in the 1966 *Batman* feature for making an atomic submarine available to a Mr. P.N. Guin. Films include *Bye Bye Birdie* and *Please Don't Eat the Daisies* and

TV appearances include *Adventures of Superman, The Twilight Zone, Wagon Train, The Untouchables, 77, Sunset Strip, My Favorite Martian, Bewitched, The Addams Family,* more *Batman,* and *Dobie Gillis.*

Olan Soule, here a waiter, had appeared in *It Happened at the World's Fair* as the gun-totin' father of Yvonne Craig. His credits include dozens of bit parts and walk-ons in films and TV episodes, including the fawning reporter in the opening scene of *This Island Earth.*

Playing cops were Richard Reeves and Ralph Lee. Reeves, a tough-looking guy who had played dumb hoods in numerous episodes of *Adventures of Superman,* had previously appeared in *Blue Hawaii*. Bit player Lee played a typical silver alien in a *Lost in Space*. Both Reeves and Lee would be back for *Harum Scarum.*

During filming it was old home week on set; Presley socialised with Ann-Margret, Nick Adams, and new-found buddy Gary Crosby, *Girl Happy* co-star and son of Bing. Unlike Elvis, Bing Crosby was the complete opposite of his public persona, a cold, selfish, loveless man who made the lives of his four sons by his first wife (including Gary, his lookalike) a misery by constantly belittling them and denigrating them in public. When he remarried in 1957 after a clumsy courtship, he and his new wife swept away all trace of the boys along with his first wife's belongings and started a new family (for which he'd been actively shopping since their mother's death in 1952). However, his private life and public persona were skilfully managed, and the public would hear no ill of him. A compliant Hollywood gossip press, knowing that in those more trusting days any bad stories about favorite public figures would only make the teller of tales look small, generally backed off or collaborated with the myth, and the Crosby boys' lives were blighted, some terminally; both Gary Crosby's brothers committed suicide. When your father is one of the most beloved entertainers in America, and he perpetually puts you down in the press, the private pain of being alternately mocked, criticised, slandered and ignored becomes unbearably public. In fact, diligent research after Crosby's death (he died within weeks of Elvis) revealed that his sons were far better men than he had ever been.

Like Frank Sinatra and an army of lesser crooners, Bing Crosby had a tough time being dethroned by a younger, fresher and more sincere new face, even though he had enjoyed genuine talent and a lengthy run in the limelight, and the genial, affable nice guy mask slipped a bit when interviewers asked him about Presley. In 1975, a millionaire many times over from careful investments during his two decades as the main man, he snapped "He never contributed a damn thing to music" and added coldly "He was successful--hard to account for".

For Gary Crosby, who had tried to follow in his father's footsteps as an entertainer singing similar fare to his dad, but found that style of music dead in the water, it must have been an enjoyable act of rebellion, a vengeful snub to be working with the man who had made his cruel father's style of singing redundant and old hat. But all he had really wanted was his father's love and respect, two things perpetually denied him.

But in 1965, Elvis was now thirty years old. "I was sitting in the Colonel's office one day and the 'phone rang" said Mary Ann Mobley. "It was *Time* magazine calling, and they were offering to put Elvis on the cover. Colonel Tom said `Well, that'll be twenty five thousand dollars'. And the *Time* guy said `You don't understand, this is *Time* magazine'. And the Colonel said `You don't understand. We don't need you'!". *Time's* sulky reviewers had been at the forefront of trashing Presley's music and films with snide, snobbish put-downs in the past. Revenge, so sweet...

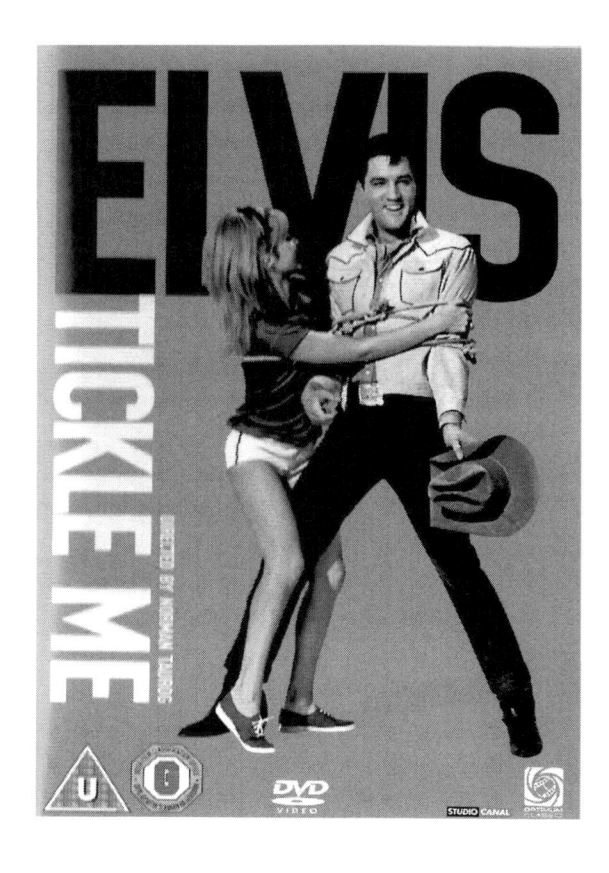

Tickle Me (1965)

wr. Ellwood Ullman, Edward Bernds, dir. Norman Taurog, pr. Ben Schwalb (Allied Artists)

with Elvis Presley (Lonnie Beale), Jocelyn (Jackie) Lane (Pam Merritt), Jack Mullaney (Stanley Potter), Edward Faulkner (Brad Bentley), Julie (Julia) Adams (Vera Radford), Merry Anders (Estelle), Bill Williams (Deputy), Grady Sutton (Mr. Dabney), Dorothy Konrad (Mrs. Dabney), Connie Gilchrist (Hilda/ masseusse), John Dennis (Adolph/chef), Lou Elias (Henry/gardener), Laurie Benton (Janet), Linda Rogers (Claire), Ann Morell (Sybil), Jean Ingram (Evelyn), Francine York (Mildred), Eve Bruce (Pat), Jackie Russell (Gloria), Angela Greene (Donna), Peggy Ward (Dot), Dorian Brown (Polly), Inez Pedrova (Ophelia), Barbara Werle (Barbara), Allison Hayes (Mabel), Lilyan Chauvan (Ronnie), Lori Williams, Diane Bond, Red West

Elvis sings: "It's a Long, Lonely Highway" (on bus, over titles); "It Feels So Right" (in nightclub); "Easy Question" (to girls at picnic); "Dirty, Dirty Feeling" (in stables with girls); "Put the Blame On Me" (in western fantasy sequence, to Jocelyn Lane); "I'm Yours" (at luau); "Night Rider" (in stables with girls); "I Feel That I've Known You Forever" (serenading Jocelyn Lane); "Slowly but Surely" (finale to Jocelyn Lane)

Allied Artists' three top money-making films were *55 Days in Peking, El Cid,* and... *Tickle Me?* As the press had so blithely pointed out to Elvis after *Roustabout*, he was a sure-fire box-office banker whose--as *Halliwell's Filmgoer's Companion* pointed out disinterestedly--"popularity with teenagers survived a host of bad movies". Elvis, who wanted to be taken seriously as an actor in his youth, was furious when the trade press pointed out that the money Hal Wallis was making for Paramount was allowing them to take chances with other actors on riskier projects. He wanted those riskier projects. But on the other hand, who remembers *Becket?*

Bizarrely described in Eric Braun's "impartial" *Elvis Film Encyclopedia* as "soft porn" (!), a view also held by the peculiar Albert Goldman in his tome *Elvis*, who thinks the mid-'60s Elvis films offered the "indiscriminating" audience "dirt", *Tickle Me* was in fact specifically marketed by Parker and Allied as a wholesome family film with the 1960s definition of sexual content toned down to a minimum (surrounded by willing women, Elvis single-mindedly pursues just one girl and never beds any of them).

Despite this pitiful innocence (or perhaps because of it), *Tickle Me*--a cheap knock-off redeemed by the efforts of everyone involved--is a far better film than it has any right to be. If the songs sound a little removed from both the picture and the soundtrack, then it's probably because most of them are removed from the proceedings by several years; *Tickle Me* is unique among the Elvis films for not having any specially prepared songs, and benefits from it--the tracks are all oldies (many with a misplaced 1950s-style echo effect) dating back to the very beginning of the '60s, the earliest recording 1960, the most recent the 1963 opener. It's fortunate that Elvis mimes from a distance as he doesn't seem to be bothering too much with the words on several occasions.

What happened was this: a title song was written but never recorded, so rendering the already irrelevant film title totally redundant. The Colonel, however, was not going to trash all his already prepared publicity materials, so *Tickle Me* it was and *Tickle Me* it stayed. Only dyed-in-the-wool Presley fans in the know could have told audiences why *Tickle Me* had a completely pointless title and why nobody asks to be tickled or indeed gets tickled! If it proves anything, it proves that audiences were going to see the films because of Presley, not because of any film producer or studio's idea of a good title! But if marketing meant nothing to Elvis film audiences, there surely were limits, and the bottom of the barrel was dangerously close...

Writers Ellwood Ullman and Edward Bernds were B-movie stalwarts from Hollywood's lowest echelons who made Sam Katzman look like Sam Goldwyn. Ullman's writing credits included Norman Taurog's *Doctor Goldfoot and the Bikini Machine* and, the year after *Tickle Me,* the last *Three Stooges* feature, *The Outlaws is Coming,* which features a skunk by the name of Elvis!

Bernds had written and directed the sci-fi cheapies *Space Master X-7, World Without End* and *Return of the Fly,* written and/or directed the slapdash low budget westerns *Escape from Red Rock, Quantrill's Raiders,* and *Gunfight at Comanche Creek,* and directed a ton of *Three Stooges* two-reelers. His career had begun with *Blondie* and *Bowery Boys* shorts (Ullman and Schwalb also had their fingers in the *Bowery Boys* pie), and his most recent film had been *The Three Stooges in Orbit.* Producer Ben Schwalb, another veteran of bottom-of-the-barrel westerns, had given the world the camp classic *Queen of Outer Space,* which Bernds had also directed.

As film credentials went, it was difficult to go much lower, and had Elvis been any kind of a film student, he might have wondered if the Colonel was setting him up as a fourth Stooge. By rights, even the title alone suggests that the audience should be watching from behind their fingers. However, credit where credit's due--proving Parker's philistine philosophy right, this swiftly shot cheapie with a *Scooby Doo* plot and clownish gags and double takes saved Allied Artists from bankruptcy and earned Presley and Parker more money than any film since *Blue Hawaii*. What it did not buy them was critical credibility or respect from Presley's peers.

But big deal. The film is genuinely sexy and funny, and has no pretensions above its creaking cartoon show plot, concerning a ghost town even phonier and dustier than the storyline. Ullman, Bernds and Schwalb had made *The Bowery Boys Meet the Monsters* together in 1954, and Ullman and Schwalb *Spook Busters* in 1957; ten years on, and they were working the same cornball material for Elvis.

Elvis is Lonnie Beale, a rodeo champion with a no-show show who is given work at the Circle Z ranch by Julie Adams' Vera Radford, a watered-down version of *Roustabout's* Maggie Moran, after he's impressed her with both his singing and self defense skills in the town bar (*Tickle Me* has all the essential Elvis film ingredients upfront).

Circle Z is actually a firm but fair health farm in cattle country for "actresses, models, career women...to get in shape", although this being an Elvis movie, very few of them need much improving! Even the film tries to explain away this anomaly, by referring to the current guests as those near the end of their stay! "We roast 'em, toast 'em, wiggle 'em, jiggle 'em, rend 'em, bend 'em, and give 'em very little to eat" explains Jack Mullaney as the film's "Blinky" figure.

Filmed swiftly in October 1964, *Tickle Me* was released in 1965 within days of the similar *Girl Happy* and deservedly made a ton of money, giving movie-goers of the time exactly what they expected from an Elvis movie. There's the standard army of bathing belles clustered around Elvis every time he sings, the comedy no-chance rival (Edward Faulkner as Brad Bentley, recreating his hard-faced, self-deprecating fall guy from John Wayne's *McLintock,* cock of the walk until Presley arrives; he co-starred more heroically with Wayne in *The Undefeated*), comic relief in the *Girl Happy* tradition from goofball roomie Stanley Potter (Jack Mullaney, doing his usual poor man's Jerry Lewis bit as the hopeless best buddy, later returned for *Spinout*), and the obligatory barroom brawl started by a seething lout (Red West) who is furiously watching his date throw herself at the hapless Elvis.

"Get your hands off my girlfriend" he rages, but Elvis raises his free hands innocently, pointing out that the girl is hanging round his neck voluntarily, which enrages the poor man even more. Although West got these roles because he was Elvis' best friend and bodyguard, he also earned them; he'd come a long way from his first flustered lines on *Wild in the Country* (even doing comedy in *Clambake*), and he's entirely convincing and professional as the glaring, short-fused troublemaker, superior to many of the wooden, unconvincing actors playing Presley's rivals in other films. When West looked pissed off, he really looked pissed off. For his part, Elvis never looked better, and the songs, because they come from Presley's musical career rather than movie career, are--without exception--excellent.

Elvis quickly shows up the adversarial Brad, who calls him a saddletramp ("I know horses" agrees Lonnie, "and the ones with the long ears are usually jackasses!"), but is in turn swiftly humiliated in front of the girls and gym teacher Pam Merritt (Jocelyn Lane), whose beautiful butt and legs he meets before her equally appealing face. The delights on display from herself and her charges cause him to blunder oafishly through nearby garden furniture, with guitar and saddle contributing to the chaos, while the girls giggle at him. It's a superb piece of physical comedy that comes off just right.

The romance follows the usual pre-set path for a Presley movie, but is no less entertaining for it. Even though the pair of young lovers are clearly lost the minute they clap eyes on each other, there's the pouty, scowling forced indifference and flirty verbal sparring as they antagonise each other, followed by the almost-nearly embrace and succumb to lip-lock that keeps getting interrupted.

A trip to the ghost town leads to a fantasy wild west saloon bar scenario, with Brad as a card cheat, Stanley as the barman, Pam as a showgirl, and Elvis/Lonnie as the milk-drinkin' Panhandle Kid ("Leave the bottle"), turning into a heroic romantic fantasy when he steps in to save Pam from Brad's unwanted attentions with a shoot-out for which he ultimately needs to dispense a handy band-aid... But whose fantasy is it? Either way, it ends with the couple's first kiss.

Next comes capitulation to force of nature followed by the Big Misunderstanding and the inevitable rejection courtship dance (as performed by Yvonne Craig in *It Happened at the World's Fair,* Ann Margret in *Viva Las Vegas,* and Nancy Sinatra in *Speedway,* to name but three), this time amusingly performed by Jocelyn Lane's Pam with the benefit of closing windows, pulled blinds, and firmly shut doors. Finally, Elvis thinks he's worn her down with his serenading and she's melting, when flump, down comes the last set of blinds. But the foregone conclusion is obvious to everyone but Lonnie and Pam, even to those watching their first formula Elvis film.

With the premise and the romance in place and the cast of characters established, the cobwebs are blown off the Poverty Row plot. It turns out that Pam's grandfather was a crazy old coot who hid a stash of gold dollars somewhere in the ghost town's haunted hotel, consarn it, and now the dagnabbed bad guys are trying to get their mitts on it before poor Pam. After a couple of botched kidnap attempts (Lane puts up a welcome spirited resistance when they try to drag her off in their car, kicking the car door shut several times as the struggling heavies, their work cut out for them, try to bundle her in), Pam eventually and inadvertently delivers herself into their clutches. When Elvis is coerced into an embrace with Vera Radford, Pam naturally walks in at the worst possible moment, and there follows the Big Misunderstanding sequence of events. Pam flounces off to the ghost town with Elvis and Stanley in hot pursuit, but a sudden storm sends the sodden threesome into the haunted hotel for the night, where the villains of the piece, all disguised in various Hallowe'en B-movie monster outfits, wait to indulge in the usual timeless old dark house scare stunts while one and all attempt to find the old man's money.

Anyone familiar with Laurel and Hardy, the East Side Kids/Bowery Boys, Abbott and Costello, or indeed the Three Stooges (and in 1965, most were) knew exactly what to expect from the old haunted hotel scenario, and they weren't to be disappointed. Everyone creeps around shivering and yelping and accidentally scaring each other for a while, and it's all embarrassingly amusing (particularly when Lane gets her nightdress harmlessly trapped, but daren't turn round to see what's restraining her until a bemused Elvis appears at the skylight).

Several nice touches at this point include our heroes trying to jimmy open an encouraging-looking chest while the would-be crowbar that Stanley rips off the wall turns out to be a lever that releases the coins, and the assumption that mean ol' Brad might be the cliche head villain being amusingly overturned when he shows up to rescue them ("I may be a louse" he announces bizarrely, "but I'm not a crook!"; he actually hasn't done anything lousy except have the misfortune to be on the wrong side of the film's title when it comes to getting the girl!).

Although *Tickle Me* was made for next to nothing, it's one of those films that has improved with age. The now retro-look of the clothes, set designs and furnishings give the film a style that at the time was effortless, natural, invisible, and cost peanuts. Today, the small sets and backdrops look charmingly naive, and the paper-thin plot covers a film that is surprisingly substantial (plenty of comedy, music, fight scenes, female flesh, pulp mag thrills, running gags and action). Unlike more costly efforts, there's not a dud scene in the show; even the short-cut stock footage for the rodeo scenes is integrated skilfully (the announcer amusingly announcing Lonnie's name with more despair and indifference each time as Presley's preoccupation with Pam's rejection results in pratfall after pratfall).

The film is colorful, well-paced, and never dull, and mixes the comedy, music, romance and adventure perfectly, and leading lady Jocelyn Lane is a doe-eyed, corn-haired beauty, one of the most stunning women to grace an Elvis film (no mean accolade in a competitive genre). Ullman and Bernd's Z-movie background actually works in the film's favor, as the end result has no higher pretensions to sink it; most of the cringe-inducing scenes in other Elvis films occur when the writer or director has ideas or opinions above the film's needs or requirements. *Tickle Me* is like a daft old uncle--nothing to say, just here to entertain. And best of all, there isn't a cute little kid in sight.

There are lots of corny visual gags that are genuinely funny, including Stanley getting up from a bench and innocently tipping Brad and his dinner into the dust, and Elvis' delayed reaction bit when he discovers a ghost in a closet in the haunted hotel. Merry Anders, as a starving diet-breaker, has a great scene with wealthy benefactors the Dabneys (Grady Sutton and Dorothy Konrad), spearing herself a chicken with a toasting fork through the bushes, and then pushing her luck too far and spearing Mrs. Dabney's butt on a greedy second attempt! Nyuk-nyuk--"Why, you...!".

There are also running gags--Elvis unintentionally but effortlessly steals Brad's action at every turn, and twice Elvis goes to Pam's rescue and she concusses him instead of the villains (when she finally gets it right at film's end, Elvis gasps "Hey, how'd that happen?"). Then there's Elvis' "Strictly business" reassurances to Pam every time she discovers one of the spa guests snuggling up to him. "Keep your eyes right on the target" says Lonnie on the archery range, but the girl with the bow is staring deep into his eyes. "Like this?". Later, he's helping another smitten female onto a horse. "You're the boss, not the horse" instructs Lonnie. "Got it?". "I'm the horse and not the boss" drones the girl dreamily as Presley paws her.

"He was such a gentleman, and surprisingly shy" said lead actress Julie Adams in an interview with Tom Weaver. "There was a scene in the picture where I pursued him around a desk and kissed him. All his friends from Memphis were standing around--all 'the guys'--and I suddenly felt like I was at a party where we were playing post office and the boy was very bashful! But I was quite in awe of him because he would do a musical number in one take. And the most fun he had in the picture was when he and all his friends staged a fight scene and tore up a barroom! They had great fun doing that!".

Julie (or Julia) Adams (real name, Betty May Adams), although she played in a wide variety of films, will always be best known for her role as the female interest in the sci-fi horror classic *The Creature from the Black Lagoon* (even though the film's most notorious scenes, those in the water, were performed by a stunt swimmer). There was little logic or pattern to her career choices, if choices they were, as she flitted from low budget movies to big budget star vehicles, from low-class, lowbrow schlockmeisters like William Castle and Albert Zugsmith to big names like Anthony Mann, and between conservative film projects with Glenn Ford, Jimmy Stewart and John Wayne to bizarre experimental indulgences like *The Last Movie* with Dennis Hopper.

Returning from Peru and the druggy disaster that was Hopper's post-*Easy Rider* downfall she went straight to work as geriatric Jimmy Stewart's ridiculously too young wife on the saccharine sit-com *The Jimmy Stewart Show* (1971-'72). Other TV work included a single season in the cast of 1958-'59 western *Yancy Derringer* and 1982 firefighters drama *Code Red*, with guest spots on *Cheyenne, Dick Powell Theater, 77, Sunset Strip, Surfside Six, Hawaiian Eye, Twelve O'Clock High, The Girl from UNCLE, McMillan and Wife, Ironside, Night Gallery, Kolchak--the Night Stalker, Streets of San Francisco, Quincy, The Incredible Hulk, Vegas, Murder She Wrote,* and *Diagnosis: Murder.*

Jocelyn Lane, as the stand-offish but secretly attracted gym teacher, was formerly British-based Jackie Lane. Her sojourn in America got off to a fairly good start, with guest parts in episodes of *The Man from UNCLE, Amos Burke--Secret Agent, The Wild Wild West, The Girl from UNCLE,* and *It Takes a Thief*, after a small film role in *Sword of Ali Baba*. However, despite a *Playboy* spread and various other promotional puffs, subsequent films became more and more downmarket (westerns with TV actors and directors, Italian sex comedies), culminating in the role of a biker chick in *Hell's Belles*, with Jeremy Slate of *Girls! Girls! Girls!* and Angelique Pettyjohn of *Clambake*. This is one of the most ridiculous films ever made, but great fun, and Lane again is beautiful... but when she found herself in a Larry Buchanan movie in 1970, she must have known it was time to throw in the towel.

She had not made herself popular on the *Tickle Me* set; Francine York, Linda Rogers and Ann Morell all felt snubbed by their lead actress, and Sonny West observed the frost first-hand. "I thought Jocelyn Lane was gorgeous, but she didn't want anything to do with the rest of us" laughed Linda Rogers with interviewer Tom Lisanti. "Oh please, we were so beneath her! She especially didn't like me. In fact, I would tease Elvis about her. Jocelyn just ran around with her nose in the air". Despite all this young girlish competitive resentment behind the scenes (or was it method acting!?), Lane gives a spirited and enjoyable performance.

By 1965, Merry Anders (real name, Merry Anderson) was mostly appearing in lurid horror films, with *Tickle Me* standing out like a feather duster in an abbatoire amid such titles as *House of the Damned* and *Legacy of Blood*. She was also in the infamous *Women of the Prehistoric Planet,* with Wendell Corey and Irene Tsu. Her films had been more varied but equally undistinguished in the 1950s, as had her regular TV roles in forgotten series like *The Stu Erwin Show, It's Always Jan,* and *How to Marry a Millionaire*. TV guest shots at around this time included *Cheyenne, 77, Sunset Strip, Surfside Six, Hawaiian Eye, The Addams Family* and *Get Smart*.

"They wanted a Joan Blondell-type" for *Tickle Me,* Anders told interviewer Paul Woodbine, so "I came on the set and I went through all my wardrobe fittings to be this slightly overweight woman. Then I got a call (for another movie where) I had to lose weight because I had to do a scene in a bathing suit. I finished that Thursday noon and then started eating to gain twelve pounds by the following Monday!" (in fact, she's shapely and attractive in *Tickle Me*).

As ever, Anders' memories of the shoot are as happy as most actresses on the Presley pictures. "He treated you so well--like royalty" she gushed. "My daughter and my mother were on the set and Elvis came over and said `Do you mind if I steal this little love for a couple of minutes?'. He took my daughter over and showed her the set and talked to her. He came back, pulled up the director's chair, sat down, and talked to my mom".

The films of character actress Connie Gilchrist (real name, Rose Gilchrist) included *Some Came Running,* with Frank Sinatra and Dean Martin, and *Say One for Me,* with Bing Crosby and Debbie Reynolds. On television, she had co-starred in the 1950s *Long John Silver* series. Bill Williams (real name, Bill Katt), the husband of actress Barbara Hale and the father of actor William Katt, was best known as TV cowboy hero Kit Carson in the early '50s. Ed Faulkner had previously had a minor role in *G.I. Blues*. Grady Sutton, who specialised in older luckless doofus types, was back for *Paradise, Hawaiian Style*. As a young man, he had played a hapless bridegroom in the *Laurel and Hardy* feature *Pardon Us*. He was a frequent foil for W.C. Fields. Comedy actress Dorothy Konrad appeared in an episode of *The Monkees* at around this time. Elderly Lilyan Chauvin was still playing old ladies as late as the 1990s, when she appeared in an episode of *Friends* as Joey's grandmother.

The film was littered with beach bunny types from the period, including Linda Rogers (*Winter-a-Go-Go*), Barbara Werle (back for *Harum*

Scarum), Lori Williams (a regular dancer in Elvis and beach movies) and Diane Bond, a bit player from *The Beverly Hillbillies* best known as the "girl in the polka-dot bikini" from *Pajama Party*. Bond also turned up in the scenery of *Swingin' Summer, In Like Flint,* and *Barbarella*. Allison Hayes, of course, had been around a little longer, and was best known for her B-movies of the 1950s, including the legendary *Attack of the 50 Foot Woman*.

Francine York, although not a household name, has an extraordinary resume in the world of pop culture. She has appeared in five Jerry Lewis films and worked for such Z-grade producers as Arthur Pierce, Sam Katzman, Larry Buchanan, Ted V. Mikels and Fred Olen Ray. She played the Bookworm's moll Lydia Limpet in *Batman,* the goddess Venus in *Bewitched,* an Amazon queen in *Lost in Space,* and Lois Lane's mother in the 1990s *Superman* series *Lois and Clark: New Adventures of Superman*. Other TV includes *The Untouchables, My Favorite Martian, Burke's Law, The Wild Wild West, I Dream of Jeannie, Bewitched, Mission: Impossible, It Takes A Thief, Land of the Giants, The Name of the Game, Kojak, Police Story, Jason of Star Command,* and *Riptide*. Add on the daytime soaps, and she's been working continuously for four decades.

Tickle Me wasn't the steak Elvis was looking for, but a burger prepared to perfection can be just as rewarding, to the bankbook and to the audience at least, who despite the film's close proximity to the release date of *Girl Happy,* came in droves. As audiences flocked to see *Girl Happy* and *Tickle Me,* which premiered within weeks of each other, *Harum Scarum, Frankie and Johnny,* and *Paradise, Hawaiian Style* were all in various stages of preparation.

Harum Scarum (1965)

wr. Gerald Drayson Adams, dir. Gene Nelson, pr. Sam Katzman (MGM)

with Elvis Presley (Johnny Tyronne), Mary Ann Mobley (Princess Shalimar), Fran Jeffries (Aishah), Jay Novello (Zacha), Theo Marcuse (Sinan), Michael Ansara (Prince Dragna), Phillip Reed (King Toranshah), Billy Barty (Baba), Wilda Taylor (Amethyst), Gail Gilmore (Sapphire), Brenda Benet (Emerald), Vicki Malkin (Sari), Joey Russo (Yussef), Jack Costanzo (Julna), Dirk Harvey (Mokar), Larry Chance (Captain Herat), Barbara Werle (Leilah/ maidservant), Ryck Ryden (Mustapha), Suzanne Covington (Naja), Richard Reeves (Bedouin), Maja Stewart (movie princess), Hugh Sanders (Ambassador McCord), Robert Lamont (President), Judy Durell (cashier), Ralph Lee, Red West

Elvis sings: "Harem Holiday" (over titles); "Desert Serenade" (in film sequence); "Go East, Young Man" (on stage); "Mirage" (to handmaidens in palace); "Kismet" (at lakeside to Mary Ann Mobley); "Shake That Tambourine" (in courtyard to crowds); "Hey, Little Girl" (to Vicki Malkin); "Golden Coins" (in fantasy sequence to Mary Ann Mobley); "So Close, Yet So Far" (from jail cell); "Harem Holiday" (on stage to close)

Sam Katzman's second and last Elvis movie was a ridiculous pantomime fantasy, and the last gasp of the Ali Baba-style sword-and-sandal adventure films that had gradually become cheaper and more formulaic with each subsequent entry. Katzman had made his fair share of these already, including *The Magic Carpet, Thief of Damascus, Siren of Bagdad, Prisoners of the Casbah,* and *Slaves of Babylon,* and Gerald Drayson Adams was a prolific low-budget scribe who could turn his pen to any type of adventure yarn, and did.

Elvis is Johnny Tyronne, a Vegas singer and film star (not a stretch) who goes on a goodwill tour to the kind of Hollywood Middle Eastern states that existed in movies before anyone in sandals became a terrorist. There, he becomes involved in a fairytale adventure of intrigue and swordplay (now very much a stretch--Elvis is floundering as much as Johnny). Poor Elvis looks like he's been dropped into an episode of *The Time Tunnel,* an image not dispelled by the opening scenes of an audience watching his exploits on a cinema screen or the use of two of that series' favorite bad guys, Michael Ansara and Theo Marcuse.

The film is lavish by Sam Katzman standards, mainly because the sets came from *King of Kings* and half the wardrobe from *Kismet.* However it didn't stop it from being twinned on a double bill with Japan's *Ghidorah, the Three Headed Monster!* (I'm not sure what the crossover appeal is for both Godzilla films *and* Elvis films, but I suspect it might just be me! Single figures, anyway...). Elvis, initially looking forward to being made up like Rudolph Valentino (his idol Tony Curtis had starred in *Son of Ali Baba* in 1952, scripted by... Gerald Drayson Adams), seems not so much embarrassed by the fun, as just awkward. All the traditional Hollywood ingredients are present, including a supporting cast of paint-by-numbers *Arabian Nights* stereotypes, and there is never the slightest hint that Elvis or any other cast member is in any real kind of danger (Adams had done this sort of thing many times before, including *The Desert Hawk,* directed by Fred De Cordova, who would make Presley's *Frankie and Johnny* the next year).

Despite being plunged into an existing Hollywood genre, a few ingredients of the Elvis formula are dripped into the mix too--there are cute kids to be cared for (Vicki Malkin and Joey Russo), a good girl in the form of beauty queen Mary Ann Mobley (last seen in *Girl Happy*) and a bad girl in the form of Fran Jeffries. Portraying three dancing girls along for the ride are Wilda Taylor from *Roustabout,* soon to dance yet again in *Frankie and Johnny,* Brenda Benet, prolific TV guest star (*I Dream of Jeannie, The Green Hornet, The Girl from UNCLE, Wonder Woman, The Incredible Hulk*) and the future wife of twice Elvis co-star Bill Bixby, and beach movie babe Gail Gilmore (real name, Gail Gerber), who had also appeared in *Girl Happy.*

Gilmore, a trained ballet dancer and teacher, made four other films that year, including *The Girls on the Beach* with Lesley Gore and the Beach Boys, *Beach Ball* with Benet and *Girl Happy's* Chris Noel, and weird sci-fi teen movie *Village of the Giants,* with Joy Harmon, before pairing off with, and disappearing into the colorful world of *Easy Rider* screenwriter Terry Southern. Raised to the sounds of classical music and jazz, Gilmore was completely unfamiliar with pop music, and even Elvis, until she started making movies throughout 1965. Barbara Werle, who plays Mobley's maidservant, had previously appeared in *Tickle Me* and would make a third Elvis movie appearance in *Charro.*

From the *Arabian Nights* box of tricks we have character actor Jay Novello in one of his larger parts as the stereotypical fixer and fleecer, fearful for his life but never too scared to grasp for spare change, and Billy Barty as a colorful midget pickpocket. As was often the case in these sort of yarns, morality is topsy-turvy in fairytale land; ordinarily, Elvis would be pursuing and subduing a purse thief stealing from innocent spectators rather than acting as decoy and helping him escape with his Fagin-like aides and corrupted urchins. Here, it's all portrayed as a jolly romp.

Novello was always being cast as a shifty, sniveling type and spent much of his career in front of the camera begging for his life; his TV roles include shots in *The Naked City*, *The Untouchables*, *77, Sunset Strip*, *Hawaiian Eye*, *Bourbon Street Beat*, *Twelve O'Clock High*, *Combat*, *I Spy*, *Land of the Giants*, *McCloud*, *Ironside*, *Kojak*, and *Streets of San Francisco*. Before that, he had cowered and cringed for his sins in the Saturday morning serials, in such gems as *King of the Mounties* and *Captain America*. Who could forget his awful demise in Irwin Allen's 1960 version of *The Lost World* ("Eaten alive! Horrible, horrible!")? He grovelled his way through numerous westerns as bandits and cheats, usually pleading forlornly not to be shot in cold blood. He was brutally typecast, but if he minded, it didn't seem to show in his enthusiastic performances.

Billy Barty was what might today be called a midget wrangler--he was often recruited to provide dwarf actors for other productions, and it was he who rounded up the hordes to play the Munchkins in *The Wizard of Oz*. Despite no longer being a young man, he displays extraordinary skill, energy and vitality in *Harum Scarum*'s set pieces, a born circus performer in an era when society offered little else but approving, condescending laughter.

Richard Reeves frequently played heavies, and was a familiar fixture in the *Adventures of Superman* series of the '50s and the slightly more grown-up gangster show *The Untouchables*. He had already appeared in bit parts in *Blue Hawaii* and *Girl Happy*, and also turned up in episodes of *My Favorite Martian*, *The Munsters*, *The Addams Family*, *Batman* and *I Dream of Jeannie*. Child actor Joey Russo played bit parts in *The Man from UNCLE*, *Lost in Space*, and several sit-coms of the period.

Villains Michael Ansara and Theo Marcuse were also in their element. Ansara spent most of the 1950s and 1960s playing various bad guys of ethnic origin in countless westerns and sci-fi TV shows, playing everything from Red Indians to Red Menace. He would don an Arab head-dress again for "The Arabian Affair" a few months later in *The Man from UNCLE*, and later "The Prisoner of Zalamar Affair" for *The Girl from UNCLE* (alongside Brenda Benet), and made several appearances in wife Barbara Eden's TV series *I Dream of Jeannie* as, first, King Kamehameha, and then an evil blue-skinned djinn. He played heartless warriors in everything from *The Outer Limits* to *Bewitched*. Irwin Allen used him frequently in his pulp sci-fi series, and *Star Trek* cast him as a Klingon in "Day of the Dove", a role he reprised in the spin-off series *Star Trek--Deep Space Nine* in the '90s. Other TV included *The Untouchables*, *Burke's Law*, *Mission: Impossible*, *The Name of the Game*, *McCloud*, *Police Story*, *Fantasy Island*, *Buck Rogers in the 25th Century*, *Simon and Simon*, *Mike Hammer*, and *Hunter*.

Theo Marcuse also did a fair amount of sci-fi, with bit parts in *The Twilight Zone, The Outer Limits,* and *Voyage to the Bottom of the Sea,* and more prominent guest shots in *The Invaders, The Time Tunnel* and *Star Trek.* He benefited more from the 1960s spy genre, appearing several times in *The Man from UNCLE* and episodes of *Get Smart, I Spy, Amos Burke--Secret Agent,* and *The Wild Wild West,* as well as Nancy Sinatra's spy film *The Last of the Secret Agents,* and Doris Day's foray into the secret agent field, *The Glass Bottom Boat.* He also appeared in the first episode aired of *The Monkees.*

Both Ansara and Marcuse were the sort of busy and prolific performers whose faces were so well known to the public that, either consciously or in an almost subliminal fashion, they became virtual visual reference points in films and TV of that period, creating their own stereotypes through the sheer number of their appearances. Marcuse plays Sinan, usurper for hire, who is supported by a small army of impressively towering scimitar-wielding goons, monstrous thugs named the Assassins, who charge around like the minions of the Yellow Peril bad guys of the serials (inevitably, one of their number is Red West).

Playing the rightful king who the bad guys are trying to dispose of was Phillip Reed, performing with a very plummy English voice for an Arab potentate! But then, didn't all fairytale kings speak with an English accent? Interestingly, the good king is an Amish-like, anti-progress Khomeni/Bin Laden type of figure who doesn't allow western influences in his kingdom (the land Elvis visits is said to be living "two thousand years" in the past). Even more amusingly, the villainous Sinan wants to overthrow him so that the Western world can come into their region and drill for oil! How times change--in Hollywood, at least.

As usual in these fables, the choice for the masses is between two despots, one benevolent tyrant with a beautiful daughter, one torturing self-interested exploiter; we see the good king at one point casually ordering executions, while the designated bad guy hands out whippings and beatings. Democracy and free elections are never an option in fairytale-land--it's always about putting the next person on the throne.

Director Gene Nelson (who had already directed Elvis in *Kissin' Cousins* for Katzman) was a former dancer, and the action and fight scenes are as choreographed as the actual dance numbers. Presley's performance is clearly and visibly being rushed, and so is he; Mobley also looks lost without guidance. It's left to the television actors more used to the pace of a fast shoot to carry the can, and Ansara in particular is calm and collected. Marcuse and Novello are clearly in control of scenes in which Elvis should be dominant and in charge of the situation.

Nelson went on to direct for television, and continued the Middle East theme by handling the pilot and first few episodes of the magical television sit-com *I Dream of Jeannie,* starring Michael Ansara's then-wife Barbara Eden (who had herself worked with Elvis in *Flaming Star*) and employing many of the same Hollywood cliches. He did not get on with the cast, and it was a thoroughly unpleasant experience for him that ended in a he-goes-or-I-do stand-off with volatile and temperamental series lead Larry Hagman (who stayed).

Harum Scarum's only obvious failing--and it may have been down to the lack of time and money as much as Nelson's directorial choices--is that too many of Elvis/Johnny's performances are filmed in longshot from a distance; Presley gets few close-ups when he's singing except for the best song, "So Close Yet So Far", a moving ballad sung from behind bars in the inevitable jail cell, the only time the Presley voice is exercised in all its glory. Otherwise, the songs--although Elvis' voice is always welcome--are as banal and unmemorable as ever.

"With four pictures a year it was like a factory" protested Hill and Range's Freddy Bienstock in Alanna Nash's book *The Colonel,* making odd claims that the Elvis movie scripts went through ten or twelve drafts, a curious and unlikely scenario given the speed of production and the studio's pump-'em-out attitude toward them--actually three a year. "I would mark those scenes where a song could be done... I'd wind up with four or five songs for each spot from seven or eight songwriting teams, and then I would take them to Elvis and he would choose which one to do. But there was no way to have better music" he insisted lamely, "because from the moment one picture was finished, we would have to get started on the next one".

But one way to have had better music would have been for the Colonel not to have locked Elvis in to Bienstock and the Hill and Range company exclusively; it is a matter of record that many possible offerings never reached Elvis. And just how bereft of inspiration were seven or eight writing teams?

Ben Weisman, who managed to squeak over fifty songs into the Elvis movies over the years, confirmed Bienstock's approach in the Clayton and Heard interview book *Elvis--By Those Who Knew Him Best,* pointing out that Elvis either gave a yes or no on the movie songs, never attempting to change the lyrics or the music. And yet, he also notes that when Elvis was recording "Loving You", he took over thirty attempts before he was satisfied with it. Ten years later, it seems Elvis, despairing over his material, hardly cared.

"What can't be disputed" write Dirk Vellenga and Mick Farren quite rightly in their 1988 book *Elvis and the Colonel*, "was that even by the standards of the most lightweight Hollywood musical, the songs in the Elvis movies of the '60s were mediocre if not awful... The movie music was cut on the cheap and in the shortest possible time. In all of 1964, Elvis spent just four days in the recording studio. Even when he did get into the studio, the tracks were cut in minimal time and, from the evidence of the resulting records, with minimal care. The session of February 24th, 1965, when Elvis laid down ten tracks for *Harum Scarum* in a single day, proved to be the rule rather than the exception. An added irony was that such slapdash work was being done at the very time when everybody around Elvis should have been acutely aware that new bands like the Beatles and the Rolling Stones were starting to breathe down their man's neck".

Although substantiation of such thoughts seem hardly necessary, Vellenger's and Farren's opinions were backed up elsewhere. Said Nashville musician Charlie McCoy, "I was hired to pick guitar on the *Harum Scarum* album in 1965. I was sixteen years old. I had a bit of a mixed emotion because when I first got the call, I was thrilled, but then, as you know, most of the movie music wasn't so hot, and I was disappointed. I noticed the producer from L.A. cut everything completely dry. We said something about it, and he said `Don't worry about it, we'll add echo later'. I don't think they ever did. When they did the next movie soundtrack album, *Frankie and Johnny*, they got their old team back, but Scotty talked them into keeping me on. So I ended up doing the soundtracks for seven Elvis movies".

Even Tom Parker, in a rare attack of aesthetic concern, expressed misgivings about the finished film, and suggested confirming it as a tongue-in-cheek comedy by having the movie narrated by a talking camel! Trust Parker to take a tolerable film and make it intolerable. Fortunately, his suggestions were ignored (besides, he had been pipped at the post in the talking camel narration stakes by the 1947 feature *Slave Girl*, starring Yvonne De Carlo). He had been incapacitated by back problems during the shooting of this and *Girl Happy*, and was--for the first time--beginning to contemplate retirement. The love affair with Sam Katzman was over, but Parker was still thinking profit and percentage rather than quality, and it was this attitude that ultimately did for Elvis and killed Parker's golden goose.

Still, *Harum Scarum* is by no means as bad as some have made out--the story is a lively caper, no better or worse than a dozen similar sword-and-sandal yarns before it. It's true, the dialogue is absurdly silly, but Elvis' character mocks it all the way through--it's as if Elvis is trapped in the bad movie from the opening film-within-a-film scene, and knows it. In that respect, it's a fish-out-of-water film; a few years later, Woody Allen would play the same game with the hilarious *Sleeper* and *Love and Death,* throwing his New York nebbish persona into a fascist future world and the time of Napoleon respectively, while another comic film maker of the 70s, Mel Brooks, would offer up *Blazing Saddles* and *Young Frankenstein* in the same spirit. *Harum Scarum* is by no means as downright funny as these, or even comparable in quality, but it's a forerunner in spirit, if not actual ambition and intent.

As the film is in no sense to be taken seriously as anything other than an escapist diversion, serious criticism is redundant. It is what it is, and on a rainy afternoon it's as much fun as any Hollywood fantasy in the same vein.

Frankie and Johnny (1966)

wr. Alex Gottleib, from Nat Perrin, dir. Frederick de Cordova, pr. Ed Small (UA)

with Elvis Presley (Johnny), Donna Douglas (Frankie), Harry Morgan (Cully), Sue Ane Langdon (Mitzi), Nancy Kovack (Nellie Bly), Audrey Christie (Peg), Anthony Eisley (Clint Braden), Robert Strauss (Blackie), Jerome Cowan (Wilbur), James Milhollin (store manager), Joyce Jameson, Wilda Taylor, Larri Thomas, Judy Chapman, Dee Jay Mattis

Elvis sings: "Come Along" (over titles); "Petunia, the Gardener's Daughter" (with Donna Douglas on stage); "Chesay" (with Harry Morgan at gypsy camp); "What Every Woman Lives For" (serenading Donna Douglas, Sue Ane Langdon, and Nancy Kovack during show); "Frankie and Johnny" (with various cast members on stage); "Look Out Broadway" (with Douglas, Morgan, and Christie in dressing room); "Beginner's Luck" (at riverside picnic in fantasy sequence to Donna Douglas); "Down By the Riverside" (onshore by steamship); "When the Saints Go Marching In" (onshore by steamship); "Shout It Out" (on stage); "Hard Luck" (in street with young boy on harmonica); "Please Don't Stop Loving Me" (on deck to Donna Douglas); "Frankie and Johnny" (second performance with various cast members on stage); "Everybody Come Aboard" (with various cast members to close)

As his films became cheaper and more and more ridiculous, Elvis retreated--much to the amazement and frustration of the "Memphis Mafia"--into the peculiar and offbeat religious cults that were flourishing in the mid-to-late '60s, as the counter culture kids embraced the peace and love philosophy and dress sense of Jesus, but rejected the authoritarianism, puritanism, respectability and plain old-fashionedness of the mainstream church.

Neither spiritual or enlightening, this was, in reality, the same supernatural bullcrap that had been fed to the gullible since time immemorial by charlatans and hucksters through the ages--which was why the wily old Colonel spotted it instantly for what it was. Today, in its current form it is termed "New Age" and embraces drivel ranging from homeopathic medicine to feng shui, but in fact dates back to the very oldest ages, and has only had scientific fact and empirical proof to combat it in the last one hundred years or so. It is science and medicine, of course, that should truly be called "New Age"--wizards and warlocks, soothsayers and astrologers, prophets and fortune tellers, and witch doctors and snake-oil salesmen have been around since the cave paintings.

While Presley insisted to interviewers that he remained committed to mainstream religion, his "search for the meaning of life" became increasingly and worryingly bizarre, mostly due (it seems, reading from Guralnick and Nash) to the influence of his hairdresser, of all people, whose fascination with various gurus was passed on to a desperately receptive Elvis Presley during lengthy grooming sessions (Parker referred to the hairdresser, Larry Geller, to his face as a hypnotist and "fellow snowman"). However, Elvis found a soul-mate on the set of *Frankie and Johnny* in shy and sensitive Donna Douglas, the curvy blonde Southern belle from the *Beverly Hillbillies* TV series, who--said her colleagues--returned to the set of her TV show disillusioned and devastated that she and he had not become more than fellow searchers for the meaning of life. "They exchanged books and ideas" said Elvis biographer Peter Guralnick, discussed mutual gurus, "and meditated together". Co-star Sue-Ane Langdon confirmed their mutual attraction.

"She didn't realise every girl he worked with fell in love with him, plus a million he didn't work with" generalised *Hillbillies* creator and producer Paul Henning. "I wouldn't interpret it as love or infatuation" insisted Douglas, "but I was going through a rough time in my life then".

Frankie and Johnny itself is a corny period piece set on a Mississippi riverboat in the 1800s. Based on a popular ballad dating back to 1904, popularised by Mae West, and filmed previously thirty years earlier with *Showboat's* Helen Morgan, it was an odd vehicle for Presley (who filmed it in the summer of 1965), but a brave attempt by United Artists to do something different from the Paramount/Wallis formula without ditching the Presley persona or girl troubles theme that the Elvis audience expected.

Unfortunately, when the film was released to the indifferent masses in 1966, the timing was off. Way off. While the rest of the world stared goggle-eyed at flower-power, *Batman,* secret agent movies, swingin' London, and events in Vietnam, Elvis was marching around singing "When the Saints Come Marching In" and "Down by the Riverside". Nobody could accuse the producers of fad-following opportunism.

Louisiana-born Donna Douglas (real name, Doris Smith) was a beauty queen winner and game show hostess who graduated to bit parts on TV shows as varied as *Twilight Zone* and *Mister Ed* to *Boris Karloff's Thriller* and *Pete and Gladys* before she secured the role of Elly May Clampett on *The Beverly Hillbillies,* the 1960s' most successful TV sit-com, and a series which seems to haunt this book as we proceed through the decade, number one show that it was (her co-star Max Baer was one of many young actors--including Ty Hardin, Vince Edwards, Pat Boone and Robert Conrad--who often played football with Elvis). Other early roles for Douglas included *Michael Shayne, 77, Sunset Strip, Surfside Six, The Aquanauts,* and *Route 66.*

Sour, dour Harry Morgan is today best known for his long-running role as Colonel Potter on 1970s sit-com *MASH,* during which time he also appeared in numerous TV movies. He had been in many TV series before that, including *December Bride, Pete and Gladys, The Richard Boone Show, Kentucky Jones,* and *Dragnet,* and his numerous film credits included *High Noon, The Glenn Miller Story,* and *Inherit the Wind.* Sue-Ane Langdon had played a similar character to the one here in *Roustabout;* Robert Strauss had previously appeared in *Girls! Girls! Girls!,* where more details can be found.

At around this time, Joyce Jameson played roles in *The Twilight Zone, My Favorite Martian, Burke's Law, The Munsters, The Man From UNCLE,* and *The Girl From UNCLE.* Character actress Audrey Christie's films included *Carousel* and *Splendor In The Grass.* Most often seen in musicals, she made this appearance either side of Debbie Reynolds and Doris Day vehicles. On TV, she's hung out in the Aaron Spelling stables, with *Honey West, Starsky and Hutch* and *Charlie's Angels* on her resume.

Nancy Kovack was never very happy with her career in terms of the roles she was offered, but she told interviewer Tom Weaver that she enjoyed almost every minute of it, and no doubt--she fell into a profitable and prolific career almost by chance, traveled the world from Italy to the Middle East, acted in some of television's best-remembered series and worked with some of cinema's most well-known names. Here, for the only time in her career, she's a redhead. Initially a contract player for Columbia, her dozen or so films were mostly soapy melodramas and westerns, but also include *Diary of a Madman* with Vincent Price, the Ray Harryhausen fantasy *Jason and the Argonauts,* the first of Dean Martin's *Matt Helm* spy films, *The Silencers,* and *Tarzan and the Valley of Gold.* For TV, she appeared in the pilot of *Bewitched* and several other episodes, as well as two *Man from UNCLE* stories (one bit part, one major), and episodes of *Voyage to the Bottom of the Sea, Burke's Law, Honey West, Twelve O'Clock High, Batman, I Dream of Jeannie, I Spy, The Invaders, Star Trek, Get Smart, It Takes a Thief, Hawaii Five-O,* and *The Invisible Man.* Usually blonde, with fashion magazine looks, she eventually retired when she married conductor Zubin Mehta of Three Tenors fame.

Anthony Eisley (formerly Fred Eisley) had starred in the TV detective series *Hawaiian Eye* with Robert Conrad in the early '60s, but had never really been able to escape the B-movie/Z-movie circuit, despite changing his name to something more stylishly Hollywood. Eisley probably has the most bizarre acting career to rival anybody, his films at around this time including the Hawaiian-set *One Way Wahine* with Joy Harmon, an Italian spy film called *Lightning Bolt,* a brazen *Time Tunnel* rip-off titled *Journey to the Center of Time,* the self-explanatory amateurish schlock-fest *Dracula vs. Frankenstein,* and the giant gorilla film *The Mighty Gorga,* all of which have to be seen to be believed. One of his films, *The Tormentors,* took fifteen years to get a release; at least three others were released despite being unfinished! He began his movie career filming *The Wasp Woman* with Roger Corman, and ended it mixing with the likes of Herbert Strock and Fred Olen Ray ("Can you imagine? Some guy sees *The Mummy and the Curse of the Jackals* and says `I've got to use that actor!'" he laughed in an interview with Tom Weaver). TV work included guest shots in cult series *Honey West, The Wild Wild West,* and *The Invaders.* He has basked in his notoriety, with a remarkably healthy and sanguine attitude about the direction his career took.

Elvis is not really convincing as Johnny, a gullible gambler who--working in the surroundings he does--should really know better. Ditto his best buddy, the considerably older songwriter played by Harry Morgan, who not only throws away his own money, but provides Elvis with cash to lose as well. Always better suited to comedy than drama, Morgan fires off his quips with the same mechanical professionalism he would employ ten

Elvis, with Donna Douglas, Anthony Eisley, and Nancy Kovack

years later on *MASH*. The script is full to brimming with wry, loaded remarks about the stupidity of gambling, and justly so, but it's mostly sledgehammer wit, and no doubt still water off a duck's back to life's real world incurable gamblers. Two gypsies who kickstart the storyline by telling Johnny that a red-haired woman will bring him luck, do everything but bang the guys' heads together.

As the showgirl Frankie, Donna Douglas--so perfect in *The Beverly Hillbillies* all those years--is plainly out of her depth, miming her songs badly, and even occasionally slipping into her Elly May accent, which--given the film's locale--she would have been well-advised to keep. Oddly, she doesn't look infatuated with Elvis, or Johnny, or her part, or her opportunity--she just looks bored.

Elvis is on auto-pilot. As with the previous *Harum Scarum,* the two leads are carried through the film, almost on shoulders, by the professionalism and experience of the supporting cast. A good example of this comes from uncredited character actor James Milhollin, memorable as the department store manager in the famous "After Hours" episode of *The Twilight Zone* and excellent as wicked lawyer Alfred Slye in the *Batman* story featuring Liberace, who is here unbilled as the crooked New Orleans dress-seller who offloads three Madame Pompadour costumes on the leading ladies as one-off originals with just another ten to go! His broad, theatrical style graced numerous 1960s TV shows, including two other *Twilight Zones, My Favorite Martian, Bewitched, The Beverly Hillbillies, Get Smart, Lost in Space, The Man from UNCLE,* and *The Girl from UNCLE.* Morgan, Christie, Langdon and Strauss in particular are giving their all while at the same time simply going through the motions for a routine film made by an uninspired director.

The riverboat and Mardi Gras locales would put some life into the movie, and Elvis' voice is as gorgeous as ever, but *Frankie and Johnny* is still, like *Harum Scarum,* just another rainy afternoon movie. Director Fred De Cordova was another old timer plodding toward the retirement pastures, and had been directing movies regularly from 1945, mostly long-forgotten romantic comedies for Warners and Universal, but his most infamous achievement had been the notorious Ronald Reagan vehicle *Bedtime for Bonzo* and its sequel *Bonzo Goes to College.* He had drifted into television, where he worked on the likes of *My Three Sons, Leave It to Beaver,* and *The Jack Benny Show,* but in 1965 had returned to films to make the comedy *I'll Take Sweden,* with Bob Hope, Tuesday Weld, Frankie Avalon, and Jeremy Slate. Now in his fifties, he was yet another middle-aged man making teen movies, and would soon semi-retire to Johnny Carson and producing *The Tonight Show.*

The story is another clodhopping caper through romantic misunderstandings, resorting to the old ploy of the masked ball where all the female protagonists are wearing the same outfit. In contrast to the usual resolution of such films, everyone ends up trapped in a rotten relationship with a poor choice in partner, albeit the ones they wanted. Langdon's Mitzi, the tart with a heart, goes home empty-handed, but lonely.

The music, when period, is adequate but redundant, while things look up toward the end when Elvis performs more typical fare. "Shout It Out", "Hard Luck" and "Please Don't Stop Loving Me" are fine. The title ballad is performed twice, but the fatal shooting is neither fatal nor deliberate (the escape clause the oldest in the book), and despite all the warnings about the dangers of gambling, Frankie secures Johnny only on the understanding that she won't try and change his destructive ways! Happy times ahead, then...

"I haven't seen all the Elvis Presley movies" said two time co-star Sue-Ane Langdon, "but I do think *Frankie and Johnny* was one of the best he ever made. He had a good back-up cast with Harry Morgan and Donna Douglas. He sang real well and seemed more relaxed in this one. It was a really nice cute movie. The business today is relatively impersonal. I don't think we grow to love our stars. They are not projected as loveable people for the most part. There are no charming men". Not in *Frankie and Johnny* either though, just louts, crooks, and idiots and the silly girls who chase them!

Paradise, Hawaiian Style

Paradise, Hawaiian Style (1966)

wr. Allan Weiss, Anthony Lawrence, dir. Michael Moore, pr. Hal Wallis (Paramount)

with Elvis Presley (Rick Richards), James Shigeta (Danny Kohana), Suzanna Leigh (Judy Hudson), Marianna Hill (Lani), Donna Butterworth (Jan Kohana), Julie Parrish (Joanna), Linda Wong (Lehua), Irene Tsu (Pua), Jan Shepard (Betty Kohana), Grady Sutton (Mr. Cubberson), Doris Packer (Mrs. Barrington), John Doucette (Mr. Belden/FAA), Mary Treen (Mrs. Belden), Gigi Verone (Peggy/ stewardess), Don Collier (Judy's date), Philip Ahn (Lani's father), Robert Ito (Pua's boyfriend), Deanna Lund (Danny's nurse), Edy Williams (secretary applicant/beach girl), Red West (stunts), the Jordanaires, the Mello Men

Elvis sings: "Hawaii USA" (over titles); "Queenie Wahine's Papaya" (with Donna Butterworth at Kohana home); "Scratch My Back" (with Marianna Hill at restaurant); "Drums of the Island" (to Irene Tsu on river); "Dog's Life" (on helicopter with Julie Parrish); "Datin'" (with Donna Butterworth at Kohana home); "House of Sand" (at beach party); "Won't You Come Home, Bill Bailey?" (Butterworth only, at show); "Stop Where You Are" (on stage at party); "This Is My Heaven"/"Drums of the Island" (grand finale)

A decidedly chubby-faced Elvis sleepwalks his way through a by now familiar formula as helicopter pilot Rick Richards (a more shallow, two-dimensional version of *Blue Hawaii's* Chad Gates) in this otherwise entertaining return to Hawaii with all the usual plot elements in place--fawning women, cute kids, best buddy, comic relief old folk and romantic misunderstandings. By this time, producers were not simply reworking the usual formula for Elvis pictures into new material--like a TV series in its third or fourth season that returns to the most successful storylines of the first year, they were blatantly recreating the more successful Presley movies for a second go-round. *Paradise, Hawaiian Style* took Elvis back to the Islands, while his next effort, *Spinout,* would take him back to the racetrack of *Viva Las Vegas.* It was preferable to, and more suitable than *Frankie and Johnny,* at least.

Elvis is in uniform again at the start of the film, but this time he's been sacked from his job as an airline pilot for inappropriate behavior with overheated stewardesses, and has now exhausted all avenues of employment with the major airlines. Rejecting crop-dusting disdainfully (the job he held in *It Happened at the World's Fair*), he persuades best buddy Danny Kohana (James Shigeta), who runs an air charter operation, to invest in a couple of helicopters to exploit the tourist trade. For the first hour, nothing much happens as Elvis hops from island to island where he has a collection of secret girlfriends, each unaware of the others, each touting for business for him as he strings them along. Amazingly, all this nothingness is very pleasant and relaxing. In the last half-hour there is a hint of jeopardy as first Rick and little Jan, Danny's daughter, are missing overnight (thanks to the machinations of scheming girlfriend Marianna Hill), and then Danny comes to grief while taking his daughter home. Rick goes to the rescue, and all is forgiven (Rick's travails having put the business at risk).

It's enjoyable fluff to pass the time with, but there's a distinct impression of everybody, from Presley and Wallis on down, just going through the motions--as indeed they were. Wallis certainly felt confident enough to promote Michael Moore, assistant director on *King Creole* and *Roustabout*, and Norman Taurog's assistant on *G.I. Blues, Blue Hawaii,* and *Girls! Girls! Girls!*, to direct the human traffic. Whether Taurog was unavailable, or whether Wallis thought he could save a few bucks on a film that could direct itself, it is difficult to guess, although the latter seems more likely. Either way, once the aerial photography and dance numbers had been taken care of by their respective supervisors, Moore had little else but an hour or so of TV-standard camera-pointing to achieve.

"Michael Moore never gave us any direction" said Irene Tsu, who played native girl Pua in several major scenes. "The guy was terrified of everybody, most of all Elvis. He never directed Elvis at all, and let him do whatever he wanted". Although filmed on location, *Paradise, Hawaiian Style* rarely even bothers with establishing shots of the characters, settling for 'planes and helicopters arriving and departing (so we are at least spared the usual long-shots of doubles and stand-ins).

Paradise, Hawaiian Style is so sure of itself it's almost lazy, but audiences by now knew what to expect, and it's fortunate indeed that Wallis and his writers had got the formula down pat. There's nothing else but the formula though, and the result is ninety minutes of surprisingly watchable inconsequential Elvis Presley wallpaper. The girls are particularly weak, with Linda Wong, Jan Shepard and Irene Tsu barely registering, and Suzanna Leigh, magazine model-beautiful but cold, interesting only because of her blondeness and British accent. Marianna Hill as Lani is invisible and unlikeable, even though she gets a musical number with Elvis. Only Julie Parrish as Joanna gives the impression that she could have done so much more if the script had offered it.

"I was a bit awed working with Elvis" said Parrish. "It probably hampered me a little bit because I really was a huge fan of his. I was in every Elvis fan club around when I was a teenager". A role like Laurel Goodwin's in *Girls! Girls! Girls!* could have been expertly filled by Parrish.

However, that was unlikely to happen--Parrish claimed she made the fateful "mistake" of resisting the advances of Wallis, who had plans for her that went far beyond the requirements of the filming. Laurel Goodwin had said she suffered similar unwanted attentions, but had been fortunate that Wallis had been distracted by personal matters. Parrish was apparently not so lucky, and suffered the usual cliched pushy threats of the stereotypical middle-aged movie producer.

Ironically, Parrish (real name, Ruby Joyce Wilbar) had appeared alongside Wallis' earlier nemesis Stella Stevens in the Jerry Lewis film *The Nutty Professor*. She then co-starred in the snowbound beach movie *Winter-a-Go-Go,* and played in most of the major TV shows of the period on the guest-star circuit, including episodes of *The Untouchables, Dobie Gillis, My Three Sons, Temple Houston, Gunsmoke, Burke's Law, Ben Casey, The FBI, Gidget, Bonanza,* and *Star Trek* (again ironically, appearing in the episode incorporating Laurel Goodwin's pilot footage, "The Menagerie"). Poor Julie--after Wallis, she then, according to an interview she gave to Tom Lisanti, had to fight off the clumsy advances of William Shatner.

She followed *Paradise, Hawaiian Style* with a turn as an inappropriately blonde co-star for Frankie Avalon and Fabian in William Asher's race car teen movie *Fireball 500* (Annette Funicello did not want another brunette alongside her), made with his usual beach movie regulars. Reviving her career at the close of the '70s, she did more TV, with roles in *The Rockford Files, Laverne and Shirley, The Fall Guy, Murder She Wrote, Hunter, Hotel,* and, like so many '60s starlets in the '80s, the soaps--*Dallas, Dynasty,* and *Capitol*. In the 1990s she had a recurring role in *Beverly Hills 90210*.

British-born Suzanna Leigh (real name, Suzanna Smyth) was toiling in British and French TV when she heard Wallis was in London and literally banged on his hotel room door for a screen test. A few months later she was in Hawaii. Callously used as a political pawn between the American and British actors' unions, she was embroiled in a dispute over whether she could make a second Elvis film, *Easy Come, Easy Go,* and frustrated and impatient, threw in the towel, returning--as it turned out--to a less than dazzling career in Britain, where her highest profile was in the delightfully lurid and cheesy Hammer horror films. She resurfaced when Elvis died to sell her non-story that she didn't sleep with Presley to Britain's sleazy tabloid the *News of the World*.

Marianna Hill (real name, Marianna Schwarzkoff) made an inevitable (and excellent) *Batman* appearance that same year as *Paradise, Hawaiian Style,* and went on to appear in somewhat stronger fare as the movies grew up, including *Medium Cool, Thumb Tripping, El Condor, High Plains Drifter, The Last Porno Flick,* and *The Godfather, Part II.* Cult TV shows to feature her included *77, Sunset Strip, The Untouchables, The Outer Limits, Star Trek, Mission: Impossible, I Spy, Hawk* (an early Burt Reynolds vehicle), *The Name of the Game,* and *Kung Fu.* Hill's credits were all eclectic, daring, and offbeat, and included a 1961 hoot called *Married Too Young* co-written by Ed Wood.

"After a day's filming the crew and some of the actors would go to dinner in the hotel" said Parrish. "But never Elvis. His entourage and Colonel Parker always surrounded him and kept him isolated. I had a great time hanging out with the crew and with Irene Tsu, Marianna Hill, and Linda Wong, who played my rivals for Elvis. There was definitely no rivalry amongst us off the set, and I never had that with anyone I worked with up until that time".

"I wanted to work with Elvis so badly..." echoed Irene Tsu. "I was very nervous during my audition, but Hal Wallis offered me my choice of roles. I chose Pua because she was featured in one of the film's most lavish production numbers, 'Drums of the Island'. As the scene started, they blasted the song from these huge boom boxes hidden along the banks of the river. As we sailed along, Elvis just lip-synched to himself. Nobody told me what to do, so I decided to just sit there and look pretty. Our heads kept going back and forth. Elvis was looking one way and I was looking another. It looks pretty silly".

Tsu did find herself invited into the inner sanctum for dinner, "but it was very uncomfortable. He would be sitting there with Colonel Parker and his entourage. Nobody really had a conversation. It was more like trying to say something to entertain Elvis. It was horrible, and I felt sorry for Elvis, so I stopped going".

Jan Shepard, who--unlike young fans Parrish and Tsu--had known Elvis in 1959, when she appeared alongside him in *King Creole,* felt the same way. "He was not unfriendly, just very withdrawn, and kept to himself between takes--not as outgoing and fun-loving as before. We scarcely saw him. Of course there was a whole different group of guys--he was now surrounded by an entourage. He was preoccupied with theology books and seemed to be questioning his role in the scheme of things. One time he asked about Dolores Hart, and we had a little bit of a conversation. When we reminisced about *King Creole,* he said `honey, that was my favorite picture'". Tsu also confirmed that he was going through his spiritual phase during filming.

Chinese-born Irene Tsu began her Hollywood career as a dancer, and--in her own words--"decoration" in films such as *Flower Drum Song* (co-starring James Shigeta*), Cleopatra, Take Her, She's Mine, Sword of Ali Baba,* and beach movie *How to Stuff a Wild Bikini*. She also appeared in John Ford's troubled last picture, *Seven Women*. On TV, she found work on *Perry Mason, My Favorite Martian, The Man from UNCLE* (twice), *Voyage to the Bottom of the Sea,* and *I Spy,* again in minor roles as decoration. Her first major role was in the laughable pulp sci-fi turkey *Women of the Prehistoric Planet,* alongside Wendell Corey, from Elvis' first film, *Loving You,* and Merry Anders from *Tickle Me*.

Tsu's next film was the Doris Day spy comedy *Caprice,* directed by Frank Tashlin, who had given Julie Parrish her start, and further TV followed in series such as *My Three Sons, Laredo,* and *The Wild Wild West*. Another *Man from UNCLE,* a memorable two-parter titled "The Five Daughters Affair", and released in cinemas as *The Karate Killers,* gave Tsu one of her best remembered roles as a geisha who rescues a young girl from both UNCLE and bad guy adversaries THRUSH.

Like Marianna Hill, Tsu has always been risk-taking and unconventional, never playing her career by the book, and frequently going down paths other actresses might have balked at. In 1968 she took a role in John Wayne's controversial pro-Vietnam film *The Green Berets* (even though she felt John Wayne didn't like her), upset everybody again by doing a high-profile ad campaign (something you're only supposed to do at the very beginning or very end of your career), and in the '70s went on location in the Far East to star in two martial arts movies. Although during the 1970s she made appearances in numerous forgettable films, she kept herself in the public eye through TV, guest-starring in such series as *The Name of the Game, Cade's County, Mission: Impossible, Cannon, Hawaii Five-O, Ironside, Wonder Woman,* and *The Rockford Files*. 1980s TV work included *Airwolf, MacGyver* and *Trapper John,* and in the '90s, *Baywatch Nights, E.R.,* and *Star Trek – Voyager*.

As Danny Kohana, James Shigeta is so strong that he pushes bored Elvis off the screen with his energy and enthusiasm. Although Hawaiian by birth, Shigeta naturally spent his career playing mostly Chinese or Japanese parts in mostly undistinguished films and TV; television roles included episodes of *The Naked City, Burke's Law, I Spy, The Green Hornet, It Takes A Thief, Mission: Impossible, Matt Helm, Ironside, The Young Lawyers, Hawaii Five-O, Streets of San Francisco, The Rockford Files, Fantasy Island, T.J. Hooker, Magnum p.i., Greatest American Hero, Masquerade, Simon and Simon, Matt Houston, Murder She Wrote,* and *Renegade*. He's often remembered as the unlucky executive made an example of in *Die Hard*.

Young Donna Butterworth had previously appeared in the Jerry Lewis film *The Family Jewels*. She's fine as the token kid, although a toe-curling performance of "Won't You Come Home, Bill Bailey?" is a ludicrous sight best saved for the cutting-room floor and her parents' private home movies collection.

The comedy tourist on this occasion was Grady Sutton, a competent character actor who had just appeared in *Tickle Me* and specialised in nervous ninnies, and here plays a skittish sales rep who is uncharacteristically treated quite disrespectfully by Elvis' character. His TV work includes a very funny bit as a mesmerised bank manager in a *Batman* episode guest-starring Tallulah Bankhead.

Treated equally badly by Rick, but deservedly so, is later client Mrs. Barrington, who gives as good as she gets with her parasol when her showdogs--which Danny and Rick have ill-advisedly agreed to transport loose in the helicopter when all others refused--arrive bruised and battered from their ordeal... but not as bruised and battered as poor Elvis and Julie Parrish, who battle to stay aloft while Rick serenades the dogs, running an FAA inspector and his wife off the road in the process. "Elvis hated this song" laughed Parrish, "But we had a good time filming the scene. He couldn't stop laughing while he was recording it. I just had to sit there while Elvis sang that song for hours while they filmed from different angles". When the dog-laden helicopter lands, in long shot, it is quite clearly bereft of either Parrish or the dogs, who magically reappear as they alight. Elvis had already suffered a humiliating experience singing to a hound dog on *The Steve Allen Show* in the mid-'50s, and bizarrely, but typically, one of Presley's idols, Dean Martin, had been similarly infuriated to find himself singing to animals in the Wallis-produced Martin and Lewis vehicle *Three Ring Circus* ten years earlier as well. Wallis' philosophy hadn't changed much at all--milk the name, deliver them doing what they do best, and don't waste money on much else.

Portraying Mrs. Barrington the dog owner was character actress Doris Packer, who specialised in playing snooty, stuffy, pompous grand dames and appeared memorably in several episodes of *The Beverly Hillbillies* as the similar Mrs. Fenwick. John Doucette, the FAA man, was often cast as figures of some authority (he was royalty in *Get Smart,* and Ulysses in *The Time Tunnel*). Elvis regular Mary Treen (the hat shop lady in *Girls! Girls! Girls!* and another tourist/wife in *Fun in Acapulco*) plays his dreadful wife. As ever, James Gavin appears to be the only helicopter pilot in Hollywood.

In blink and you miss them roles are the prolific Philip Ahn (of *Kung Fu* fame; his resume goes all the way back to Universal's *Buck Rogers* serial in 1939) in a brief and pointless scene as Lani's father, beautiful twinkle-eyed redhead Deanna Lund (Valerie Scott in *Land of the Giants*) as a nurse, Robert Ito (co-star of 1970s murder mystery series *Quincy*) as Pua's escort at the festival dinner, and the aforementioned Jan Shepard as Danny's wife.

One of the dancers in the sandcastle scene (also in the secretary hiring sequence) is ambitious starlet Edy Williams, then turning up in most of the cult TV series of the period, *Burke's Law, Batman* (twice)*, The Man from UNCLE, The Beverly Hillbillies* and *Lost in Space* among them. She later secured a role in *Beyond the Valley of the Dolls,* and (briefly) married the director, breast-fixated sex film producer Russ Meyer. She has appeared in various states of undress in low-budget movies over four decades, including such extraordinary titles as *Doctor Alien, Bad Girls from Mars,* and *Hollywood Hot Tubs!* Somewhat more prominent is fellow starlet Gigi Verone as a sympathetic stewardess in the pre-titles set-up. The scenes of Elvis wallowing in the Polynesian culture are lavish, colorful, and spectacular, and he was genuinely interested in the efforts made by the Polynesian Cultural Center in Oahu, who were providing many of the locations, to enlighten him.

There is, of course, a brawl with a drunken lout, and while Red West gets his usual licks in, the main cause of the trouble is Suzanna Leigh's insensitive and stupid date, an uncouth loudmouth played by Don Collier who ends up with his face in the sweets trolley. As Leigh's Judy Hudson, a pilot reduced to working as a secretary for Danny and Rick, is pretending to be married to keep wolfy Rick at bay, she is, of course, the one who ends up with him--apparently--at the film's end, when all the girls converge on the same giant party night. The game's up, the girls will get commission for putting business Rick's way, and Elvis is whisked away before he can even consummate the film's resolution with a kiss, to perform the grand finale--almost in recognition that the resolution of the storyline is pretty much a formality. The FAA inspector's change of heart has a similar let's-get-this-over-and-done-with feel about it.

Presumably, Judy's obvious intelligence and ability to fly a 'plane was a lacklustre attempt to excuse the army of blank canvasses in bikinis and other brainless bimbos in the frame, but as Judy ends up answering the 'phone in the office it's not terribly convincing. The girls in Elvis movies were often nothing more than attractive scenery, and for the films that they were, this was not only acceptable, but right. However, *Paradise, Hawaiian Style* is irritatingly sexist in an old-fashioned way, particularly in the scene where Rick interviews the secretaries not for their meagre office abilities but for their potential for sexual escapades--all of them beaming vacuously and posing like the models they are. When the inevitable bespectacled bore starts boasting of her actual qualifications to do the job properly, Rick shunts her aside bluntly for Danny to deal with later. When the ubiquitous Edy Williams and her bosom buddies are joyfully gyrating on the beach to Elvis grooving his way through "House of Sand" it's party time, acceptable and pleasurable, but when the women are applying for jobs and then overtly being made to look empty-headed and being put down in their everyday lives, it's a different situation entirely, and *Paradise, Hawaiian Style* is unable to make the appropriate distinction.

Shot like a travel ad, the film is a little more leering than usual, possibly a sign of the times, as the mainstream media was now responding to the counter culture's free love philosophy with the more daringly overt sexual overtones of the spy movies. Although *Paradise, Hawaiian Style* is nostalgically cute and coy by contemporary standards, the age of 1950s-style innocence was firmly in the past by 1966, and the Tulsa McLean/Toby Kwimper persona was not going to cut it in the mid-'60s, even in an Elvis film.

Elvis was also beginning to feel the heat from newer, fresher acts... although these did not include Tom Jones or Peter Noone (of Herman's Hermits), both of whom he met socially at this time. It was after Elvis and his entourage returned from Hawaii to film the Hollywood interiors that Presley finally met a new act he did grudgingly admire--the Beatles, fresh from the success of their ground-breaking swinging '60s movie *A Hard Day's Night*. Today, the Beatles movies look even more outdated than the Elvis films, and are virtually unwatchable except as artefacts, whereas at least the Elvis films still work on their own terms. At the time, though, it was humiliating that Elvis appeared to be left behind.

Diane McBain (l) and Shelley Fabares (r) with Elvis in Spinout

Spinout (1966)

wr. Theodore Flicker, George Kirgo, dir. Norman Taurog, pr. Joe Pasternak (MGM)

with Elvis Presley (Mike McCoy), Shelley Fabares (Cynthia Foxhugh), Deborah Walley (Les), Diane McBain (Diana St. Clair), Jack Mullaney (Curly), Jimmy Hawkins (Larry), Carl Betz (Howard Foxhugh), Warren Berlinger (Philip Short), Will Hutchins (Tracy/motorcycle cop), Cecil Kellaway (Mr. Ranley), Una Merkel (Mrs. Ranley), Frederic Worlock (Blodgett the butler), Dodie Marshall (Susan), Dave Barry (Harry/manager), Red West, Nancy Czar, Thordis Brandt, Deanna Lund, the Jordanaires

Elvis sings: "Spinout" (over titles); "Stop, Look, Listen" (at club); "Adam and Evil" (at club); "All That I Am" (to Diane McBain); "Never Say Yes" (rehearsal at club); "Am I Ready?" (to Shelley Fabares); "Beach Shack" (at pool party); "Spinout" (at evening party); "Smorgasbord" (at evening party); "I'll Be Back" (finale at club)

The second of Elvis' three motor racing films was a childishly funny romantic comedy, slight and silly, but relentlessly entertaining. With heavy-handed humor pitched somewhere between a Jerry Lewis film and a Doris Day film, and performances to match, Elvis plays a rock and rollin' race car driver who plays a war of nerves with a millionaire (Carl Betz) who wants him to drive his new car, and his daughter (Shelley Fabares) who wants to drive him to the altar. Meanwhile, Elvis--as Mike McCoy--is also romantically pursued by a flighty journalist writing a book on eligible men (Diane McBain) and his tomboy drummer Les (Deborah Walley).

Making up the band are comedy relief buddies Larry and Curly (Jack Mullaney and Jimmy Hawkins, named after two of the Three Stooges; one assumes only legal problems prevented boyish Walley from being named Mo, although what one makes of substitute handle Les depends on one's individual level of cynicism). What makes this frantic and colorful 1960s time capsule work--apart from the fact that it is a frantic and colorful 1960s time capsule--is a wonderful cast and the advantage that despite the cornball developments, the film defies convention and goes for a surprise ending. If you've not seen the film yet, stop here.

Not only does Elvis *not* drive the car in the climactic race, but he doesn't get the girl, evading all three of them, each of whom get married off to other cast members. Equally surprising, and pleasantly so, is that although *Spinout* can't resist dropping in the inevitable comedy oldsters, there are no patronised ethnic groups, no loveable animals, and no cute kids. And unusually, while the opening scenes confirm he's no eunuch, instead of pursuing a girl, Elvis is either trying to escape them, or oblivious to them.

In short, *Spinout* is different enough from the usual Elvis fare to be interesting, but delivers the expected formula and ambience. It's a dumb, dumb film, but dumber still is the audience that takes it seriously. The film moves smartly along, ducking and diving every attempt to make sense of the plot, the broad performances telling all but the slowest member of the audience that this is nothing more or less than a fizzy, silly bit of fluff to take your mind off your problems... or perhaps, just take your mind.

"For myself, I am allergic to racing cars and suffered from a surfeit of Elvis' jiving bimbos" sighed Eric Braun in his *Elvis Film Encyclopedia*. "Norman Taurog again does a professional job, but oh, those noisy cars". Poor dear! In fact, despite being produced in the usual manner of long shots filmed on location and close-ups of the actors in dummy cars in the studio, the race is excellent--and quite frankly, if you don't like racing cars and dancing girls, there's not much point in sitting through Elvis films!

Even better are the party scenes, a poolside affair where Red West can be seen throwing a young woman into the water, and an indoor soiree with some amazing '60s fashions jiggling around with pretty girls inside them, and filmed on a set later used for one of the *Man from UNCLE* movies, *The Karate Killers*, aka "The Five Daughters Affair", which features Elvis girls Diane McBain and Irene Tsu in its cast.

The likeable Shelley Fabares had been a teen idol star herself in the 1950s, appearing in the rock and roll movies *Rock, Pretty Baby* and *Summer Love*, and from 1958 to 1963 co-starring as one of the kids in *The Donna Reed Show* (she even had her own hit record in 1962). Carl Betz was her father in that series too, so *Spinout* doesn't get much credit for subtle casting--Betz went straight from the series' final episode in 1966 to *Spinout!*

After appearing in *Ride the Wild Surf* with Fabian, and *Hold On* with British pop star Peter Noone, Fabares appeared in three Elvis films altogether (having already appeared in *Girl Happy,* as gangster's daughter Val, she later played gold-digger Dianne Carter in *Clambake*), and alongside the Donna Reed years, they are probably her most notable achievements. "Doing those pictures with him were some of the happiest experiences I ever had professionally or personally" she told interviewer Tom Lisanti. "Even if the films weren't great--they were okay, and perfect for what they were, at that time--the experience of doing them was extraordinary".

She spent the 1970s flitting from one short-lived sit-com to another, was cast for three years in the long-running comedy *One Day at a Time* between 1981 and '84, and finally found a hit show all to herself in 1989 titled *Coach,* a dreadful sit-com which inexplicably ran throughout much of the 1990s. She was more suited to light roles than dramatic, but still managed to pay the rent with guest parts in *The Twilight Zone, The Ghost and Mrs. Muir, McCloud, Ironside, Barnaby Jones, Police Story, The Rockford Files, Vegas, Fantasy Island, The Incredible Hulk, Matt Houston,* and *Murder She Wrote.* She married Mike Farrell of *MASH* fame.

Diane McBain started her acting career at Warner Brothers, appearing in numerous TV shows including *Maverick, The Alaskans, Bourbon Street Beat, Sugarfoot, 77, Sunset Strip,* and *Hawaiian Eye,* and later graduating to a co-starring role as socialite Daphne Dutton in the short-lived detective series *Surfside Six.* She played "her first movie bad girl" in the camp classic *Parrish,* and from then on was virtually typecast. Film and TV roles poured in, including guest shots on such cult shows as *Burke's Law* (four times), *The Man from UNCLE* (twice, once alongside *Blue Hawaii's* Angela Lansbury), *The Wild Wild West* (twice), *and Batman* (twice), in one of which she appeared colored completely pink (with pink poodle) as "Pinky Pinkston" in a team-up tie-in episode with her old *Surfside Six* co-star Van Williams, then playing *The Green Hornet.* However, after *Spinout,* she found herself being offered only B-movies, albeit future schlock classics such as *Thunder Alley* (another race car movie, this time with Fabian and beach babe Annette Funicello), hilarious drugs drama *Maryjane* (in which she plays a prim schoolteacher secretly dealing drugs, again with Fabian), and *The Mini-Skirt Mob* (an anodyne biker movie with *Girls! Girls! Girls!'* Jeremy Slate in the cast).

Many more in the same vein followed, including the self-explanatory *I Sailed to Tahiti With an All-Girl Crew.* The 1970s saw her turning up in such cult series as *Land of the Giants, The Mod Squad, Barbary Coast, Charlie's Angels, Police Story,* and *Hawaii Five-O,* while in the '80s she found herself in *Dallas, One Day at a Time* (with the wonderful name of Foxy Humdinger) and *General Hospital.* Other TV roles came along in *Matt Houston, Knight Rider, Airwolf,* and *Sabrina, the Teenage Witch,* followed by more B-movies such as *Puppet Master 5* and *Invisible Mom II.*

"Elvis was extremely good-looking, very sexy, and a major gentleman" said McBain. "I had not been a fan of Elvis, so I didn't know what to expect. I was really impressed by him. He was a joy to work with, especially in the scenes when he'd sing to you. Can you think of anything nicer than being serenaded by Elvis?". For other actresses, such as Millie Perkins, Julie Parrish, and Irene Tsu, it was a cause of major embarrassment, as they struggled to look fascinated by the miming of an equally embarrassed Elvis. Shelley Fabares, on the other hand, found it provoked a you-had-to-be-there moment and a major case of the giggles for both herself and Elvis, when his breath started flicking her hair style around by accident, and neither of them could get through their romantic moment without cracking up.

"I was never a subtle-type chick" said Deborah Walley in *Beach Blanket Bingo,* and she certainly proves her point with her performance as the tomboy drummer in *Spinout,* one of the film's highlights. In a sea of '60s beach movie starlets, Deborah Walley was an original, one of a kind. Spotted by a Columbia talent scout, she went from playing Chekov in New York to Gidget in Hollywood within the space of a few months when she was cast in *Gidget Goes Hawaiian* in 1961 alongside James Darren.

An enthusiastic and energetic actress who excelled at light comedy, she made a couple of Disney films before signing on for a succession of beach movies and similar fare throughout the '60s. She appeared frequently alongside the likes of Frankie Avalon and Tommy Kirk in such teen titles as *Beach Blanket Bingo, Sergeant Deadhead,* the wonderfully hare-brained *Ski Party* (template for numerous 1980s teen comedies), the infamous *Ghost in the Invisible Bikini,* and *It's a Bikini World,* and ended up married to *Beach Blanket Bingo* co-star John Ashley.

A regular role in the often funny two season sit-com *Mothers-in-Law* from 1966 to '68 alongside Eve Arden and Kaye Ballard turned out to be something of a mixed blessing. A sort of *Lucy Show* without Lucy produced by Desi Arnaz, it gave her little to do, as the two leading ladies inevitably consumed all the screen time, leaving her in a nothing role as a sort of glorified bit player (she was also the runner-up for the equally bland role of Lucy's daughter on *The Lucy Show* a few years earlier). Other TV roles included spots in the cult shows *The Naked City, Route 66,* and *Burke's Law,* as well as *Wagon Train, Gomer Pyle,* and *Love, American Style.*

Ironically, while playing the frustrated tomboy surrounded by all the glamor girls, it was Walley who became the object of Elvis' attentions when not filming, although as with Donna Douglas earlier, it was primarily due to a shared interest in Presley's obsession with mystic mumbo-jumbo. Slight in stature and susceptible to bad ideas, she was perfect for Presley, but smart enough to know that she had no future with him. She was seeking freedom, after all, not the stifling seclusion of life with the Memphis Mafia. Walley had something of a spinout of her own as the '60s crashed and burned, tumbling headlong into the wild side of hippie culture and narrowly avoiding becoming a casualty of the era's excesses (she took several acid trips during those years). She left acting to raise her children from a second marriage at the end of the '70s, but accepted two gimmicky retro roles in *Simon and Simon* (the producers of which had a thing about hiring faces from the '60s) and 1990s beach descendant *Baywatch*.

"Some film experiences were wonderful" she told interviewer Kim Holston. "I loved working with Norman Taurog and Elvis was wonderful, which was quite something, because I really didn't think too much of him when I started *Spinout*, and we became fast friends during the filming".

Jack Mullaney kept himself employed throughout the '60s as the sit-com stooge of choice, securing regular supporting roles as best buddy on a variety of comedy series one after the other (*The Ann Sothern Show, Ensign O'Toole, My Living Doll,* and *It's About Time*), although none of them lasted more than a couple of years. Mullaney had previously appeared in *Tickle Me* in the same sort of second banana role.

Jimmy Hawkins was a child actor during the early '50s in a sit-com called *The Ruggles*, and later took supporting roles in *Annie Oakley* (on which the very young Shelley Fabares once guested) and *Ichabod and Me*, another forgotten sit-com. He had recurring roles on Fabares' *Donna Reed Show* gig and the *Ozzie and Harriet* sit-com. Hawkins had previously appeared in *Girl Happy*, again with Fabares, once more as a sidekick. Neither Mullaney or Hawkins did much after *Spinout*.

Carl Betz, fresh off *The Donna Reed Show*, went straight from *Spinout* into a new series, the title role in contemporary law drama *Judd for the Defense*. He often played manipulative bad guys in shows like *Mission: Impossible, The Name of the Game,* and *McCloud*. Warren Berlinger, who has some good bits of business as Betz' comic relief aide, was soon to be stuck in TV, ploughing through guest shots in dreary shows like *Ironside, Emergency, Murder She Wrote, Simon and Simon, Knight Rider,* and *Misfits of Science*. He also worked for Stephen Cannell, appearing in episodes of *The Rockford Files, The A-Team,* and *Riptide*; one of his last roles was in an episode of *Friends*. Here, he has a thankless early nerd role, but makes the most of it.

Will Hutchins, playing a friendly gourmet cop who makes out with Walley's Les, was the star of the 1957-'61 western series *Sugarfoot*. Hutchins would be back for *Clambake* as--yes, the comedy sidekick. Among the girls were Dodie Marshall, later seen in *Easy Come, Easy Go*, Nancy Czar, also in *Girl Happy*, Deanna Lund, also in *Paradise, Hawaiian Style*, and Thordis Brandt, a *Man/Girl from UNCLE* bit player later seen in *Live a Little, Love a Little*. Next door neighbors the Cranleighs were played by Hollywood veterans Cecil Kellaway and Una Merkel, both old pros at playing old timers. Ditto, Frederic Worlock, their butler.

Originally titled *Raceway,* the title was changed when a songwriting team composed of Ben Weisman, Sid Wayne, and Ed Wood ingenue Dolores Fuller submitted a song called "Spinout" that was used as the title song. This didn't stop some idiot calling it *California Holiday* in Britain.

Easy Come, Easy Go (1967)

wr. Allan Weiss, Anthony Lawrence, dir. John Rich, pr. Hal Wallis (Paramount)

with Elvis Presley (Ted Jackson), Dodie Marshall (Jo Symington), Pat Harrington Jnr. (Judd Whitman), Pat Priest (Dina Bishop), Skip Ward (Gil Carey), Frank McHugh (Captain Jack), Elsa Lanchester (Madame Neherina), Diki Lerner (Zoltan), Sandy Kenyon, Ed Griffith, Read Morgan, Mickey Elley (army buddies), Jonathan Hole (assessor), Elaine Beckett, Shari Nims (boat girls), Kay York (Tanya), Robert Isenberg (artist), and the Jordanaires

Elvis sings: "Easy Come, Easy Go" (over titles); "The Love Machine" (in nightclub); "Yoga Is As Yoga Does" (in yoga class with Elsa Lanchester); "You Gotta Stop" (at party); "Sing, you Children" (at party); "I'll Take Love" (finale with Pat Harrington and Dodie Marshall at club)

"This isn't a very popular view" mused Elvis associate Lamar Fike, "but the Colonel's formula was correct. The serious stuff--the movies that didn't have many songs in them--flopped. As far as the movie years were concerned--and by that I mean the '60s--they might have been years of incredible frustration (for Elvis), but they were also years of incredible money". Said relative Billy Smith "The fact that the money was still coming in from the movies meant that the Colonel was going to ride that horse 'til it dropped". But with the appropriately titled *Easy Come, Easy Go*, the horse's legs were beginning to buckle...

Although not the last in this style, *Easy Come, Easy Go* was the last of the Hal Wallis-produced Elvis movies, a foregone conclusion after it failed to recoup its costs, the first Elvis film not to make a profit. Paramount had already lost faith in its once profitable star, having pretty much decided that *Paradise, Hawaiian Style* would be Presley's swan song, and made little attempt to promote it. Writing again was Alan Weiss, once again paired with Anthony Lawrence, his partner on *Roustabout* and *Paradise, Hawaiian Style*. The plot is more frivolous and less grounded in reality than *Roustabout*, but there's more to the story than their previous collaboration on *Paradise, Hawaiian Style*, which was carried by the scenery. Directing was John Rich, who had made *Roustabout* with a young and enthusiastic Presley in earlier, happier days, but had belatedly seen the writing on the wall and failed to desert the sinking ship in time.

By 1967, Elvis was angrily resigned to his fate film-wise (having now given up on the over-ambitious fantasies about serious films that he once entertained), and as it turned out, Presley, looking like an overweight, puffy-cheeked cartoon chipmunk, spent six weeks making a film that neither he nor Rich wanted to make, and that both Wallis and Parker felt ambivalent about. Record sales were hurting, and Presley felt vulnerable, outdated, and directionless--a mood which this film could have done little to dissipate, for reasons to be discussed.

It was not a happy time. Various members of the entourage were feuding with Priscilla and each other, the Colonel had stepped up his war of nerves with Presley's hairdresser guru Larry Geller (both Geller and Presley were convinced, probably wrongly, that the comedic yoga scene satirising trendy faddism was inserted in the script deliberately by the Colonel to mock the foolishness of it all), and as Wallis and Parker played one-upmanship games for the last time, Presley was kept in Palm Springs, as per his contract, for the full two months agreed to, despite filming finishing two weeks earlier.

Happily, none of this behind-the-scenes bad feeling comes across in the film, a typical what-a-wacky-world-we-live-in late '60s endeavor aimed at the sort of audience not actually living in that wacky world, and written by men who could only guess at it, peering through the sweet shop window at the candy inside.

Elvis plays former navy frogman and minesweeper Ted Jackson, who takes up fortune hunting when he spots a sunken wreck potentially full of booty while on his final mission. Unluckily for him, happy-go-lucky fun-seeker Dina Bishop (Pat Priest) and her sour-faced blond boyfriend Gil Carey (Skip Ward) are also aware of the wreck, and the race is on to claim salvage. For this, all parties need to secure diving equipment from the loopy Captain Jack, a marine supplies store owner and former kiddie TV show host (of the good ship Lollipop) who has a powerful phobia about actually being on water. If you can accept the absurdity of the Cap'n having the only appropriate diving equipment not just in his shop, but in the whole coastal area, then you can enjoy the escapades that follow.

With the usual misunderstanding of mixed-up motives (except that here, Elvis' intentions are base rather than noble), Elvis teams up with the other woman in the inevitable lust triangle, a flighty arty type named Jo Symington (the film plays that favorite '50s/'60s card of having Elvis looking for a Joe Symington who knows about the ship's cargo, until pleasantly surprised).

Jo's interest in the artistic endeavors of the brainless bouncing bubbleheads she hangs out with not only provides Elvis/Ted with his first exposure to the faddists of the swingin' '60s, for whom she wants to provide an arts center (they already seem to have one, in her house), but also a charitable use for the ship's fortune when finally recovered. When Ted's true motives for finding the wreck are uncovered, he snaps "Would you like me any better if I hated money, grew a beard, and stood on my head?" (the latter a reference to kooky Jo's favored method of relaxation-- few of the exceptionally well-scrubbed hippies, incidentally, other than best buddy Judd, are actually bearded, or even long-haired!).

Elvis struggles manfully from the off with the film's various indignities--heading for shore with his military buddies in the film's opening, he is obliged to mime badly (he mimes badly throughout every number) while using an oar as a mock guitar. Plainly embarrassed, he clearly realises the absurdity of the situation, and abandons the idea mid-song, playing around with the oar and his colleagues self-consciously. It's not often you can see Elvis the actor visibly squirming behind Elvis the character.

The film opens like a bad copy of *G.I. Blues,* complete with sexist banter over a spinning wheel with girls' photos and 'phone numbers on, but as the uniforms fade into the background, *Easy Come, Easy Go* soon takes the well-worn path of every other Elvis film that opens with him leaving the service. His long-time-no-see best buddy in this instance is, preposterously, a horn-blowing beatnik, who greets Ted and his uniformed buddies fulsomely, and with not the slightest shred of disdain or disinterest a real '60s hippie might have demonstrated to a man in uniform (then again, he is still a beatnik, rather than an actual hippie, even though it's 1967!).

Similarly, Jo and her pals are more beach party bingo than Haight-Ashbury, all smartly dressed in wonderful 1960s fashions rather than the penniless rags the script suggests. The yoga scene that so infuriated Presley and Geller (with frizzy-haired oldster Madame Neherina "yearning to communicate across a void of spiritual isolation") looks more like a dance class where something's been added to the drinking water, but even less convincing are the scenes where Elvis/Ted picks up a guitar, looking for all the world like a really bad Elvis impersonator for hire. The driving force behind rock and roll without whom no other rock performer would have existed might as well still be grasping the oar for all the conviction he musters.

Later, as Elvis wanders through Symington's large home (like many 1960s hippies, she is plainly quite well-off), he sees a performance piece with a kissing couple having a huge vat of spaghetti tipped over them ("It's called a happening!" sighs a bubblehead, rapturously), and then a multi-colored rainbow recreation of Yves Klein's famous work involving bikini'd paint-covered girls rolling their bodies along a white canvas (Klein's models were blue only and completely naked, but this film is about two years too early to dare to show Elvis gawking at nudity). Indeed, the total absence of drugs use, stoned idiots, and naked lovemaking only adds to the Hollywood unreality of the hippie/pop art sequences. Musically, the film is spartan, with a paltry six songs including the opening titles, and two of them novelty songs, the comedy yoga bit and a rousing parting-the-sea (of kids) revivalist hand-clapper more suited to a traveling tent show than a hippie orgy (even a Disney-ish cleaned up one).

Chorus girl and nightclub singer Dodie Marshall had worked as a dancer on such series as *Shindig* and *Hullabaloo* and had big ambitions that she was entitled to. She is superb in *Easy Come, Easy Go*, vibrant, sexy, energetic, likeable, and clearly talented, one of Presley's prettiest and most desirable leading ladies. She had appeared in minor roles on *My Favorite Martian* and *The Man from UNCLE*, and parlayed a minor one-line, two scene role dancing maniacally in the closing scenes of *Spinout* into a starring role in this following Presley film. She showcases beautifully a fine wardrobe of enviable 1960s fashions on a gorgeous body in both *Spinout* and *Easy Come, Easy Go*, dances like there's no tomorrow, and is as sexy as Ann Margret when she wears a pair of tiny white shorts.

"I want to be a star and I see no reason to conceal it" she announced to the world proudly. "I want to get to the top of my profession and it's more than just an expression of ego. I have the desire and some of the qualifications and I hope I can acquire the others". Amazingly--because she got good reviews and she was excellent in the film--she promptly disappeared.

Originally cast as Dina Bishop was Britisher Suzanna Leigh, who had portrayed Judy Hudson in *Paradise, Hawaiian Style* but impatiently dropped out to pursue offers in Europe when she became a pawn in a spiteful dispute between American and British actors' unions--the American union refused to allow Leigh to play the role because, apparently, Charlton Heston had been refused permission to take a role in Britain by the nabobs of Equity, the British actors' union. American actress Pat Priest, who had just finished two TV seasons as Marilyn Munster in the successful sit-com *The Munsters,* stepped into the role, the second time in her career she had benefited from another actress' unavailability. When Beverly Owen, who had originally accepted the role of the Munster daughter, became unhappy in her personal life and wanted to leave Hollywood and return home, the producers had kindly released her from the series, and Priest--who had worked her way up through various guest star roles on other shows, including bits with Bob Hope and Jack Benny, and episodes of *Dobie Gillis, Doctor Kildare, Perry Mason, Death Valley Days, My Favorite Martian* and *Voyage to the Bottom of the Sea*--had taken over. It was regular work, but as anonymous as her previous work, overshadowed as she was as the non-monster Munster, by the other cast members, all comedy caricatures of Universal movie creatures. The role in *Easy Come, Easy Go* had gone some way in compensating for a recent career disappointment of her own, when despite seeing out the *Munsters* series, she found herself replaced in the feature film *Munster, Go Home* by the younger Debbie Watson. It was all part of the Hollywood wheel of fortune, but it had hurt her, and apparently her sympathetic supporting cast on the show as well.

Having spent her time on *The Munsters* in demure 1950s-style dress, her appearance in *Easy Come, Easy Go* as a scheming, immoral bikini-clad seductress is a revelation in all senses. She and her fellow beach babes look very desirable in their encounter with the navy, but the role itself is as nondescript and shallow as that of Marilyn Munster. Her previous film roles had been uncredited bit parts, but she might well have wished her next film to leave her name off the credits as well--it was the schlock sci-fi Z-movie *The Incredible Two-Headed Transplant*. A few more TV appearances followed *The Munsters,* including *The Lucy Show, Mannix, Ironside, Mission: Impossible,* three *Bewitched,* and *The Mary Tyler Moore Show,* but it was soon clear that *The Munsters* would be the highpoint of her career and she retired to marriage, motherhood, and *Munster* memorabilia shows.

"Elvis was wonderful to work with" she told sit-com buff Stephen Cox for his book on *The Munsters.* "He never argued with anybody and was not temperamental. He treated me beautifully. Incidentally, I bought his car from him... for 4,000 dollars. Do you know what it would be worth today if I still had it? I remember the keys had a keychain that said EP. The keychain alone would be worth a fortune today". Priest must be the only person who came into Elvis' orbit and wasn't *given* a car.

Elsa Lanchester, who has just one scene as the demented Madame Neherina, and Frank McHugh, wonderful as silly Cap'n Jack (get a load of his mad laugh), were both veteran old-timers who were professional enough to ignore the film's troubles and any odd behavior from younger, less experienced cast members, and just come in, practice their craft, make a meal of their opportunity, and collect the money. Lanchester was, of course, best remembered for *The Bride of Frankenstein,* the camp classic of 1935, but she had kept busy since in movies, and thirty years later had recently appeared for Disney in *Mary Poppins* and *Blackbeard's Ghost,* racking up camp credentials in two editions of *Burke's Law* and as another crazed eccentric in an episode of *The Man from UNCLE,* "The Brain Killer Affair". Her role as Madame Neherina was more in the same vein, and the role is so silly it almost seems as though she has strayed out of a Disney film. Frank McHugh had been playing light relief roles since the end of the silents, and like Lanchester, kept steadily employed, often but not always in musicals (one of these memorable exceptions was his poignant role in *The Roaring Twenties,* alongside James Cagney). Although his character has the potential to be, like Neherina, thoroughly annoying, he never is. He is a wonderfully silly character, typical of 1960s TV eccentrics and like something out of *The Avengers.*

Pat Harrington Jnr., the son of comedian Pat Harrington, had followed in his father's footsteps as a game show host/participant and comedy performer, usually in broad, loud, outrageous character parts. He had appeared on *The Steve Allen Show* and *The Danny Thomas Show* during the 1950s, flitted around through various guest roles in the '60s (including the inevitable *Man from UNCLE,* twice, once as his recurring character from *The Tonight Show,* Guido Panzini) and spent nearly ten years in the sit-com *One Day at a Time* as Schneider the building superintendent, a typical Harrington role, which ran from 1975 to 1984 and won him an Emmy. The role of beatnik buddy Judd Whitman was a walk in the park.

Skip Ward, on the other hand, was the sort of muscular young actor cast for his looks. He appeared as a race car driver in the B-movie *Road Racers,* a seaman in the *Voyage to the Bottom of the Sea* feature film, as a footballer in *The Beverly Hillbillies,* and as a surfer in *Batman.* He later went on to produce sports programs and TV movies.

Of the bit players, Sandy Kenyon was better known for straight-faced dramatic roles, although he often appeared in uniform. Read Morgan was a stunt-man who often took monster roles in shows like *The Outer Limits.* Giving Elvis the bad news about his treasure trove uncredited is Jonathan Hole, who snobbishly delivered bad news with relish (or received it with stifled horror) from behind a desk throughout the '60s in virtually every sit-com and light-hearted show on the air. Shari Nims, one of the boat girls, appeared as a ridiculous-looking orange-skinned alien in the *Star Trek* episode "The Apple". She and her colleague look much more appealing here!

Diki Lerner does an amusing, swishy, over-the-top turn as the wild-eyed artist Zoltan (the old timers behind this picture had not missed the fact that there was a large homosexual element in the art world), a typically deranged character who, while Elvis is foolish enough to leave his red sports car unattended for a few minutes, turns the vehicle into a dismantled and dismembered "automobile mobile" just as our heroes need to beat Didi and Gil to the premises of Cap'n Jack. Lerner, actually a mime and traditional vaudeville-style specialist, had previously appeared in a fondly-remembered spooker from *Boris Karloff's Thriller,* "The Weird Tailor", as a shop mannequin that comes to life, and then as a dancing fool in the later episode "The Innocent Bystanders".

The golden, oblong, fur-lined, surfboard-seated rattletrap the threesome are forced to borrow until the other car can be reassembled is an amusing creation of car customiser George Barris, best known for creating the *Batman* TV series' Batmobile and the Munster Koach for *The Munsters.* Barris and his wife were good friends of Elvis, who was a frequent client (Priscilla stayed with them during her first trip to the U.S. from Germany when Elvis came out of the army), and this particular creation would later turn up in the *Batman* TV series itself the following year, for further use as the Joker's means of transport in "The Joker's Last Laugh"/"The Joker's Epitaph" and "Surf's Up! Joker's Under!" (with Skip Ward as one of the Joker's surfer henchmen).

Much of the pop art of the 1960s was stunning, and some fabulous and genuinely mind-expanding work was created during that decade that changed the way everybody--even, subliminally, the detractors--looked at the world, but such anything-goes-experimentalism inevitably attracted no-talents, charlatans, and opportunists who have prospered and multiplied with each passing decade, often to the detriment of traditional art thanks to the buffoonery of the art world. Much of the rubbish started to appear with the increase of drugs use and abuse as the '60s wore on, which presumably dulled or distorted critical faculties, combined with a sort of emperor's new clothes stance adopted by the unsure, and much of the disdain levelled at the pop art phenomenon was less about trying to appreciate the ideas than understandable rage and bafflement at the stupid amounts of money involved in the buying and selling of it. It may be legitimate to display a pile of soup cans or building bricks in a creative environment to let the world see them in a different way, but it should not increase the value of them!

But what we are seeing in *Easy Come, Easy Go* is the familiar spectacle of the puzzled and confused middle-aged writers and directors in Hollywood who neither liked or understood the massive changes the world was going through in terms of art and fashion during that tumultuous decade, writing out their frustrations in entertainment for middle-America.

This half-true, half-witless portrayal of 1960s pop art in TV and film was everywhere at this time, and it only ever concerned itself with the phonies, and never identified, or even acknowledged, the talent. A classic example is "Pop Goes the Easel", a 1965 episode of pulpy detective series *Honey West,* in which a pop art soup can is confused with the real thing, an art dealer offers thousands for a cardboard cut-out, and the villain of the piece makes his money selling pop art to ignorant suckers to finance a stunning fine art collection (which, interestingly, includes Picasso and Monet among the more traditional names, thus proving that yesterday's rebel is today's mainstream). The idea that an art dealer might patronise pop art to a gullible outside world while secretly coveting the Old Masters was frequently revisited, and also gets an airing in the *Man from UNCLE* episode titled--what else?--"The Pop Art Affair".

In a wonderfully funny *Batman* episode "Pop Goes the Joker" (not one with Barris' car), in a scene that would be recreated in the 1989 *Batman* feature film, the villainous harlequin of the comics prances around an art gallery vandalising the conventional works on display with a paint-filled spray-gun. This immediately increases their value to the wealthy suckers who flock to buy the mess that's been made. Cesar Romero gives a hilarious performance as the Joker, hailed as a new artistic genius, quizzically turning to the assembled connoisseurs for justification for his outrageous actions whenever they are questioned, visibly relieved when it comes forth every time. Similar cynical scams are perpetrated in episodes of *Top Cat* ("Dibble's Double", with turtle tracks), *The Monkees* ("Art for Monkees' Sake", with a beatnik accidentally smearing a shirt with paint and declaring it a work of art) and Britain's *Randall and Hopkirk (Deceased) aka My Partner, the Ghost* ("Somebody Just Walked Over My Grave", with bicycle wheels) to name just three of many examples. By the time *The Simpsons* got around to satirising modern art (Homer's barbecue gone wrong is hailed as a work of genius in "Mom and Pop Art"), the same reactionary old jokes had suddenly acquired a validity that was unfair back in the 1960s.

However, the main thing wrong with *Easy Come, Easy Go* is Elvis. Apart from his appearance, with the constant pill popping and poor diet visibly making its mark, he looks bored rather than bemused (as the script asks), comes across as selfish and surly (something that hadn't been seen in the screen Elvis since *Jailhouse Rock*), and in the film's worst moments, slightly goofy. He was now just that little bit too old to be playing baffled and naive.

Unfortunately, baffled and naive are what he and the writers are, all three of them playing at struggling to understand the 1960s counter-culture through a sort of pointing finger parody that only existed in Hollywood movies trying to figure it out. Instead, the finger points back at them, confirming Elvis as ten years out of date, a sort of condescending older brother to the happy hipsters and bogus beatniks gyrating around him. The mistake did not go un-acknowledged--*Clambake* and *Speedway*, the last of this sort of film, would both send Elvis back through time to an early-'60s, rather than late-'60s milieu.

Double Trouble (1967)

wr. Jo Heims, from Marc Brandel, dir. Norman Taurog, pr. Judd Bernard, Irving Winkler (MGM)

with Elvis Presley (Guy Lambert), Annette Day (Jill Conway), Yvonne Romain (Claire Dunham), John Williams (Uncle Gerald), Norman Rossington (Archie Brown), Chips Rafferty (Arthur Babcock), Monty Landis (Georgie), Michael Murphy (Morley/American tourist), Leon Askin (Inspector De Groote), John Alderson (mysterious man), Stanley Adams (Captain Roach), Walter Burke (First Mate), Helene Winston (Gerda), Monique Lemaire (desk clerk), the Weire Brothers, and the G-Men.

Elvis sings: "Double Trouble" (over titles); "Baby, If You'll Give Me All Your Love" (in disco); "Could I Fall in Love" (to Annette Day); "Long Legged Girl" (impromptu performance on deck of ship to passengers); "City by Night" (to Yvonne Romain in nightclub); "Old MacDonald" (comic version on truck to Annette Day); "I Love Only One Girl" (at carnival); "There's So Much World to See" (to Annette Day)

A dismal late entry attempting to pointlessly return to Elvis' just out of the army period, *Double Trouble* marries themes from *G.I. Blues* and *Kissin' Cousins* to a vacation spot Elvis never got to outside of Germany, the rest of Europe.

Although the public never knew it during Presley's lifetime, the bogus Colonel Parker was later discovered to be a Dutchman with a false name as well as a false title, and not only possessed no passport, but as an illegal immigrant with a shady background, was unable to pursue one. *Double Trouble* indeed.

Here, a host of British-born character actors residing in Hollywood are dropped into the Disney-esque middle-American version of Europe for a dated, thin yarn that wheels out all the predictable faces and cliches of the 1960s jet-set era, including the sinister, threatening carnival where only half the people are there to blindly have fun while the other half brazenly menace and terrorise the leads, and a tiresome song and dance number that wheels out every stereotypical foreign country cliche in the history of cinema (here come the Germans--and look, they're all wearing lederhosen, hats with feathers in them, and carrying swilling tankards of beer!).

Although it looks, sounds, and feels like a British-made cheapie, it's actually been shot on the MGM backlot in the U.S., on the same European village sets employed in countless episodes of *Combat* and *The Man from*

UNCLE. Regular viewers of those shows will have no trouble recognising the narrow back streets or the arched bridge across the river.

It's an insightful look at how America--thanks to Hollywood--viewed Europe at the time; every single character from the briefest bit player to the leading roles is odd, weird, crooked, ugly, wicked, corrupt, mad, menacing, or merely eccentric. At least the jet set era exploits presented in *I Spy* and the *UNCLE* franchise made Europe look like fun. No-one would leave the shores of America if they took their lead from *Double Trouble*.

If the reader still hopes to be surprised during a first viewing, he or she should view the film before reading further, as we now need to discuss the plot.

Made before *Easy Come, Easy Go*, but released afterwards, *Double Trouble* is one of the last, and most certainly the least, of all Elvis' happy-go-lucky movies. It's more dreary-go-sappy. While preferable to the dreadful mistakes perpetuated toward the end of Presley's film career, it is easily his most minor effort, a tired and cliched caper movie made at the end of the fad for both caper movies and America's fascination with Europe. It looks like a glamour-free backlot episode of third season *Man from UNCLE* filmed by Walt Disney, and one almost expects Mary Poppins or 101 dalmatians to hove into view (author Brandel was story editor on the short-lived cliche-strewn James Bond knock-off *Amos Burke--Secret Agent*).

Once again, as with *Girl Happy*, Jeff Alexander's heavy-handed score suits the heavy-handed script, with blaring musical cues to guide the snoozing audience ("Rule, Britannia" booms out every time Britain or the British appear), although this time there can be no defense of potential satirical intent.

When cutting corners in sunny locales (*Fun in Acapulco, Paradise, Hawaiian Style*), producers still ended up with a bright and breezy film, as cheap and cheerful as it might appear. But when recreating the post-war austerity of drab and shabby Europe on a low budget, one simply ends up with a drab and shabby film (*Double Trouble* is so cheap, the establishing shot of London doesn't even move--not so much a travelogue, as Elvis sometimes called his films, as a postcard).

As admirable and foolishly ambitious as it might have been to attempt to put Elvis' trademark character (here a modestly successful singer named Guy Lambert, but as American as apple pie as ever) into new surroundings, away from America and the sunshine, and floundering in a gloomy, mocked-up Europe, audiences must have wondered what Elvis Presley had come down to. If Elvis was going to visit film-land's version of

Europe, one wonders why he wasn't dropped into one of Hollywood's recreations of swingin' London so ruthlessly satirised by the *Austin Powers* franchise. The only answer has to be cost, but the result is that both Elvis and MGM look cheap and down on their luck.

Europe is presented not as a bright, exciting, cultured environment full of history and tradition, but a scary and stupid near-medieval world where no-one is normal or trustworthy, and every action is foolish, foreign and inexplicable. The intimidating, masked, threatening Hallowe'en-ish carnival is light years away from the playful scamming of the fairground in *Roustabout* or the colorful eccentricity of the chautauqua in the forthcoming *Trouble With Girls,* and more like Mexico's annual Day of the Dead. *Carnival of Souls* would be less unpleasant.

Of the leading ladies, Annette Day, supposedly discovered on the Portobello Road (but most likely in the imaginations of MGM's publicists), promptly disappeared, while French-born Yvonne Romain had spent her career so far in mostly lurid minor British horror films. She fared little better in the U.S., where, before making this Elvis film the following year, she had co-starred in the sex comedy *The Swinger* alongside none other than Ann Margret (whose career was being dragged downward by besotted admirer and former benefactor George Sidney in one of a string of silly sex kitten roles).

British actor John Williams had been toiling at the bottom of cast lists in Hollywood for almost a decade before he attracted attention by appearing in both Hitchcock's *Dial M for Murder* and Billy Wilder's *Sabrina* in the same year, 1954. Another Hitchcock, *To Catch a Thief,* followed in '55, and another Billy Wilder, *Witness for the Prosecution,* in 1957. Williams was invariably cast either as the ubiquitous representative of Scotland Yard, or as an urbane gentleman criminal, and kept busy throughout the '50s, '60s and into the '70s in these sort of roles, but inevitably his opportunities were limited. Director Taurog had previously used him in Hal Wallis' Jerry Lewis film *Visit to a Small Planet* in 1959, also starring Joan Blackman.

On TV at around this time he was well-cast as a slightly too old William Shakespeare in "The Bard", a satirical *Twilight Zone* episode, and played a recurring police inspector role in the short-lived series *The Rogues.* When *Columbo* went to Britain, in 1972's "Dagger of the Mind", Williams was the murder victim. There is a career of obvious limitations to be had for those handful of Britishers willing to exploit the American perception of jolly old Britain, guv'nor, but only if one plays up to the stereotype rather than complaining about it. Like Maurice Evans and Bernard Fox, to name but two, Williams milked it for all it was worth, and so could hardly object that he always played the same role. Here, he plays the stuffy guardian of Annette Day's childlike love interest, but even his dapper Uncle Gerald turns out to be a cold-hearted murderer and the instigator of the confusingly told plot, which is gussied up with comedy jewel smugglers (Norman Rossington and Chips Rafferty; the credits seem uncertain who is who, so mine have gone by the script) and seafaring swindlers (Stanley Adams and Walter Burke).

The two women, intended murder victim Jill (Day), and worldly femme fatale Claire (Romain), both behave like bunny-boiling stalkers with the word Trouble written across their faces like a Tex Avery cartoon character. Jill is about to turn eighteen, although she still behaves like a twelve-year-old, while the beautiful Claire sends out warning signs simply by always being on her own wherever she turns up. Why Elvis would want either one of them--both oxymoronic hard-to-get groupies--is a mystery when wiggly go-go-booted dolly birds are gyrating all around him every time he picks up a guitar.

The revelation that Day's Jill is stand-offish because she's hiding her true age is not only highly unlikely behavior for jailbait, but was a somewhat tactless story idea given that those who knew him were well aware of Presley's preference for waif-like barely legal youngsters; he was about to marry Priscilla. Consequently, his character's horror at discovering Jill is a few days off eighteen (in reality, Presley had been counting the days to Priscilla's coming of age for months) can only provoke laughter. As everyone knows, Elvis liked 'em young. Uncle Gerald wants to bump wide-eyed Jill off before her birthday so that he can filch her inheritance; his surname is Waverly, despite--or perhaps, because of-- the same name already being familiar as that of the British boss of UNCLE, the franchise's fad then at its peak.

Standard unconvincing murder attempts in the form of unlucky accidents follow as the comic relief smugglers hide their stolen diamonds in Day's luggage (of course) and bungle all attempts to get it back (of course). Presley's best buddy is the gurning Monty Landis, absurdly cavorting around Elvis with a guitar and Beatle-cut despite being plainly over forty, if not fifty years of age. The one normal-looking person, a vacationing American of course (Michael Murphy), provides the film's only genuine surprise twist when he turns out to be a hired assassin.

Murphy, here a bland villain, went on to do a considerable amount of work for Robert Altman, becoming a regular fixture in many of his films. The Weire Brothers are a hopelessly unfunny trio of comedians in the silent movie tradition, but whatever it is they think they've got, they haven't, and whatever it is they think they're doing, they're not. In a movie revelling in national stereotypes, they do nothing to put paid to the cliche that the Germans have no sense of humor.

Monique Lemaire cornered the small market in bit parts as young French women in the '60s, appearing in episodes of *77, Sunset Strip, The Rogues, Perry Mason, Voyage to the Bottom of the Sea, Combat, Twelve O'Clock High, Batman, The Rat Patrol,* and *The Time Tunnel* (as Marie Antoinette). Britisher John Alderson lurks around silently (and for good reason, we discover, when he finally opens his mouth) as the film's red herring.

Once again, a mediocre Elvis movie is enhanced and carried by a colorful collection of character actors. Norman Rossington usually stayed in Britain to exploit the Ealing image (Chips Rafferty was Australian), while John Alderson and Walter Burke were two other British-born actors finding work as Hollywood Brits. Alderson arrived in the early '60s, and went straight to television, turning up in *The Untouchables, Cheyenne, Combat, Voyage to the Bottom of the Sea, The Man from UNCLE, The Girl from UNCLE, Mission: Impossible, I Spy, The Wild Wild West,* and *The Time Tunnel* (as Little John in their "Revenge of Robin Hood" entry, one of the rare occasions he was able to make an impact). Why he is so bad here is inexplicable. Character actor Walter Burke turned up a few years earlier, in such series as *The Untouchables, The Outer Limits* (in which he appeared twice, once as a gothic hunchback), *77, Sunset Strip* (three times, in a recurring role as a safecracker), *Hawaiian Eye, Bourbon Street Beat, The Twilight Zone, The Detectives, The Munsters, Bewitched, Branded, Batman, Lost in Space* (as a Gepetto-like toymaker), *Voyage to the Bottom of the Sea* (as a leprechaun!), *The Lucy Show, I Spy, It Takes a Thief, Mission: Impossible, I Dream of Jeannie, The Wild Wild West, Ironside, Night Gallery, Ghost Story,* and *Police Story*. One of those odd-looking actors who exploited his appearance to secure a variety of unusual roles, there was no Williams-like typecasting for him.

Austrian-born Leon Askin had memorable bad guy parts in *The Man from UNCLE,* and found series work in the recurring role of the evil General Burkhalter in mid-'60s wartime-set sit-com *Hogan's Heroes*. Typecast by his appearance and accent in "Boris" roles (*My Favorite Martian, I Spy, The Monkees, It Takes a Thief* and *Mission: Impossible* were just a handful of such parts), he later returned to Europe to direct theater. Monty Landis frequently played broad comedic Brit-roles, including episodes of *The Monkees, Get Smart, Batman,* and *The Girl from UNCLE* (alongside Chips Rafferty in "The Paradise Lost Affair"; Rafferty also appeared in *The Monkees*).

Stanley Adams, another expansive and expressive theatrical performer, essayed two well-remembered character parts in TV sci-fi at this time, appearing as the Tribble salesman Cyrano Jones in *Star Trek's* legendary "The Trouble With Tribbles" and as the Carrot Man in the infamous "Great Vegetable Rebellion" for *Lost in Space*. Other roles included *The Twilight Zone, The Untouchables, The Detectives, McHale's Navy, Honey West, Batman, The Ghost and Mrs. Muir,* and *Kolchak--the Night Stalker*. Adams and Burke provide the film's one single, solitary laugh-out-loud moment at the film's close, when they scuttle their ship with *Looney Tunes*-style explosive results and make their escape in a slowly sinking lifeboat, Adams barking orders through a megaphone as they sink beneath the waves.

    For the film's young lovers, the ending has a James Bondish quality to it, as they float into the sunset on the wreckage oblivious to thoughts of food, water, and rescue, and finally enjoying a peaceful moment together. But even this small army of comedic supporting characters couldn't add color to this dismal, drab enterprise, although it would be considerably poorer without them, and they remain the most interesting items of discussion where *Double Trouble* is concerned.

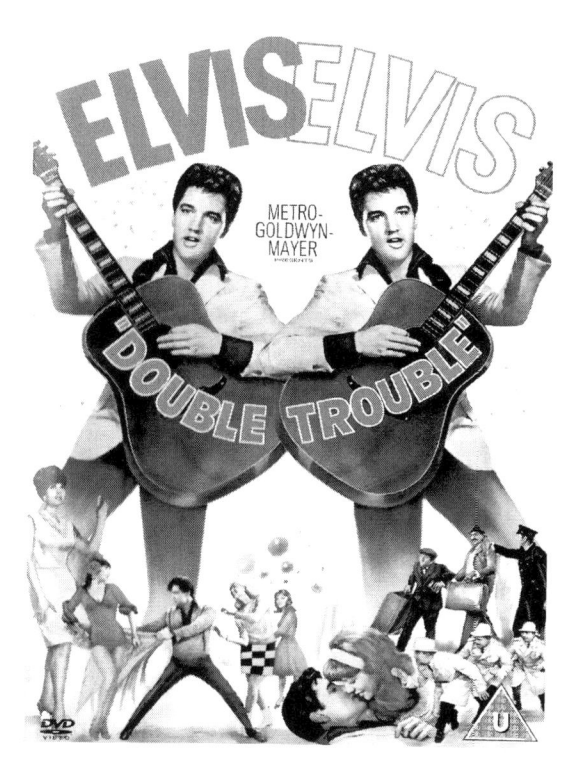

Clambake (1967)

wr. Arthur Browne Jnr., dir. Arthur H. Nadel, pr. Arnold Laven, Arthur Gardner, Jules Levy (UA)

with Elvis Presley (Scott Heyward), Shelley Fabares (Dianne Carter), Will Hutchins (Tom Wilson), Bill Bixby (James Jamieson III), Gary Merrill (Sam Burton), James Gregory (Duster Heyward), Suzie Kaye (Sally/Tom's girlfriend), Amanda Harley (Ellie/Duster's secretary), Jack Good (hotel manager), Hal Peary (hotel doorman), Marj Dusay (sandwich girl), Sue England (cigarette girl), Red West (ice cream seller), Lee Krieger (bartender), Angelique Pettyjohn (Gloria), Olga Kaye (Gigi), Arlene Charles (Olive), Lisa Slagle (Lisa), Sam Riddle (race announcer), Steve Cory (bellhop), Robert Leib (Barasch), Melvin Allen (crew), Herb Barnett (waiter), Lance Le Gault (dancer)

Elvis sings: "Clambake" (over titles); "Who Needs Money?" (with Will Hutchins on the road); "A House That Has Everything" (to Shelley Fabares on the beach); "Confidence" (to kids in playground); "Clambake" (at clambake); "You Don't Know Me" (solo); "Hey, Hey, Hey" (with girls fixing the boat); "The Girl I Never Loved" (solo on beach)

Although Wallis and Paramount had seen the writing on the wall and perceptively bailed with the prophetically titled *Easy Come, Easy Go*, there were still other opportunities to be had at other studios, and with *Clambake*, while all the usual ingredients of an Elvis film remained in the recipe, a new team of producers arrived on the scene.

Arthur Gardner, Jules Levy, and Arnold Laven were old WWII army buddies who had all pursued careers in Hollywood and, in the early 1950s, teamed up together to make their own movies independently of the majors. Gardner was a producer, Levy a producer and script supervisor, and Laven a dialogue coach and director.

Backed by United Artists from the start, they made three routine but lurid crime films in the pulp novel manner, *Without Warning, Vice Squad,* and *Down Three Dark Streets*. A brief foray into science fiction followed, including an above-average creature feature, *The Monster That Challenged the World*, a typical monster from the sea yarn built around the usual formula, but executed with a degree of competence not usually found at the shallow end of the sci-fi pool (Levy, Gardner and Laven were not known for throwing money around, and were notoriously tight with their expenditure, but the monster was of a surprisingly high quality for low-budget SF).

Unfortunately, in the eyes of Hollywood, science-fiction of whatever degree of quality was perceived as the lowest rung of the ladder, and the trio drifted into TV for a few years, where they worked on *The Rifleman, The Detectives, The Law of the Plainsman,* and *The Big Valley.* At the same time, they managed to turn out an occasional movie, including a 1962 version of *Geronimo* and *The Glory Guys,* a 1965 film ten years in the making, from an early Sam Peckinpah script (Peckinpah had worked for them on *The Rifleman*).

Clambake was an extraordinary project for the trio to take on, bizarre and out of character, particularly as they had spent the whole of the 1960s almost exclusively devoted to westerns (indeed, after *Clambake,* Laven would continue to direct westerns throughout the '60s, until spending the 1970s and '80s in television, taking, it seemed, any work he could find-- some westerns, but mostly cops and robbers and super-heroes, and finally, series for Stephen J. Cannell). However, the producers had an eye for a popular format (indeed, never moved beyond it), had worked with other entertainers (Rat Packers Sammy Davis Jnr. and Dean Martin had appeared in their films), and knew other actors who had worked with Elvis (notably Barbara Stanwyck, but also Richard Egan and Wendell Corey, both of whom spoke highly of Presley).

Having had a lengthy and mutually profitable relationship with United Artists, it is entirely plausible that knowing their affinity for formula and tight budgets (the two Wallis/Paramount Elvis essentials), UA approached the trio to oversee their final commitment to Colonel Tom as a favor that would benefit both parties; UA must have seen the declining grosses for the Presley pictures, and for Gardner/Levy/Laven it was another movie opportunity, however lame, and not television. And anyone who could handle Sam Peckinpah could certainly handle the Colonel.

Clambake had nothing to do with the wild west, and very little to do with clambakes. Set in Miami, Florida, it's a frantic, manic rehash of *Blue Hawaii* and *Girl Happy* (even the director's credit is jiggling wildly), right from the opening scene with a red sports car whizzing along a sunny highway. Elvis is Scott Heyward, son of blustering Texan oilman Duster Heyward (James Gregory), anxious to defy his father's well-intentioned hand-outs and make his own way in the world unaided by his father's financial advantage. More to the point, he also wants to find a woman who wants him for himself, rather than his wealth.

"Just once, I'd like to know it's me and not my money... not my car", Elvis/Scott laments to wacky comedy relief Will Hutchins, who, as water-ski instructor Tom Wilson, is failing miserably to score with Marj Dusay's sandwich girl, drooling over Scott's automobile at the gas station. Wilson, like most of us, is unable to afford such whiny self-indulgences, and is happy just to get on any way he can. He willingly--greedily, hungrily--agrees to exchange places with poor-little-rich-boy Scott, and in an off-key, badly mimed duet, they set off for the Shore Hotel, Hutchins in the traditional red sports car Elvis drove during the credits, Presley on the motorbike.

Scott soon spots the girl of his dreams--*Girl Happy*'s Shelley Fabares in her third and final Elvis film--but irony of ironies, she's a scheming and deceitful gold-digger with her sights firmly fixed on millionaire sleazeball James Jamison as she recreates her *Spinout* persona. Jamison is played broadly with just the right mix of cash-bought charisma and unpleasantness by Bill Bixby, who--despite his looks and TV fame as banal nice guy in the 1963-'66 sit-com *My Favorite Martian*--was bravely playing an unsympathetic character. Jamison sets his sights on her in return, and Elvis is left lookin' like a big-eyed mournful hound dog.

While Hutchins' Tom inadvertently sabotages Jamison's efforts at every turn, Elvis/Scott mopes around lecturing Fabares in song (the hummable "A House That Has Everything"). As Dianne Carter, Fabares exhibits just the right degree of camp self-consciousness in her face and body language, a living fluttery-eyed romance comic cartoon girl. These sort of films are harder to make than cynics might realise--so much depends on the performers capturing just the right level to play at, and the entire cast of *Clambake* are spot on. They are real-life comic strip characters come to life, none more so than James Gregory, who makes a meal of his role as Texan oilman Duster Heyward, a three-dimensional bushy-moustached caricature straight out of a Hanna-Barbera cartoon pitched at just the right level to get away with the key scene where Elvis confronts his father and finds respect rather than anger.

The only straight part goes to Gary Merrill, well-cast and perfectly likeable as genial businessman Sam Burton, who sees in Scott a surrogate son and gives him the chance to prove himself in the climactic speedboat race, an event of which sort was now an essential part of the mix since *Viva Las Vegas*. Naturally Scott is up against the smarmy Jamison, who can't resist rubbing Heyward's nose in it in front of the gradually defrosting Dianne. What he doesn't know, and what brings the entire cast of characters together at story's end, is that Scott has perfected Heyward Oil's million dollar failure, a protective super-strong resin nicknamed goop. The race and girl are won, father and son united, and the humiliated Jamison slinks off with no tail between his legs.

Clambake was hardly a tirade against capitalism, and so cannot be accused of the two-faced dishonesty found in similar money-ain't-everything Hollywood fare. Clearly in *Clambake,* it is. Hutchins/Wilson loves every minute of his masquerade as the son of a millionaire, and has the time of his life, Fabares gets her millionaire husband, and Scott returns to his former life having not proven very much at all. He may have got a girl to love him for himself, but she's still marrying money!

What the film does do with good humor is mock the ugly hypocritical side of wealth--the fawning hotel manager (pop producer Jack Good), the two-faced doorman (character actor Hal Peary), the empty life of seducer Jamison/Bixby, a walking, talking example of the old truism that money can't buy you charm, or love, or even always victory. Scott's rejection of his father's money and proffered nepotism (Duster wants him to "come home" and take up the position of vice-president of Heyward Oil) has more to do with reflecting Presley's search for self-justification than any trendy late-'60s position against wealth. Presley had seen poverty. He had no time for posturing middle-class hippies and pretentious rich boy rebels. *Clambake* is honest enough to admit that money makes the world go round, and that cash-flow is only no problem if you have enough of it, something the formerly dirt-poor Elvis and his family knew all too well.

Plainly, *Clambake*--in it's clumsy, simplistic fortune cookie manner-- was also addressing the dilemma that was playing constantly on the mind of Elvis Presley. What was it all for? Who could he trust? These two questions influenced his every thought and action in his personal life throughout the 1960s. Although he would remain interested in bogus spiritual alternatives to the more conventional religious upbringing he had been raised with (he insisted to the press that such interests were in addition to traditional religion, not a substitute, and they probably were), the worst of the introspective faddism phase with crackpot cults and shady gurus was over. Much to the relief of the Memphis Mafia and the Colonel, the despised Larry Geller was no longer so influential, and in retreat.

Unfortunately, the decline of the search-for-the-meaning-of-life obsession coincided with the rise of his pharmaceutical dependency. Not only did he miss the first of his recording sessions for the *Clambake* soundtrack songs, but for the first time ever he failed to meet the agreed start date for the film (he had been late to the set for the first time--twice on consecutive days--on *Easy Come, Easy Go*).

When he did show up on the revised date, a week later in March 1967, he was overweight, visibly unwell, and soon to be concussed after a fall caused by too much pill-popping. Needless to say, the Colonel was beside himself with rage at the unprofessionalism and incompetence of the entourage. All problems were now to go to Joe Esposito, Godfather of the Memphis Mafia, not to Elvis, and no pills, self-help books, or hypnotic hair stylists were to go anywhere near Elvis, he decreed. Geller's hairdressing sessions, once lengthy philosophical forums of supposedly revelatory introspection lasting whole mornings, would now be chaperoned half-hours (Elvis himself had also wised up somewhat). Sackings in the near future were gravely hinted at, a paring down of personnel with no malice intended, Parker insisted, just a natural and necessary streamlining. Sadly, none of these threats stemmed the flow of prescription drugs into the Presley bloodstream.

Bill Bixby, reputedly one of Hollywood's nice guys, albeit a bit of a pot-head, was certainly unharmed by his two roles in the Elvis movies as clumsy, comical no-goods (he was back for *Speedway*, as a similarly smarmy best buddy). Although they didn't help his film career, he had a successful and highly profitable run in television until his death in the early '90s, starring in such long-running series as *The Courtship of Eddie's Father* (1969-'72), *The Magician* (1973-'74), and as the tortured alter-ego of *The Incredible Hulk* (1978-'82), before a couple of misfires persuaded him to turn his hand to directing. Throughout the whole of the 1970s and early '80s he was never not on television (unlike many TV stars who wisely rest a couple of seasons, he went straight from one series to the next, barely pausing to do Disney films, game shows and TV movies inbetween), and was employed constantly for the rest of his life. His life was touched by tragedy--his ex-wife, Elvis dancing girl Brenda Benet, killed herself after the accidental death of their child.

Will Hutchins played a small role in *Spinout* as the policeman boyfriend of drummer Les, and like Jeremy Slate in *Girls! Girls! Girls!* and Dodie Marshall in *Easy Come, Easy Go* was promoted from bit player and let off the leash in a later film, here to play the best buddy/comic relief role of Tom Wilson. He was a former Warner Bros. contract player who had starred in the 1957-'61 western series *Sugarfoot* and guested in other Warners series of the period, including *77, Sunset Strip* and *Surfside Six*.

James Gregory's numerous TV roles included guest shots in shows such as *Dick Powell Theater, The Untouchables, Star Trek, The Wild Wild West, Mission: Impossible, Ironside, The Name of the Game, Kolchak--the Night Stalker, Hawaii Five-O, Night Gallery, McCloud, Columbo,* and *Police Story*. He had just appeared in three of the four Dean Martin *Matt Helm* spy spoofs as McDonald, head of the good guy organisation ICE.

Movie tough guy Gary Merrill was more used to melodramas (some with his then-wife Bette Davis) and various flag-waving he-man military adventures, than anything involving gyrating teenagers. However, the quality of the films he was offered (he had always been a supporting player) declined sharply during the 1950s, attempts at TV series failed, and by the time of *Clambake,* his career was struggling, and he was mostly doing sci-fi at a time when the genre was unfairly looked down on.

He had just made *Around the World Under the Sea* and *Destination: Inner Space,* stood in for an ailing Richard Basehart on a *Voyage to the Bottom of the Sea* episode involving amphibious "menfish" (*Clambake* writer Browne would contribute a "frost men" yarn to the series), and surfaced spluttering from all the underwater escapades to perform well in the costly pilot for *The Time Tunnel.* From his perspective, *Clambake* at least returned him to the mainstream. He handles the straight scenes well, but looks decidedly uncomfortable when the hordes of bimbos arrive to help fix up the boat and he's obliged to look jolly (it looks suspiciously like one of those get-togethers where very little gets done!). Gary Merrill didn't do gaiety very well.

Suzie Kaye danced her buns off in the mid-'60s after a film debut in the big budget musical *West Side Story* in 1961 as Rosalia. After a one-line bit part with Sandra Dee in *Tammy and the Doctor,* she got her first major role in the infamous 1966 cheapie *Women of the Prehistoric Planet* ("I wound up doing a Mambo with flaming red hair on a rocket ship" she told Tom Lisanti). Following in quick succession were *Wild, Wild Winter* with Gary Clarke, *Girl Happy's* Chris Noel and Steve Franken, *Clambake* (for which she wisely went blonde), *It's a Bikini World* with Deborah Walley of *Spinout* and Tommy Kirk, and *C'mon Let's Live a Little* with Bobby Vee and Jackie De Shannon, all of them distinguished by being early '60s-style films put into production in the middle of the peace and love hippie period. Despite virtually growing up on the New York revue show *Star Time Kids* in the 1950s, TV afterwards was sparse, with Kaye just missing out on key roles in *Rowan and Martin's Laugh-In* and *The Mod Squad.* As times changed, Kaye spent the early half of the 1970s in the New York soap *Love is a Many Splendored Thing* before retiring.

"Elvis Presley was divine--what a dream" Kaye told Tom Lisanti for his interview book *Drive-In Dream Girls.* "This was before his comedown, so he was so handsome. Both men and women loved him. He was so sweet and a total gentleman. He also paid attention to you if you had a problem. While we'd be waiting for a shot to be set up, we'd talk in a corner, and he'd listen. He wasn't just fluff".

Several familiar faces flit through *Clambake* in minor roles. At around the same time as appearing as hanger-on Gloria in *Clambake* with Elvis, Angelique Pettyjohn was playing other bit parts on such cult TV shows as *The Green Hornet, Batman* (the episode guest-starring the Green Hornet and Elvis girl Diane McBain), *Get Smart,* and *The Girl from UNCLE,* but would become best known for her role as the lustful dominatrix barbarian girl in the well-remembered *Star Trek* camp-fest "The Gamesters of Triskellion". In *Get Smart* she was known as Charlie, a male spy who adopted the brilliantly effective disguise of a shapely young woman (no-one could quite figure out how he did it!).

After being billed simply as Angelique in bit parts for sleazy exploitation fare such as *The Touch of Her Flesh* and *The Love Rebellion, Clambake* was her bid for movie respectability, and she used her full name when listed in the opening credits for what is essentially just another decorative walk-on. Unfortunately, nothing came of it, and following her *Star Trek* she drifted into endless roles as white trash and hookers in the likes of *Hell's Belles* (with Jocelyn Lane and Jeremy Slate), *The Mad Doctor of Blood Island* (a low, low-budget Phillipines horror film with Deborah Walley's then-husband John Ashley), *The Curious Female, Up Your Teddy Bear,* and *Dragon Lady,* the titles of which speak for themselves.

By the late '70s she was dancing in strip clubs, and by the early 1980s, she was making porn films. By the mid 1980s, her *Star Trek* notoriety had caught up with her, and she was appearing at conventions signing autographed photos and turning up, frequently without much clothing, in straight-to-video fare such as *The Lost Empire, Biohazard,* and *Sorority Girls and the Creature from Hell,* no doubt directed by young men still drooling over *Star Trek's* busty, boss-eyed space slut Shahna.

Marj Dusay, seen as the sandwich girl at the gas station, is rather unfairly best known for her own part in an infamous *Star Trek* episode, "Spock's Brain", another classic for all the wrong reasons. Despite this, she's had many other small or recurring roles in TV over the years, and got a rare chance to shine as William Holden's pragmatic girlfriend in Clint Eastwood's little-known gem, *Breezy.*

Lee Krieger, who plays Walter the barman, had appeared in *My Favorite Martian, The Munsters, McHale's Navy, Combat,* and *Get Smart.* Sue England, the cigarette girl, did many offscreen voiceovers for the 1960s

Irwin Allen sci-fi shows, notably two evil female robots for *Lost in Space*. She had previously appeared in *Loving You* as a sorority girl.

For Lance Le Gault, *Clambake* represented his first on-screen credit as assistant to the choreographer, while Red West got to play a comedy bit as an ice-cream seller rather than his usual punch-up scene, as scriptwriter Browne, slavishly following the formula even when it made no sense, has Presley and Hutchins stop by a playground to help a moppet conquer her fear of heights with "Confidence", a dreadful kid-infested musical number. It's the lowpoint of an otherwise thoroughly entertaining film, which songwise gives Elvis two romantic if undistinguished ballads and several wild dance scenes, always preferable to the ghastly novelty songs like the duet that blights the movie's start.

"There was a party after the film was completed" *Shindig* producer Jack Good told Jerry Hopkins, "with Lance Le Gault's band playing, and Elvis wouldn't sing. Slowly, Lance got him into a blues thing, "Let it Roll", and he was terrific. I thought what a shame he doesn't do that sort of thing in the film".

Still, Elvis was by now no longer quite so deferential as he had been ten years earlier. Felton Jarvis, one of his record producers, told a story about the soundtrack and that dire opening duet, for which Elvis had asked for the Jordanaires to provide a chorus. "Well, the director of the picture was there, and he says `Elvis, I don't think you understand where the song's going to be used in the picture. In this particular scene, you're riding down the highway on a motorcycle. The voices can't sing along with you. Where would we put the singers?'. Elvis thought a second and said `Put 'em the same damn place you put the band!'. That was the end of that".

There were no hard feelings, though, quite the reverse. There were pie fights and water fights, with director Arthur Nadel getting in on the act, turning up in protective rain gear on the last day of filming and going home dry and untouched, only to be pied when wearing his end-of-shoot party tuxedo later that evening. Turning up on the set unannounced was *Big Valley* actor and future *Six Million Dollar Man* Lee Majors, one of Presley's football buddies, who dressed up as one of the red-jacketed, fez-wearing waiters in the hotel bar as a gag to surprise Elvis. He has a silent cameo in the movie, uncredited and concealed under a huge moustache!

Screenwriter Arthur Browne may have been rewriting *Blue Hawaii* to order, but he managed to put his own slant on the proceedings to create yet another slight variation on a theme. If Browne, Nadel, Gardner, Levy and Laven had proven anything, it was that the Elvis film had by now become so formulaic that anyone could produce a credible copy of the Wallis/Elvis popcorn movie effortlessly. It was as much a genre with its own clearly-defined rules and ingredients as a western, cop film, or Disney adventure, and you defied them and denied them at your peril. The Elvis film, as the likes of *Viva Las Vegas, Girl Happy,* and now *Clambake* had demonstrated, didn't even need Hal Wallis any more--but, ironically, *Clambake* would be the penultimate example of the form.

Speedway (1968)

wr. Phil Shuken, dir. Norman Taurog, pr. Douglas Laurence (MGM)

with Elvis Presley (Steve Grayson), Nancy Sinatra (Susan Jacks), Bill Bixby (Kenny Donford), Gale Gordon (R.J. Hepworth), William Schallert (Abel Esterlake), Carl Ballantine (Birdie Kebner), Victoria Meyerink (Ellie Esterlake), Ross Hagen (Paul Dado), Poncie Ponce (Juan Medala), Harry Hickox (grill chef), Robert Harris (Lloyd Meadow), Harper Carter (Ted Simmons), Carl Reindel (Mike), Michele Newman (Debbie Esterlake), Courtney Brown (Carrie Esterlake), Dana Brown (Billie Esterlake), Patti Jean Keith (Annie Esterlake), Christopher West (Billie Jo), Charlotte Considine (Lori), Gari Hardy (Kenny's date), Beverly Powers (Mary Ann), Sandy Reed (race announcer), Burt Mustin (janitor)

Elvis sings: "Speedway" (over titles); "Let Yourself Go" (in disco); "Your Groovy Self" (Nancy Sinatra only, in disco); "Your Time Hasn't Come Yet, Baby" (to kids); "He's Your Uncle, Not Your Dad" (with Bill Bixby and Gale Gordon in tax office); "Who Are You? Who Am I?" (to Nancy Sinatra); "There Ain't Nothin' Like a Song" (with Nancy Sinatra, in disco)

The last and probably least of the sunny, shiny, Elvis movies of the '60s, and the last to be overseen by director Norman Taurog, sees Elvis back on the racetrack (stock cars this time) and teamed once again with his *Clambake* co-star Bill Bixby (history refuses to organise itself for the historians, and the next chapter's *Stay Away Joe* preceded it). *Speedway* is another 1960s time capsule, with some groovy discotheque sequences making up for the rather boring racetrack scenes (Quentin Tarantino, an avowed Elvis fan, would later pay tribute to the set design for the famous nightclub sequence in *Pulp Fiction*).

For some reason, the film's opening credits make a huge deal out of showcasing a slew of racing drivers of the era, but who only appear in the movie encased in their cars or as background extras. This might have made some sense if it wasn't for the fact that Presley does all his driving in front of a projection screen in a mock-up (or at least, one presumes so; hopefully, the film-makers wouldn't be so incompetent as to put Elvis behind the wheel and then not prove he's there).

Bixby was again playing the same broadly comedic second-rater he portrayed in *Clambake,* another no-good gambling-addicted so-called best buddy in the style of Gary Lockwood's Danny Burke in *It Happened at the World's Fair*. The feeling of been-here-done-that continues as newcomer Phil Shuken, previously writing episodes of *The Beverly Hillbillies,* drops in all the standard ingredients--the never-in-with-a-chance rival (the virtually absent Ross Hagen), comical oldster (Gale Gordon, about whom, more later), loyal pals (including an Asian-American one, the improbably named Poncie Ponce, last seen on the 1959-'63 TV series *Hawaiian Eye*, starring Red West's buddy Robert Conrad), plus gyrating dolly birds, and cute kids by the truckload... literally, as veteran supporting player William Schallert plays a debt-totalling racer fallen on hard times who lives in a wagon with a small army of loveable scamps.

The film grinds achingly to a halt every time Schallert and his moppets are onscreen (although their introductory scene with the disappearing hot dogs is amusing), and this is the last gasp for the conventions of the all-encompassing something-for-everybody family film, although there is much to enjoy. This was Presley's last of the genre and Disney--the last practitioner--would fold up that particular tent just under ten years later (many of his last featuring Elvis admirer Kurt Russell). From hereon, demographics and target audiences became the norm.

Presley was much more professional, and a little bit happier, on *Speedway* than he had been on *Easy Come, Easy Go* and *Clambake*. This was partly due to his abandonment of mysticism and the effectiveness of the Colonel reading the riot act after the *Clambake* debacle, but mostly because he had just found out to his great joy that Priscilla was pregnant.

The ice queen swiftly melted on this occasion is the lovely Nancy Sinatra, who--while no Ann-Margret--is a step up from the usual two-dimensional invisible girls, and plays Doris Day to Presley's Rock Hudson with impressive comedic ability and no motivation at all for her eventual and inevitable change of heart (one very funny sequence has Elvis angling to get himself in kissing position as she flounces round his trailer trying to talk business, the same coy mating dance previously seen with Yvonne Craig in *It Happened at the World's Fair* and Jocelyn Lane in *Tickle Me*).

In previous Presley fantasies such as *Easy Come, Easy Go* and *Clambake*, the seduction is simplistic but sequential, and progresses logically, but scriptwriter Shuken offers Sinatra no such transitional moments. She just capitulates to Presley's charms because it's an Elvis film and the formula says she must. As in *Paradise, Hawaiian Style*, it's viewed as compulsory convention for Elvis to get the girl. This is quite right and as it should be, but some motivation would be appreciated.

Elvis had already met Nancy during the *Welcome Home Special* featuring daddy Frank, and they were already--and remained--good friends. It was Nancy Sinatra who Elvis rang and spoke to for over an hour when Priscilla gave birth, and she told Elvis biographer Albert Goldman that they shared a love only for practical jokes, notably emerging from

Presley's trailer after innocent horseplay with deliberately ruffled hair and clothes in disarray to tease onlookers.

She had made her film debut in the 1964 beach movie *For Those Who Think Young,* starring James Darren and Pamela Tiffin, appeared in the troubled *Ghost in the Invisible Bikini* for AIP, made the obligatory *Burke's Law* appearance, and enjoyed a top ten hit with her signature song "These Boots Were Made for Walking". She also provided the theme song for the fifth James Bond movie *You Only Live Twice,* one of the series' best and most enduring intros (Tarantino uses her other well-known song, the morose offbeat ballad "Bang Bang, My Baby Shot Me Down", to open his feature *Kill Bill 2*).

She had also made the 1966 spy spoof *The Last of the Secret Agents,* in which she had been menaced by spy movie regular and Elvis' adversary from *Harum Scarum,* Theo Marcuse, and at around the same time had guested on an episode of 1960s TV mega-hit *The Man from UNCLE* (as the delightfully named Coco Cool in "The Take Me to Your Leader Affair") in which she'd briefly duetted with David McCallum. Even the Colonel had to concede that Sinatra would have to sing in the film, and she provides one superb paean to the swingin' '60s ("Your Groovy Self") and briefly duets with Elvis at the film's close.

The burger bar/disco hang-out sequence in which the compulsory performance spotlight fortuitously falls on a reluctant Elvis and then shy Nancy is blissfully and naively absurd, as both temporarily ditch their characters to turn out spontaneous yet blistering professional numbers unfailingly backed by the house band. In fact, the musical numbers in *Speedway* are all okay, even the usually awful obligatory song with the kids. However, watching Elvis seduce Sinatra with the song "Who Are You, Who am I?" is professional old timer Burt Mustin, who made his first film at age 67 and spent the next thirty years playing old coots, here embracing his janitor's mop dreamily. He kills the scene stone dead by painfully and laboriously crooning the song's last line himself. It's what the fast forward button was made for.

Elvis, looking slim and relaxed, plays race car driver Steve Grayson, but is, of course, as usual, Elvis by any other name, and the film exploits Presley's well-publicised penchant for giving away extravagant gifts to anyone who strayed into a certain radius (he was a huge fan of the TV show *The Millionaire,* in which the title character does just that; the show was later reworked by Stephen Cannell in the 1980s as *J.J. Starbuck*).

In fact, had Presley's ludicrous generosity already not been a matter of record, the story would not have held water for a second, as Grayson lavishes station wagons and wedding parties on wasters and waitresses alike. No doubt his ever-worried, taxman-loathing, frugal father Vernon would have approved of the next development in the wafer-thin plot, as Grayson's generosity is punished by the pursuit of the Inland Revenue for 145,000 dollars in back taxes after Bixby's waste-of-space Kenny botches the accounts. Pursuing the cash is the typecast Gale Gordon, the wonderful comic actor who portrayed the penny-pinching bank manager Mr. Mooney in *The Lucy Show* throughout the 1960s.

Gordon was a veteran vaudevillian who was astonishingly lithe for his years, despite his blustering old man appearance. He frequently took acrobatic prat-falls for *The Lucy Show* that would have hospitalised lesser men his age, and on one occasion cartwheeled across the stage while supposedly in a hypnotic trance! Here, he's under-exploited, appearing in only one scene with the cast, and literally 'phoning in the rest of his performance as Sinatra's IRS boss from behind a desk or from his bed. It was no more than a couple of day's work away from Lucille Ball's studios, if that, although he does get to strut his stuff in the film's most embarrassing scene, an otherwise under-rehearsed song and dance debacle in the Inland Revenue office, as a bunch of old fools in suits perform an old-style Hollywood musical number patriotically praising Uncle Sam. Even the respectful, flag-loving Presley must have blanched at this.

Only Gordon as Mr. Mooney, sorry, R.W. Hepworth, makes this awful nadir bearable, going through his traditional three point Mr. Mooney routine from the *Lucy Show* song and dance sequences (dragged into the show, he flusters, reluctantly joins in, then sheepishly gets into it) and it would still have been better left on the cutting room floor. One song, "Five Sleepy Heads", does end up cut, leaving Elvis only the one song inevitably sung to a moppet.

Chief recipient of Elvis/Grayson's lavish generosity as the struggling father of the small army of urchins is TV veteran William Schallert, then best known as the English teacher of *The Many Loves of Dobie Gillis* (1959-'63) and the long-suffering father in *The Patty Duke Show* (1963-'66). Despite both these shows occupying his time for the best part of the 1960s, he still found space in his schedule to guest in other series, including *77, Sunset Strip, Surfside Six, Route 66, Combat, The Lucy Show, Bewitched, Mission: Impossible, The Wild Wild West,* and a well-remembered *Twilight Zone,* "Little Girl Lost". He also had a recurring role in the cult comedy series *Get Smart*. In the 1970s he was in numerous TV movies and guest shots, as well as playing the lawyer father of the heroine of *The Hardy Boys/Nancy Drew Mysteries,* and was still working during the 1980s, turning up in episodes of *Magnum p.i., Simon and Simon, Hotel,* and *Murphy Brown,* and keeping busy as one of a small army of cult TV veterans appearing in Joe

Dante's films, specifically *Twilight Zone--the movie, Gremlins, Innerspace,* and *Matinee*. His career spanned forty years during which he looked exactly the same from start to finish, and included one of the earliest flying saucer films, *The Man from Planet X,* Roger Corman's *Gunslinger,* and Albert Zugsmith's Red Menace fever dream *Invasion USA*.

Despite treading well-trod, over-familiar ground, *Speedway*--unlike the films that followed--gave audiences the switch-off-your-brain-and-enjoy entertainment they paid for and expected, and while Presley's films deteriorated from this point, the formulaic Presley vehicle that *Speedway* represented grew old but never tired. The films that followed the traditional format had always delivered, but it was 1968, and the go-go portion of the decade was folding up the tent and getting ready to go-go into the history books.

Accompanying Presley in the caravan out of town that year were *The Monkees, Batman, The Man from UNCLE,* Maxwell Smart, *Lost in Space,* and genie Jeannie; fantasy TV was about to be replaced by the fad for 'relevance'. Films, pop music and comics were also visibly, dramatically changing in style; *Easy Rider* would soon oust the Hollywood traditionalists, pop groups would become rock groups and start making "concept albums", Marvel Comics--who had pioneered the notion of comics as pop art--would start dumbing down, while the delightfully naive and childish DC Comics would charmlessly try to mature. Although the 1960s had been perceived as a time of newness, change, and youth (which it was), it was paradoxically actually at the end of the '60s that most of the old guard (and attitudes) in the various media retired, having had their last creative hurrah. Much mocked at the time and since, the mid-'60s had been a brief period of vacuous color, vacuous adventure, and equally vacuous girls that would eventually be wistfully missed by those lucky enough to have experienced it.

The escalation of the Vietnam war, along with the Manson murders, Kent State, Altamont, and Watergate were just around the corner and America would spend the first half of the 1970s intellectually and reflectively whipping itself before retreating spent into historical revision and nostalgia. Elvis Presley's puzzling over the past would be done within a cocoon of bright lights, loyal fans, and over-indulgent but powerless protectors in Las Vegas, a Disneyland for adults. But inbetween the so-called *Comeback Special* and the Vegas shows, came those very strange years, that peculiar few months in pop culture during 1968 and 1969 which belonged neither to the '60s or the '70s...

And so it was goodbye to all this…

...and all this...

...and as they say on the internet...

...if you liked those...

...then you might like these...

3. the dreadful mistakes

Stay Away Joe (1968)

wr. Burt Kennedy, Michael Hoey, from Dan Cushman, dir. Peter Tewkesbury, pr. Douglas Laurence (MGM)

with Elvis Presley (Joe Lightcloud), Burgess Meredith (Charlie Lightcloud), Joan Blondell (Glenda Callahan), Katy Jurado (Annie Lightcloud), Thomas Gomez (Grandpa), Quentin Dean (Mamie Callahan), L.Q. Jones (Bronc), Susan Trustman (Mary Lightcloud), Anne Seymour (Mrs. Hawkins), Angus Duncan (Lorne Hawkins), Douglas Henderson (Congressman Morrisey), Henry Jones (Hy Slager), Michael Lane (Frank), Buck Kartalian (Bull), Warren Vanders (Hike), Maurishka (Connie), Caitlin Wyles (Marlene), Marya Christen (Billie-Jo), Jennifer Peak (Little Deer), Sonny West (Jack), Michael Keller (Orville), Brett Parker (Deputy Mattson), Dick Wilson (used car salesman), Harry Harvey Snr. (Judge Nibley), Robert Lieb (rodeo announcer), David Cadiente, Joe Esposito, the Jordanaires

Elvis sings: "Stay Away" (over credits--to the public domain tune of "Greensleeves"!); "Stay Away, Joe" (at party); "Dominic" (over sequence chasing girls); "All I Needed Was the Rain" (during downpour)

Stay Away Joe was released three months before *Speedway*, but undoubtedly belonged to the late '60s canon rather than the early-to-mid-'60s (reality stubbornly refusing to arrange itself for the benefit of retrospective cataloguing!). One's heart sinks as soon as the movie begins, as we are assaulted by a barrage of unfunny fun. Elvis is in his usual movie persona of a decent kind of guy who has tipped over into small-time trouble, but this is that awkward animal the comedy western, further complicated by a contemporary setting, late-'60s moral confusion, and the notion that Elvis and his deep Southern voice might pass for Native American Joe Lightcloud, the Stay Away Joe of the title who returns home periodically between ill-considered adventures. This is Elvis' second film as a Native American (after *Flaming Star*), and also his second as a rodeo rider (after *Tickle Me*; only Elvis could herd cattle in a sports car!).

Why was *Stay Away Joe* made, and who was it made for? The plot, dialogue, performances, set-pieces, and even background music conspire to make the Native Americans look like idiots, but this sort of comedy caricature went out with *F Troop* (and those send-ups were set safely in the

Old West--this is the present day, at a time when American society was finally starting to see the Natives as legitimate American citizens).

The Native American characters in this movie scoff at city folk, shrink from work, drool over hundred dollar bills, have neither guile nor education, fight and gamble, frolic in that curiously non-sexual '60s way (a couple of would-be nude scenes have no nudity), brawl and booze, and have comedy morals (Elvis starts an enormous punch-up in order to steal away with another man's willing girlfriend, and unlike the innocent ambiguity of the earlier Elvis movies, we are left in no doubt that they have had sex together). All the white characters are cynical stuffed shirts, ignorant white trash, or stuffy, uptight prigs.

The kindest comments one can make about *Stay Away Joe* are that it is a healthy antidote to the Noble Savage cliche that was about to manifest itself over the next few years, and that it would never have been made over the next few politically correct decades. On the other hand, one could also say that it was thoughtless offensive turkeys like this that caused the birth of political correctness in the first place.

Stay Away Joe does not reject PC fussiness and eggshell-walking in a pleasing, amusing, rebellious way, but simply displays poor taste and judgement. In fact, it's extremely difficult to work out exactly what *Stay Away Joe* is trying to say or do. There's a welfare theme to the napkin-sized storyline (a local Congressman is pinning his political future on supplying the locals with breeding stock, but Elvis spends the movie trying to replace a prize bull after it gets cooked and eaten during a drunken party), but the film's attitude is neither conservative and hostile, nor condescendingly liberal and sanctimonious. It's not satire, because there's no truth to it and it doesn't have a target, or even an opinion. It's not political, because the film doesn't take a side. It's not witty (there are perhaps two funny lines in the whole movie), the slapstick is forced and unfunny (one fight is conducted with slide-whistle sound effects), and it's farcical only in a bad way.

Anything good to say? Elvis' voice is rich and strong for the handful of vocals, and some of the frantic, foot-tappin' music's okay, if undermined by the continuous air of contrived chaos. However, the musical interludes were getting fewer and fewer at this point. "Stay Away" is a ludicrous dirge sung over the credits to the public domain tune of "Greensleeves", the title track is so-so, and "Dominic" plays over a sequence in which Elvis pursues a couple of girls around the landscape who are trying to get caught (which is at least preferable to seeing him sing it to the bull, which goes by that name); only the bluesy and atmospheric "All I Needed Was the Rain" is worth a second play.

Faced with appearing in a stiff, some of the old timers do what they always do in such circumstances, and try to make their individual roles into showcase cameos. There's no hope for Burgess Meredith and his eye-shadow or Thomas Gomez and his flowerpot hat, who both come off looking ridiculous (Meredith looks like a parody of Peter Sellers doing his wonderful turn in *The Party*), but Joan Blondell's gun-totin' slovenly drunken slut and Anne Seymour's stuffy and proper mother-in-law make a meal of their opportunities.

Seymour is often cast as coarse harridans, and is a revelation as the terror-stricken but determinedly polite society woman, never once giving into the temptation to revert to a cartoon snob or comedy mother-in-law; this is a three-dimensional portrait of a good woman trying hard for her son. Blondell, on the other hand, has no option but to go for broke, and gives one hundred and ten percent as a shotgun-wielding two-faced old tart. The oddly named newcomer Quentin Dean plays Blondell's sexy dense daughter, dumbly following in her savvier, sharper mother's zig-zag footsteps. Caught in bed with this dimwit virgin (for the first time in his movies, Elvis' recurring promiscuous character isn't choosy), Presley gets the chance to do some real comedy.

Katy Jurado, a long way from *High Noon* and *Broken Lance,* and still to redeem herself in Peckinpah's moving *Pat Garrett and Billy the Kid,* is already playing a woman who gets through the day by putting on a variety of different performances--angry dissatisfied wife, judgemental mother, fawning hostess--but other cast members have less to work with, reduced to trying to create an air of carefree wackiness in a non-stop party atmosphere where nothing is happening (rather than hide this failing with zooms and edits, the camera pans forlornly over the antics in endless tracking shots, like a party guest looking in vain for action or amusement). A typical late-'60s mess, the end of the party sequence even switches between three different musical scores, each signifying nothing. Red West's cousin Sonny West and the Colonel's aide Joe Esposito are among the revelers.

Elvis/Joe eventually replaces the government bull with a dozy, constantly sleeping lump of indifference, and while he sells his car piece by piece to hold on to the herd, his mother is selling it cow by cow to furnish their modest tumbledown shack for the arrival of her daughter's future mother-in-law (a much coveted toilet arrives, but without plumbing, while father wallpapers the outside of the house--sideways). Then the pistol-packin' Blondell pursues Elvis to the Lightclouds' paper palace to ensure the cradle-robber does the decent thing--unaware he hasn't had the chance to be indecent. In the film's highlight scene, the entire structure, now riddled with Blondell's bullet-holes and carpet-covered pits made by several careless heavy steps, slowly but surely tumbles to the ground like a Laurel and Hardy finale...

As Elvis movie girl and TV's Batgirl Yvonne Craig remarked about her *Batman* co-star Burgess Meredith, he was a man with about six different careers, even though he would be best remembered as Batman's arch enemy the Penguin; other memorable roles include a near-sighted librarian in a famous *Twilight Zone*, a crooked, henpecked mortician in *McCloud*, a mad scientist in *Return of Captain Nemo*, and--among his dozens of films-- Sylvester Stallone's manager in the *Rocky* saga. Covered in fake tan and varying degrees of eyeliner that change between scenes, *Stay Away Joe's* feckless father is not his finest hour.

Film actress Joan Blondell, now middle-aged, had drifted into TV guest shots during the 1960s (*Dick Powell Theater, The Twilight Zone, The Untouchables, Burke's Law, The Man from UNCLE, The Girl from UNCLE, The Guns of Will Sonnett, The Lucy Show*), and by the time of this film, she was on her way to a decade of TV movies. In the previous forty years she had made around a hundred movies including *The Public Enemy* with James Cagney, but mostly musicals and comedies as blowsy bimbos.

Of the supporting players, Henry Jones rarely seemed out of work in either TV guest shots or feature film bit parts. The sort of character actor who today doesn't exist any more, he turns up, does his eccentric Henry Jones bit, and goes home. TV includes *The Twilight Zone, The Untouchables, Lost in Space, Bewitched, The Man from UNCLE, Voyage to the Bottom of the Sea, The Six Million Dollar Man,* and many others, including numerous westerns and a co-starring role in the sit-com *Phyllis*. This was western veteran L.Q. Jones' third outing with Presley, following *Love Me Tender* and *Flaming Star* in the '50s. It's not that odd that Jones should be in three of Presley's four westerns; it's tough to find any western film he isn't in! Bit player Brett Parker also appears in the same director's *The Trouble With Girls*.

Only three years earlier, writer Michael Hoey had been the dialogue coach on *Tickle Me*. Given Hoey's involvement with producer Douglas Lawrence's appalling *Live a Little, Love a Little* the same year, the few sequences that work may well be the contribution of uncredited co-writer Burt Kennedy, who went on to write and/or direct a string of mildly amusing comedy westerns at this time, including such well-cast but inconsequential time-wasters as *Support Your Local Sheriff* in 1969 and *Support Your Local Gunfighter* in 1971, both starring James Garner (and the latter co-starring Joan Blondell), *The Good Guys and the Bad Guys* and *Young Billy Young,* both starring Robert Mitchum, and Frank Sinatra's *Dirty Dingus McGee*. Prior to this Presley fiasco, he had been involved with several similar projects, including *Mail Order Bride* with *The Beverly Hillbillies'* Buddy Ebsen in 1963, *The Rounders,* with Henry Fonda, Glenn Ford and Sue Ane Langdon in 1965 (he worked with both Fonda and Ford again), John Wayne's *The War Wagon* in 1967, and--again with Wayne, and Ann Margret--*The Train Robbers* in 1975, all of them distinguished by the recurring use of favorite stock players and all alternating between grimmer, revenge westerns which were also star vehicles for iconic figures (including, in the better-than-it-ought-to-be *Hannie Caulder,* Raquel Welch).

Occasionally, Kennedy veered away from westerns, but he always swiftly returned, and there was always plenty of material waiting for him. The glut of television westerns in the 1950s and early '60s had made the form weary, over-familiar, and ripe for parody. Following the surprise box office success of the embarrassing *Cat Ballou* in 1965, there were almost as many comedy westerns being made as serious ones in the 1960s and early '70s, mainly because the best known box office western heroes, now rapidly ageing, were all out of place in the wild west now inhabited by Eastwood and Peckinpah; John Wayne, for example, was now gently sending himself up (with the aid of Hal Wallis, who made the veteran actor his post-Elvis project and secured him his Oscar, for the superb *True Grit*).

Elsewhere, however, the comedy western trumpeted its self-doubt. Uncertain of their worth, these loud cries for attention were almost all as coyly brash, heavy-handed and vulgar as this effort, and this seems to be the only context into which Presley's Joe Lightcloud and *Stay Away Joe* clearly fit, although Kennedy plainly either departed the project early, or came in late to try and fix it. Ironically, the best tribute to the dying first wave of westerns came not from these clumsy attempts to dismiss them to Boot Hill with raucous insincere laughter, but from Peckinpah himself--with 1962's *Ride the High Country,* the final film of both Joel McCrea and Randolph Scott, a noble, poignant swan song to rival John Wayne's final film, *The Shootist.*

Live a Little, Love a Little (1968)

wr. Dan Greenberg, Michael Hoey, dir. Norman Taurog, pr. Douglas Laurence (MGM)

with Elvis Presley (Greg Nolan), Michele Carey (Bernice), Don Porter (Mike Landsdown), Rudy Vallee (Mr. Penlow), Dick Sargent (Harry), Celeste Yarnall (Ellen), Sterling Holloway (milkman), Eddie Hodges (delivery boy), Mike Keller (art director), Joan Shawlee (new tenant), Mary Grover (landlady), Emily Banks (Penlow's receptionist), Merri Ashley, Phyllis Davis (secretaries), Ursula Menzel (perfume model), Susan Henning (mermaid model), Morgan Windbell, Benjie Bancroft (motorcycle cops), Susan Shute, Edie Baskin, Gabrielle, Ginny Kaneen, Thordis Brandt (models), Vernon Presley, Red West

Elvis sings: "Wonderful World" (in beach buggy over credits); "Edge of Reality" (dream sequence); "A Little Less Conversation" (to Celeste Yarnall); "Almost in Love" (to Michele Carey)

The third and last Elvis movie produced by Douglas Laurence, who had previously overseen *Speedway* and *Stay Away Joe*, was a rather sorry attempt to bring the beach movie Elvis into the sexually liberated late '60s. Hollywood during the years 1968 and 1969 often seems to be little more than a visual representation of the death throes of the '60s; watching films made during this period is like watching a much-loved friend expire slowly and with senility. All the mistakes that followed the joy of the '60s, from the fashions to the philosophies, are on display here in all their unfortunate glory. At least the chaos and confusion of the early 1970s would produce an array of dazzling, thoughtful, intelligent and evocative movies before Lucas and Spielberg took American cinema into the toy shops. But for the '70s to begin, the 1960s had to die. The '60s did not go without a fight, and a small army of turkeys preceded the gems of the early 1970s to prove it. *Live a Little, Love a Little* was one of those films.

Shooting was supposed to start early in 1968, but was delayed when Presley's long-time buddy, actor Nick Adams, was found dead from a drugs overdose in suspicious circumstances, a supposed but suspect suicide. Adams carried on a colorful life, to put it tactfully, and the mystery of his demise was never satisfactorily resolved. A month later, work began with the recording of the film's four musical numbers, including the well-known "A Little Less Conversation" and the bizarre "Edge of Reality", for that perennial 1960s favorite, the dream sequence, which features Elvis dancing with a guy in a dog suit (Elvis meets Scooby-Doo) to an age-of-Aquarius style arrangement.

Elvis, fresh from the *Comeback Special,* looks fantastic, and visually the film is a treat, not the least because of the groovy bright yellow beach buggy his character drives throughout most of the movie. Elvis portrays Greg Nolan, a freelance photographer who meets Michele Carey's free spirit artist on the beach one morning. Several warning flags immediately go up--an immediate offer of sex, a furious and wicked response when he declines, the revelation that she goes by several different names depending on her mood, and her being accompanied by an enormous and bothersome Great Dane (in real life owned by Elvis himself) which she orders to chase him into the sea. This delightful package is tied up in a string of lies.

In 1968, we were supposed to find all this intriguing, compelling, wacky, challenging and charming, but scary Carey is alarming rather than alluring, and makes the deadly duo from *Double Trouble* look relatively stable in comparison. Despite this, Elvis is drawn into her web effortlessly, as the audience watches this bunny boiler lead him around like a second slobbering pet dog (in fact heavy-lidded, heavy-sideburned Elvis looks so dumb and bored in this film that the dog comes across as the smartest living thing in the film; Presley can barely be bothered to stand upright).

This is only the beginning of his, and our, embarrassments. She drugs him unconscious for four days (a pill-popping episode eerily similar to some of the scares we later found out Elvis had endured in the '60s, with himself and others) and, even when second Darrin from *Bewitched* Dick Sargent shows up as the supposedly dead husband (as it turns out, neither deceased or married), Elvis still fails to make an Elvis-shaped hole in the wall by fleeing.

His reward is to find that Carey has, posing as his sister, had the locks changed on his apartment and given away his home! She's also lost him his job by knocking him out for four days (for some hazy reason this is the excuse for the token fight scene with Red and Sonny West and others), and so Elvis--now financially dependent on her while he pursues two new jobs--is obliged to set up home with her (after she tells yet another pack of lies).

Ultimately, Presley secures two new photographic jobs in the same building--one with a thinly disguised girlie mag empire based on *Playboy* and run by Don Porter (where Elvis is obliged to dress casual) and the other at a very conservative advertising agency run by former crooner Rudy Vallee (where he must wear a suit and tie). The film's only entertaining moments are provided by Elvis' frantic scampering up and down the stairs and elevators between the two places of employment while simultaneously remembering to change clothes. When Elvis/Greg picks up a gorgeous model (Celeste Yarnall) from one of Porter's parties, scary Carey is ahead of him again, ruining his chances. Needless to say, after a further bout of sabotage, deceit and prickteasing, Elvis succumbs, and the audience is left to contemplate their future together. As with so many Elvis films, one can't imagine the story continuing after the credits have rolled. Elvis has left the movie.

This unbelievable pile of crap came from a novel with the equally unbelievable title of *Kiss My Firm But Pliant Lips,* and--again, unbelievable--this was very nearly the title of the film as well, which was written by the book's author, Dan Greenburg, and the same Michael Hoey who had adapted *Stay Away Joe.* Imagine Elvis fans telling their buddies they'd just been to see *Kiss My Firm But Pliant Lips...!*

Of course, her stupid role was not the fault of sexy Texan Michele Carey, who went on to co-star with Presley's old nemesis Frank Sinatra in the comedy western *Dirty Dingus Magee* a couple of years later. She had been stunning in the Howard Hawks western *El Dorado* alongside John Wayne and Robert Mitchum, filmed in '65 but released in '67, and appeared in another swingin' '60s film this year, Joe Pasternak's *The Sweet Ride,* playing another high maintenance bimbo. TV included '60s spy shows *The Man from UNCLE, Amos Burke--Secret Agent, The Wild Wild West,* and *Mission: Impossible.* A few TV movies followed, along with two *Starsky and Hutch* episodes and bit parts in movies like the notorious and unflattering *The Choirboys.* This latter role, brief and vulgar, was degrading and creepy, like the film itself. She had worked with big names in the 1960s, and deserved more.

Silver-haired Don Porter regularly worked in films, recurring TV roles, guest shots in series, and numerous TV movies, and is blandly, vaguely recognisable to casual viewers. He spent the '50s in a sit-com titled *Private Secretary* with Ann Sothern, and when the format changed after four modestly successful seasons he was dropped only to be swiftly rehired in a new role for another two seasons in what was now titled *The Ann Sothern Show.* In the mid-'60s he played the father of Cindy Carol's Gidget in the colorful and pleasant *Gidget Goes to Rome* (a film loaded with Elvis movie co-stars), and later the father of Sally Field's TV incarnation of Gidget.

Rudy Vallee had been a heart-throb radio singer in the 1930s, and never let anybody forget it. He made a run of forgettable films subsequently, and this was another of them. A singer, bandleader, and supposed idol of females everywhere before even Sinatra, Rudy Vallee left a trail of irritable co-stars wherever he went, at least in his later years. The cast of *Batman* were mortified to find themselves trapped with him for a three-part episode, Lucie Arnaz loathed him when he guested on *Here's*

Lucy, and Elvis himself, embarrassed by his leching, said to his guys "if I ever become like him, shoot me like a dog!". He also appeared in several episodes of *Alias Smith and Jones,* a series which also featured a guest-shot by Michele Carey.

Celeste Yarnall was another actress smitten with Elvis. "I adored Elvis" she gushed to interviewers. "When I met him for the first time, he immediately put me at ease. I was introduced to him right on the soundstage. I thought I was dreaming. He was exquisitely handsome and looked fabulous. I don't think people knew how incredibly beautiful and absolutely electrifying he was--the epitome of the word charismatic. We had to film our kissing scene first, and neither of us heard the director say `cut'! Elvis wouldn't let me go! All the lights were being turned off and Norman Taurog is yelling `Lunch, everybody! Elvis, you can let her go now!'. He wouldn't let me out of his embrace and I'm cracking up! He was warm and full of love. Flirting was an understatement. Elvis had the ability to make you feel like you were the most special person in the world. He had this tremendous desire to please people. He was far more handsome in person... He held jam sessions on the set and would play cars with George Barris or play football with 'the boys', who traveled with him everywhere". Onscreen however, the kiss is one of those just-shy-of-the-lips Hollywood kisses. Yarnall also glimpsed Presley's serious, spiritual side when Martin Luther King was murdered. "We watched the funeral in his trailer", she said. "He cried".

Yarnall was an elegant-looking blonde, usually cast in sexpot roles; she had a similar function as here in the timely 1969 sex satire *Bob and Carol and Ted and Alice.* She started out with a bit part in *The Nutty Professor* and various ads and modelling jobs and then started turning up in TV, including episodes of *Ozzie and Harriet, Gidget, The Defenders, Burke's Law, Bewitched, The Wild Wild West, Hogan's Heroes, The FBI, Bonanza, It Takes a Thief, Mannix, The Survivors, Love, American Style, The Bold Ones, Columbo,* and *McMillan and Wife.* She had memorable roles as naive beauties in cult shows *The Man from UNCLE* ("The Monks of St. Thomas Affair"), *Star Trek* ("The Apple"), and *Land of the Giants* ("The Golden Cage"), before ending her career, for financial reasons, with such downmarket horror productions as *Beast of Blood* and *The Velvet Vampire.* She became a successful businesswoman during the 1970s, and returned to acting briefly in the late '80s/early '90s, appearing in various film roles and episodes of *Knots Landing* and *Melrose Place.*

Michele Carey and Celeste Yarnall are the only female cast members with significant roles. Former glamour girl Joan Shawlee was playing matronly roles by this time, and appears in a cameo as the new occupant of Elvis' apartment. Susan Henning, from the Elvis *Comeback Special,* appears briefly in a photo-shoot sequence, wearing Doris Day's mermaid outfit from *The Glass Bottom Boat*. Among the models is Thordis Brandt, a busy bit player of the 1960s, often in background decoration roles, and mostly associated with the spy genre, particularly *The Girl from UNCLE,* on which she appeared five times in four different roles. However, her largest role was in an episode of *The Green Hornet,* as a gangster's ill-fated girlfriend.

Live a Little, Love a Little remains yet another example of why it was time to move on from the innocent feel-good sun and sand movies of the '60s. Peel away the stylish 1968 advancements in photography, editing, and camerawork and you find *Girl Happy* and *Tickle Me* underneath, but what a difference a mere three years make as society and cinema struggles to redefine women... whether they want to be redefined or not. Nominally directed by virtual traffic cop Norman Taurog, but almost certainly seriously influenced by the support staff of cameramen, cinematographers, and designers, it was a genuine and brave attempt to revamp the Hal Wallis era for the age of Aquarius. In this, it was just as confused as *Easy Come, Easy Go,* but at least Elvis wasn't on the outside of the candy store looking in this time. As the least ambitious of the misguided efforts to find a new formula for the Elvis film, it has, alongside the ensemble cast effort *The Trouble With Girls,* the backhanded compliment of being the least lousy of his last few movies... but only because the others--*Stay Away Joe, Charro, Change of Habit*--were so unbelievably off the mark.

Charro (1969)

wr. Charles Marquis Warren from Frederic Lewis or Louis Fox and Harry Whittington, dir. Charles Marquis Warren, pr. Charles Marquis Warren (NGP)

with Elvis Presley (Jess Wade), Ina Balin (Tracy), Victor French (Vince), Solomon Sturges (Billy Roy), Paul Brinegar (Opie Keetch), Tony Young (Lt. Rivera), Lynn Kellogg (Marcie), Barbara Werle (Sara Ramsey), James Almanzar (Sheriff Ramsey), James B. Sikking (Gunner), Harry Landers (Heff), Charles H. Gray (Moody), John Pickard (Jerome Selby), Garry Walberg (Martin Tilford), J. Edward McKinley (Henry Carter), Robert Luster (Will Joslyn), Christa Lang (Christa), Robert Karnes (bartender), Duane Grey, Rodd Redwing

Elvis sings: "Charro" (over titles)

Charles Marquis Warren was a writer, director and producer best known for his westerns, some for cinema, most of them for TV. He produced and directed the first season of *Gunsmoke* in 1956, the longest running TV western series ever (twenty years), which was developed from the radio series of the same name on which he also worked. He also wrote numerous episodes of *Gunsmoke,* and from 1958 to '60 performed the same multi-tasking function on the *Rawhide* series that made Clint Eastwood's name. He then created and executive produced *Gunslinger* in 1961, developed and executive produced *The Virginian's* first season in 1962, and executive produced *Iron Horse* in 1966.

He was considered a better writer than director by western buffs, but despite controlling every aspect of the series he worked on, he was never so devoted to them that he didn't mind moving on to new pastures, leaving all his long-running series to fend for themselves as soon as he'd taught them to fly. His career at the camera had begun in movies in 1951, and *Charro* was a curious one-off return to the big screen after years of security in television. Born in 1912, he was another old-timer by the time he got to Elvis, and was firmly entrenched in TV westerns when Elvis had been making *Love Me Tender* and *Flaming Star.* One can only speculate on what drew him to such a curious project, although the cinema release of his previous work, the Glenn Ford TV movie *Day of the Evil Gun,* might have provided the impetus, as might witnessing the success of former colleague Clint Eastwood in Italian-made westerns.

Shot during July and August of 1968, in both Hollywood and Phoenix, Arizona, with a mostly dreary, uninspired choice of cast, *Charro* was a non-event for Presley fans and western fans alike. Despite

Peckinpah's *Wild Bunch*, the Italian-made westerns, and the revitalisation of John Wayne's career (partly with the aid of the ever-astute Hal Wallis, who had redefined Wayne as Rooster Cogburn), there were a fair number of bad, inconsequential westerns being made at this time (this was the year of *Paint Your Wagon*, the abomination so magnificently sent up in *The Simpsons*), and *Charro*--unlike the hideous *Butch Cassidy and the Sundance Kid*, also that year--couldn't even show box office in its defense. Needless to say, the fact that Presley was in the lead allowed the critics to have a field day, making a meal of a mundane mediocre film that they would otherwise have completely ignored.

Elvis plays reformed bad guy Jess Wade, a sort of western version of his early roles in the 1950s, but with obligatory stubble. The Hacketts, a pair of outlaws he used to ride with, have lured him back to the town of San Reco in Mexico (actually Apache Junction in Arizona) to frame him for their latest theft, a valuable cannon of historical significance and monetary value. A huge reward is offered for its return, and the Hacketts plan to deliver Jess dead and the cannon safe to claim it.

Left in the desert to die, Jess inconveniences the Hacketts by surviving, and returns to San Reco for revenge. With the dumber of the Hacketts incarcerated, the gang threaten to turn the cannon onto the town unless Wade releases him. When the cannon is fired and the sheriff--Wade's one true friend--is killed in the blast, his grieving wife shows Wade's wanted poster to the townspeople. Now Jess is obliged to prove himself, patch things up with the town, make amends to the people who believed in him, and bring the Hacketts to justice to clear his name. Ina Balin is the saloon owner who has a shady romantic past with both Wade and the sanest of the Hackett brothers, James Almanzar is the town sheriff who trusts him and deputises him when he suffers injury, Elvis movie regular Barbara Werle is the sheriff's wife, and Victor French and Solomon Sturges are the Hacketts.

Some actors and actresses suffer from typecasting, others never really make their mark. Ina Balin (real name, Ina Rosenberg) never really found her niche, jumping from one type of film to the next. Prior to *Charro*, her films had included *The Comancheros* with John Wayne, *The Patsy* with Jerry Lewis, and *The Greatest Story Ever Told* with everybody. TV had included episodes of *Twelve o'Clock High*, *Get Smart*, *Voyage to the Bottom of the Sea*, and later *Streets of San Francisco*, *Alias Smith and Jones*, and *The Six Million Dollar Man*. She was heading for TV movies.

Victor French, who had a recurring role on *Get Smart* as Agent 44 throughout the late '60s, went on to have a profitable relationship with TV star and producer Michael Landon, joining the cast of his long-running series *Little House on the Prairie* (which ran from 1974 to '83) and then co-starring with him in *Highway to Heaven* (from 1984 to '89). Solomon Sturges, who plays the deranged half of the Hacketts and played a few minor roles in TV westerns and cop shows before disappearing from the reference books, was the son of director Preston Sturges. His last work was for two Stephanie Rothman drive-in films for Roger Corman.

Barbara Werle, who had played various bit parts in the Elvis movies during the '60s, went from this film to a co-starring role in the short-lived series *San Francisco International Airport.* James B. Sikking had over two hundred minor film and TV roles to his credit (including the assassin in *Point Blank*) before making his mark as reactionary nutcase Howard Hunter in the 1980s series *Hill Street Blues,* a ground-breaking template for many ensemble series to follow. The rest of the cast of *Charro* was composed of mostly western veterans, including Paul Brinegar, famous as Wishbone, the comedy relief cook in Warren's *Rawhide* (1959-'66). Rodd Redwing's many westerns included *Flaming Star.*

Charro looks, feels, and plays like one of the nondescript cheap knock-offs that inevitably follow a huge success, and that is exactly what it was--an attempt to duplicate the look and feel of the Italian western. Furthermore, it has the air of a self-indulgent star vehicle for a major player's ego, which it certainly wasn't. Elvis never made a single decision of his own where his movie career was concerned, and *Charro* was no exception. Any actor from the biggest name to the smallest could have played Jess Wade, but Presley guaranteed a certain amount of box-office and critical attention, even at this point. But *Charro* is as false as a two dollar bill, and Elvis did himself no favors by associating himself with it.

The Trouble with Girls (1969)

wr. Arnold and Lois Peyser, from Day Keene, Dwight Babcock, and Mauri Grashin, dir. Peter Tewkesbury, pr. Lester Welch (MGM)

with Elvis Presley (Walter Hale), Marlyn Mason (Charlene), Nicole Jaffe (Betty), Sheree North (Nita Bix), Edward Andrews (Johnny), John Carradine (Mr. Drewcolt), Vincent Price (Mr. Morality), Joyce Van Patten (Maude), Dabney Coleman (Harrison Wilby), Anissa Jones (Carol), Pepe Brown (Willy), Anthony Teague (Clarence), Bill Zuckert (Mayor Gilchrist), Med Flory (police constable), Pitt Herbert (Mr. Perper), Robert Nichols (Mr. Smith), Patsy Garrett (Mrs. Gilchrist), Kevin O'Neal (Yale), John Rubinstein (Princeton), Chuck Briles (Amherst), Helene Winston (Olga), Frank Welker (Rutgers), Mike Wagner (Chowderhead), Linda Sue Risk (Lily Jeanne), Brett Parker (iceman), Charles P. Thompson (cabbie), Leonard Rumery, William Paris, Kathleen Rainey (farmhands), Hal J. Pederson (soda man), Duke Snider, Pacific Pallisades High School Madrigals

Elvis sings: "Swing Down, Sweet Chariot"; "Aura Lee"; "Clean Up Your Own Back Yard"; "Signs of the Zodiac" (all on stage in tent show; last accompanying Marlyn Mason); "Almost" (on piano, to close)

...and the following period pieces are sung by various cast members: "When You Wore a Tulip"; "Hello Susan Brown"; "Here We Go Round the Mulberry Bush"; "Rocked in the Cradle of the Deep"; "Toot Toot Tootsie, Goodbye"; "I'm Always Chasing Rainbows"; "Nobody's Baby"; "Darktown Strutters Ball"; "The Whiffenpoof Song"

Although the title makes it seem like a sun, sea and sand movie from Elvis' early '60s period, *The Trouble With Girls* is nothing of the kind. The trouble with *The Trouble With Girls* is that the title has nothing to do with the movie, which in itself is not too bad an entertainment, but is just not an Elvis movie. Elvis movies had often been carried by their supporting casts, but this was the only one that actually belonged to the co-stars; some, such as Vincent Price and John Carradine, performed their cameos without ever performing alongside Presley, or perhaps even meeting him!

The setting is a sort of traveling talent show, an upmarket carnival or lowbrow arts festival named a Chautauqua (pronounced sha-tor-cwa) after the New York state such affairs originated in. The first had been in the early 1870s, but they had fallen out of favor by the 1940s. Although the film itself--an amalgam of *Frankie and Johnny* and *Roustabout*--is set in the 1920s, you'd never know it from looking at Elvis or any of his co-stars, despite several attempts to set the time period with knowing pop culture references. Elvis plays the organiser of the chautauqua, a pragmatic, opportunistic, white-suited, cigar-chewing big shot, who brings his cross-country distraction to a small town in Iowa and becomes involved in the petty and trivial lives of the bored locals. The main event of the occasion turns out to be unplanned--the murder of storekeeper and local creep Harrison Wilby (Dabney Coleman), which Presley's Walter Hale attempts to exploit to his own ends. The romance, if that's the right word for the movie's interminable dog and cat fight between Presley's Hale and Marlyn Mason's ass-pain Charlene, is yet another Presley film example of Hollywood's late-'60s confusion over contemporary women (and this is supposed to be 1927 anyway); all the supposed attributes that the writers pile onto this scatty loudmouth only serve to make her thoroughly undesirable. There is no pleasure in seeing Elvis get the girl at the end of the movie as she's been so thoroughly unpleasant throughout.

What occurs is a series of quirky vignettes, some featuring Elvis and advancing the story, some featuring the other players from the movie's extensive cast. American cinema had just discovered observational character comedy that was more concerned with capturing the atmosphere of an occasion than telling a story, and some of it worked and some of it didn't; one of the better examples would be Michael Ritchie's 1972 beauty pageant satire *Smile*. For the first thirty minutes, Elvis wanders around with Edward Andrews looking for his part in the movie; so many minutes pass between Presley's appearances that one can easily forget he's in it. He only sings twice, the first a superb gospel number, the second a nice piece hampered by the tricksy distracting camerawork popular at the time. Peter Tewkesbury directs throughout like a teenage film student who's just bought his first camera and is trying to score points with his tutor.

As *The Trouble With Girls* owes so much to it's supporting players, we should take a look at them. Cast at the insistence of director Tewkesbury, singer and dancer Marlyn Mason came from television (a recurring role in *Ben Casey* and guest shots in *My Three Sons, Gomer Pyle, Burke's Law, Doctor Kildare, The Man from UNCLE, Bonanza, The Big Valley, Laredo, The Fugitive, The FBI, The Invaders, Hogan's Heroes, I Spy,* and *Mannix*) and returned as soon as her Elvis movie was finished, guest-starring in numerous TV movies and episodes of *Ghost Story, Ironside, Mission: Impossible, The Mod Squad, Banacek, Streets of San Francisco, Cannon, Barnaby Jones, The Amazing Spider-Man, Wonder Woman, Project UFO, Vegas, Dynasty, Hardcastle and McCormick,* and *Scarecrow and Mrs. King* and co-starring in the short-lived detective series *Longstreet* during the 1971-'72 season. As Tom Lisanti points out in his book *Drive-In Dream Girls,* Mason played "sexy, kooky, naive or evil characters", a variety of offbeat types, and the above program titles only skim the surface. She also played Broadway and Vegas.

Initially perceived as a Marilyn Monroe type, from the mid-'60s onwards, Sheree North made a career out of playing brow-beaten, world-weary, tired-eyed, long-suffering wives, whores and girlfriends for ageing action men. In most films her characters brought such miseries down upon herself, either through her actions (*The Outfit*) or her inaction (*Lawman*). Although stereotyped, her avoidance of the bimbo circuit allowed her several good roles and character parts, even if they were often similar. Her characters never escape their tiresome, tragic, empty lives. She finally got some laughs playing Kramer's mother in *Seinfeld*, albeit another sad, sleazy broad.

Nicole Jaffe (carelessly misidentified as Joyce Van Patten in the film's trailer) gave up acting to become an agent, but not before she'd secured her place in pop culture history by becoming the voice of Velma Dinkley in the *Scooby-Doo* cartoons. Although others took up the role in the '80s and '90s she reclaimed the role at the turn of the century for some of the straight-to-video features. She considered Elvis "an incredibly sexy, lonely, sad person with the most magnetic eyes I'd ever seen". Ironically, featured further down the cast is Frank Welker, one of the busiest voice actors in the business and the voice of Freddy.

Edward Andrews had a dual career, playing loveable chumps in comedy films and sweaty villains in dramas. He was thoroughly horrible in episodes of *The Twilight Zone* (an informer, and later a hit-and-run driver), *The Invaders* (a sleazy reporter), and *The Name of the Game* (a slumlord), delightfully daffy in such comedy films as *The Absent-Minded Professor, The Thrill of It All,* and *The Glass Bottom Boat,* as bumptious figures of authority. Numerous TV roles included many for Quinn Martin and Universal.

Dabney Coleman spent the 1960s playing nondescript bit parts in series like *The Outer Limits, I Dream of Jeannie* and *The Invaders* before growing a moustache and carving a niche for himself as opinionated slimeballs, *The Trouble With Girls* being one of the earliest examples, albeit clean-shaven; such films as *Nine to Five* and *The Beverly Hillbillies* (as Drysdale) eventually followed, alongside critically acclaimed but short-lived TV series such as *Buffalo Bill* and *The Life and Times of Slap Maxwell,* although he paid his dues throughout the 1970s in a fair number of bad TV movies.

Joyce Van Patten specialised magnificently in fragile, broken flowers and bitter harridans and unlike so many actresses who like to make excuses for the weak, wretched women they portray, Van Patten seems to relish playing slightly offbeat, deranged nutjobs. Here, she's the daffy, self-important swimmer who finds the dead body. A courageous, up-for-anything actress, she was an over-zealous nun in a soup kitchen in *Columbo,* the wealthy, shrewish wife of a crooked mortuary owner in *McCloud,* a lonely police groupie in *The Rockford Files,* a lost and frightened newly-bereaved widow in *Lou Grant,* and a shrill, fearful wife in the mini-series *The Martian Chronicles,* to mention just a handful of her portrayals of tragic, damaged goods. A treasure of a character actress, her appearances in film and TV are few, but when she shows up, she steals the show.

Child actress Anissa Jones was then starring in the long-running saccharine sit-com *Family Affair,* which had begun in 1966 and would cease production in 1971. She died tragically from drugs-related causes five years later, in 1976. Child actor Pepe Brown went straight from this film to the supporting players of a short-lived variety show hosted by Pat Paulsen in 1970.

Putting in brief but amusing cameos were Vincent Price and John Carradine, both known primarily for their roles in the horror genre, but also for rarely turning anything down. Both come up roses here, Price quoting dialogue from the classics, Carradine getting the best line in the movie (asked if he thought Romeo and Juliet had pre-marital relations, he pompously replies "Only in the Des Moines company!"). Both took almost any role in any film offered them, in the full confidence that their craft and professionalism would protect them from a negative end result--which it always did.

Carradine and Price consequently appeared in some awful rubbish, but their attitude also ensured that they never missed a good role either, and both had enjoyed many (Carradine had played in *Stagecoach* and *The Grapes of Wrath* before descending into Z-movies). They also had no qualms about doing TV, and both have subsequently left their mark on the small screen too, mostly in cult series that still air today (Price did *Batman, F Troop, Get Smart, Voyage to the Bottom of the Sea, The Bionic Woman, Columbo* and *The Snoop Sisters,* Carradine did *Johnny Ringo, The Twilight Zone, My Favorite Martian, The Munsters, The Beverly Hillbillies, Branded, The Green Hornet, Lost in Space, McCloud, Kung Fu,* and *Starsky and Hutch,* and both did *UNCLE*). Price even turns up in *Beach Party.* Neither were they shy about lending their vocal talents alone; Carradine voiced a living brain for *Wonder Woman,* and Price worked alongside both Michael Jackson and Scooby-Doo!

Bill Zuckert, Med Flory, and Pitt Herbert were busy bit players with literally hundreds of small roles between them. Kevin O'Neal was the younger brother of actor Ryan O'Neal, but never secured similar fame. He had small roles in episodes of *The Twilight Zone* and *The Time Tunnel*. John Rubinstein later co-starred in the late-'80s murder mystery series *Crazy Like a Fox* and has made numerous TV guest appearances before and since, notably as a crooked art dealer in an early *Frasier*. Robert Nichols' many roles include the `Blinky' part in *This Island Earth*. Patsy Garrett went from this film to the cast of the TV series *Nanny and the Professor*, which ran from 1970 to '71, a last gasp of the 1960s-style sit-com. Helene Winston had previously appeared in *Double Trouble*. Frank Welker is known for providing voices for virtually every cartoon series on the air from the 1970s to the present. Tewkesbury had previously used bit player Brett Parker in *Stay Away Joe*.

The 1968 TV special had revitalised Elvis and thrilled his fans, but there was only one reason that the movie projects ground to a halt, and one reason only. Memphis Mafia member Alan Fortas put it in a nutshell. "All of his movies made money, but by the time he got to *The Trouble With Girls* and *Charro* there was a noticeable decline in profits, and an even more noticeable decline in Elvis' interest in movies". Looking at a film like this, one simply asks--what's the point? True, Elvis is surrounded by some classy character actors, and had been for all his recent efforts... but these films--*Stay Away Joe, Charro,* all of them, post *Speedway*--could have been devised for anyone. They weren't Elvis films, they were just films with Elvis in them. Indeed, in many respects, the fact that they became Elvis films may actually have obscured any other values they might have possessed. *Stay Away Joe* and *Live a Little, Love a Little* were bona fide stiffs, but *Charro* might have fared better as a plain ordinary minor western, and *The Trouble With Girls,* while never box office gold, was an intriguing slice of Americana at a time when America was looking beyond the Old West and the modern day big cities for their material. And in that respect, as the 1960s gasped their last and the 1970s loomed, Elvis got out of the movies just in time. Or, strictly speaking, five movies too late. But he got out.

Change of Habit (1969)

wr. James Lee, William Schweitzer, Eric Bercovici, from John Joseph, Richard Morris, dir. William Graham, pr. Joe Connelly (Universal/NBC)

with Elvis Presley (John Carpenter), Mary Tyler Moore (Sister Michelle), Barbara McNair (Sister Irene), Jane Elliot (Sister Barbara), Regis Toomey (Father Gibbons), Ed Asner (Lt. Moretti), Robert Emhardt (the Banker), Nefti Millet (Julio Hernandez), Rodolfo Hoyos (Mr. Hernandez), Laura Figueroa (Desiree), Ruth McDevitt (Lily), Doro Merande (Rose), Timothy Carey (shopkeeper), Leora Dana (Mother Joseph), Richard Carlson (Bishop Finley), Lorena Kirk (Angela), Virginia Vincent (Miss Parker), Bill Elliott (Robbie), Ji-Tu Cumbuka (Hawk), A. Martinez, David Renard

Elvis sings: "Change of Habit" (over titles); "Rubberneckin'" (to kids at clinic); "Have a Happy" (to kids in the park); "Let Us Pray" (finale in the church)

Change of Habit was Elvis Presley's final film, and sadly, probably his worst. It's very difficult to understand a film like *Change of Habit*--or indeed, a beautiful song like Mac Davis' "In the Ghetto", recorded by Elvis that same year--without first understanding the peculiar little pocket of popular culture that was formed in a half decade between the end of the 1960s and the middle of the 1970s.

To say that Europe and America had not treated the black people of the world well is something of an understatement, the detail of which is a matter for the history books, not this one. However, the changes of 1960s habits had included the somewhat overdue civil rights movement, and black people had been responding to their second rate status in society with both hope and optimism (in the form of that remarkable orator Martin Luther King) and anger and hatred (in the form of the likes of Malcolm X and other angry firebrands like him) throughout the 1960s. In the media, producers like Sheldon Leonard and Gene Roddenberry, and performers like Sammy Davis Jnr., Harry Belafonte, Sidney Poitier, Robert Culp and Bill Cosby, and Richard Pryor pushed painfully forward inch by inch.

The reaction of white people to the integration of black people into the mainstream, which had to be achieved with acts of political force, and the subsequent riots in the city ghettoes that followed, was neatly divided between just two possible responses. The first was the racist response, to begrudge everything with fear, anger, and resentment, and the other was with acceptance, understanding, remorse and guilt for the injustices so long swept under the carpet. This latter, liberal view, admirable in itself, ultimately resulted in the fifty years of squirmy, condescending political correctness that has kept Western society walking on eggshells ever since, even in the face of such blatantly offensive ugliness as gangsta rap, the sentiments of which would never be tolerated from white performers.

But if the road to hell is paved with good intentions, then the ribbon-cutting ceremony began when the late '60s and early '70s let loose a veritable flood of hand-wringing, banner-waving, well-intentioned social conscience plays, books, films, TV episodes and even comic books that were known by the catch-all nickname "relevance". It wasn't just about race and/or racism; drugs, pollution, poverty, slumlords, police brutality, political corruption, the bogeyman of over-population, all became subjects to be confronted by every film star, TV character, writer of merit, even super-hero. This was the buzzword for the pop culture that followed the fluff and fantasy of the '60s--was it relevant? As irrelevant as most of these efforts are today, many of them painfully dated, patronising, and occasionally even misguided, they were, at the time, the only possible intelligent response from the white world.

Given the amount of work required to make such huge changes in society from the early '60s on, these improvements, slow and modest though they were, were made relatively swiftly and effectively, with each decade showing definite advances in tolerance and understanding both because of, and in spite of, the excesses of liberal angst, which often took the form of a sort of arm-around-the-shoulder reverse racism as progressives trampled over each other to offer tea and sympathy to the oppressed masses. One example of this excessive pity shows itself in the haunting lament of "In the Ghetto", beautifully performed and sung by Elvis, which makes the common unintentionally racist assumption that the poor black woman in the song resents and regrets her pregnancy, and sees her children as a financial burden. Women of any race who choose to give birth rarely see their young as unwelcome arrivals, whatever the hardships they might face as they grow. Ethnic society was perceived by both right-wing racists and liberal progressives as a problem to be dealt with. Those people, needless to say, quite rightly didn't see themselves as the problem, although this wasn't particularly clear to white society at the time.

All of this matters in the context of this book because popular culture of this period was awash in well-meaning but ultimately condescending attempts to understand and appreciate the newly-discovered justifiable complaints of the so-called minorities, and *Change of Habit* was a particularly mealy-mouthed product of it (Europe was far less tolerant during this period, and ultimately took its cue from American pop culture, albeit later; there was less political impetus for change in Europe, and ultimately when it came, political correctness hit much harder and sometimes more foolishly).

To put things in perspective, the late-'60s/early '70s flood of always American films, TV series, individual TV episodes, songs, plays and comic-books that so sympathetically confronted the problems of ethnic groups (often represented by burning ghettoes and/or angry young men raging at the white world) were all written and produced by predominantly well-intentioned white men trying to understandably distance themselves from the other, racist response that was fuelling and perpetuating the bad feeling. Even as late as the appearance of the extraordinarily popular *The Cosby Show* in the 1980s, some liberal critics were still complaining that this banal sit-com was not being honest because it didn't confront the reality of most black peoples' lives in the U.S.--as if black people weren't entitled to watch insipid, phoney aspirational shows of happy family life, wealth and success in the era that produced *Growing Pains, Full House, Family Ties, Facts of Life,* and *Dallas* and *Dynasty* for the white folk.

From 1969 to the mid-1970s, every TV show had what was disparagingly but with depressing accuracy called a token black character in the regular cast, and every drama series had an episode (or even maybe two or three) where the white lead would find himself immersed in an ethnic world for the duration of that one story--during which he would be both tourist and the man in charge, sorting out the problems he uncovered, making life a little better for the small number of non-white characters he encountered in that story (not always black--sometimes Hispanic, Mexican, Chinese, Japanese, Native American), and metaphorically patting everyone on the head as he departed for the more usual white-dominated storylines for the rest of the season.

These actors, writers, directors and producers meant well, and were usually quite genuinely trying to do their bit for racial harmony, but these early first steps--of which *Change of Habit* was a part--look alarmingly indulgent and condescending today (the classiest, most three-dimensional examples of relevant TV were on such Universal series as *The Name of the Game* and *The Bold Ones*). Comedy handled the issues better (although *All in the Family*'s Archie Bunker, like the British counterpart his series sprang from, may have harmed as much as helped, by making its racist leading character begrudgingly likeable in a boorish Ralph Kramden/Fred Flintstone way). Far more popular with black audiences were the rash of cinema films at the time, insultingly, honestly and revealingly nicknamed blaxploitation, which at least put black leading men (and women) at the forefront of stories about cleaning up the ghettoes and closing down the activities of drugs dens and violent pimps (and which also didn't shy away from implicating the white men in their part of the problems)--*Shaft,*

Superfly, Slaughter, Coffy, Black Belt Jones, Black Caesar, Across 110th Street, Bucktown, Cleopatra Jones, Friday Foster, Foxy Brown... black actors and actresses had never worked so hard, so much or so often.

Although made for the cinema, *Change of Habit* was as close to a TV movie as Elvis ever got. Producer Joe Connelly had previously worked with partner Bob Mosher on the whitebread *Leave it to Beaver* and spoof sit-com *The Munsters*. In a twist almost too absurd to be true, they had written hundreds of scripts for the *Amos n' Andy Show* in the 1950s, which--although not much different in content or attitude to most contemporary sit-coms with a predominantly black cast--was widely condemned as racist by those brave enough to declare themselves qualified to speak for everyone else. It's also worth noting that the *Munsters* pilot, "My Fair Munster", was one of TV comedy's earliest digs at the cliches of intolerance, with uptight neighbors complaining about the Munsters being "different" in very familiar terms.

Almost everybody working on *Change of Habit* was either already in or on TV, or on their way there, and while the film certainly featured quality performers (particularly among the reliable character actors further down the cast), it had the look and the feel of being made for the small screen (New York is the familiar Universal backlot). The NBC network was involved, as was Universal, and the movie was part of the deal that included the *Comeback Special* (absurdly, the money for that legendary piece of television and rock music history was a fifth of that found for this silly, dated, forgotten film). It was Presley's last and most inappropriate acting role (as an idealistic young doctor working in a poverty-stricken neighborhood), and it indicated clearly where Elvis was heading had he not finally forsaken film for Vegas. As depressing as some of his rambling stage sets later became, the TV and cinema of the 1970s would have surely been far worse (and far more frequently revisited).

The biggest problem with *Change of Habit* is not the fashionable social concern for non-whites on the breadline (as usual in an Elvis film, other ethnic groups figure more prominently in the storyline than African-Americans). Nor is it even Dr. Elvis, who is reduced to co-star status in his own movie, as the film invites the audience to follow and empathise with the three nuns into whose lives Elvis is dropped into; it's the only Presley film not told from the Presley character's perspective. The biggest problem is accepting bubbly, personable Mary Tyler Moore as a nun, an even greater leap across the credibility canyon than accepting Elvis as a free clinic medic.

Even then, the story is offensively stupid; the three nuns enter the community they seek to gain the trust of by ditching their religious identification and posing as regular, everyday women (rather like alien invaders posing as Earth people). They swan into the area with gleeful condescension, piously considering themselves better than everyone else around them, winking at the audience with giveaway remarks in the manner of the 1950s Clark Kent, and work as nurses while perversely trying to gain the trust of the locals before admitting who and what they are, brazenly telling lies to cover up their frequent slips.

Told to rely on her own resources, the first thing Jane Eliot's character does without her nun's habit is exploit her feminine wiles to dupe the local males into bringing her furniture in off the street. She dolls herself up, pouts and flutters her eyelashes, and draws six beaming idiots across the road to work up a sweat on her furniture. She's quite nasty about it too, sitting in one of the chairs in the street, smirking and not lifting a finger. When the guys expect the payback she's flaunted, she's saved only by the arrival of the local moneylender, Robert Emhardt's slimy Banker, and his even tougher muscle. One is left with the nagging feeling that six new misogynists have just been created in the space of half-an-hour with Sister Stupid.

Meanwhile, Tyler Moore cavorts shamelessly with poor Dr. Elvis (who could do better), as if on vacation from the convent, and only Barbara McNair's Sister Irene seems to be remembering her true identity, even while Eliot's Sister Barbara chooses to abandon hers for her new calling as cartoon cut-out protest movement organiser. The protest movement of the late 1960s was almost always represented by Hollywood as all-purpose, anti-everything campaigners carrying non-specific placards, rather than people with a specific cause. Professional rabble-rousers undoubtedly were prolific at this time, but they were hardly non-controversial in their noise-making; Sister Barbara belongs to their jargon-spouting number, eccentric colorful scenery, not to be taken seriously.

For all that happens to them during the course of the film, next to the irritatingly effervescent Mary Tyler Moore, the drab and dull performances offered by Barbara McNair and Jane Eliot make them virtually invisible. Despite the fact that the nuns' scheme is dishonest and clearly failing (all three nuns are a menace to themselves and others), the unimpressed and dubious old guard are portrayed as a collection of bitter, mean-spirited bigots--the disapproving local priest, Father Gibbons (Regis Toomey) is a very un-Christian misery who keeps the doors of his church locked so that he can display valuable religious artefacts without worrying about their theft, and two disapproving old dears (Doro Merande and Ruth McDevitt) are comedy relief hypocrites full of zealous disgust even as their dirty minds work overtime making mountains out of molehills, spiritual descendants of the finger-clicking fuddy-duddies of the 1950s rock and roll films.

The film boasts a minimal amount of trendy 1970s buzzwords that still manage to stand out like psychedelic beacons of the era ("where it's at", "way out", and "you're too much" all get an airing) and lays its cards on the table when Eliot asks Presley poker-faced whether he believes "the riots, the student unrest, are not really the death throes of an old order, but the birth pains of a new one?".

Although it can't end quickly enough, one gets the distinct feeling that several cuts have been made to get the film down to an excruciating 87 minutes, notably a storyline involving a local market where the goods are apparently overpriced, and the sleazy storekeeper (an unbilled Timothy Carey) short-changing the elderly customers. This is so truncated that it barely makes sense and begs the question that the volatile Carey might have removed his name. Also dealt with far too simply is Emhardt's Tarantino-esque ribs-beating, face-smashing, leg-breaking moneylender, who in reality would have escalated the violence he promises, but instead is seen off effortlessly by one nun and a vague threat and dropped from the plot. This is a guy who has held the neighborhood in terror for years.

Another cop-out, to excuse the pun, is Ed Asner's loveable understanding street cop, not a non-existent figure certainly, but an unconvincing rarity here, and even rarer in the '60s. Asner himself is as always wonderful, struggling manfully with absurd dialogue of writer's rant, and making his comic relief character totally three-dimensional against all the odds. He's never seen dealing with any of the real vice on the block, even though the whole film centers around it, just coping with the local eccentrics. When a rapist attacks Tyler Moore (we're told rapes are a regular occurrence here), it's not Asner, but Dr. Elvis who charges to the rescue, getting his obligatory fight scene in (several Elvis ingredients from the 1960s are here in this movie, cunningly disguised for the 1970s, including the cute kid and funny senior citizens).

What never convinces for a minute is that Elvis and Tyler Moore could be an item, habit or no habit. You have to wonder where the controlling Colonel Parker was while all this was going on; even *Viva Las Vegas*--which Parker loathed--was still undeniably Elvis' movie. This is Tyler Moore's, from start to finish; Elvis is special guest star.

Mary Tyler Moore's career began in the 1950s as the Hotpoint elf and a pair of legs on the *Richard Diamond* detective drama. She guested in shows such as *77, Sunset Strip, Surfside Six, Hawaiian Eye, Bourbon Street Beat, The Aquanauts,* and *Wanted--Dead or Alive,* but struck gold when she was cast as the TV wife in the superb *Dick Van Dyke Show*, a 1961-'66 sitcom literally ten years ahead of its time, boasting 1970s-style format, gags and storylines in the feelgood fantasy and slapstick era of *Leave it to Beaver, Ozzie and Harriet,* and *Mr. Ed.*

Everything she learned from comic genius Dick Van Dyke about sympathetic reactive comedy and the comedy of embarrassment was put to use ten years later when she married TV executive Grant Tinker and they formed MTM Productions to make *The Mary Tyler Moore Show,* a wonderful sit-com (also co-starring Ed Asner) from which sprung everything that was good about 1970s TV, cultivating spin-offs, writers, formats and styles that pushed the envelope and primed the audience for a new level of quality that spread from MTM programming right across the television landscape; many of MTM's comedy writers landed at Paramount to create the likes of *Taxi, Cheers,* and *Frasier,* while dramatists such as Steven Bochco gave MTM *Hill Street Blues* and then *L.A. Law* and *NYPD Blue* to 20th Century Fox (whose *Simpsons* phenomenon also began with former MTM staffers). It is no exaggeration to say that two thirds of everything good about American television for the rest of the 20th century only came about because of MTM Productions (the other third owes the ubiquitous Stephen J. Cannell).

Barbara McNair was a singer who peaked with her own TV variety show from 1969 to 1971. She also appeared in *I Spy* and the final first-run episode of *Mission: Impossible,* and played the wife of Sidney Poitier's Virgil Tibbs character in the spin-off films from *In the Heat of the Night, They Call Me Mister Tibbs* and *The Organisation.* After making various one-off appearances in TV, Jane Eliot co-starred in the short-lived 1977 series *Rosetti and Ryan* and appeared in the long-running prime-time soap *Knots Landing* during the 1980-'81 season before becoming a regular player in daytime soaps.

Ed Asner starred in MTM's first major dramatic success, in the title character of *Lou Grant,* a spin-off built around his *Mary Tyler Moore Show* character; prior to that he had played hoods, thugs, slobs and cops, as his two Elvis film roles--in *Kid Galahad* and *Change of Habit*--are testimony to. He would appear in two more white-scripted melodramas with a black theme, *Halls of Anger* and *They Call Me Mister Tibbs,* both 1970. Numerous TV guest shots included *The Untouchables, The Outer Limits, Route 66, Gunsmoke, Voyage to the Bottom of the Sea, The Fugitive, The Invaders, The Girl from UNCLE, The Wild Wild West, The FBI, The Name of the Game, The Mod Squad,* and *Ironside.* He relished playing the opposite of what he was, a vocal advocate of left-wing ideals, and appeared in Oliver Stone's *JFK* in a small but significant role as a right-wing racist.

Robert Emhardt had also played a minor role in *Kid Galahad*. He excelled as sleazy bad guys, making memorable appearances in *The Untouchables, The Invaders,* and *The Man from UNCLE* to name but three of many. Veteran actor Regis Toomey previously co-starred in *The Mickey Rooney Show, Four Star Theater, Richard Diamond, Letter to Loretta, Burke's Law,* and *Petticoat Junction*. A. Martinez, typecast, appeared in numerous cop shows and TV movies in the 1970s, invariably as a troubled youth. Equally typecast, Rodolfo Hoyos, Hollywood's live-in South America bad guy.

Leora Dana, the Mother Superior, had worked alongside Frank Sinatra and Dean Martin in *Some Came Running*. Ruth McDevitt often played wacky old women and had a recurring role in *Kolchak--the Night Stalker*. Doro Merande co-starred in the 1960-'61 sit-com *Bringing Up Buddy* as an interfering aunt, and both she and McDevitt loved to play easily shocked old biddies, because in reality they were both intelligent and amusing character actresses.

Timothy Carey usually portrayed hoods and gangsters, and was superb in early '70s crime thriller *The Outfit*. A genuine eccentric, he'd take any role in any film (although his appearance always typecast him as pure evil), and while he played slimeballs in the likes of *The Killing* and *East of Eden,* he also appeared in William Asher's beach movies *Bikini Beach* and *Beach Blanket Bingo,* the Monkees film *Head,* and a barrel-full of bizarre exploitation sleaze. He milked sadistic bit parts in *The Untouchables* for all they were worth, and is very funny as a scuzzy key-holder in an early '70s *McCloud,* making a meal of his single scene. Other TV included episodes of *Rawhide, Gunsmoke, Daniel Boone, The Name of the Game, Baretta, Starsky and Hutch, Charlie's Angels, Greatest American Hero,* and *Mike Hammer*.

Richard Carlson was a veteran of 1950s B-movies, notably sci-fi creature features like *It Came from Outer Space* and *The Creature from the Black Lagoon*. He later moved into directing (*The Detectives*) and writing (*O'Hara, U.S. Treasury*). Ji-Tu Cumbuka played a heavy in many 1970s films and TV shows.

Although it's a mortifying thought, *Change of Habit* really needed to be a three-hour mini-series to cover all the ground it stakes a claim to, but the format didn't exist back then. The result is a bizarre hybrid of mismatched leads, misjudged scenes (the shots of the nuns jettisoning their habits are filmed like a lingerie fantasy), unexplored ideas and unresolved storylines, unsatisfying even to the limited audience such soapy mawkishness might appeal to. It would have been wonderful if Elvis could have ended his movie career with one really impressive contemporary adult-themed film to stand alongside the *Comeback Special* (the aforementioned mob thriller

The Outfit had a leading role played by Joe Don Baker that would have been perfect for Elvis) but instead it fizzled out with another dismal addition to his post-Paramount list of embarrassments. So--Viva *Viva Las Vegas!*

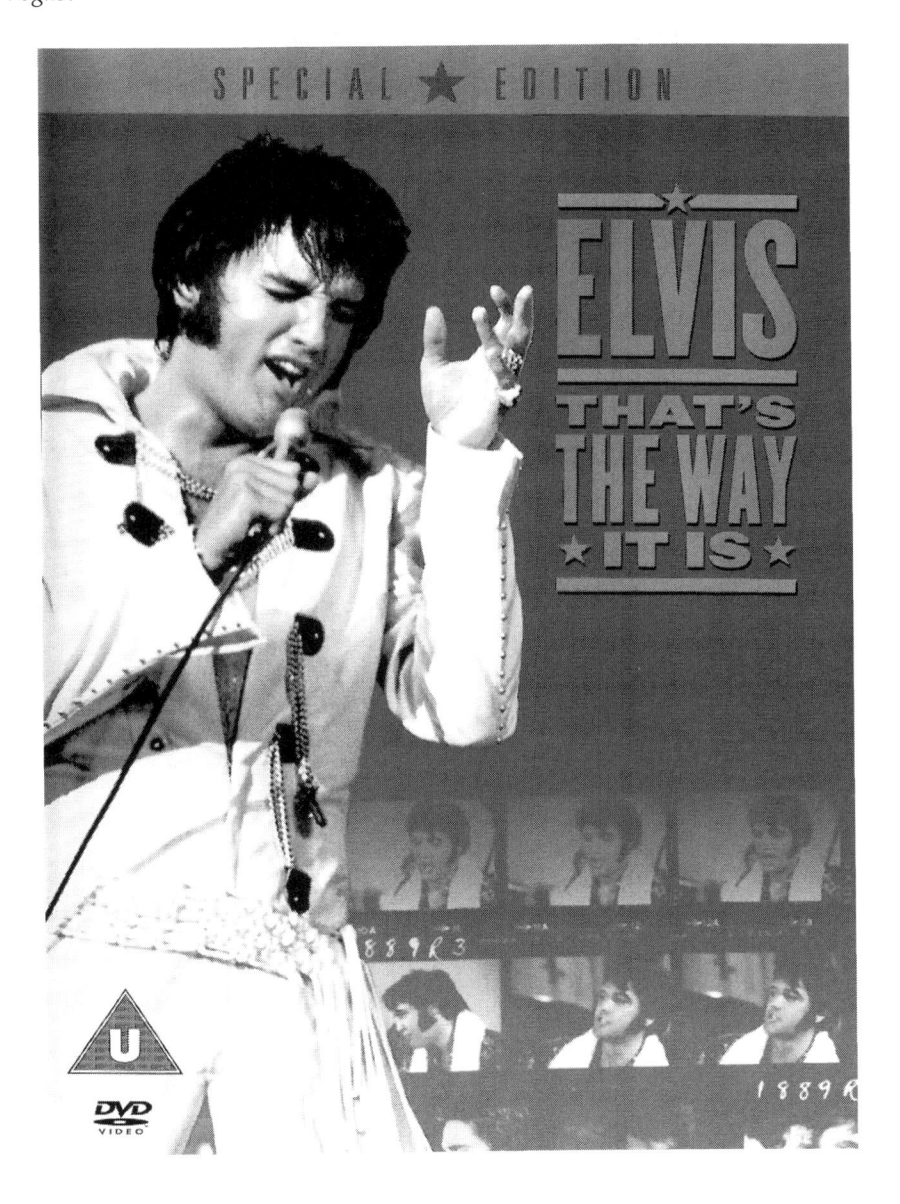

appendix 1--the documentaries

Elvis--That's the Way It Is (1970)

dir. Denis Sanders, pr. Herbert Solow (MGM)

Special Edition 2001: ed. Michael Solomon, prod. Rick Schmidlin (Turner/W. Bros)

New to MGM, producer Herb Solow had just left Paramount, formerly Desilu, where he had been involved with the television series *Star Trek* and the comedy series of the wonderful Lucille Ball. Now he was involved with another American icon.

The better of the two fly-on-the-wall behind the scenes documentaries, this is rather slow when Elvis isn't on stage. In 2001, it was re-edited with hindsight and rediscovered footage into a less pointless, less cynical, more useful and entertaining product that focussed more on Elvis and less on Elvis-related incidentals and phenomena. Although the opening title sequence uses dated film tricks to needlessly jazz things up, the actual concert footage is mostly free of artifice. This was more due to the Colonel than the director, as we shall see.

That's the Way It Is serves its purpose, more valuably than anyone could have known at the time, of putting 1970s Elvis' stage performance on record for posterity. It's extraordinary to think just how important this casually shot, randomly edited footage has become; anyone remotely interested in Elvis as a person would push aside diamonds and rubies to grab hold of this rare film of the man himself, images and performances once discarded on the cutting room floor but which transcend any book ever written about him to show the real person, in person. Above all, it offers indisputable evidence that Elvis Presley was an okay guy.

The film's greatest value is to put the lid on some of the arguments that have raged over the years. Firstly, it puts the lie to sleazy garbage like the Albert Goldman book by showing that Elvis was fundamentally an ordinary, decent individual. The guys in the band tend to laugh a little too readily at Presley's every utterance, but that's them, not him. He's king of the hill, but he doesn't seem to be abusing his position (possibly, but not definitely, because the cameras are there; there are anecdotal stories of Presley regally demanding lights for cigarettes and expecting to be the center of attention, although on the evidence of the *Comeback Special* footage, his position and occasional obvious irritation was justified).

That's the Way It Is demonstrates Elvis' skill and dominance of the proceedings, showing how he instructed the musicians and backing singers, and how he directed his stage shows while they were in progress-- uniquely, the running order for the songs was never set in stone. It is often overlooked that Elvis judged the mood of the audience, and indulged his own moods, while the show was proceeding, with the backing players and singers waiting for their next fleeting, almost unnoticeable cue; they had to know the repertoire backwards.

And it also shows beyond a shadow of a doubt that Elvis enjoyed the sort of music he was now performing... whether the rock and roll purists liked it or not. As in the *Comeback Special,* his performance of the old material is lazy and indulgent. To say that his rendition of "Hound Dog" is perfunctory is an understatement! It's only when he performs his more mundane MOR 1970s material that he seems to come to life and feel the music and sentiments of the words. At other times, he's playing about, breezing through his back catalogue without any thought to the lyrics he's singing. Elvis, while still a dynamo on stage, had grown old with his audience.

The generous concert footage, although it takes its time coming, is taken from six different performances, opening with "That's Alright Mama", then "I've Lost You", ("You ain't nothin' but a...") "Hound Dog", "Heartbreak Hotel" ("Well, since my baby left me..."), "Love Me Tender" (with some outrageous flirting with the audience--"Hang loose, I'll be with you in a minute..."; "I'm sorry I couldn't make it up there, ma'am"), the mundane pop anthem "I Can't Stop Loving You", "Just Pretend", "The Wonder of You", an oddly upbeat "In the Ghetto", the weak "Patch it Up", the parents' party anthem "You've Lost That Lovin' Feeling", and "Chain Gang". Then Elvis rips into "One Night", a light-hearted "Don't Be Cruel" and "Blue Suede Shoes", and then back into the middle of the road with "You Don't Have to Say You Love Me", an almost self-parodic performance of "Suspicious Minds" (as well it should be), and a delightfully loose "Can't Helping Falling in Love". The gentle rippling discussions of a polite and mannered after-show party run over the closing credits as Elvis schmoozes and gladhands his guests with the knowing self-assuredness of a seasoned professional as he works the room with what seems to be genuine pleasure.

There are some nice candid moments with offstage Elvis, but most fascinating and valuable is the footage of Elvis interacting with the audience... teasing them with false intros, sideways offhand remarks and bits of business with the band and back-up singers, and heartfelt body language deliberate (as in "One Night"), or inadvertent (the famous vibrating left leg). At one point, after dealing with a helplessly sobbing young girl completely overwhelmed by her close proximity to the man himself ("Please kiss me!!" she pleads), he is next confronted by a much more confident, experienced and self-assured woman, the other female's polar opposite. "You want to get serious, or just play a little bit?" Presley sneers good naturedly. "Yes!" she announces emphatically and unhesitatingly, with a determined assurance that most men will only hear once or twice in their lives. But Elvis has simply brushed it off and moved on. Imagine a star of that magnitude walking amongst an audience today (the memorable walkabout in "Love Me Tender" was originally left on the cutting room floor--twice).

Having taken the blame for the perceived failings of Presley's thirty-odd theatrical films, it was the Colonel who saved *Elvis--That's the Way It Is* from being the dated waste of time and space it occasionally appears to be when Elvis is offscreen. On viewing the first cut, the Colonel dashed off a letter to MGM president James Aubrey. As self-serving as Parker's criticisms were, he was surprisingly tactful in his three-page letter of complaint concerning the first edit, and absolutely right on every point ("...the slurs on *Blue Hawaii* and *G.I. Blues* should be completely removed, as these were two of the most successful films... and they do not deserve to be mentioned as just trash... There is no reason to show an abundance of steaks in a truck in this picture when perhaps in Dalton, Georgia, where the picture may be showing, a family saved up money... and relinquished their hamburger for that night so they could see Elvis"). Parker knew exactly what the snide and cynical Sanders was doing, but cleverly played dumb in his correspondence. Further details of Parker's complaints can be found in the Guralnick book.

A clearer example of Sanders' agenda can be ascertained by looking at other films of the early '70s, a period when fantasy images from Doris Day to the forthcoming *Star Wars* had taken a back seat in favor of down-to-earth almost *cinema verite* portraits mocking the dreary populace inhabiting more unsophisticated territories such as the suburbs, or more particularly rural communities outside the city. See, for example, the attitude toward the common man in such wonderful gems as *Dillinger, Badlands, Prime Cut,* or *Jackson County Jail,* to name but a handful. No film of the era was complete without a nudging stop at a hillbilly hoedown or county fair (the corny street parade had now replaced the sinister funfair as the menacing chase locale), often with the happy and willing participation of the locals, supporting players at their own event.

Readers and researchers may be confused that many reference works list different songs in a different order. This is because the revised *Special Edition* now in circulation only appeared in 2001 after outtake footage found in the vaults at Turner in 1986 (and released on video as *Elvis: the Lost Performances* in 1992) had been re-edited into a second, far superior cut (with, of course, the benefit of hindsight and a damn sight more respect than that proffered by Sanders). In actuality, bearing in mind that the Colonel sent the film back to MGM to be re-cut to the specifications referred to above, the *Special Edition* is actually the third version of the Sanders film, although only the second to be shown publicly. And, as with the *Comeback Special* and the *Elvis--Aloha from Hawaii* satellite special, it seems the best material was originally left on the cutting room floor. Forty percent of the *Special Edition* (re-edited by Rick Schmidlin) is new footage, including nine songs originally excised, including the aforementioned "Love Me Tender" walkabout. Imagine how much dross was cut out of the original to accommodate this material. Imagine Sanders leaving out performance footage to include irrelevant interviews with gushing fans. But then Elvis was still alive, visible for the price of a ticket and taken for granted as the grand old man of rock and roll. He was going to go on forever.

The infamous book by Elvis' former bodyguards Red and Sonny West that shocked America but came too late to save their wayward friend from his mistakes. Tame stuff today.

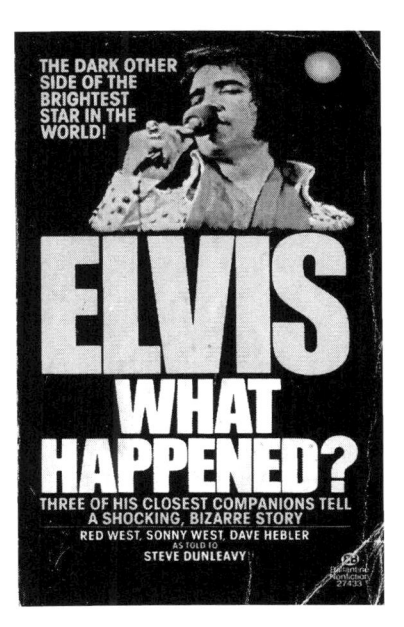

Elvis on Tour (1972)

dir. and pr. Pierre Adidge, Robert Abel (MGM)

Surprisingly, given the detail and accuracy of the Colonel's complaints about *Elvis--That's the Way It Is,* this second documentary made two years later not only duplicates all Sanders' mistakes and misjudgements, but keeps them intact in the finished product. Despite this, many reference sources cite this as the superior product.

Elvis on Tour is exactly what it says on the label, but if the packet isn't exactly empty, let's just say the contents have settled a little. Either Adidge had precious little film in the can or he didn't have much skill at editing-- much of the footage is like blooper outtakes without the bloopers, including overlong sequences with a supporting comedian deservedly bombing (his two writers get an end credit with him!) and then some bumbling civic dignitaries.

Even though this is chunky Vegas Elvis, and the music is from that period when Presley was performing all the wrong material in all the wrong ways (footage was filmed throughout April 1972), it's hard to believe that life with Elvis Presley could have been this tired, depressing, and tedious; Memphis Mafia member Lamar Fike holds it up as a perfect example of how much was kept from the public at that time, and how little people knew about the real Presley while he was alive.

Dismal and misjudged performances of his own hits and other peoples are interspersed with mind-numbingly dull footage of backstage preparations and dreary exteriors (only one scene is amusingly revealing; a welcome wagon of screaming girls all grasping copies of the same album cover--surely the handiwork of the Colonel). At one point Adidge inserts some very '70s footage of the soft drinks and popcorn being mass produced (remember Parker's nailing of the steaks-in-Vegas sequence in the Sanders film), as if aware of, and playing up to, his film's own banality. Yes folks, Elvis is a product, too (pause for epiphany).

Adidge goes out of his way to film every dull, flat, uninspired interior and exterior to create an almost suicidal atmosphere of emptiness. If there's a naked street, block of granite, boring individual, bare wall, or large piece of plastic, Adidge will lovingly shoot it at length. The *Woodstock*-style split screen technique does the work no favors either, replacing one screen showing nothing with three screens showing nothing.

It's hard to believe that anyone could make footage of one of the 20th century's most charismatic figures boring, but *Elvis on Tour* manages it, and makes the effort to do so. As if in realisation that they've got nothing, the producers insert montages (by the young Martin Scorsese, no less) of '50s Elvis, movies Elvis, and anything else they can whip up, to pad it out and liven it up, but the only times the film comes alive are during a performance of "Dixie" and an impromptu jamming session as Elvis sings gospel with his band.

However there is no sense at all of what made Elvis great, no sense of his talent, his uniqueness, his humility, his sexuality, his humor--despite the endless shots of screaming girls, who could be howling at anyone from the Beatles to a two-bit evangelist. Nor is there any hint of his dark side, his down moments. Instead, one finds one's mind wandering, reflecting on the aspects of Elvis Presley that are nowhere to be found in this dismal record of Elvis' most downbeat period. Any one of dozens of still photos from this period will tell you more than this film.

A detached disinterest from documentary makers coerced into tackling a subject they don't care for, then gradually being drawn into the possibilities, can be an advantage or disadvantage. Neither Abel or Adidge were much taken with Presley, and were semi-burnt-out from a recent assignment filming '60s rock and roller Joe Cocker over a period of months. The last thing these committed dedicated acolytes to the potential of film wanted to do was follow around an overweight has-been in Vegas who had made a string of--echh--commercially successful and popular feelgood movies for the popcorn market, and their disdain and disinterest shows in the footage and their editorial choices. Possibly, the enthusiasm of the critics and the fans came from the interview sequences (which the Colonel had confidently assumed Elvis would not give), which--we must remember--were revealing opinions, attitudes, and approaches to his music that had at this point never before been revealed. Fans and interested parties were viewing not beach bum girl-chasin' movie Elvis, or gyrating, audience-manipulating stage Elvis (although there's plenty of that), but candid, actual Elvis (Adidge and Abel had genially informed Elvis that the minute he started playing to the lens, they'd turn the cameras off--although wasn't that the real Elvis too?). Apparently, we mere mortals are far too easily impressed to see through any artifice.

Interestingly, this film--in which the cynicism towards, and unspoken criticism of Presley is overwhelming--received excellent reviews from the areas of the press and public who should have been resenting it ("At last-- the first Elvis Presley movie" said respected rock bible *Rolling Stone*). There are two key moments that sprinkle magic dust over the proceedings, one musical, one casual, caught on camera. Neither are from the stage. The musical moment is the aforementioned gospel jam session; the candid glimpse of the human Elvis comes when Presley and some of the boys are languidly chit-chatting in the car and Elvis breaks out in his wicked, sexy smile as they laugh and joke. Just Elvis and his entourage, the Memphis Mafia, the good ol' boys, chilling out in a private moment, the casual confidence of a female-free masculine guys' reverie, alive, yet frozen in time. Life is good. Over the next four years, everything will fall apart. Our knowledge that the end is so near makes this moment powerfully poignant.

appendix 2--the Elvis impersonators; Elvis on TV

Elvis Presley did not do TV for the simple reason that "the Colonel" quite deliberately priced him out of the market (although it's doubtful he could, or would, do the same today). In early 1955, *Arthur Godfrey's Talent Scouts,* scouting for talent, had sent him packing. Just ten years later, in May 1965, pop music magazine *Shindig,* unable to get the real thing, devoted an entire show to Elvis cover versions. In January, 1959, and again in January, 1962, *Dick Clark's American Bandstand* had devoted its entire show to the Presley phenomenon.

Presley's actual early TV appearances were a mixed bunch, from the highs of *The Dorsey Brothers' Stage Show,* where Presley made the first of a series of dynamic appearances on January 28th, 1956, *The Milton Berle Show,* and *The Ed Sullivan Show* (in the fall of 1956) to the lows of *The Steve Allen Show* earlier that July. Exposing him to a wider public nearly killed the future of rock and roll in its tracks, from the debacle of the hound dog incident that Steve Allen was still talking around to the day he died, to the idiocy of filming Elvis from the waist up on *The Ed Sullivan Show,* a decision the director was still defending with contra-dick-tory myth and legend forty years later (apparently Elvis' trousers were tight enough to outline his manhood, yet the offending appendage was somehow swaying at mid-thigh as well).

Not that Parker would have minded if this had been the end of Elvis as a teen idol and purveyor of sexual hysteria. He and Hal Wallis regarded rock and roll as a fad, and to protect the longevity of Presley positioned him as a family entertainer. In the event, Presley did successfully grow older with his audience, but mostly he ensured that rock 'n roll was here to stay. Rock and roll will never die because of Elvis--everything else happened thanks to him (as John Lennon memorably pointed out, "Before Elvis, there was nothing"). Ironic, as he was much more popular when he came out of the army than before.

And while it took until 1960 for Presley to appear in his own fictionalised account of his army years in *G.I. Blues,* comedy legends Nat Hiken and Phil Silvers had been quick to jump on the bandwagon with "Rock and Roll Rookie", a heavy-handed but unavoidably obvious entry in the Sgt. Bilko series *The Phil Silvers Show,* in which rock star "Elvin Pelvin" (Tom Gilson) gets sent into Fort Baxter and the greedy, scheming mitts of Silvers' finagler Ernie Bilko! The episode may at least have made "the Colonel" wince.

Silvers had been in the audience during the young Elvis' earliest and most unsuccessful foray into Vegas a couple of years earlier, and was no doubt as perplexed by this new phenomenon as all the other old vaudevillians of his generation. Although *Bilko,* as the public knew it, had a young audience, Silvers' poke at the pelvis of Elvis was neither cash-in fawning or savagely hostile, but rather simply opportunist and playing up to the general bemusement felt about the Elvis phenomenon by anyone over thirty in the 1950s. As such, it was rather silly and tiresome in its pandering to the puzzled masses, and despite being bereft of the usual celebrity walk-ons in other episodes (such as the Ed Sullivan and Bing Crosby episodes), wasn't really clever enough for satire. Neither spiteful or reverent, it was simply trying to be topical, and the army setting of the series made the plotline not just a natural, but virtually inevitable.

In January 1957, one year after Elvis' first TV broadcast from New York, Tommy Sands appeared in a *Kraft Television Theater* production as *The Singing Idol.* Ironically, as so often happens, the unintended consequences of what was supposed to be adverse criticism caused it to become a part of what it was critiquing and produced a hit record, "Teenage Crush" (the same thing happened again when little Ricky Nelson sung--badly--on his sit-com *Ozzie and Harriet,* and subsequently gained a hit single and pop music career). However, the *coup-de-grace* came in the form of Broadway musical and later 1962 film *Bye Bye, Birdie,* an energetic and colorful production about the departure of a teen idol into the army, with the only failing being its cruel and unjustified portrayal of a pop star plainly meant to be Elvis as an arrogant, tone-deaf egotist.

It's impossible to dislike a film toplining Dick Van Dyke, Ann Margret, and Paul Lynde all doing their standard party pieces, but Conrad Birdie, played charmlessly by Jesse Pearson in a suspiciously familiar gold suit, is the exact opposite of everything we know Elvis to have been. Clearly, the vicious anti-Presley media coverage had done its job well in perpetuating the prejudices against Presley in the face of all the evidence. If it had been a little more sympathetic toward Elvis, and a little less presumptuous about his personality, the film could have doubled its audience. The sad thing about this unwarranted slur on Presley is that the rest of the film is so overwhelmingly enjoyable, with Ann Margret of all people prophetically cast as the high school girl who wins a PR contest to administer a farewell kiss to the preening and posturing Birdie who, in one sequence, leaves a trail of swooning girls in the school grounds that resembles the fainting soldiers at Fort Knox in *Goldfinger.*

The script is witty, the performances wonderful, and the storyline is actually about the girl Kim McAfee (Ann-Margret) and her boyfriend Hugo (Bobby Rydell), and Van Dyke's songwriter character and his romantic entanglement with Janet Leigh, with the obnoxious Birdie an afterthought, the McGuffin that triggers all the story developments. Among the film's many highlights (it never drags), Dick Van Dyke sings "Put on a Happy Face" to girlfriend Janet Leigh, with animated and supernatural assistance, Trudi Ames (of *Gidget Goes to Rome*) initiates a magnificently staged ensemble piece as the kids 'phone each other with the latest high school gossip, and the blatantly gay Paul Lynde (as the father!) makes a meal of the infamous parental complaint "Kids", the song he was born to sing, while Maureen Stapleton as Dick Van Dyke's suffocating mother sings back-up with her head in the (electric) oven.

All the songs and dance sequences are superb, but for the caterwauling of the ersatz Elvis, who comes across more like an evil Frankie Avalon of the mirror-world. The film does capture and illustrate quite well the frustration many young men felt at the time as they watched their girlfriends lusting after not only Elvis, but the small army of pop stars, movie stars, and TV stars who followed in his wake, but paradoxically, Elvis was unique in having male admirers as well. There were so many better targets for satirical attack at this time, so many genuinely phoney teen idols on the scene that it seems ludicrous to have pilloried one of the few genuine people of the period so brutally.

It's all extremely silly fluff bearing a strong resemblance to the likes of *Grease,* but with the inescapable advantage of actually belonging to that period. Columbia, who produced this picture, was--tellingly--the only major that didn't cut itself a slice of the Elvis movie pie, but what they did have at this time were the distribution rights to the Hanna-Barbera cartoons, and in a shameless flurry of product placement there can be seen Huckleberry Hound, Yogi Bear, and Flintstone merchandise as far as the eye can see. Less than two years later, Ann Margret and director George Sidney would be making *Viva Las Vegas.* If Elvis had been played sympathetically, even as the subsidiary plot point that Conrad Birdie is (it is said Parker turned the role down for Presley on financial grounds), this film would still be remembered and enjoyed by mainstream audiences today.

For the real Elvis on TV, we are left with the treasured so-called *Comeback Special* on NBC and the infamous satellite special from Hawaii. Both shows have been released on DVD in their original as-shown versions and, most significantly, restored all-available-footage versions, with much material until then unseen, and it is quite alarming to see what a hash was made of the original transmissions and how fortunate we have been to have the unused material survive.

The Elvis *Comeback Special* as it has come to be best known starts badly, with lethargic, under-rehearsed dancers... Elvis is clowning around and sending himself up, looking embarrassed and insecure, and launches into a medley of oldies. The orchestral backing occasionally lets it down, particularly on "Can't Help Falling in Love". The highlight is "Jailhouse Rock". Presley clearly has a self-deprecating sense of humor about his classics, almost to the point of offending his audience, and "Love Me Tender" is a notable victim.

A gospel segment is completely ruined by some hideous dancing that evokes unwelcome memories of just about every dreadful light entertainment "spectacular" of the '60s and '70s. A jaw-droppingly bad *Frankie and Johnny*-style sequence with Elvis in the big bad city throws in every horrible cliche imaginable and looks like amateur night; producer Steve Binder gets full credit for defying the Colonel's hopes for a Christmas Special in the Bing Crosby tradition and setting up the improv sequences, but must also take the blame for this cringe-inducing debacle. A restored bordello sequence, completed but excised by the sponsor (Elvis still a victim of nervous censorship, even in '68) is fascinatingly bad, with supposedly alluring whores bowing to the TV rule that they must always look cheap and unattractive, and thus resembling drag queens (late-'60s cosmetics choices not helping). Only dancer Susan Henning, the blonde Elvis dances with, comes out looking good.

Much of the best footage, we now realise, was considered too raw and candid and was never aired in '68 at all, when the emphasis was on lavish, phoney, stage musical/TV variety show presentation ("They ruined it" wailed record producer and '60s pop icon Phil Spector--"You should have seen it before they edited it"). The supposedly professional artifice and so-called polish that replaces and eliminates any and all casual spontaneity and realism dates the show horribly, and in the uncut, unedited DVD footage that we now all can see (some of it previously seen on the 1991 video *Elvis: the Unguarded Moments*) Elvis can be seen making fun of the dismal contrivances planned with the best of intentions. Really, Elvis just wants to sing and have fun--and he does. The restored untouched version is a joy, although unbelievably, the slimmer budget version of the *Comeback Special* DVD omits the candid performances and offers only the wretched 1968 broadcast. Caveat emptor!

Elvis--Aloha from Hawaii is even worse in its aired version, and consequently even more rewarding in its restored, untouched form. It seems insane today, and a perfect example of how the world in the 1970s took Elvis for granted, that NBC could be showing bland travelogue footage of Hawaii instead of actual footage of Elvis performing, but there are endless dreary montages of nobodies doing nothing while Elvis sings unseen. It's bizarre to think that Asia saw it live, Europe saw it a few hours later, and America saw it four months late and only in truncated, bastardised form until the DVD release thirty years later.

With the rehearsal footage included on the DVD, Elvis historian Dave Marsh makes the important observation that "everyone, but most especially Americans, missed much of the best that *Aloha* had to offer" and that "the NBC Special serves as a period piece" with "the insert songs and the multi-screen editing mak(ing) it feel, in a sense, more dated, more locked into a specific past... *it works around Elvis' music* (my italics)... *periodically cutting away* (to) *eliminate Elvis' interaction with the audience...*". The content is typical 1970s MOR mixed with a few classics; the highlight is the irony of Elvis flirting with the audience throughout his performance of "Suspicious Minds".

Television's love of technology for the sake of it (if it's there it must be used) matched with its innate disregard for, and lack of trust in its own material means that very often television producers are compelled to give artistic expression to their own egos and urges to interfere, unable to let the performances speak for themselves. This mindset was particularly prevalent in the 1970s, when the most modest and mediocre broadcasts were often more about showing off the now primitive contemporary camera tricks and video technology than trusting the entertainers they were supposed to be accommodating to entertain their public. As Marsh points out, "since almost everyone who's ever written about the *Aloha* special knew only this version, that explains the disdainful critical reception it received in America... it is only in the full-length re-edited versions... that what Elvis really achieved can be seen".

Nevertheless, there are some horrible musical choices, including "Welcome to My World", "I Can't Stop Loving You" and the Beatles' "Something". Some of the dated '70s arrangements grate, but the Presley voice even triumphs over the appalling selection of "My Way", that whiny, unintentionally funny self-pitying hymn to middle-aged melancholia, the theme song of every drunken loser who ever cried into his beer. Saving the day are "Can't Help Falling in Love With You" and "I'm So Lonely I Could Cry"... and of course Presley's always moving "American Trilogy", which even crass 1970s presentation can't castrate. More valuable than anyone could ever have known at the time is the unedited video footage of broadcast standard showing Elvis arriving in Hawaii (for the cameras of course). Gold dust. Pure undiluted Presley with no editing to anyone's specific agenda or judgement.

For Elvis as myth, at the forefront is Kurt Russell's bold attempt to recreate the King in *Elvis--the Movie* (actually, Elvis--the TV movie); only

Larry Geller and Charlie Hodge appear in person, with actors representing everyone else. Russell was a former child actor best known for his Disney films and a handful of TV guest appearances in American institutions of the '60s such as *Lost in Space* ("The Challenge"), *The Fugitive* ("Nemesis" and "In a Plain Paper Wrapper") and *The Man From UNCLE* ("The Finny Foot Affair"). He also appeared several times in *Dick Powell Theater*. As a youngster he had worked with Elvis, appearing in two scenes of *It Happened at the World's Fair* in 1964 as the young lad who kicks Elvis in the shin (literally) and then the groin (metaphorically). Shortly before he began his 1980s career as a sci-fi action hero (in films like *The Thing* and *Escape from New York*) he made this TV movie widely considered to be the best execution possible of a bad idea--a biopic of Elvis' life, Hollywood-style (Russell's actor father, Bing Russell, who also appears in his two *Fugitive* outings, plays Vernon).

This effort by the ABC network was followed the next year by *Elvis and the Beauty Queen* on NBC, where executives obviously assumed that now the ice had been broken they could fish in the same hole. Stephanie Zimbalist of *Remington Steele* fame was the poor choice to portray Linda Thompson, Presley's most devoted post-Priscilla girlfriend, and Don Johnson of *Miami Vice* the even worse casting choice for Elvis. Exonerated from guilt for having left Elvis to his drugs in despair and departed before the fateful night Ginger Alden shared his bed, Thompson herself was the driving force behind this shabby exercise. It was a foolish move as until then she had been seen in a good light by distraught Elvis admirers, considered blameless and helpless in his final years, one of the few good things he had in his life. Now she could possibly be perceived as jumping on the bandwagon with this sordid trash, which concerned itself only with Presley's most unpleasant and unhappy years.

Warners' 1981 docu-drama *This is Elvis* was one of those uncomfortable hybrids that mixes newsreel footage with actors playing Elvis and his friends and family. Joe Esposito, Linda Thompson, and Vester Presley were the only genuine participants, with Joe Esposito, Jerry Schilling, and the Colonel getting their names on the behind-the-scenes credits. One sequence has Elvis singing the maudlin ("I did it...") "My Way" while a montage of his movies runs--a magnificently inappropriate and unintended irony, as he didn't do it his way at all, as this book and many others are at pains to point out.

Priscilla got into the act with 1988's *Elvis and Me,* based on her 1985 book of the same name with Sandra Harmon, executive producing for New World Television, with Jerry Schilling taking the technical advisor role. Dale Midkiff (later star of the syndicated series *Time Trax* and *The Magnificent Seven*) portrays Elvis, with Susan Walters as Priscilla and Elvis impersonator Ronnie McDowell singing the songs (as he did in the Kurt Russell film). As might be expected, Elvis gets a pretty rough ride!

Since then, Priscilla has found it more advantageous to pay tribute to the Presley myth in assorted coy and sugar-coated documentaries of the sort whose scripts read like very carefully considered press releases, each and every word cautiously selected and vetted to balance gingerly on the fence. Sadly, there seem to be only two ways to make biography-style programs on TV today--whitewash or hatchet job. Objectivity is an alien word, the hope for accuracy a joke.

Most of Elvis' other "appearances" on TV have been affectionate posthumous digs at the "Elvis is Alive" industry. Elvis is still alive in episodes of *ALF* ("Suspicious Minds", 1988), *Charles in Charge* ("Duelling Presleys", 1989), *Murphy Brown* ("The Morning Show", 1989), *Full House* ("The King and I", 1991), *Cheers* ("Uncle Sam Wants You", 1991), *Eerie, Indiana* ("Foreverware", 1991), Cannell's *Renegade* ("The King and I", 1994), and *Sliders* (the 1995 pilot). In 1992, the short-lived legal series *Civil Wars* featured a divorce case in which the wife was divorcing her husband because he thought he was Elvis. A distasteful episode of a '90s sit-com titled *The Naked Truth* (about an idealistic girl who works for a tabloid rag) featured an episode concerning a vial of Elvis Presley's frozen sperm ("a twenty-five year old Elvis popsicle")!

And then there are the Elvis impersonators (or tribute artists). The blond-haired Cartoon Network character *Johnny Bravo* (who lives in Aron City) is shamelessly modelled vocally on Elvis for the amusement of a generation that barely knows or cares who Elvis Presley was. In 1986, Pete Willcox, one of the busiest of the Elvis impersonators on TV (he had memorably appeared in the aforementioned early *Murphy Brown* as one of the title character's running joke unsuitable office assistants, and others above), secured a regular role in the short-lived Stephen Cannell series *The Last Precinct,* as an Elvis-obsessed cop. And an entire army of Elvis impersonators were recruited for "Sophia's Wedding", a two-part 1980s *Golden Girls* episode, one of them a young and unknown Quentin Tarantino. In Britain, the sit-com *Father Ted* featured an episode in which the three leads, fighting over who should enter a dress-up competition as Elvis, compromise by going as "the three ages of Elvis".

In "The Once and Future King" (1986), an episode of the 1980s version of *The Twilight Zone,* Jeff Yagher plays Elvis impersonator Gary Pitkin, who, after his car is run off the road, finds himself offered a ride by the original Elvis Presley on July 2nd, 1954--the day before Presley's legendary recording session for Sun Records. The clever twist here is that Elvis believes Pitkin to be his twin brother Jesse, who in reality died at birth.

Pitkin revels in his opportunity to meet his hero ("It ain't gonna be all good" he warns him. "There's gonna be some people who just want to use you. There'll be drugs, and scandals, and liars and cheats... but it doesn't have to happen that way..."), but discovers Presley's music to be less than revolutionary on the eve of the birth of rock and roll.

For some reason, Pitkin assumes that history will not take its course without his intervention, and he may be right--when he attempts to show Elvis what his act should look like, the young Presley takes offence at "the devil's music", and in the ensuing struggle when Pitkin's 1980s-level insults get the better of him, is accidentally killed--comically impaled on a broken guitar. Pitkin the professional impersonator now sees no option but to take Presley's place, and ensure that the birth of rock and roll occurs as it should... but it gives him no pleasure to steal the life of his idol. In a chilling endpiece, we discover that the ill-advised and unpopular (to some) slide into conservatism and convention by the older Presley is to be explained by Pitkin's guilt, as he gradually attempted to live the more mainstream career that the original Elvis Aaron Presley had supposedly once intended... an unlikely but compellingly irresistible assumption for pop historians from the Twilight Zone!

Of course anyone who knows anything about Elvis at all is aware of the truck-sized holes in this assertion, as Presley's opinions on every part of his career are well-documented and contradict the yarn's premise (interestingly, the end credits reveal that the Presley estate co-operated in this fascinatingly heretical fantasy!), but if the episode has any failing at all, it is the unavoidable one that Yagher, like all those other erzatz Elvis impersonators, is no Elvis. It remains one of the great ironies of modern history that one of the most singularly individual and unique pop icons of the 20th century should have had a twin brother that died at birth. There were very nearly two of him.

Two other TV series offered equally fanciful but marginally more tolerable alternative scenarios on the birth of rock and roll. The *Quantum Leap* episode "Memphis Melody" (1993) takes place one day after the *Twilight Zone* story, on July 3rd 1954, and has time traveler Sam Beckett (Scott Bakula) materialising in Elvis Presley's body just as he is saved from some thugs by old friend Red West (John Boyd West, the spit of his dad). Sam must prevent hopeful singer Sue-Ann Winters (Mary Elizabeth McGlynn) from marrying an intolerant and ultimately violent future husband and persuade her to follow her dream instead, while at the same time ensuring that his efforts don't hinder the key developments of Presley's rise to the top--"Please--please tell me you know these songs, Sam!" begs invisible companion Al (Dean Stockwell) after Sam has botched the fateful Sun Records session. Inevitably the distraction of helping Sue-

Ann break free of her lack of confidence does indeed get in the way of recorded recording history; Sue-Ann is to attend Presley's formerly solo audition...

"You've just turned the King of Rock and Roll into Donny and Marie!!" howls Al in anguish as he despairingly consults his computer with mounting horror to assess the ongoing damage to the future of popular music. "`Jailhouse Rock' will be recorded by Tony Orlando and Dawn!!!".

"Memphis Melody" also confronts the grim end to Presley's career that must occur if the 1950s are to be set alight. "In three years he's gonna meet Priscilla, they're gonna get married, and they're gonna have a little baby, and you don't want to jeopardise any of it!" snaps Al. "Yeah, but what about what happened to Elvis later on?" speculates Sam. "Maybe if he'd been with Sue-Ann, things would have ended differently than they did".

Most episodes of *Quantum Leap* are set in our real world, but this story is a weirdly fictionalised account of Presley's turning point in history, with the Sue-Ann character a bizarre amalgam of Elvis' girlfriend at the time, Dixie Locke, with Anita Wood, who did have show-biz aspirations, but didn't enter Presley's life until some years later.

In the short-run television series of the film *Bill and Ted's Excellent Adventure/s,* which lasted just seven episodes in 1991, it was Elvis who was suffering a crisis of confidence in the episode "Hunka Hunka Bill and Ted".

Realising that they know nothing about the King of Rock and Roll, Bill and Ted (now played by Evan Richards and Christopher Kennedy, who had already produced cartoon voices for the duo for an equally brief animated series in 1990) travel back to 1954 and find a disillusioned Elvis (Todd McDurmand) about to throw in the towel for lack of recognition of his talents. In an effort to raise his self-esteem they bring him forward in time to 1991 to participate in an Elvis impersonator contest which they naturally feel he's bound to win. Unfortunately, Elvis has not yet perfected his unique based-on-instinct natural singing style, and having provided the worst impression of his future self, he loses! "Ted--we totally killed rock and roll, dude!" laments Bill.

Back in 1954 they discover that the now despondent Elvis has taken another trucking assignment to Chicago on the night that his famous performance for the Louisiana Hayride show should occur, and their desperate attempts to talk him out of it succeed in getting him fired from his job...

Between them, these two episodes are just likely to revive the musical if they get shown often enough! Both feature wonderful spontaneous musical numbers that ultimately expose Presley's unique style to the money men (Gregory Itzin, Stephen E. Miller) who gave him his break and save the day--*Quantum Leap* in a coffee shop rendition of "That's Alright, Mama", complete with swaying kids, Dean Stockwell's invisible Al boogieing on the counter alongside Sam's Elvis, and the soda shop owner on harmonica, and *Bill and Ted* with a confidence-boosting pop video-style rendition of "All Shook Up" in a bowling alley, again accompanied by an army of bouncing bobby-soxers.

"Colonel" Tom, absent from both of the above as they precede Presley having management, would get a seeing-to portrayed by Beau Bridges in the dismal 1993 TV movie *Elvis and the Colonel*.

In 1990, the simply titled TV series *Elvis* (known more distinctively as *Elvis--Good Rockin' Tonight* in some foreign markets) retold the story of Presley's early years in half-hour episodes and would have worked its way through the complete story had it lasted more than two months on the air. It was an interesting, original and unusual idea for a series but somehow the public missed it. As *The Complete Directory to Primetime Network and Cable TV Shows* says, "though not a ratings success, it was a TV first... Never before had the true story of a real-life superstar been dramatised in a weekly series; and never had the birth of rock and roll been treated with such reverence and authenticity. It was as if the innocent and vital young Elvis, almost forgotten in his later years of dissipation and decline, had come back to life...".

It may have been an awareness of those later years, and knowledge of story developments to come, that made the series a non-starter; perhaps it was just too painful to watch in weekly segments, knowing how the story would end. For whatever reason, the series began in February 1990 and closed in March, final episodes being run off in at the end of the TV season in May. This was a shame, as Michael St. Gerard (who also played young Elvis in the *Quantum Leap* episode) was perfectly cast in the lead, an uncanny lookalike and the best fictional Elvis to date. Bizarrely, Gladys Presley was played by Millie Perkins, thirty years earlier the young slip of a girl from *Wild in the Country*. Filmed in Memphis, Priscilla Presley co-produced.

All of these were celebrations of Elvis' life in one way or another, respectful acknowledgements of his achievements. The closest any production came to sneering at him was the 1997 TV movie *Elvis Meets Nixon*, based on the 1994 book *The Day Elvis Met Nixon*, by E. "Budd" Krogh, which--to be fair--was documenting one of the maddest and most ridiculous episodes in Elvis mythology.

It is true that Elvis met Nixon, and it is an easy moment in rock and roll history to make fun of. But every major artist has his `what was he thinking?' moment--Mick Jagger meeting the Archbishop of Canterbury, for example, Roger Daltrey doing TV commercials on his salmon farm, David Bowie's thoughtless remarks about the Nazis--and Elvis--ironically, given the manner of his death--was genuinely against drugs and didn't compromise his opinion at a time in pop culture when it would have been far too easy to go with the flow, abandon his previously held convictions, and "drop out, turn on, and tune in".

While so many rock stars have done anti-drugs propaganda to appease record company executives or authority figures, and lectured kids while indulging, or having indulged, in the full range of recreational drugs, Elvis, as in all his public stands, was completely genuine and consistent in his views. Agree or disagree, he was no hypocrite, but like so many people vehemently against drugs abuse, he had no understanding of them, which was why his end was so upsetting--he genuinely did not see prescription drugs as being as lethal as the illegal variety (even though he often obtained them illegally).

Consequently, as Elvis unravelled during the last few years of his life, his friends and family were presented with the ludicrous sight of a severely drugs-dependent Elvis, exhibiting all the trademark dishonesty of the addict, railing against drugs pushers and drugs abusers with the zeal of the TV cops he desperately wanted to emulate. In the final decade of his life, Presley was obsessed with securing a legitimate police badge and joining the war against drugs; unfortunately, he was too doped to the gills to participate...

Someone called Rick Peters grasps the short straw to take on the impossible task of replicating Elvis, and plays him as a hick buffoon, capturing none of the man's presence, talent, humility, or sexuality, while Curtis Armstrong of *Moonlighting/Revenge of the Nerds* notoriety is a one-man Memphis Mafia, presumably an amalgam of Joe Esposito, Marty Lacker and Jerry Schilling among others. Bob Gunton is properly dense and sly as Nixon, and the guy playing Vernon (Denny Doherty) is a dead ringer. The film understands how anachronistic and deeply out of vogue Elvis was in the 1970s, and there is a touching and clever scene in a hippie head shop as an unknown and unmolested Presley surveys the record racks of talentless and now-forgotten non-entities on display with bemusement and bafflement, but *Elvis Meets Nixon* is ultimately better working with the far less complex machinations of the Nixon faction than the deceptive simplicity of the Presley mindset.

Elvis--the Early Years, with Jonathan Rhys-Meyers as Elvis, is a two-part mini-series from 2005 which demonstrates that fascination with the Presley story remains as potent, fascinating and relevant to contemporary audiences as ever. Rhys-Meyers is no more Elvis than Russell or St. Gerard were, and the story plays safe by detailing only--as the title suggests--the early years.

Sometimes Elvis seems as busy in movies in the afterlife as he was in the 1960s. Among the numerous films to reference Elvis over just the last few years are such titles as *Wild at Heart* (1990), *Honeymoon in Vegas* (1992), *Finding Graceland* (1998), *Elvis Has Left the Building* (2000), *3000 Miles to Graceland* (2001), *Bubba Ho-Tep* (2002), and *Eddie Presley* (2004). All of these concern themselves with one or more of three Elvis themes--Elvis still being alive somewhere, someone deeply influenced in a life-changing way by Elvis, or an Elvis impersonator. These films are beyond the scope of this book, and in one or two cases, the author's last vestiges of sanity!

Johnny Bravo (right, with other Cartoon Network characters) spoke like Elvis and came from Aron City, named after Elvis' middle name.

appendix 3--an Elvis chronology; relevant dates for the period covered

January 1935 - Elvis Aron Presley born

1945- Elvis gets his first guitar

1948 - the Presleys move to Memphis

October, 1954 - Elvis appears on radio show *Louisiana Hayride*

May, 1955 - Elvis signs with `Colonel' Tom Parker, his future manager

1955 - *Grand Prize Saturday Night Jamboree* (KPRC-TV, Texas)

January 1956 - *Dorsey Brothers Stage Show*

February 1956 - *Dorsey Brothers Stage Show* x 3

March 1956 - *Dorsey Brothers Stage Show* x 2

April 1956 - successful screen test for film producer Hal Wallis

April 1956 - *The Milton Berle Show*

June 1956 - *The Milton Berle Show*

July 1956 - *The Steve Allen Show*

August 1956 - *Love Me Tender* starts filming

September 1956 - *The Ed Sullivan Show*

October 1956 - *The Ed Sullivan Show*

November 1956 - *Love Me Tender* premieres

January 1957 - *The Ed Sullivan Show*

January 1957 - *Loving You* starts filming

May 1957 - *Jailhouse Rock* starts filming

July 1957 - *Loving You* premieres

October 1957 - *Jailhouse Rock* premieres

March 1958 - *King Creole* starts filming

July 1958 - *King Creole* premieres

May 1960 - *GI Blues* starts filming

May 1960 - *The Frank Sinatra--Timex Welcome Home, Elvis Special*

August 1960 - *Flaming Star* starts filming

August 1960 - *GI Blues* premieres

November 1960 - *Wild In The Country* starts filming

December 1960 - *Flaming Star* premieres

March 1961 - *Blue Hawaii* starts filming

June 1961 - *Wild In The Country* premieres

July 1961 - *Follow That Dream* starts filming

November 1961 - *Kid Galahad* starts filming

November 1961 - *Blue Hawaii* premieres

April 1962 - *Girls! Girls! Girls!* starts filming

April 1962 - *Follow That Dream* premieres

August 1962 - *It Happened At The World's Fair* starts filming

August 1962 - *Kid Galahad* premieres

November 1962 - *Girls! Girls! Girls!* premieres

January 1963 - *Fun In Acapulco* starts filming

April 1963 - *It Happened At The World's Fair* premieres

July 1963 - *Viva Las Vegas* starts filming

October 1963 - *Kissin' Cousins* starts filming

November 1963 - *Fun In Acapulco* premieres

December 1963 - *Love Me Tender* television premiere

March 1964 - *Roustabout* starts filming

April 1964 - *Kissin' Cousins* opens, after sneak previews in Feb and March

June 1964 - *Viva Las Vegas* premieres

June 1964 - *Girl Happy* starts filming

October 1964 - *Tickle Me* starts filming

November 1964 - *Roustabout* premieres

March 1965 - *Harum Scarum* starts filming

April 1965 - *Girl Happy* premieres

May 1965 - *Frankie and Johnny* starts filming

May 1965 - *Tickle Me* premieres

August 1965 - Elvis meets the Beatles

August 1965 - *Paradise, Hawaiian Style* starts filming

November 1965 - *Harum Scarum* premieres

February 1966 - *Spinout* starts filming

March 1966 - *Frankie and Johnny* premieres

June 1966 - *Double Trouble* starts filming

July 1966 - *Paradise, Hawaiian Style* premieres

September 1966 - *Easy Come, Easy Go* starts filming

November 1966 - *Spinout* premieres

March 1967 - *Clambake* starts filming

March 1967 - *Easy Come, Easy Go* premieres

April 1967 - *Double Trouble* premieres

June 1967 - *Speedway* starts filming

October 1967 - *Stay Away Joe* starts filming

November 1967 - *Clambake* premieres

March 1968 - *Stay Away Joe* premieres

June 1968 - Elvis tapes the NBC `comeback' special

July 1968 - *Live a Little, Love a Little* starts filming

July 1968 - *Charro* starts filming

October 1968 - *Live a Little, Love a Little* premieres

October 1968 - *The Trouble With Girls* starts filming

December 1968 - the Elvis `comeback' Special airs on NBC

March 1969 - *Change of Habit* starts filming

March 1969 - Charro premieres

August 1969 - the Elvis `comeback' Special is repeated

September 1969 - *The Trouble With Girls* premieres

November 1969 - *Change of Habit* premieres

November 1970 - *Elvis--That's the Way It Is* premieres

January 1973 - *Elvis--Aloha from Hawaii* is beamed live by satellite around the world appendix 4--closure

"This is, after all, just another Presley movie", wrote writer and critic Renata Adler wearily in the *New York Times* review of *Speedway*, ironically the last of the traditional 1960s Elvis films, "which makes no use at all of one of the most talented, important, and durable performers of our time. Music, youth, and customs were much changed by Elvis Presley twelve years ago; from the twenty-six movies he has made since he sang `Heartbreak Hotel' you would never guess it". The final tally would be thirty-one.

In the early 1970s, as Presley's movie career drew to a close, Paramount producer Hal Wallis' rival, MGM's Joe Pasternak, producer of *Girl Happy* and *Spinout,* two of the most polished and downright most fun of Elvis' happy-go-lucky feelgood movies, suggested that "Elvis should be given more meaty parts. He's thirty five years old, he's a man, he's got guts, he's got strength, he's got charm. He would be a good actor. He should do more important pictures". But truthfully, all the evidence suggests that Elvis was best at playing Elvis.

"The idea of tailoring Elvis for dramatic roles is something we never attempted" Wallis admitted quite candidly. "Because we didn't sign Elvis as a second James Dean, we signed him as a number one Elvis Presley". "Wallis made Elvis in Hollywood" summed up Lamar Fike, one of Presley's Memphis Mafia to journalist Alanna Nash. "And Wallis eventually ruined him". But did he?

Once the beach movies of the early '60s gave way to spy capers and biker films, there was no-one else making the sort of pleasant, wholesome films Elvis did except for Disney, who was aiming at a younger audience. And in the mid-'60s, although there was precious little money on the screen, Elvis was the highest paid movie star in the world. Writer and Presley fan Dave Marsh, author of the over-the-top DVD notes for the *Hawaii* satellite special, perceptively called them "the last great series of Hollywood star vehicles", although with Wayne and Eastwood among those prolific in the '70s, and Stallone and Schwarzenegger pumping them out in the '80s, "last" may be presumptuous (especially when one looks at the resumes of, say, Jim Carrey, Will Ferrell or Jennifer Aniston, to consider more recent recurring names).

Yes, Elvis was out of date during the late-'60s, but when one looks at what was *in* fashion, who had the last laugh? *A Hard Day's Night* may have been groundbreaking and refreshing at the time, but today it is an anachronistic curiosity, whereas the Elvis films at least offer nostalgic easy viewing. *Spinout* and *Clambake* are still fun to watch, but as wonderful as the Beatles' timeless music is to listen to, try sitting through the animated Yellow Submarine feature today.

"Elvis was ruined by the Colonel and Hal Wallis" stated Memphis Mafia member Marty Lacker flatly. "They didn't let him develop. If they had only let him continue in the same vein as *King Creole*--the way he delivered that scene where he broke that bottle and said `Now you know what I do for an encore...'. But they kept putting him in crap".

In a sensible and rational interview with *Films and Filming* magazine titled, apparently without irony, "Following No Formula" (and promoting *True Grit*), Hal Wallis told interviewer David Austen "The Presley films were made, of course, for strictly commercial purposes. He is one of the most popular entertainers in the world and... you have to give the Presley fans, who are legion, what they want, and they want to hear him sing. One of the least successful films was *King Creole*, which was our favorite. But we went on to make others, *Blue Hawaii* was probably the biggest grosser, and that's what the fans wanted. Working with Presley was a very pleasant experience. Over the years I never had any problems with him. He did want to do some straight acting roles, without any songs, but that would have been quite a gamble. He recently made one, *Charro*. It'll be interesting to see how that does. Now we could have gambled, and put him in a straight acting part, and even today (1969), with the proper story and the proper set-up, I might do something like that. I had a story a while back that I was playing around with, for John Wayne and Presley, where Wayne was the old gunfighter and he was the young gunfighter, and if that could be developed, it would be a good story and could be done without music".

Even Dean or Brando would have had trouble turning their surly arrogant irritability into the soap opera rage Presley was required to turn on in *Love Me Tender*, his acting debut, but Elvis was at least good enough to attempt anything Hollywood's scriptwriters could throw at him. However, with the exception of the semi-autobiographical *Loving You*, and the superb musical interludes of *King Creole*, the one uniting factor of all Presley's pre-army 1950s films is that his role could have been played by almost any young actor of the moment. And as the 1960s took form, the era of actors like Dean and Brando, who Elvis idolised, was ending. Presley's last two Fox pictures--*Flaming Star* and *Wild in the Country*--were only modest hits in comparison to the others, and, said Albert Goldman, "mark the end, for all practical purposes, of Elvis' career as a serious film actor. Neither film received the sort of notices that would have encouraged Elvis in his acting ambitions; more importantly, neither picture made much money. At this point, Colonel Parker (and) Hal Wallis... could say to Elvis `I told you so'."

"At first it was something new for him" said Red West to Jerry Hopkins. "After a while, it got to be the same, a pick-up from the last movie. It really got so he didn't enjoy doing them. At first he liked making movies, but when the scripts didn't get any better and the songs were all the same... some of the films he couldn't wait 'til they were through. He liked *Wild in the Country*... He liked *King Creole* and *Flaming Star,* and I can't think of too many more he enjoyed doing."

But, admitted Lamar Fike, "People say if Elvis had been a more astute businessman or taken more interest in the workings of his career, he would've been a much bigger star, but God Almighty, he made more money than anybody I know of, and next to Jesus and Coca-Cola, nothing's any better known than Elvis Presley."

The argument may rage forever. Where Dean is concerned, we'll never know what films a fuller, more mature rebel without a cause might have been making in the 1960s (he looked like the sort of young lad whose looks would have declined early), and it's easier to name a good Brando film from the '70s than it is the '60s, *The Godfather, Last Tango in Paris, Superman*, and even *The Missouri Breaks* being a little better than anything he did after *Mutiny on the Bounty* in 1962. An unconventional but perceptive perspective was offered by writer Michael Streissguth (talking to fellow music journalist Alanna Nash for her book *The Colonel*), who doubted Elvis' musical preferences would have survived the mad creativity of the mid-'60s.

"By dumb luck, the movie years had the effect of preserving Elvis economically while the wild music environment passed over..." he suggested, presumably referring to Liverpool, psychedelia, and Woodstock. "Elvis was not spent from years of musical rejection, so when the time was right and people were ready to see him in concert, he was fresh and ready to pounce on the opportunity... inadvertently giving us the great Elvis music of the very late '60s and early '70s".

For all the perceived failings of the early '60s Elvis Presley movies, they have their virtues too, as I hope this book has demonstrated. And what films would or should Elvis have been making in the 1960s? We never suffered through an Elvis Presley secret agent story (caper film *Double Trouble* comes closest), and he never made a sci-fi film or a war movie (imagine Presley in *Fantastic Voyage* or *Kelly's Heroes*). And thanks to the Colonel, we never saw Presley as part of an unfunny star-studded blockbuster, or making a cameo appearance on *Batman* or *Rowan and Martin's Laugh-In*. We never saw Elvis drop in for a *Lucy Show* or visit the *Beverly Hillbillies* mansion; John Wayne did both. Sammy Davis Jnr. appeared in *Batman, I Dream of Jeannie* and *Charlie's Angels,* Chad and

Jeremy and Lesley Gore did *Batman,* Sonny and Cher turned up in *The Man from UNCLE,* the Standells, whoever they were, performed at the home of *The Munsters,* Rick Nelson sung in *McCloud.* It might have been fun to see Elvis in any of these, but what might it have led to? A rock and roll star accused of murder on *Hawaii Five-O?*

Don't laugh--Presley met series star Jack Lord in Hawaii, and gifted his wife one of his belts. Could Lord possibly *not* have said "You know, you ought to come on our show...!". It's hard, if not downright ludicrous to imagine Elvis as a sit-com dad or a TV detective, but had he abandoned music for acting, this could well have happened, and drive-in movies and TV guest-shots would have followed as surely as night follows day.

Looking at 1970s cinema with hindsight, it's laughable to imagine Elvis Presley in a Nic Roeg film (although *Performance* was yet another Tuesday Weld turn-down), or a Martin Scorsese drama, or a Woody Allen comedy, or a Robert Altman icon demolition job. Elvis as *Easy Rider?* Elvis was pro-Church, pro-flag and anti-drugs. Elvis in *Electra Glide in Blue* then? Difficult to respect his *authoritah.* Much has been made of the fact that the Colonel talked Elvis out of co-starring in *A Star is Born* with Barbara Streisand, but what a disaster that would have been. Even assuming that the audience for Streisand was the same as Presley's, which is hugely doubtful, how many Elvis fans would wish to see a movie in which Presley sacrifices his career for *hers!?* And surely nobody wanted to see Elvis as Hank Williams, another Parker thumbs-down.

The big budget Hollywood films of the time, all forgotten now, were deplorable dinosaurs produced by people making the same sort of dreadful, disastrous choices of subject and casting that some of the final few Elvis films had been. Paramount, shortly after ending their arrangement with Elvis, began throwing millions down the drain with endless turkeys, and the other big studios were doing the same. At the same time, the lower budget, more contemporary films of that time were going through their redneck phase, with small-town America being presented as bigoted, time-warped, and sinister, with particular emphasis on the South as being outdated and dangerous, lawless not in a clean-up-Dodge sort of way, but a *Deliverance/Southern Comfort/Jackson County Jail* sort of way. If you were a woman stranded in the South, you'd be raped and shot. If you were a man... well, you'd be raped and shot.

The bitter truth is that Elvis was not an actor, he was a movie star, and thanks to *Easy Rider* and its copyists, this was not a good time to be "country". Elvis might have pulled off *Dirty Harry* (Frank Sinatra and Paul Newman had already turned it down before it was reluctantly handed to Clint Eastwood), but although brother-in-law and Memphis Mafia member

David Stanley has said Presley enjoyed the *Dirty Harry* films, Elvis was probably too law and order even in the unlikely event of him being reunited with Don *Flaming Star* Siegel (imagine Elvis throwing away his police badge at the end!).

Nor was Elvis the next Jack Nicholson. If Presley had been doing '70s cinema, the Colonel would have had to come to terms with the declining box office fortunes of his protege and the inevitability of an ensemble cast, and it would have been films like *The Poseidon Adventure, The Towering Inferno,* or--heaven help us--the *Airport* movies that provided him with his opportunities. Can Captain Elvis land the 'plane safely? Elvis in *Cannonball Run,* anyone? *Every Which Way But Loose? Convoy?* If he'd walked on to a Sam Peckinpah set, they'd have ended up shooting each other.

Or perhaps he would have helped launch a small pocket industry of films running against the prevailing trends and made himself seriously uncool. The analytical, intellectual, anti-Nixon, flag-questioning controversy and complexity of American cinema in the early '70s must have mystified him--patriotism to Elvis meant "my country, right or wrong", not "he serves his country best who questions it most", although he shouldn't be underestimated; his favorite film was said to be *Doctor Strangelove.* Still, in the 1970s, he was more likely to be watching *True Grit* than *Klute.*

What was actually happening in Hollywood was that as the 1970s started, the movie stars of the family film era were starting to turn reluctantly to television, among them Rock Hudson, Jimmy Stewart, Doris Day, James Garner, Glenn Ford, Henry Fonda, and many more from the old school (the one hold-out was John Wayne, still making movies after turning down *Gunsmoke* ten years earlier, some of them with Hal Wallis).

This mass migration of disenfranchised, disenchanted movie stars to television ("The little uglies have taken over" complained Rock Hudson, looking at the rise of Dustin Hoffman and Al Pacino!) was good news for the small screen, for these old-timers still had the prestige to bring with them enough clout to demand quality scripts and budgets, and Universal's TV series in particular were in their prime during the early '70s. Their 90 minute format for the classy and ground-breaking *The Name of the Game* had produced feature films up to cinema standards on a weekly basis at a time when the movie studios were in thrall to a new generation of film-makers who had no use for yesterday's names.

It was also good timing, as the movie-goers of that bygone era were now the settled stay-at-homes during the 1970s. If we are to be honest with ourselves, then Elvis--had he dropped out of music altogether and never done the so-called *Comeback Special*--would have been heading for the small screen as well. It's mind-boggling to imagine, but entirely probable, that 1970s Presley would have ended up doing two seasons as a straight-arrow TV cop, a two-part *Charlie's Angels*, three *Love Boats*, and a couple of *Fantasy Islands*.

This is not quite such a glib and frivolous supposition as it seems. In the early 1970s, with his dreams of serious acting a dim and distant memory, Presley and one of his karate buddies, Ed Parker, had developed a vague notion of producing a martial arts film, starring Presley, to cash in on the revived fortunes of the sport encouraged by the Bruce Lee films, the *Kung Fu* television series, and the black exploitation action films. From the *Billy Jack* movies to the *Master of Kung Fu* and *Iron Fist* comic books, martial arts were seriously in vogue. None of this plotting or planning was being done with the approval of the Colonel, who--when he found out about it--not only disassociated himself from the project (primarily because he felt this other Parker was a fellow opportunist), but pointedly insisted on having his non-involvement put in writing, a clear not-so-subtle message to Elvis as to what he thought of the idea.

Turning Presley and Ed Parker's wish list into some sort of practical reality was Rick Husky, who had briefly met Elvis back in 1960 during a wild publicity stunt for his school newspaper and had since remained friends while becoming a prolific and successful writer and producer in 1970s TV, primarily but not exclusively with Aaron Spelling, a man whose opinion of the mass audience was about as low as you could go. Although he threw money at his shows, and was known for paying the highest rates to his guest stars, Spelling's mindset made Wallis and Katzman look like philanthropists of the *avant garde*.

At this time, Husky's credits consisted of *The Mod Squad, Cade's County,* and *The Rookies,* but by the late '70s his name was associated almost exclusively with Spelling and such high profile shows as *Starsky and Hutch, Charlie's Angels, Vegas,* and *T.J. Hooker*. Husky knew Presley's buddy Jerry Schilling from college, and his path had crossed infrequently with Presley over the years (a 1976 episode of *Charlie's Angels,* produced and co-written by Husky, includes an "ex-con" character named Joe Esposito!). Somewhere in a parallel world, it is a girdled Elvis Presley clinging onto the bonnet of an L.A. police car for dear life in the opening credits of *T.J. Hooker*.

Despite a first meeting during which Parker was adversarial and Presley stoned, Husky went away and wrote out a thirty page premise for their project which embraced all Presley's favorite fantasies. Elvis would be a former CIA agent running a karate school who would come blasting out of retirement when an old friend is ruthlessly disposed of by drug dealers. It was daft, dumb, wholly derivative, and undoubtedly commercial, although fans of the rock and roll Presley would have been distraught and what was left of Presley's dwindling credibility would have been gone forever. Ultimately, Ed Parker's desire for a more documentary approach involving his school and students won through, but mercifully, nothing came of any of it.

Bearing in mind the Colonel's explicit non-involvement in this nonsense, the incident also puts the lie to the belief that Presley's career would have been somehow stellar if the conniving carny con-man had never entered the picture. He may have been a reprehensible greedy manipulator, but bearing in mind that his naive young client wanted recognition as an actor (where he had severe limitations) more than for his music (where he had few), the Colonel made the best of the small number of choices available to him in the 1960s, and also probably the right ones. The controlling old devil certainly seems to have made more right decisions than wrong ones, and if he didn't always push Elvis to the best possible place, he certainly steered him away from several bad choices.

The fact is that in early 1965, the soundtrack album for *Roustabout* sold more copies than the latest albums from the Beatles and the Beach Boys. And a few months later, his gospel single "Crying in the Chapel" (released in desperation by a product-starved RCA) held the number three slot in the singles charts; as recently as 2007, an Elvis compilation box-set held the number two spot in the U.K. The Colonel's biggest failing was not in Hollywood, but in his machinations in the music business which restricted Elvis' available choice of material--but Elvis played as much a part in that as Parker.

Presley wasn't a film producer or scriptwriter, but he knew good music inside out and back to front. He may have been locked into his movie contracts, but exclusive song providers Hill and Range had weaker manacles around his wrists. Where his music was concerned, he could have defied the Colonel if he'd cared to make the effort. So: the weakest aspect of his movies--the music--was as much Presley's fault as anyone's.

At this point, in 1973, would-be karate master and super-cop Presley was seriously losing it. He was divorced, drugs-dependent, worryingly overweight, out of fashion, ignoring advice, drifting apart from the wily Colonel Parker, rambling incoherently on stage, making poor musical choices, shaking hands with Nixon, abandoning friends like the Wests, finished in films, and headed towards the nauseating spectacle of CBS' *Elvis in Concert* footage and the events of August 8th, 1977 with a remorseless inevitability. However, had he lived, the Spelling scenario was not the only possibility when we look at the subsequent directions of Elvis' buddies such as Red West and Lance Le Gault, and beach movie contemporaries James Darren (a co-star in *T.J. Hooker*) and John Ashley, all of whom went to work with intelligent populist Stephen J. Cannell.

Presley's old high-school buddy and part-time bodyguard Red West had been working regularly during the 1960s as a bit-player and heavy, not just in Elvis Presley's films, but other productions as well, in particular those of the brusque and outspoken Robert Conrad, a feisty former boxer and ex-Warners contract player. Conrad, formerly of *Hawaiian Eye*, found success with his TV series *The Wild Wild West,* a dull sci-fi spy caper set in the 1860s and created by a florid, witty, shaven-headed, mountainous homosexual named Michael Garrison who plunged down his marble staircase to an accidental death mid-way through the show's run. Unlike its colorful creator, and despite some wonderful guest stars and the talents of the leads, the series itself was a dreary affair, enlivened only by the numerous brawls in which Red West specialised, but hugely successful in the ratings, and West went on to be virtually guaranteed a role in Conrad's various subsequent series and TV movies (Conrad had been a close friend of the late Nick Adams, the Elvis hanger-on for whom Red West also stunted).

Although he spent more time in the '70s with Presley than with Conrad, after Presley died, his working relationship and friendship with Conrad helped keep him employed; virtually every Conrad project found a role for Red West. He even had a regular co-starring gig, in a show called *The Duke* (1978), but this mundane detective show lasted only a few weeks on the air. One of West's final roles was in 1994 as a grey-haired, pot-bellied country sheriff in a brief blink-and-you-miss-it scene for Oliver Stone's notorious indictment of media excess *Natural Born Killers,* written and then disowned by Elvis buff Quentin Tarantino.

Conrad had made two of his many series--*Black Sheep Squadron* and *The Duke*--with television producer Stephen Cannell, who specialised in offbeat and sardonic detective series in the '70s and smash-and-crash vigilante shows like *The A-Team, Riptide,* and *Hardcastle and McCormick* in the '80s, before retiring to write novels when big budget movie franchises like *Die Hard* and *Lethal Weapon* stole his thunder (Conrad's own last gasp in a successful thirty year career was the short-lived *High Mountain Rangers* series in 1988).

West guest-starred in many of the Cannell series, including *Tenspeed and Brownshoe, Greatest American Hero, The A-Team, Hardcastle and McCormick,* and *Hunter,* many more than once, and had recurring roles in Conrad's two Cannell series, *Black Sheep Squadron* and *The Duke.* He also appeared in episodes of *Mission: Impossible* (with Conrad), *Battlestar Galactica, Simon and Simon* and *Magnum p.i.*

Cannell and his *Black Sheep* colleagues Frank Lupo and Donald Bellisario at Universal later branched out on their own, dominating the action/adventure genre during the early 1980s, turning out that decade's version of the Republic serials, and running a fairly boisterous boys' club that had already found work for former beach movie stars like James Darren, who was now directing, and John Ashley, who was now producing. Just as the beach movies and Elvis films had been the honey pot for hopeful starlets to buzz around in the early 1960s, so the dozen or so TV series of the Cannell/Bellisario/Lupo troika provided regular work for ambitious and shapely young lookers in the early '80s, who, if they appeared in one such show, were guaranteed to turn up in half-a-dozen others (several '60s starlets turned up in them too).

Cannell's shows were escapist nonsense, but they were likeable, witty and hip, and just as Schwarzenegger and Stallone stood tall above the likes of Chuck Norris and Steven Seagal, so Cannell stood above Aaron Spelling and Glen Larson on the small screen (with Bellisario and Lupo's solo efforts falling somewhere between the two camps).

Former r&b singer Lance Le Gault, brought to Hollywood as Elvis' assistant choreographer and stand-in, had stayed thin and gaunt while Elvis ballooned, and also found steady employment in this corner of Hollywood, playing a regular role for Cannell in the 1980s as the eternally frustrated pursuer of *The A-Team* in that series' first few seasons and then taking recurring roles as another military hardass in Bellisario's *Magnum p.i.* and an ice-cold bounty hunter in Lupo's *Werewolf* series. While embracing right-wing populism and old-fashioned values, all these paint-by-numbers series (with the single exception of the bleak and silly *Airwolf*) shared a healthy and intelligent attitude to women and minorities (without being pathetically politically correct) that the other providers of 1980s escapism (Spelling and Larson) sometimes did not, and their sensible marriage of the best of left and right politics, and rejection of the worst of same, provided the finest moving wallpaper American TV could offer.

While Steven Bochco, MTM, and the classier sit-coms provided the food for thought, Cannell and his buddies were offering guilt-free mind candy for the more discerning couch potatoes which, by embracing humor and rejecting faddism, have stood the test of time in a way in which other 1980s shows such as *Dynasty, Cagney and Lacey,* and *Miami Vice* have not. With so many connections to the sun and sand/white knight/adult playground philosophy of the Elvis movies of twenty years earlier, not to mention the near-constant presence of West and Le Gault and the Colonel-friendly streak of conning and scamming that runs through all the Cannell productions, it is almost certain that this area of television could, and perhaps would have found something for a middle-aged Elvis to do.

Sadly, the efforts of Red and Sonny West to save Presley from his bad habits came too late. Sacked for having the temerity to try and make him confront his problem just months before Presley died, they dashed out, with Dave Hebler and ghost writer Steve Dunleavy, the tell-all book *Elvis--What Happened?* that revealed his difficulties to the world only weeks before Elvis succumbed (read it today, and you'll find nothing terribly spiteful or shocking). Trapped in a time-warp within his own private kingdom, with courtiers whose answers to his problems were deferential indulgence, shallow self-help platitudes and crackpot cults and pills instead of the professional help and common sense confrontation he needed, on August 8th, 1977, the king was dead.

* * * * *

It's important to recognise just how little anyone knew, or cared to know, about the real Elvis Presley at this point. At around the time of Presley's death, two books preceded the avalanche of tell-alls from know-nothings that flooded the shops in the aftermath of the inevitable.

The first was *Elvis--What Happened?* which came out both too soon to make huge profits for Red and Sonny West, and too late to help Elvis (which the Wests, with some claim to credibility, claimed was its intention), and the second, appearing in 1981, was the scandalous and simply-titled *Elvis* by Albert Goldman.

This sleazy and sordid tome was reviled by Elvis fans, firstly for confirming the truths that had become self-evident and undeniable in the wake of Presley's demise to still disbelieving fans, and secondly for doing so in a thoroughly unpleasant, unsympathetic, mean-spirited and one-sided manner. It's not so much the content of the Goldman book that jars (although plenty was wrong), it's the tone and manner of its revelation. Plainly fascinated by Elvis while claiming to be disgusted, Goldman had overreacted to the West/Hebler expose and his journalistic impulse to dig the dirt kicked in with a vengeance.

As with most people who try to pass judgement on others by psycho-analyzing them *in absentia*, Goldman revealed as much about himself as about Presley, particularly when discussing Presley's sex life and supposed sexual preferences, which taken on face value were little different from any other man invited to indulge his every whim. What hang-ups Elvis did possess (shyness, voyeurism, mother love, macho posturing--nothing too different from the average male) were as much a part of his religious upbringing, youthful naivete, and 1960s sexual hypocrisy as any personal problems, particularly when viewed from the vantage point of the late-1970s. A master at making mountains out of molehills, it is surprising just how little damaging detail Goldman managed to unearth from the hundreds of men and women who had actually encountered Elvis. Strip away the snide sensationalism of his writing style and you have in *Elvis*, curiously, a portrait of a very ordinary man—which Elvis wasn't.

Having never met Elvis, Goldman judges him from second-hand information tricked out of a few people who had done so (the list of named--and name--interviewees makes thin reading, and many denied, perhaps wishfully, having spoken to him; Lamar Fike, his main source, certainly regretted it), and comes to some extraordinarily presumptuous conclusions about Presley the private person with very few qualifications to do so at all. Looking over the list of names in the acknowledgements it is clear that most of these people would never have spoken to Goldman during his four years of lazy and selective research if they had known what sort of a repugnant tome he intended to produce--not a truthful, objective look at the real Elvis at all, as Peter Guralnick would offer two decades later in a two volume biography that brought the real Presley to life, but a sensational, selective and pseudo-psychological hatchet job of assumption, idiocy, embellishment and innuendo. To look at his credits, one wonders how he fell to this sort of journalism.

One clue came from Elvis fan Sid Shaw, a Britisher who produced Elvis memorabilia, and who received a 'phone call one night from a fan reading him a review--"a very flowery, verbose account written by, it seemed, an Elvis groupie. I said I thought it was some woman madly in love with Elvis". The caller then revealed he had been reading an article by Albert Goldman! Said Shaw, "Whereas John Lennon was assassinated by a fan with a gun, Goldman chose the pen". Most of the revelations Goldman repeated and elaborated on--and often absurdly pontificated upon--were relatively recent at the time, and so he was able to extract maximum shock value from his ridiculous extrapolations from fans still struggling to deal with the actual facts. Every opportunity to shame or belittle Elvis is jumped on and blown out of proportion, and his bitchy physical descriptions of the men, and spiteful, unnecessary remarks about the women give his text the queeny, homo-erotic tone of a spurned lover.

Perversely however, although he gets some of his detail wrong (misspelling the names of Ben Weisman, Deborah Walley and one of

Robert Conrad's TV shows, suggesting that the Katzman films followed Wallis' abandonment of Elvis, when in fact they appeared simultaneously during the Parker/Wallis association etc.), the greatest virtue of the Goldman book, if one dare suggest a virtue, is his analysis and understanding of the music business, the history of rock, and the Elvis films.

If he hadn't been so personally consumed with dissecting Elvis the person so irrationally he could have produced a worthwhile study of Elvis the icon. His take on *Jailhouse Rock* and *G.I. Blues* in particular are insightful enough to make one wish he had reviewed the later films as well, but in keeping with Elvis literary tradition they are airbrushed out of the big picture as irrelevancies--twenty million dollars worth of irrelevancies at the 1960s box office. Was Hal Wallis really so out of touch with his audience?

But Goldman was one of the few to acknowledge that Presley himself was more interested in movie stardom than becoming a rock and roll icon, and that he aged in mortal years. Tough love for Elvis fans at the time, even if it was tougher still for the smitten Goldman to psycho-analyse his own demons.

Whatever Dave Hebler's motives might have been (and it's worth remembering that tabloid reporter Steve Dunleavy, who carelessly referred to Presley as "white trash" on an NBC's tribute special in 1978, transcribed the Hebler/West book from interviews), it's doubtful that the Wests had anything other than Elvis Presley's health and survival in mind when they produced their book *Elvis--What Happened?* After twenty years of service and devoted friendship, what else could Red West do? He was certainly entitled to be bitter, but when one sees that awful, dreadful footage of Presley stumbling through *Elvis in Concert* weeks away from death while Charlie Hodge fawns over him like a devoted nurse, one understands. No disrespect to Hodge, who had no power, and was one of the few Graceland regulars to have a musical background, but Red West would never have let things get to that point, and that's why he was no longer there. Although many fans scorn *Elvis--What Happened?*, it's actually a very sympathetic, honest, poignant and heart-felt work, despite Dunleavy's obvious disdain for all others involved.

As for the other rambling tell-all tomes from so-called insiders, an endless stream of drivel to rival the *Star Trek* industry, they are mostly beneath contempt, particularly those that came from people Elvis himself held in contempt.

Perhaps the last word on the Elvis movies should go to songwriter Ben Weisman. "Some people today mock his movies, but I say that his movies were much healthier than a lot of the movies today. Every artist wants to do something of a serious nature, but still, Elvis is going to be remembered for all the fun movies he made. Elvis movies were fun. They were healthy. And his movies always made money. People forget that a lot of folks loved his movies. The critics can say whatever they want, but the bottom line is--the public loved his movies".

appendix 5--sources and bibliography

It's one thing knowing something--it's another thing entirely being able to back it up when it's stated in cold, hard print. Now you've got to prove you know it. Fortunately, Elvis Presley is probably the most studied, documented, researched, and occasionally lied about and/or misunderstood human being of the 20th century (with perhaps JFK coming in a close second?). So many people have been interviewed, so much film exists, and so much detail has been accumulated, that it is not difficult to weed out the malice, misunderstandings, and misjudgements.

Clearly, a dozen or so good reference works and some common sense will inform anyone that Elvis Presley was a flawed, decent, likeable, vulnerable, and--it has to be said--beautiful man with the full compliment of human emotions, desires, virtues, attributes and failings, and a massive, unique talent. All the factual information and anecdotes in this book were either sourced from, or are confirmed by, the following publications (and yes, the first three are mine, further supported by additional sources).

All the movies discussed were watched many, many times both before and during the writing of this work, and will continue to be until I'm no longer able to do so! All films or television episodes referred to in this text have been viewed, in many cases, many times (with the possible exception of films or TV episodes referred to only by title as credits information). The opinions--supported by the evidence--are mine (although not exclusively).

Abbott, Jon. *Irwin Allen Television Productions, 1964-1970.* North Carolina: McFarland, 2006

Abbott, Jon. *Stephen J. Cannell Television Productions.* North Carolina: McFarland, 2009

Abbott, Jon. *20th Century Time Travel Television and Movies,* forthcoming

Archerd, Army. *Clambake* set report. *TV Star Parade,* August 1967

Austen, David. *Following No Formula,* interview with Hal Wallis. London: *Films and Filming.* December 1969

Baker, Trevor. *The Little Book of Elvis.* Carlton

Biskind, Peter. *Easy Riders, Raging Bulls.* London: Bloomsbury, 1999

Braun, Eric. *The Elvis Film Encyclopedia*. London: Batsford, 1997

Bret, David. *Elvis--the Hollywood Years*. London: Robson Books, 2001

Brooks, Tim, and Earle Marsh. *The Complete Directory to Primetime Network and Cable TV Shows, 1946 – present.* New York: Ballantine, 1999

Chartrand, Harvey F. interview with Harold J. Stone, *Filmfax*, no. 90, April/May, 2002

Clayton, Rose, and Dick Heard. *Elvis By Those Who Knew Him Best*, London: Virgin, 1994

Cox, Stephen, *The Beverly Hillbillies*. New York: Harper Collins, 1993

Cox, Stephen, *Dreaming of Jeannie*. New York: St. Martin's Press, 2000

Cox, Stephen, *The Munsters*, New York: Backstage Books, 2008

Douglass, Greg, interview with Dolores Fuller, *Outre* nos. 16 and 17, 1999

Dunleavy, Steve, and Dave Hebler, Red West, Sonny West. *Elvis--What Happened?* New York: Ballantine, 1977

Eisner, Joel. *The Official Batman Batbook*. London: Titan Books, 1997

Fagen, Herb, interview with Sue-Ane Langdon, *Filmfax* no. 55, March/April, 1996

Feeney, F.X., quoting Adler, *New York Times*, *Movie Icons: Presley*, Koln: Taschen, 2006

Fidelman, Geoffrey Mark. *The Lucy Book*. Los Angeles: Renaissance, 1999

Gregory, Neal and Janice Gregory. *How TV Reacted the Day Elvis Died, TV Guide,* August 15th, 1981

Guralnick, Peter. *Careless Love*. Boston: Little, Brown, 1999

Guralnick, Peter. *Last Train to Memphis,* Boston: Little, Brown, 1994

Halliwell, Leslie. *Filmgoer's Companion*. London: Granada, 1983

Halliwell, Leslie. *Halliwell's Film Guide*. London: Granada, 1984

Hardy, Phil, ed. *The Aurum Film Encyclopedia of the Western,* London: Aurum, 1995

Henderson, Jan Alan, interview with William Campbell, *Filmfax* no. 75/76, October 1999

Holston, Kim. *Starlet,* North Carolina: McFarland, 1988

Kinnard, Roy. *Science Fiction Serials,* North Carolina: McFarland, 1998

Levy, Shawn. *Ratpack Confidential*. London: Fourth Estate, 1998

Lisanti, Tom. interview with Shelley Fabares, *Outre* no. 16, 1999

Lisanti, Tom. interview with Laurel Goodwin, *Filmfax* no. 81/82, October 2000

Lisanti, Tom. interview with Diane McBain, *Filmfax* no. 69/70, October 1998

Lisanti, Tom. interview with Irene Tsu, *Filmfax* no. 68, Aug/Sept., 1998

Lisanti, Tom. interview with Celeste Yarnall, *Femme Fatales,* vol. 11, no. 4, April 2002

Lisanti, Tom. interview with Francine York, *Filmfax* no. 81/82, October 2000

Lisanti, Tom. *Fantasy Femmes of Sixties Cinema.* North Carolina: McFarland, 2001

Lisanti, Tom. *Drive-In Dream Girls.* North Carolina: McFarland, 2003

Lisanti, Tom, and Louis Paul. *Film Fatales.* North Carolina: McFarland, 2002

Lisanti, Tom. *Hollywood Surf and Beach Movies.* North Carolina: McFarland, 2005

Martin, Deana. *Memories Are Made of This.* Sidgwick and Jackson

McGee, Mark Thomas. *The Rock and Roll Movie Encyclopedia of the 1950s,* North Carolina: McFarland, 1990

Nash, Alanna. *Elvis and the Memphis Mafia.* London: New York: Harper-Collins/Aurum, 2005

Nash, Alanna. *The Colonel*. New York/London: Simon and SchusterAurum, 2003

Newman, Kim. *The BFI Companion to Horror*. London: Cassell, 1996

Parish, James Robert. *The Elvis Presley Scrapbook*. New Yotk: Ballantine, 1977

Parish, James Robert. *The Great Movie Series*. New York: Barnes, 1971

Peary, Danny. *Cult Movie Stars*. New York, Simon and Schuster, 1991

Phillips, Mark, interview with Celeste Yarnall, *Starlog,* April 1989

Shepard, Don, with Robert E. Slatzer, *Bing Crosby: The Hollow Man*, W.H. Allen

Siegel, Don. *A Siegel Film*. London: Faber and Faber, 1993

Stanley, David, with Frank Coffey. *The Elvis Encyclopedia*. Virgin Books, 1994/1998 (U.K.)

Tosches, Nick. *Dino*. London/New York: Virgin Books/Random House, 1992/1997 (U.K.)

Turner Classic Movies press releases on Elvis movie seasons

Vellenger, Dirk, with Mick Farren. *Elvis and the Colonel*. London: Grafton/Collins, 1998

West, Sonny, with Marshall Terrill. *Elvis: Still Taking Care of Business*. Triumph Books, 2007

Weaver, Tom. interview with Julie Adams, *Starlog* no. 167, June, 1991

Weaver, Tom. interview with John Archer, *Starlog* no. 204, May, 1994

Weaver, Tom. interview with Darlene Tompkins, *Cult Movies*, 2000, cited in *Science-Fiction Confidential,* North Carolina: McFarland, 2002

Weddle, David. *Sam Peckinpah: "If They Move, Kill 'em!"* New York: Grove Press, 1996

Weldon, Michael J. *The Psychotronic Video Guide*. London: Titan Books, 1996

Wicking, Chris, and Tise Vahimagi. *The American Vein*. Talisman

Woodbine, Paul, interview with Merry Anders, *Filmfax* no.63/64, October 1998

also--background on actress Barbara McNair: Howard, Josiah, *Blaxploitation Cinema--The Essential Reference Guide,* FAB Press, 2008; background on actress Nicole Jaffe: Lawson, Tim, and Alisa Persons, *The Magic Behind the Voices,* University Press of Mississippi, 2004; background on producer Michael Garrison: Weaver, Tom, interview with Ken Kolb, *Starlog* no. 312, July 2003, cited in *Earth vs. the Sci-Fi Filmmakers,* North Carolina: McFarland, 2005; quote from Rock Hudson: Hofler, Robert, *The Man Who Invented Rock Hudson,* New York: Carroll and Graf, 2005; some cuttings and clippings, including a useful article on *Clambake,* from fellow writer and archivist Mark Phillips; some information on *Elvis Meets Nixon* TV film and the casts of a couple of films sourced from Internet Movie Data Base; episode titles for three of the TV shows referencing Elvis sourced from Internet Movie Data Base; otherwise, no internet sites were sought or consulted.

I'd also like to acknowledge Tony Mechele, formerly of the British Film Institute, for supplying much of the background information on producer Sam Katzman's credits, initially for another job of work some years ago, but so useful here as well.

© Jon Abbott, 2014

All promotional materials, publicity stills, and DVD sleeves reproduced in this book are from the author's private collection, and are copyright their respective commercial sources. They are used solely for their intended function, and there is no intention to infringe on that copyright.

index

20th Century Fox 17, 31, 49, 52, 54, 55, 221, 248,
55 Days to Peking 129,
77, Sunset Strip 53, 61, 62, 65, 99, 107, 116, 124, 126, 127, 135, 136, 140, 147, 154, 161, 178, 184, 220,
300 Spartans, The 22,
2001: A Space Odyssey 83,
3000 Miles to Graceland 242,

A-Team, The 48, 163, 254, 255,
Abbott and Costello 133,
Abbott, Dorothy 31,
Abel Robert 228, 229,
Absent-Minded Professor, The 64, 212,
Acosta, Rodolfo 49,
Across 110th Street 218,
Adam 12 125,
"Adam and Evil" 159,
Adams, Beverly 112, 117, 119, 126,
Adams, Gerald Drayson 101, 138, 139,
Adams, Julie/Julia 129, 131, 134, 135,
Adams, Peter 31,
Adams, Nick 20, 27, 39, 48, 70, 97, 123, 127, 202, 254,
Adams, Stanley 174, 177, 178, 179,
Addams Family, The 39, 106, 107, 125, 127, 136, 140,
Adidge, Pierre 228, 229,
Adler, Renata 247,
Adrian, Iris 55,
Advance to the Rear 106,
Adventures of Captain Africa, The 103,
Adventures of Kit Carson 136,
Adventures of Robin Hood, The 29, 38,
Adventures of Superman, The 117, 127, 140,
"The After Hours" 149,
Aguirre, Fred 85,
Ahn, Philip 151, 155,
AIP 21, 191,
Airport 251,
Airwolf 68, 80, 95, 155, 161, 255,
Alamo, The 83,
Alaskans, The 161,
Albertson, Jack 101, 104, 106, 110, 111, 112, 117,
Albright, Lola 69, 70,
Alcaide, Chris 69,

Alden, Ginger 236,
Alderson, John 174, 178,
Alexander, Jeff 71, 121, 175,
ALF 237,
Alfred Hitchcock Presents 67,
Alias Smith and Jones 204, 208,
"All I Needed Was the Rain" 197, 198,
All in the Family 217,
"All Shook Up" 240,
"All-Star Munster" 110,
"All That I Am" 159,
Allen, Irwin 140, 187,
Allen, Melvin 180,
Allen, R.S. 119, 121,
Allen, Rusty 119,
Allen, Steve 26, 231,
Allen, Woody 144, 250,
Allied Artists 129, 131,
Almanzar, James 207, 208,
"Almost" 210,
"Almost Always True" 55, 60,
"Almost in Love" 202,
"Aloha Oe" 55,
Altman, Robert 177, 250,
Alyn, Kirk 103, 110,
"Am I Ready?" 159,
Amazing Spider-Man, The 29, 211,
Amazing Stories 68,
"American Trilogy" 235,
Ames, Trudi 233,
Amos and Andy 218,
Amos Burke – Secret Agent 116, 135, 175, 204,
Anchors Aweigh 97,
Anders, Merry 129, 134, 136, 155,
Andress, Ursula 85, 88, 93,
Andrews, Edward 210, 211, 212,
Andy Griffiths Show, The 65,
"Angel" 63, 67,
Angels With Dirty Faces 38,
Angold, Edith 41,
Anholt, Edward 72, 76,
Aniston, Jennifer 247,
Ann Margret 44, 61, 74, 81, 91, 92, 93, 94, 94, 95, 97, 98, 98, 99, 101, 113, 119, 121, 123, 127, 132, 168, 176, 190, 201, 232, 233,
Ann Sothern Show, The 163, 204,
Annie, Get Your Gun 97,
Annie Oakley 163,
Ansara, Michael 138, 140, 142,

265

Ape Man, The 102,
"The Apple" 171, 205,
"The Apple-a-Day Affair" 110,
"Appreciation" 91, 93,
The Aquanauts 76, 107, 147, 220,
"The Arabian Affair" 140,
Arabian Nights 139,
Archer, John 55,
Arden, Eve 162,
Arkoff, Sam 29,
Armstrong, Curtis 241,
Arnaz, Desi 162,
Arnaz, Lucie 204,
Arnie 116,
Arnt, Charles 52,
Around the World Under the Sea 185,
"Art for Monkees' Sake" 172,
Arthur Godfrey's Talent Scouts 231,
"As Long As I Have You" 35, 38,
Asher, William 71, 153, 222,
Ashley, John 59, 123, 162, 185, 254, 255,
Ashley, Merri 202,
Askin, Leon 174, 178,
Asner, Ed 69, 70, 215, 220, 221,
"Assignment: Earth" 98,
Astaire, Fred 33,
Atienza, Frank 55,
Atoll K 11,
Atom Man vs. Superman 103,
Attack of the Fifty Foot Woman 137,
Atwater, Edith 81,
Aubrey, James 226,
"Aura Lee" 210,
Aurum Encyclopedia of Western Films 23,
Austen, David 248,
Austin, Pamela 55, 61, 101, 105, 106, 108, 109, 110, 111,
Austin Powers (franchise/character) 13, 44, 176,
Austin Powers, International Man of Mystery 15,
Automan 79,
Autry, Gene 54,
Avalon, Frankie 126, 149, 153, 162, 233,
Avengers, The (U.K.) 170,
Avery, Tex 177,

Babcock, Dwight 210,
Baby Doll 22,

"Baby, I Don't Care" 31,
"Baby, If You'll Give Me All Your Love" 174,
Bachelor Father 62, 116,
Back to the Beach 126,
Bad Girls from Mars 157,
Badlands 226,
Baer, Max 146,
Bailey, Raymond 35, 39,
Baker, Herbert, 24, 35,
Baker, Joby 119, 125,
Baker, Joe Don 223,
Bakula, Scott 238,
Baldwin, Walter 52,
Balin, Ina 207, 208,
Ball, Lucille (Lucy) 13, 192, 224,
Ballad of Cable Hogue, The 75,
Ballantine, Carl 189,
Ballard, Kaye 162,
Banacek 83, 211,
Bancroft, Benji 202,
"Bang Bang, My Baby Shot Me Down" 191,
Bankhead, Tallulah 156,
Banks, Emily 202,
Barbarella 137,
Barbary Coast 79, 161,
"The Bard" 176,
Bardot, Brigitte 12, 25,
"Barefoot Ballad" 101,
Barnaby Jones 161, 211,
Barnett, Herb 180,
Baretta 222,
Barris, George 171, 205,
Barry, Dave 159,
Barty, Billy 112, 117, 138, 139, 140,
Basehart, Richard 185,
Baskin, Edie 202,
"The Bat Cave Affair" 110,
Bat Masterson 82,
Batman (character/franchise) 109,
Batman (serials) 102, 103,
Batman (1966 film) 126,
Batman (1989 film) 172,
Batman (tv series) 9, 13, 14, 28, 34, 39, 45, 54, 65, 66, 70, 97, 99, 107, 116, 117, 125, 127, 137, 140, 146, 147, 149, 153, 156, 157, 161, 170, 171, 172, 178, 186, 193, 200, 204, 213, 249, 250,
Batman and Robin 103,
Battlestar Galactica 79, 255,
Baywatch 163,
Baywatch Nights 155,

Beach Ball 126, 139,
Beach Blanket Bingo 162, 222,
"Beach Boy Blues" 55,
Beach Boys, the 139, 253,
Beach Girls and the Monster, The 28,
Beach Party 213,
"Beach Shack" 159,
Beaird, Barbara 49,
Beall, Barbara 72,
Beall, Betty 72,
Beast of Blood 205,
Beatles, The 10, 12, 143, 158, 229, 235, 253,
Beaulieu/Presley, Priscilla 87, 88, 90, 171, 177, 236, 237, 240,
"Because of Love" 72,
Becker, Ken 24, 28, 41, 72,
Beckett, Elaine 165,
Bedtime for Bonzo 149,
"Beginner's Luck" 145,
Beguiled, The 50,
Belafonte, Harry 215,
Bellisario, Donald 48, 255,
Beloin, Edmund 41,
Ben Casey 45, 107, 153, 211,
Benet, Brenda 126, 138, 139, 140, 184,
Bennett, Bruce 17, 22,
Bennett, Marjorie 72, 77,
Benny, Jack 169,
Benson, Sally 91,
Benton, Anne 49,
Benton, Laurie 129,
Bercovici, Eric 215,
Bercutt, Sharon 49,
Berle, Milton 126,
Berlinger, Warren 159, 163,
Berman, Pandro 31,
Bernard, Judd 174,
Bernds, Edward 129, 130, 131, 134,
Betz, Carl 159, 160, 163,
Beverly Hillbillies,The (film) 212,
Beverly Hillbillies, The (tv series) 10, 13, 34, 39, 44, 63, 64, 65, 70, 74, 106, 110, 117, 126, 137, 146, 149, 156, 157, 170, 189, 201, 213,
Beverly Hills 90210 153,
Bewitched 53, 65, 71, 76, 106, 108, 124, 125, 126, 127, 137, 140, 147, 149, 169, 178, 192, 200, 203, 205,
"Beyond the Bend" 81,
Beyond the Time Barrier 62,
Beyond the Valley of the Dolls 157,

Bice, Robert 31,
Bienstock, Freddy 142,
"Big Boots" 41,
Big Heat, The 39,
Big Valley, The 68, 107, 113, 181, 187, 211,
Bikini Beach 222,
Bilko/The Phil Silvers Show 67, 231, 232,
Bill and Ted's Excellent Adventure/s 239, 240,
Bill Dana Show, The 1265,
Billy Jack (franchise) 252,
Binder, Steve 234,
Biohazard 186,
Bionic Woman, The 83, 125, 213,
Birdman of Alcatraz, The 22,
Bixby, Bill 70, 107, 139, 180, 182, 183, 184, 189, 192,
Black Belt Jones 218,
Black, Bill 24, 25, 31,
Black Caesar 218,
Black Dragons 102,
Black Sheep Squadron 66, 79, 254, 255,
Black Star 50,
Blackbeard's Ghost 34, 170,
Blackboard Jungle, The 39,
Blackman, Joan 55, 59, 61, 69, 70, 176,
Blackwell, Otis 81,
Blair, Nicky 91, 95, 97,
Blake, Madge 24, 28,
Blazing Saddles 144,
Blondell, Joan 136, 197, 199, 200,
Blondie (character/franchise) 130,
"Blood Oath" 21,
Blood on the Sun 77,
Blue Denim 61,
Blue Hawaii 11, 38, **55—62**, *55, 58,* 63, 67, 70, 72, 83, 87, 88, 90, 105, 106, 107, 117, 118, 121, 127, 131, 140, 151, 161, 181, 248,
"Blue Hawaii" 55, 67, 74 226,
"Blue Suede Shoes" 45, 225,
Bob and Carol and Ted and Alice 53, 205,
Bob Newhart Show, The 125,
Bochco, Steven 10, 221, 255,
Bogart, Humphrey 29, 32, 70,
Bold Ones, The 205, 217,
Bonanza 61, 62, 66, 113, 114, 115, 116, 153, 205, 211,
Bond, Diane 129, 137,
Bonnie and Clyde 53,
Bonzo Goes to College 149,
Boon, Robert 41,

267

Boone, Pat 92, 146,
Bop Girl Goes Calypso 34,
Boris Karloff's Thriller 88, 107, 116, 125, 146, 171,
Born in '68 15,
"Bossa Nova Baby" 85,
Bourbon Street Beat 65, 107, 116, 140, 161, 178, 220,
Bowery at Midnight 102,
Bowery Boys (characters/franchise) 130, 133,
Bowery Boys Meet the Monsters 131,
Bowie, David 241,
"A Boy Like Me, A Girl Like You" 72,
Boyd, Pat 63,
Boyd West, John 238,
Boyne, Hazel 35,
"The Brain-Killer Affair" 170,
Brand, Neville 17, 22,
Branded 70, 90, 126, 178, 213,
Brandel, Marc 174, 175,
Brando, Marlon 14, 18, 29, 50, 248, 249,
Brandt, Thordis 159, 163, 202, 206,
Braun, Eric 129, 160,
Brenda Starr 103,
Bret, David 26, 47, 109,
Brick Bradford 103,
Bride of Frankenstein, The 170,
Bridges, Beau 240,
Bridget Loves Bernie 124,
Briles, Chuck 210,
Brinegar, Paul 207, 209,
Bring Me the Head of Alfredo Garcia 70,
Bringing Up Buddy 222,
Brix, Herman 22,
Brodie, Steve 55, 112, 115, 117,
Broken Lance 199,
Bronco 107,
Bronson, Charles 69, 71,
Brooks, Mel 144,
Brooks, Peter 119, 125,
Brown, Courtney 189,
Brown, Dana 189,
Brown, Dorian 129,
Brown, Pepe 210, 213,
Browne, Jnr., Arthur 180, 185, 187,
Bruce, Eve 129,
Bruce Gentry 103,
Bubba Ho-Tep 242,
Buchanan, Larry 135, 137,

Buck Rogers (serial) 156,
Buck Rogers in the 25th Century 59, 79, 140,
Buckner, Robert 17,
Bucktown 218,
Buffalo Bill 212,
"The Bullfighter Was a Lady" 85,
Bullitt 66,
Bullock, Harvey 119, 121,
Bundle of Joy 124,
Burke, Walter 174, 177, 178, 179,
Burke's Law 22, 39, 64, 68, 70, 99, 110, 116, 123, 126, 137, 140, 147, 153, 155, 157, 161, 162, 170, 191, 200, 205, 211, 222,
Burkhart, Monte 49,
Burnett, Don 31,
Burns, George 99,
Burns, Paul 17,
Butch Cassidy and the Sundance Kid 208,
Butham, Joe 52,
Butler, Timothy 24,
Butterworth, Donna 151, 155,
Buttram, Pat 52, 54, 110, 112, 117,
By Love Possessed 106
Bye Bye, Birdie 92, 126, 194, 232,
Byrnes, Edd 126,

"C'mon, Everybody" 91,
"C'mon, Let's Live a Little" 185,
Cadiente, David 197,
Cade's County 155, 252,
"The Cage" 74,
Cagney and Lacey 255,
Cagney, James 10, 32, 170, 200,
Call to Glory 79,
Callahan, Mushy 69, 70,
Calvert, Steve 103,
Calypso Heat Wave 104,
Cameron, David 24,
Campbell, William 17, 18, 21,
Can-Can 45, 66,
Candido, Candy 35,
"A Cane and a High Starched Collar" 49,
Cannell, Stephen J. 10, 48, 59, 115, 163, 181, 191, 221, 237, 254, 255, 256,
Cannon 155, 211,
Cannonball Run, The 125, 251,
"Can't Help Falling In Love" 55, 56, 57, 225, 234, 235,
Cano, Eddie 85,

Cape Fear 116,
Capitol 153,
Capra, Frank 63, 91,
Caprice 155,
Captain America (serial) 140,
Captain Nice 106,
Captain Video 103,
Cardenas, Elsa 85, 87, 88, 90,
Cardenas, Leon 85,
Careless Love 12, 92,
Carey, Michele 202, 203, 204, 205,
Carey, Timothy 215, 220, 222,
Carlson, Richard 215, 222,
Carnal Knowledge 99,
Carnival of Souls 176,
Carol, Cindy 204,
Carousel 108, 147,
Carradine, John 210, 213,
Carrey, Jim 247,
Carricart, Robert 63, 66, 85, 90,
Carry On (film franchise) 67,
Carson, Johnny 149,
Carson, Robert 101,
Carson, Henry 41,
Carter, Harper 41, 189,
Carter, Harry 52,
Carter, Jack 91,
Cartoon Network 237, 242,
Casablanca 29, 38,
Cash, Johnny 110,
Casino Royale 88,
Castle, William 134,
Cat Ballou 201,
"Catching On Fast" 101,
CBS 253,
Cease Fire 126,
Chad and Jeremy 249,
"Chain Gang" 225,
"The Challenge" 236,
Chance, Larry 138,
Change of Habit 12, 206, 215,
"Change of Habit" 215,
Chapman, Judy 145,
Charge of the Lancers 103,
Charles, Arlene 180,
Charles in Charge 237,
Charles, Ray 96,
Charlie Chan (character/franchise) 65,

Charlie's Angels 39, 62, 66, 83, 95, 124, 147, 161, 222, 249, 252,
Charro 12, 51, 139, 206, *206*, 207 – 209, 214, 248,
"Charro" 207,
Chartrand, Harvey 124,
Chase 125,
Chatton, Sydney 24,
Chauvin, Lilyan 35, 129, 136,
Cheers 221, 237,
"Chesay" 145,
Cheshire, Harry 24,
Cheyenne 82, 90, 124, 135, 178,
Chicago Teddy Bears, The 34,
Chiles, Linden 52, 54,
China Beach 126,
Choirboys, The 204,
Christen, Marya 197,
Christie, Audrey 145, 147, 149,
Christine, Virginia 49,
Cisar, George 31,
Citizen Kane 39,
"City By Night" 174,
Civil Wars 237,
"The Clam" 123,
Clambake 11, 28, 97, 106, 123, 132, 160, 163, 173, **180 – 188,** *185, 188,* 189, 190, 248,
"Clambake" 180,
Clarke, Gary 185,
Clarke, Ken 17, 22," 210,
"Clean Up Your Own Back Yard" 210,
Cleopatra Jones 218,
Cleopatra Jones and the City of Gold 75,
"The Climb" 91, 123,
Coach 161,
Coby, Fred 31,
Coch, Edward 41,
Cochran, Steve 77,
Cocker, Joe 229,
Cockfighter 53,
Code Red 135,
Coe, Barry 17, 22,
Coffy 218,
Coleman, Dabney 210, 211, 212,
College Confidential 117,
Collier, Don 151, 157,
Collier, Richard 72,
Colonel, The 57, 92, 142, 249,
Columbia 103, 126, 147, 162, 233,
Columbo 61, 66, 124, 125, 176, 184, 205, 213,

269

Combat 39, 65, 71, 76, 82, 83, 90, 140, 174, 178, 186, 192,
"Come Along" 145,
Comeback Special 80, 109, 193, 203, 205, 214, 218, 222, 225, 227, 233, 234, 252,
Complete Directory to Primetime Network and Cable TV Shows 240,
Computer Wore Tennis Shoes, The 65,
Congo Bill 103,
"Confidence" 180, 187,
Connelly, Joe 215, 218,
Conquest of Space 34,
Conrad, Robert 48, 123, 146, 147, 190, 254, 255, 258,
Conrad, Walter 41,
Considine, Charlotte 189,
Conway, Russ 17, 22,
Coogan, Jackie 119, 124,
Cool Ones, The 124,
Comancheros, The 208,
Convoy 251,
Corcoran, Noreen 126,
Corey, Wendell 24, 25, 27, 135, 154, 181,
Corman, Roger 21, 28, 46, 71, 102, 120, 148, 193, 209,
Corpse Vanishes, The 102,
Corrigan, Ray "Crash" 28, 103,
Corry, Will 52,
Cory, Steve 180,
Cosby, Bill 77, 78, 215,
Cosby Show, The 78, 217,
Costanzo, Jack 138,
"Cotton Candy Land" 81,
Couch, The 67,
"Could I Fall in Love?" 174,
Courtship of Eddie's father, The 107, 184,
Covington, Suzanne 138,
Cowan, Jerome 145,
Cox, Stephen 169,
Craig, Yvonne 81, 101, 105, 106, 107, 108, 109, 111, *111*, 123, 127, 132, 190, 200,
"Crawfish" 35,
Crawford, Christina 52, 54,
Crawford, Joan 54,
Crazy Like a Fox 213,
Creature from the Black Lagoon, The 135, 222,
Creature With the Atom Brain 103,
Creel, Tom 41,
Crosby, Bing 39, 47, 106, 127, 128, 136, 232, 234,
Crosby, Gary 119, 120, 127, 128,

"Cross my Heart" 119,
Crow, Carl 41,
"Crying in the Chapel" 253,
Cukor, George 27,
Culp, Robert 77, 215,
Cumbuka, Ji-Tu 215, 222,
Cummings, Jack 91,
Curious Female, The 186,
Curran, Pamela 119, 126,
Curtis, Howard 91,
Curtis, Tony 139,
Curtiz, Michael 35,
Cushman, Dan 197,
Czar, Nancy 119, 126, 159, 163,

"Dagger of the Mind" 176,
Dagwood Bumstead (character) 46,
"Dainty Little Moonbeams" 72,
Dallas 88, 90, 153, 161, 217,
Daltrey, Roger 241,
Dana, Leora 215, 222,
Daniel Boone 222,
Danny Thomas Show, The 170,
Danova, Cesare 91, 94, 95, 96, 117,
Dante, Joe 193,
Dante, Michael 69,
Darin, Bobby 92, 124,
"Darktown Strutters Ball" 210,
Darrell, Steve 17,
Darren, James 59, 106, 125, 162, 191, 254, 255,
"Datin'" 151,
Davis, Bette 70, 184,
Davis, Mac 215,
Davis, Phyllis 202,
Davis Jnr., Sammy 181, 215, 249,
Dawson, Hal K. 24,
Dawson, Jim 119,
Day, Annette 174, 176, 177,
Day, Doris 11, 12, 25, 73, 141, 147, 155, 159, 190, 206, 226, 251,
Day Elvis Met Nixon, The 240,
Day, John 31, 81,
"Day of the Dove" 140,
Day of the Evil Gun 207,
DC Comics 193,
de Anda, Robert 85,
de Cordova, Frederick 139, 145, 149,

270

De Anda, Mike 119,
De Carlo, Yvonne 143,
De Kova, Frank 63, 66,
De La Fuente, Ramon 69,
De Sales, Francis 31,
De Shannon, Jackie 185,
De Vega, Jose 55,
De Witt, Jaqueline 81,
Dean, James 14, 18, 20, 71, 247, 248, 249,
Dean, Quentin 197, 199,
Dear Brigitte 25,
Death Valley Days 169,
December Bride 147,
Dee, Sandra 61, 107, 124, 185,
Defenders, The 205,
Del Rio, Dolores 49, 50, 59,
Deliverance 250,
Demarest, William 91, 97,
Dennis, John 129,
Desert Hawk, The 139,
"Desert Serenade" 138,
Desilu 224,
Destination: Inner Space 185,
Detectives, The 65, 67, 70, 90, 107, 116, 124, 126, 178, 179, 181, 222,
Devon, Richard 69, 70,
Di Reda, Joe 17,
Diagnosis: Murder 135,
Dial M for Murder 176,
Diary of a Madman 147,
"Dibble's Double" 172,
Dick Clark's American Bandstand 231,
Dick, Douglas 49,
Dick Powell Theater 39, 53, 64, 65, 88, 135, 184, 200, 236,
Dick Van Dyke Show, The 114, 116, 221,
Dickerson, Beach 24, 28, 41, 46,
"Didja Ever" 41,
Die Hard 155, 254,
Dillinger 226,
Dino 43,
Dirty Dingus McGee 200, 204,
"Dirty, Dirty Feeling" 129,
Dirty Harry 50, 250, 251,
Disney (films) 11, 34, 64, 65, 83, 110, 162, 170, 175, 184, 188, 190, 236, 247,
Disorderly Orderly, The 106, 108,
"Dixie" 229,
"Dixieland Rock" 35, 38,
"Do Not Disturb" 119,

"Do the Clam" 119,
Dr. Alien 157,
Doctor Goldfoot and the Bikini Machine 44, 130,
Doctor Kildare 62, 68, 107, 115, 126, 169, 211,
Dr. No 88,
Doctor Strangelove 251,
"Does He Love Me, Or Does He Love My Rival?" 91,
"Dog's Life" 151,
Doherty, Denny 241,
"Doin' the Best I Can" 41, 45, 46,
Dolan, Trent 41,
Domasin, Larry 83, 87, 88,
"Dominic" 197, 198,
Donna Reed Show, The 160, 163,
"Don't Ask Me Why" 35, 38,
"Don't Be Cruel" 225,
Don't Knock the Rock 26, 28, 29,
Don't Knock the Twist 104,
"Don't Leave Me Now" 31,
Dorsey Brothers 29,
Dorsey Brothers' Stage Show, The 231,
Double Trouble 11, 79, 111, **174—179,** *179,* 203, 214, 249,
"Double Trouble" 174,
Doucette, John 151, 156,
Douglas, Donna 145, 146, 147, *148,* 149, 150, 162,
Douglas, Gordon 63, 66,
Douglas, James 41, 43,
"Down By the Riverside" 145, 146,
Dracula vs. Frankenstein 148,
Dragnet 147,
Dragon Lady 186
The Dreamers 15,
Drive-In Dream Girls 75, 107, 185, 211,
Drums of Tahiti 103,
"Drums of the Island" 151, 154,
Drury, James 17, 22,
Du Pont, Elaine 24, 28,
"Duelling Presleys" 237,
Duke, John 63, 66,
Duke, The 254,
Dukes of Hazzard, The 110,
Dulo, Jane 112,
Dumke, Ralph 24, 25,
Duncan, Angus 197,
Duncan, Johnny 103,
Dunhill, Ford 91,

Dunleavy, Steve 256, 258,
Dunne, Phillip 52, 54, 61, 66, 114,
Dunnock, Mildred 17, 22,
Durbin, Deanna 47, 119,
Durell, Judy 138,
Durfee, Minta 35,
Dusay, Marj 180, 181, 186,
Dutton, Evelyn 81,
Dylan, Bob 10,
Dynasty 39, 153, 211, 215, 255,

E.R. 155,
"Earth Boy" 72,
Earth vs. the Flying Saucers 103,
East of Eden 71, 222,
East Side Kids (characters/franchise) 103, 133,
Eastwood, Clint 50, 201, 207, 247, 250,
Easy Come, Easy Go 13, 118, 122, 153, 163, **165 – 173,** *168, 173,* 174, 183, 184, 190, 206,
"Easy Come, Easy Go" 165,
"Easy Question" 129,
Easy Rider 135, 139, 193, 250,
Ebsen, Buddy 201,
Ed Sullivan Show, The 10, 231,
Eddie Presley 242,
Eden, Barbara 49, 51, 140, 142,
"Edge of Reality" 202,
Edgington, Lyn 119,
Edwards, Vince 38, 45, 146,
Eerie, Indiana 102, 237,
Egan, Richard 17, 21, 22, 181,
Eighteen and Anxious 106,
Eisley, Anthony 145, 147, *148,*
Ekman, Britta 41,
El Cid 129,
El Condor 153,
El Dorado 204,
"El Toro" 85,
Electra Glide in Blue 250,
Elley, Mickey 1§65,
Elliot, Jane 215, 219, 220,
Elliott, Bill 215,
Elvis (book) 129, 256, 257,
Elvis (tv drama) 53, 240,
Elvis – Aloha from Hawaii 227, 233, 234, 235, 247,
Elvis and Me 236,
Elvis and the Beauty Queen 236,
Elvis and the Colonel (book) 143,
Elvis and the Colonel (tv movie) 240,
Elvis – By Those Who Knew Him Best, 142,
Elvis Film Encyclopedia 129, 160,
Elvis – Good Rockin' Tonight 240,
Elvis Has Left the Building 242,
Elvis in Concert 253, 258,
Elvis Meets Nixon 240, 241,
Elvis Presley Scrapbook, The 12,
Elvis – That's the Way It Is 223, **224 – 227,** 228,
Elvis – That's the Way It Is – the Special Edition 227,
Elvis – the Hollywood years 27, 47, 109,
Elvis – the Lost Performances 227,
Elvis – the Movie 235,
Elvis – the Unguarded Moments 234,
Elvis – What Happened? 227, 256, 258,
Emergency 107, 125, 163,
Emhardt, Robert 69, 70, 215, 219, 220, 221,
Empire 21,
Engel, Roy 91,
England, Sue 24, 28, 180, 186,
Ensign O'Toole 163,
Equity 169,
Erickson, Leif 112, 113, 115, 117,
Escape from New York 236,
Escape from Red Rock 130,
Esposito, Joe 48, 101, 105, 181, 197, 199, 236, 241, 252,
Essler, Fred 41,
Evans, Charles 85,
Evans, Maurice 176,
Every Which Way But Loose 251,
"Everybody Come Aboard" 145,
"The Eyes of Texas Are Upon You" 91,

F Troop 66, 197, 213,
Fabares, Shelley 116, 119, 121, 123, 125, *158, 159,* 160, 163, 180, 182, *183,*
Fabian 106, 153, 160, 161,
Face in the Fog, A 102,
Facts of Life 217,
Fadden, Tom 49,
Fahey, Myrna 24, 28,
Fall Guy, The 153,
Fall of the House of Usher 28,
Family Affair 213,
Family Jewels, The 155,

Family Ties 217,
Fantastic Journey 102, 124,
Fantastic Voyage 249,
Fantasy Island 39, 95, 107, 123, 124, 125, 140, 155, 161, 252,
Fapp, Daniel 85,
Farnum, Franklyn 35,
Farrell, Glenda 101, 105, 108, 111,
Farrell, Mike 161,
Farrell, Tommy 101, 106,
Farren, Mick 143,
Faster, Pussycat! Kill! Kill! 108,
Fastest Gun Alive, The 115,
Father Knows Best 62,
Father Ted 237,
Faulkner, Ed 41, 129, 131, 136,
Fay, William 69,
FBI, The 62, 153, 205, 211, 221,
Felony Squad, The 124, 125,
Ferrell, Will 247,
Fiedler, John 119,
Field, Sally 204,
Fields, W.C. 113, 136,
Fighting Devil Dogs, The 22,
Fighting Renegade 102,
Figueroa, Laura 215,
Fike, Lamar 66, 165, 228, 247, 249, 257,
Filmfax 123,
Films and Filming 248,
Finding Graceland 242,
"*The Finny Foot Affair*" 236,
Fireball 500 153,
"*First, The*" 70,
Fish, Ted 119,
Fisher, Eddie 124,
"*The Five Daughters Affair*" 155, 160,
"*Five Sleepy Heads*" 192,
Flaming Star 22, 31, 47, **49–51,** 52, 54, 56, 63, 142, 197, 200, 207, 209, 248, 249, 251,
"*Flaming Star*" 49, 56,
Flamingo Road 75,
Flash Gordon 103,
Flicker, Theodore 159,
Flintstones, The 10, 99, 110, 233,
Florey, Med 210, 213,
Flower Drum Song 154,
Fluellen, Joel 112, 117,
Flying Nun, The 89, 107,
Follow That Dream 49, 62, **63–68,** 72, 82, 90, 96, 105,

"*Follow That Dream*" 63,
Follow the Sun 22,
Fonda, Henry 201, 251,
Fong, Benson 72, 77,
Fontana, D.J. 24, 25, 31,
For Singles Only 126,
For Those Who Think Young 191,
"*Foreverware*" 237,
Ford, Glenn 106, 135, 201, 207, 251,
Ford, John 155,
Fordney, Alan 91,
Forrest, Steve 49, 50,
Forrest, William 24, 28, 31,
"*Fort Lauderdale Chamber of Commerce*" 119,
Fortas, Alan 214,
Forte Four, the 91,
Forte, Joe 24,
Four Amigos, the 85,
Four Star Theater 222,
Fox, Bernard 176,
Foxy Brown 218,
Francis, Connie 120,
Frankenstein 1970 28,
"*Frankfurt Special*" 41,
Frankie and Johnny 13, 78, 116, 117, 137, 139, 143, **145–150,** *148,* 151, 210,
"*Frankie and Johnny*" 145, 234,
Franken, Steve 185,
Frasier 214, 221,
Frawley, William 97,
Freeman, Joan 59, 110, 112, 113, 115,
French, Victor 207, 208,
Friday Foster 218,
Friday the 13th – the Final Chapter 115,
Friends 98, 136, 163,
From Here to Eternity 34,
Frome, Milton 119, 126,
Front Page, The 66,
Fugitive, The 34, 53, 65, 68, 124, 125, 211, 221, 236,
Full House 217, 237,
Fuller, Dolores 164,
Fun in Acapulco 66, 74, 85 – 90, 86,89, 118, 156, 175,
"*Fun in Acapulco*" 85,
Funicello, Annette 126, 153, 161,

G-Men, the 174,
Gaba, Marianne 41, 44,

Gabrielle 202,
"The Gamesters of Triskellion" 186,
Gardner, Arthur 180, 181, 187,
Garland, Judy 47,
Garner, James 200, 251,
Garr, Teri 91, 98,
Garrett, Patsy 210, 214,
Garrison, Michael 254,
Garrison's Gorillas 82, 95, 125,
Gavin, James 156,
Gay, Gregory 55,
Gaye, Lisa 21, 28,
Gaye, Marvin 10,
Gazzo, Michael V. 35, 39,
Geller, Larry 146, 166, 183, 184, 236,
Gene Krupa Story, The 106,
General Hospital 161,
Geraghty, Maurice 23,
Geronimo 181,
Gerstle, Frank 69,
Get Smart 34, 61, 65, 74, 77, 82, 90, 106, 124, 125, 136, 141, 147, 149, 156, 178, 186, 192, 193, 208, 213,
Get Yourself a College Girl 83, 108, 123, 126, 195,
Ghidora, the Three-Headed Monster 138,
Ghost and Mr. Chicken, The 115,
Ghost and Mrs. Muir, The 53, 82, 117, 161, 179,
Ghost Crazy 103,
Ghost in the Invisible Bikini, The 162, 191,
Ghost of Dragstrip Hollow, The 28,
Ghost Story 76, 178, 211,
G.I. Blues 14, 28, 38, **41—48**, 56, 57, 59, 61, 62, 67, 72, 74, 76, 85, 87, 93, 136, 152, 167, 174, 226, 231, 258,
"G.I. Blues" 41,
Giant Claw, The 104,
Gibbsville 70,
Gidget (film) 64, 106, 125, *196,*
Gidget (tv series) 126, 153, 204, 205,
Gidget Goes Hawaiian 125, 162, *196,*
Gidget Goes to Rome 95, 125, 126, *196,* 204, 233,
Gilchrist, Connie 129, 136,
Giles, Sandra 81,
Gilmore, Gail 119, 123, 126, 138, 139,
Girl from UNCLE, The 34, 90, 95, 108, 123, 125, 135, 139, 140, 147, 149, 163, 178, 186, 200, 206, 221,

Girl Happy 11, 14, 108, 109, 117, *118,* **119—128,** 122, 131, 137, 139, 140, 143, 160, 163, 175, 181, 182, 185, 188, 206, 247,
"Girl Happy" 119,
"The Girl I Never Loved" 180,
Girls! Girls! Girls! 28, 44, 48, 57, **72—80,** *80,* 87, 88, 90, 106, 118, 147, 152, 156, 161, 184,
"Girls! Girls! Girls!" 72,
Girls on the Beach, The 126, 139,
Girls' Town 117,
Glass Bottom Boat, The 141, 206, 212,
Glass, Ned 35, 39, 69, 70,
Gleason, Jackie 74, 75, 76,
Gleason, James 24,
Glenn Miller Story, The 147,
Glory Guys, The 74, 181,
"Go East, Young Man" 138,
Godfather, The 249,
Godfather, Part II, The 97, 153,
Godzilla (character/franchise) 139,
"The Golden Cage" 205,
"Golden Coins" 138,
Goldfinger 232,
Goldina, Marian 49,
Goldman, Albert 12, 46, 129, 190, 224, 248, 256, 257, 258,
Goldwyn, Sam 130,
Gomer Pyle 162, 211,
Gomez, Thomas 197, 199,
Good Guys and the Bad Guys, The 200,
Good, Jack 180, 183, 185,
Good Morning, World 125,
Goodwin, Laurel 72, 73, 74, 75, 76, 80, *80,* 115, 152, 153,
Goodwin, Ruby 52,
Gordon, Bert 67,
Gordon, Gale 189, 190, 192,
Gordon, Gavin 72,
Gore, Lesley 107, 139, 250,
"Got A Lot of Living To Do" 24,
Gottlieb, Alex 145,
Grabowski, Norm 112, 115, 117, 119,
Graham, William 215,
Grapes of Wrath, The 49, 213,
Grashin, Mauri 210,
Gray, Charles H. 207,
Grease 233,
Great Adventures of Captain Kidd, The 103,
"The Great Vegetable Rebellion" 179,
Greatest American Hero, The 155, 222, 254,

Greatest Story Ever Told, The 208,
Green, Al 10,
Green Berets, The 155,
Green, Dorothy 81,
Green Hornet, The 34, 77, 95, 126, 139, 155, 161, 186, 206, 213,
"Green Ice/Deep Freeze" 97,
Greenburg, Dan 202, 204,
Greene, Angela 129,
Greenleaf, Raymond 52,
"Greensleeves" 198,
Greenway, Tom 17,
Greer, Dabbs 112, 117,
Gregory, James 106, 180, 181, 182, 184,
Gremlins 193,
Grey, Duane 207,
Griffith, Ed 165,
Griggs, Loyal 72,
Grinnage, Jack 35, 39,
Grover, Mary 202,
Growing Pains 217,
"Guadalajara" 85,
Guffey, Burnett 71,
Gunfight at Comanche Creek 130,
Gunfight at the O.K. Corral 29,
Guns of Will Sonnett, The 200,
Gunslinger 193, 207,
Gunsmoke 61, 67, 114, 115, 153, 207, 221, 222, 251,
Gunton, Bob 241,
Guralnick, Peter 12, 23, 41, 68, 92, 146, 226, 257,

Hagen, Ross 189, 190,
Haggerty, Don 119,
Hagman, Larry 142,
Hale, Barbara 136,
Hale, Barnaby 91,
Hall, Snr., Arch 126,
Halliwell, Leslie 103,
Halliwell's Film Goer's Companion 64, 129,
Halls of Anger 221,
Hammer Films 88, 153,
Hammerhead 126,
Hanalei, Tiki 55,
Hanna-Barbera 9, 110, 125, 182, 232,
Hannie Caulder 201,
"Happy Ending" 81,
Hard Day's Night, A 158, 247,

"Hard Headed Woman" 35, 38,
"Hard Knocks" 112,
"Hard Luck" 145, 150,
Hardcastle and McCormick 115, 211, 254,
Hardin, Ty 38, 146,
Hardy Boys/Nancy Drew Mysteries, The 192,
Hardy, Gari 189,
"Harem Holiday" 138,
Harlan, Russell 38,
Harley, Amanda 180,
Harmon, Joy 139, 148,
Harmon, Sandra 236,
Harrington, Pat 170,
Harrington Jnr., Pat 165, 170,
Harris, Robert 189,
Harryhausen, Ray 104, 147,
Hart, Dolores 23, 24, 27, 35, 37, 74, 120, 154,
Hart, Tommy 69,
Hart to Hart 68, 75,
Harum Scarum 11, 107, 111, 117, 123, 127, 136, 137, **139 – 144** 149, 191,
Harvey, Dirk 138,
Harvey, Snr., Harry 197,
Hattie, Hilo 55,
"Have a Happy" 215,
Hawaii Five-O 65, 66, 67, 68, 124, 147, 155, 161, 184, 250,
Hawaiian Eye 61, 62, 65, 68, 82, 115, 116, 135, 136, 140, 147, 161, 178, 190, 220, 254,
"Hawaiian Sunset" 55,
"Hawaiian Wedding Song" 55,
"Hawaii, U.S.A." 151,
Hawk 154,
Hawkins, Jimmy 119, 125, 159, 163,
Hawks, Howard 66, 204,
Hayes, Allison 129, 137,
Hayes, Flora 55,
Hayle, Grace 24,
"He's Your Uncle, Not Your Dad" 189,
Head 222,
Hearn, Barbara 24,
"Heartbreak Hotel" 225, 247,
Hebler, Dave 256, 258,
Helicopter Spies, The 70,
Heims, Jo 174,
Hellman, Monte 53,
"Hello, Susan Brown" 210,
Hell's Belles 76, 135, 186,
Helm, Anne 63, 64, 67, 110, 115,
Helton, Percy 31, 34,

Henderson, Douglas 197,
Henning, Paul 146,
Henning, Susan 202, 205, 234,
Herbert, Pitt 210, 213,
"Here We Go Round the Mulberry Bush" 210,
Here's Lucy 204,
Herman's Hermits 158,
Hernandez, Tom 85,
Heston, Charlton 169,
Hewitt, Alan 63, 64,
"Hey, Hey, Hey" 180,
"Hey, Little Girl" 138,
Hickox, Harry 189,
High Chaparral, The 115,
High Mountain Rangers 254,
High Noon 147, 199,
High Plains Drifter 153,
High School Confidential 125,
High Time 106,
Highway to Heaven 209,
Hiken, Nat 231,
Hill and Range 142, 253,
Hill, Marianna 112, 117, *150*, 151, 152, 153, 154, 155,
Hill Street Blues 209, 221,
Hillbillies in a Haunted House 110,
Hillbilly Bears, The 110,
Hines, Harry 31,
His Girl Friday 66,
Hodge, Charlie 236, 258,
Hodges, Eddie 202,
Hoey, Michael 197, 202, 204,
Hoffman, Dustin 251,
Hogan's Heroes 178, 205, 211,
Holcomb, Harry 63,
Hold On 116, 160,
Holden, Jennifer 31,
Holden, William 186,
Hole, Jonathan 165, 170,
Holloway, Sterling 202,
Hollywood Hot Tubs 157,
Holston, Kim 75, 163,
"Home Is Where the Heart Is" 69,
Honey West 34, 77, 90, 95, 108, 147, 147, 148, 172, 178,
Honeymoon in Vegas 242,
Hootenanny Hoot 110,
Hope, Bob 39, 47, 76, 126, 149, 169,
Hope, Teri 85, 87,

Hopkins, Jerry 114, 187, 249,
Hopper, Dennis, 135,
Hot Car Girl 28,
"Hot Dog" 24,
Hotel 39, 83, 95, 124, 153, 192,
"Hound Dog" 225,
"House of Sand" 151, 157,
House of the Damned 136,
House of Wax 39,
"A House That Has Everything" 180, 182,
How the West Was Won 79,
How to Marry a Millionaire 136,
How to Stuff a Wild Bikini 44, 126, 155,
"How Would You Like to Be?" 81,
"The Howling Man" 82,
Hoyos, Rodolfo 49, 51, 215, 222,
Huckleberry Hound (character/franchise) 233,
Hudson, John 41,
Hudson, Rock 190, 251,
Huffaker, Clair 49,
Hullabaloo 108, 168,
Humble, Linda 81,
"Hunka Hunka Bill and Ted" 239,
Hunter 95, 125, 140, 153, 254,
Husky, Rick 252,
"Husky Dusky Day" 52, 53,
Hutchins, Will 159, 163, 180, 181, 182, 183, 184, 187,
Hutton, Brian 35,
Hyer, Martha 29,

"I Can't Stop Loving You" 225, 235,
"I Don't Wanna Be Tied" 72,
I Dream of Jeannie 53, 65, 108, 126, 137, 139, 140, 142, 147, 178, 193, 212, 249,
"I Feel That I've Known You Forever" 129,
"I Got Lucky" 69,
"I Got News For You" 119,
I Love Lucy 97,
"I Love Only One Girl" 174,
I, Mobster 77,
"I Need Somebody To Lean On" 91,
I Sailed to Tahiti With an All Girl Crew 161,
"I Slipped, I Stumbled, I Fell" 52, 53,
I Spy 61, 66, 77, 82, 90, 117, 124, 125, 140, 141, 147, 154, 155, 175, 221,
"I Think I'm Gonna Like It Here" 85,
"I Want To Be Free" 31,

I Was a Teenage Werewolf 28,
Ichabod and Me 163,
"If You Think I Don't Need You" 91, 98,
"I'll Be Back" 159,
"I'll Take Love" 165,
I'll Take Sweden 76, 149,
"I'm Always Chasing Rainbows" 210,
"I'm Falling in Love Tonight" 81,
"I'm Not the Marryin' Kind" 63,
"I'm So Lonely I Could Cry" 235,
"I'm Yours" 129,
"In a Plain Brown Wrapper" 236,
In Like Flint 107, 137,
"In My Way" 52, 53,
"In the Ghetto" 215, 225,
In the Heat of the Night 221,
Incredible Hulk, The 70, 79, 135, 139, 161, 184,
Incredible Two-Headed Transplant, The 169,
Indrisano, John 31,
Ingram, Jean 129,
Inherit the Wind 147,
Inkspots, the 96,
Innerspace 193,
"The Innocent Bystanders" 171,
Invaders, The 117, 126, 141, 147, 148, 211, 212, 221, 222,
Invasion of the Bodysnatchers 39, 50,
Invasion USA 193,
Invisible Ghost, The 102,
Invisible Man, The 147,
Invisible Mom II 161,
Ireland, John 52, 54,
Iron Fist 252,
Iron Horse 207,
Ironside 39, 66, 83, 116, 124, 135, 140, 155, 161, 163, 169, 178, 184, 211, 221,
Isenberg, Robert 165,
"Island of Love" 55,
It Came From Beneath the Sea 104,
It Came from Outer Space 222,
"It Feels So Right" 129,
It Happened At The World's Fair 48, 77, **81—84,** 84, 105, 106, 112, 115, 127, 132, 151, 189, 190, 236,
It Takes a Thief 61, 65, 107, 124, 135, 137, 147, 155, 178, 205,
It's a Bikini World 108, 162, 185,
"It's a Long, Lonely Highway" 129,
"It's a Wonderful World" 112,
It's About Time 163,

It's Always Jan 136,
"It's Carnival Time" 112,
"It's My Party" 107,
"Ito Eats" 55, 56,
Ito, Robert 151, 156,
Itzin, Gregory 240,
"I've Got to Find My Baby" 119,
"I've Lost You" 225,
Ivers, Robert 41, 43,

Jack Armstrong 103,
Jack Benny Show, The 149,
Jackson County Jail 226, 250,
Jackson, Michael 213,
Jacobs, Seaman 81,
Jacques, Ted 49,
Jaeckel, Richard 49, 51,
Jaffe, Nicole 210, 212,
Jagger, Dean 35, 39,
Jagger, Mick 241,
Jailhouse Kid 32,
Jailhouse Rock 9, 11, 13, 26, 28, **31—40,** 32, 34, 43, 54, 56, 58, 81, 90, 112, 119, 173, 258,
"Jailhouse Rock" 31, 33, 37, 234, 239,
James Bond (character/franchise) 13, 14, 88, 117, 175, 179, 191, 232,
Jameson, Joyce 145, 147,
Jarvis, Felton 1287,
Jason and the Argonauts 147,
Jason of Star Command 137,
Jazz Singer, The 97,
Jeffries, Fran 138, 139,
Jenson, Roy 49, 51,
JFK 221,
Jimmy Stewart Show, The 135,
J.J. Starbuck 191,
Johnny Bravo 237, 242,
Johnny Ringo 213,
Johnson, Arch 41, 43,
Johnson, Don 236,
Johnson, Nunnally 49,
Johnson, Rafer 52, 54,
Johnson, Walter 31,
"The Joker's Last Laugh"/"The Joker's Epitaph" 171,
Jolson Sings Again 97,
Jolson Story, The 97,
Jones, Anissa 210, 213,
Jones, Carolyn 35, 37, 39,

Jones, Dean 31, 34,
Jones, Henry 197, 200,
Jones, L.Q. 17, 22, 49, 51, 197, 200,
Jones, Tom 158,
Jordanaires, the 24, 26, 35, 41, 52, 81, 85, 119, 151, 159, 165, 187, 197,
Joseph, John 215,
Jostyn, Jay 17,
Journey to the Center of the Earth 120,
Journey to the Center of Time 148,
Judd For the Defense 163,
Jungle Jim (character/franchise) 103,
Jurado, Katy 197, 199,
"Just Pretend" 225,

Kai, Lani 55,
Kam Tong 81, 82, 83,
Kaneen, Ginny 202,
Kanter, Hal 24, 25, 26, 50, 55, 60, 91, 107,
Karate Killers, The 155, 160,
Karlson, Phil 69, 71,
Karnes, Robert 207,
Kartalian, Buck 197,
Katz, Omri 102,
Katzman, Frank 102,
Katzman, Leonard 102,
Katzman, Sam 26, 29, 57, 83, 93, 101, 102, 108, 109 110, 116, 120, 130, 137, 138, 141, 143, 252, 258,
Kaufman, William 41,
Kay, Christian 55, 61,
Kaye, Olga 180,
Kaye, Suzie 180, 185,
Keene, Day 210,
Keith, Patti Jean 189,
Kellaway, Cecil 159, 163,
Keller, Michael 197,
Kellogg, Lynn 207,
Kellogg, Ray 112,
Kelly, Gene 29,
Kelly's Heroes 249,
Ken Darby Trio 17,
Kennedy, Burt 197, 200, 201,
Kennedy, Christopher 239,
Kent, Larry 91,
Kentucky Jones 147,
Kenyon, Sandy 165, 170,
Kerouac, Jack 14, 44,
Kerr, Donald 31,

Kersh, Kathy 45,
Kid Galahad 39, 49, 61, 69—71, 221, 222,
"Kids" 233,
Kiel, Richard 112, 117,
Kill Bill 2 191,
Killer Elite, The 70,
Killing, The 222,
"The King and I" (2) 237,
King Creole 11, 33, **35—40**, *40*, 46, 56, 83, 152, 154, 248, 249,
"King Creole" 26, 27, 35,
King, Martin Luther 205, 215,
King of Kings 138,
King of the Congo 103,
King of the Mounties 140,
"King of the Whole Wide World" 69,
Kirgo, George 159,
Kirk, Lorena 215,
Kirk, Pamela (Austin) 55, 61,
Kirk, Tommy 162, 185,
Kismet 138,
"Kismet" 138,
Kiss Me Deadly 34,
Kiss My Firm But Pliant Lips 204,
Kissin' Cousins 61, 100, **101—111**, *111*, 117, 141, 174,
"Kissin' Cousins" 101,
Kitten With a Whip 99,
Klein, Yves 167,
Klute 251,
Knight Rider 79, 161, 163,
Knots Landing 205, 221,
Knotts, Don 115,
Knox, Mickey 41,
Kojak 66, 70, 90, 107, 124, 137, 140,
Kolchak, the Night Stalker 39, 66, 124, 125, 135, 178, 184, 222,
Konrad, Dorothy 129, 134, 136,
Koon, Gavin 63, 64,
Koon, Robin 63, 64,
Kovack, Nancy 145, 147, *148*,
Kraft Television Theater 232,
Kreig, Frank 31,
Krieger, Lee 180, 186,
Krogh, E. "Budd" 240,
Kruger, Fred 41,
Kruschen, Jack 63, 65,
"Ku-U-I-Po" 55, 56,
Kung Fu 154, 156, 213, 252,

L.A. Law 221,
"La Strega" 88,
Lacker, Marty 241, 248,
Ladd, Cheryl 62,
"The Lady Loves Me" 91, 98,
Lally, Mike 52,
Lamont, Robert 138,
Lanchester, Elsa 165, 169, 170,
Land of the Giants 34, 39, 79, 107, 115, 137, 140, 156, 161, 205,
Landers, Harry 207,
Landis, Monty 174, 177, 178,
Landon, Michael 208,
Lane, Jocelyn 76, 129, 132, 133, 134, 135, 136, 186, 190,
Lane, Michael 197,
Lang, Doreen 52,
Lang, Charles 72,
Lang, Christa 207,
Langdon, Sue Ane 112, 116, 145, 147, 149, 150, 201,
Lange, Hope 52, 53,
Lansbury, Angela 55, 59, 161,
Lansbury, Bruce 59,
Lanza, Mario 47,
Laramie 68, 115,
Laredo 22, 116, 155, 211,
Larson, Glen 102, 255,
Las Vegas Hillbillies 110,
Lassie 107, 115,
Last Movie, The 135,
Last of the Comanches 34,
Last of the Secret Agents, The 141, 191,
Last Precinct, The 237,
Last Porno Flick, The 153,
Last Tango in Paris 249,
Last Train to Memphis 12, 23, 41,
Latham, Jack 24,
Launer, S. John 31,
Laurel and Hardy 58, 59, 133, 136, 200,
Laurence, Douglas 189, 197 200, 202,
Laven, Arnold 180, 181, 187,
Laverne and Shirley 153,
Law of the Plainsman, The 181,
Lawman 212,
Lawrence, Anthony 112, 118, 151, 165,
Le Gault, Lance 48, 59, 79, 90, 91, 97, 98, 101, 105, 109, *111*, 112, 114, 117, 180, 187, 254, 255,
Leave It to Beaver 149, 218, 221,

Lederer, Charles 63, 64, 66,
Legacy of Blood 136,
Lee, Bruce 252,
Lee, Guy 72, 77,
Lee, James 215,
Lee, Ralph 119, 127, 138,
Legend of Custer, The 123,
Leib, Robert 180, 197,
Leiber, Jerry 33,
Leigh, Janet 233,
Leigh, Suzanna *150,* 151, 152, 153, 157, 168,
Lemaire, Monique 174,
Lennon, John 231, 257,
Leonard, Sheldon 215,
Lerner, Diki 165,
"Let It Roll" 187,
"Let Me" 17,
"Let Us Pray" 215,
"Let Yourself Go" 189,
Lethal Weapon (franchise) 254,
Letter to Loretta 222,
"Let's Have a Party" 24,
Levin, Henry 120,
Levy, Arthur 112,
Levy, Jules 180, 181, 187,
Levy, Shawn 43,
Lewis, David 69, 70,
Lewis, George J. 69,
Lewis, Jerry 11, 12, 26, 29, 47, 75, 106, 108, 119, 126, 137, 153, 156, 159, 176, 208,
Liberace 149,
Lieutenant, The 126,
Life 18,
Life and Times of 'Slap' Maxwell, The 212,
Lightning Bolt 148,
Lil' Abner (comic strip/franchise) 110,
Lilley, Joseph 42,
Lime, Yvonne 24,
Lisanti, Tom 75, 76, 107, 116, 135, 153, 160, 185, 211,
Little Caesar 29, 106,
Little Egypt 112, 117,
"Little Egypt" 112,
"Little Girl Lost" 192,
Little House on the Prairie 209,
"A Little Less Conversation" 202,
Live a Little, Love a Little 11, 163, 200, **202–206**, 214,
Lizst, Franz 96,
Locke, Dixie 239,

Lockwood, Gary 52, 54, 67, 81, 82, 83, 107, 115, 126, 189,
Logan's Run 79, 102,
Lois and Clark: New Adventures of Superman 137,
"Lonesome Cowboy" 24,
Long John Silver 136,
"Long Legged Girl" 174,
Longstreet 211,
"Look Out Broadway" 145,
Looney Tunes 179,
Lopez, Perry 49, 51,
Lord, Jack 250,
Loring, Teala 21,
Lost Empire, The 186,
Lost in Space 106, 110, 127, 137, 140, 149, 157, 178, 179, 187, 193, 200, 213, 236,
Lost World, The 140,
Lou Grant 66, 124, 213, 221,
Louisiana Hayride 239,
Love, American Style 107, 108, 162, 205,
Love and Death 144,
Love Boat, The 39, 252,
Love Bug, The 34,
Love is a Many Splendored Thing 185,
"The Love Machine" 165,
Love Me Tender 9, **17 – 23,** *18,* 24, 29, 30, 31, 54, 63, 83, 111, 200, 207, 248,
"Love Me Tender" 17, 22, 225, 226, 227, 234,
"Lover Doll" 35,
Loving You 11, 23, **24 – 30,** *28,* 31, 32, 33, 37, 63, 72, 107, 155, 187, 248,
"Loving You" 24, 142,
Lowery, Robert 103,
Lucas, George 202,
Lucy Show, The 65, 95, 106, 110, 117, 162, 169, 178, 192, 200, 249,
Lukas, Paul 85,
Lund, Deanna 151, 156, 159, 163,
Lund, Gail 24,
Lund, Jana 24, 28,
Lupo, Frank 255,
Luster, Robert 207,
Lynde, Paul 92, 232, 233,

Ma and Pa Kettle (characters/franchise) 110,
MacGyver 79, 83, 155,
Machine Gun Kelly 71,
Mad Doctor of Blood Island, The 186,
Made in Paris 196,

Madonna 20,
Magic Carpet, The 138,
Magic Sword, The 67,
Magician, The 107, 184,
Magnificent Seven, The (tv series) 2365,
Magnum p.i. 48, 95, 155, 192, 255,
Maharis, George 106,
Maier, Sigrid 41,
Mail Order Bride 201,
Majors, Lee 187,
Malcolm X 215,
Malibu Run 76,
Malkin, Vicki 138, 139,
"Mama, Never Let Me Go" 72,
Man from UNCLE, The 9, 65, 70, 76, 77, 82, 90, 95, 97, 99, 106, 108, 110, 115, 116, 124, 125, 126, 135, 140, 141, 147, 149, 155, 157, 160, 161, 163, 168, 170, 172, 174, 175, 178, 191, 193, 200, 204, 205, 211, 222, 236, 250,
Man from Planet X, The 193,
Manimal 88,
Mann, Anthony 135,
Mannix 107, 169, 205, 211,
Many Loves of Dobie Gillis 39, 107, 127, 153, 169, 192,
Marcuse, Theo 138, 140, 141, 191,
Margie 107,
"Marguerita" 85,
Mariachi Aguila 85,
Mariachi Los Vaqueros 85,
Mark of Zorro, The 77,
Married Too Young 28, 154,
Mars Needs Women 107,
Marsh, Dave 235, 247,
Marshall, Dodie 159, 163, 165, 168, *168, 173,* 184,
Martian Chronicles, The 213,
Martin, Dean 12, 26, 29, 42, 43, 47, 75, 99, 119, 124, 126, 136, 147, 156, 181, 184, 222,
Martinez, A. 215, 222,
Marvel Comics 9, 193,
Maryjane 161,
Mary Poppins 170,
Mary Tyler Moore Show, The 169, 221,
MASH (tv series) 147, 149, 161,
Mason, Marlyn 210, 211,
Masquerade 155,
Master of Kung Fu 252,
Matinee 193,
Matt Helm (character/franchise) 75, 99, 126, 147, 184,

Matt Helm (tv series) 155,
Matt Houston 83, 95, 124, 155, 161,
Matthau, Walter 35, 38, 39,
Mattis, Dee Jay 145,
Maurishka 197,
Maverick 116, 161,
Maxwell, Jenny 55, 60, 61, 62, 87, 106, 107,
Mayer, Torben 41,
Mayfield, Curtis 10,
McBain, Diane 76, *158,* 159, 160, 161, 186,
McCallum, David 191,
McCloud 95, 124, 140, 161, 163, 184, 200, 213, 250,
McClure, Tip 41,
McCoy, Charlie 143,
McCrea, Ann 72,
McCrea, Joel 201,
McDevitt, Ruth 215, 219, 222,
McDowall, Roddy 124,
McDowell, Ronnie 237,
McDurmand, Todd 239,
McGlynn, Mary Elizabeth 238,
McHale's Navy 107, 178, 186,
McHugh, Frank 165, 169, 170,
McIntire, John 49,
McKee, Tom 31,
McKinley, J.Edward 207,
McLintock 60, 131,
McLuhan, Marshall 78,
McMillan and Wife 95, 135, 205,
McNair, Barbara 215, 219, 221,
McNear, Howard 55, 60, 63, 65, 85, 90,
Mean Streets 95,
"Mean Woman Blues" 24,
"The Meanest Girl in Town" 119,
Medium Cool 153,
Mehta, Zubin 147,
Mejia, Carlos 85,
Melcher, Hannah 41,
Mello Men 81, 151,
Melrose Place 205,
Memphis Mafia 45, 66, 105, 114, 115, 134, 145, 162, 183, 184, 214, 228, 230, 241, 247, 248, 250,
"Memphis Melody" 238, 239,
"The Menagerie" 74, 153,
Menzel, Ursula 202,
Merande, Doro 215, 219, 222,
Meredith, Burgess 197, 199, 200,
Merkel, Una 159, 163,

Merrill, Gary 180, 182, 184, 185,
Mesa of Lost Women 125,
"Mexico" 85,
Meyer, Russ 109,
Meyerink, Victoria 189,
MGM 25, 31, 33, 49, 81, 93, 101, 107, 112, 119, 120, 160, 174, 176, 189, 224, 226, 228, 247,
Miami Vice 236, 255,
Michael Shayne 147,
Mickey Rooney Show, The 222,
Middleton, Robert 17, 22,
Midkiff, Dale 236,
Mighty Gorga, The 148,
Mike Hammer (character/franchise) 34,
Mike Hammer (1980s tv series) 140, 222,
Mikels, Ted V. 137,
Milhollin, James 145, 149,
Miller, Lester 112,
Miller, Stephen E. 240,
Millet, Nefti 215,
Milletaire, Carl 31,
Million Dollar Duck, The 34,
Millionaire, The 191,
Milton Berle Show, The 17, 231,
Mims, William 52,
Mineo, Sal 106,
Mini-Skirt Mob, The 76, 161,
Mioni, Fabrizio 119, 122, 125,
Miracle on 34th Street 105,
"Mirage" 138,
Misadventures of Merlin Jones, The 65,
Misfits of Science 163,
Missile to the Moon 44,
Mission: Impossible 34, 76, 82, 83, 90, 95, 116, 123, 124, 137, 140, 154, 155, 163, 169, 178, 204, 211, 221, 255,
Missouri Breaks, The 249,
Mr. Ed 146, 221,
Mr. Lucky 107,
Mr. Roberts 107,
Mr. Terrific 77,
Mitchell, Cameron 22,
Mitchell, George 69, 70,
Mitchum, Robert 200, 204,
Mobley, Mary Ann 83, 107, 108, 119, 121, 123, 126, 128, 138, 139, 141,
Mod Squad, The 107, 161, 185, 211, 221, 252,
Moebus, Hans 52,
"Mom and Pop Art" 172,
Mommie Dearest 54,

Monkees, The 13, 61, 77, 117, 124, 136, 141, 172, 178, 193,
"The Monks of St. Thomas Affair" 205,
Monroe, Marilyn 76, 93, 113, 212,
Monster That Challenged the World, The 180,
Montevecchi, Lillian 35,
Montgomery, Elizabeth 71,
Moody, Ralph 69,
"Moonlight Swim" 55, 121,
Moonlighting 241,
Moore, Joanna 63, 65, 67, 107,
Moore, Michael 90, 115, 151, 152,
Moore, Scotty 24, 25, 31, 143,
Morell, Ann 129, 135,
Morgan, Harry 145, 146, 148, 149, 150,
Morgan, Helen 146,
Morgan, Read 165, 170,
Morin, Alberto 85,
"The Morning Show" 237,
Morris, Jeffrey 69,
Morris, Richard 215,
Morris, Wayne 70, 71,
Morrow, Vic 39,
Mosher, Bob 218,
Mother Goose-a-Go-Go 67,
Mothers-in-Law 65, 162,
Mott, E.M. "Bitsy" 41, 52,
Move Over Darling 25,
MTM 221, 255,
Mullaney, Jack 129, 131, 159, 163,
Mummy and the Curse of the Jackals, The 148,
Mundy, Ed 17,
Munster, Go Home 169,
Munsters, The 10, 65, 77, 106, 110, 116, 117, 125, 140, 147, 169, 171, 178, 186, 213, 218, 250,
Murder She Wrote 59, 79, 83, 95, 135, 153, 155, 161, 163,
Murderer's Row 99,
Murphy Brown 192, 237,
Murphy, Michael 174, 177,
Murray, Rick 91,
Muscle Beach Party 195,
Mustin, Burt 189, 191,
Mutiny on the Bounty 249,
"My Fair Munster" 218,
My Favorite Martian 64, 65, 106, 125, 127, 137, 140, 147, 149, 155, 168, 169, 178, 182, 186, 211, 213,
My Living Doll 163,
My Partner, the Ghost 172,

My Six Loves 62,
My Three Sons 61, 62, 97, 107, 125, 126, 149, 153, 155,
"My Way" 235, 236,
My World and Welcome to It 124,

Nadel, Arthur H. 180, 187,
Naked City, The 53, 66, 83, 116, 124, 140, 155, 162,
Naked Truth, The 237,
Name of the Game, The 64, 65, 82, 95, 116, 137, 140, 154, 155, 163, 184, 212, 217, 221, 222, 251,
Nanny and the Professor 214,
Napier, Alan 52, 54,
Nash, Alanna 57, 92, 93, 142, 146, 247, 249,
Nash, Bob 91,
National Lampoon's Animal House 95, 120,
Natural Born Killers 254,
NBC 215, 218, 233, 234, 236, 258,
"The Nearness of You" 72,
Nelson, Gene 101, 109, 124, 138, 141, 142,
Nelson, Ricky/Rick 232, 250,
"Nemesis" 236,
"Never Say Yes" 159,
New Dick Van Dyke Show, The 53,
"New Orleans" 35, 38,
New World Television 236,
New York Times 247,
Newman, Michele 189,
Newman, Paul 250,
News of the World 153,
Neyland, Anne 31,
Nichols, Barbara 120,
Nichols, Robert 210, 214,
Nicholson, Jack 251,
Night Gallery 95, 135, 178, 184,
"Night Rider" 129,
Nightmare in Wax 67,
Nims, Shari 165, 170,
Nine to Five 212,
Nixon, Richard M. 114, 241, 251, 253,
"No More" 55,
No Time To Be Young 28,
"Nobody's Baby" 210,
Noel, Chris 119, 126, 139, 185,
Noone, Peter 116, 158, 160,
Norris, Chuck 255,
North, Sheree 210, 212,
Novello, Jay 138, 139, 140, 141,

"Number Twelve Looks Just Like You" 61,
Nun's Story, The 22,
Nutty Professor, The 75, 153, 205,
NYPD Blue 82, 221,

O'Brien, Joan 81, 82, 83, 123,
O'Curran, Charles 38,
O'Connell, Arthur 63, 68, 101, 105, 111,
O'Hara, U.S. Treasury 222,
O'Neal, Kevin 210, 213,
O'Neal, Ryan 213,
Oakland, Simon 63, 65,
Ocean's Eleven 66, 116,
Odd Couple, The 125,
Odets, Clifford 52,
Ogles, Pam 63,
"Old MacDonald" 174,
Olen Ray, Fred 137, 148,
On the Road 44,
"The Once and Future King" 237,
"Once Is Enough" 101,
Once Upon a Time in America 53,
"One Boy, Two Little Girls" 101,
"One Broken Heart For Sale" 81,
One Day At a Time 160, 161, 170,
One of Our Spies is Missing 107,
"One Night" 225, 226,
One Spy Too Many 107,
One Step Beyond 76, 90,
"One Track Heart" 112,
One Way Wahine 148,
Orbison, Roy 115,
Organization, The 221,
Orrison, Jack 52,
Ortega, Francisco 85,
Our Man Flint 108,
Outer Limits, The 65, 115, 140, 141, 154, 170, 178, 212, 221,
Outfit, The 212, 222, 223,
Outlaw Women 125,
Outlaws is Coming, The 130,
Owen, Beverly 169,
Ozzie and Harriet 116, 126, 163, 205, 221, 232,

Pacific Pallisades High School Madrigals 210,
Pacino, Al 251,

Packer, Doris 151, 156,
Paget, Debra 17, 21, 23, 28, 32,
Paint Your Wagon 11, 208,
Paiva, Nestor 72,
Pajama Party 108, 137, *196*,
Pakula, Alan J. 53,
Palacios, Adele 85,
Palm Springs Weekend 194,
Papa's Delicate Condition 74,
"Pappy, Won't You Please Come Home?" 101,
Paradise, Hawaiian Style 39, 78, 90, 117, 118, 136, 137, *150*, **151–158**, 163, 165, 168, 175, 190,
"The Paradise Lost Affair" 178,
Paramount 24, 29, 38, 42, 47, 49, 54, 56, 74, 90, 111, 112, 119, 129, 146, 151, 165, 180, 181, 221, 223, 224, 247, 250,
Pardon Us 136,
Paris, William 210,
Parish, James Robert 12,
Parker, Colonel Tom 13, 17, 20, 23, 25, 26, 27, 29, 30, 31, 32, 33, 35, 36, 42, 47, 49, 50, 55, 56, 87, 92, 93, 100, 101, 102, 104, 105, 112, 113, 115, 119, 128, 129, 130, 131, 143, 145, 146, 154, 165, 166, 174, 181, 183, 184, 190, 191, 199, 220, 224, 226, 227, 228, 229, 231, 233, 234, 236, 240, 248, 249, 252, 253, 255, 258,
Parker, Brett, 197 210, 214,
Parker, Ed 252, 253,
Parrish 161,
Parrish, Julie 125, *150*, 151, 152, 153, 154, 155, 156, 161,
The Party 199,
Pasternak, Joe 119, 120, 159, 204, 247,
Pat Garrett and Billy the Kid 199,
"Patch It Up" 225,
Patsy, The 208,
Patty Duke Show, The 192,
Paul, Gloria 31,
Paulsen, Pat 213,
Peak, Jennifer 197,
Pearl, Minnie 57,
Pearson, Jesse 232,
Peary, Hal 180, 183,
Peckinpah, Sam 22, 70, 74, 75, 181, 199, 201, 208, 251,
Pederson, Hal J. 210,
Pedrova, Inez 129,
Pendleton, Steve 24,
Pepper, Cynthia 61, 101, 107, 108, *111*,
Pereira, Hal 85,
Performance 250,
Perkins, Millie 52, 53, 161, 240,
Perrin, Nat 145,

Perry Mason 68, 107, 115, 116, 126, 155, 169, 178,
Pete and Gladys 146,
Peter Gunn 70,
Peters, Erika 41,
Peters, Rick 241,
Petra, Hortense 101,
Petticoat Junction 222,
Pettyjohn, Angelique 135, 180,
"Petunia, the Gardener's Daughter" 145,
Peyser, Arnold 210,
Peyser, Lois 210,
Peyton Place (film) 53,
Peyton Place (tv series) 61,
Phantom of the Opera, The 102,
Phillips, Sam 117,
Phyllis 200,
Pickard, John 207,
Pierce, Arthur 137,
Pioneer, Go Home 64,
Pirates of Tripoli 103,
Playboy 43, 44, 105, 109, 116, 135, 203,
Please Don't Eat the Daisies 126,
"Please Don't Stop Loving Me" 145, 150,
Pocket Full of Miracles 91,
"Pocket Full of Rainbows" 41,
Point Blank 209,
"Poison Ivy League" 112,
Poitier, Sidney 215, 221,
Police Story 66, 70, 76, 82, 83, 95, 116, 124, 125, 137, 140, 161, 178, 184,
Police Woman 79, 124,
Polynesian Cultural Center 157,
Ponce, Poncie 189,
"Poor Boy" 17,
"The Pop Art Affair" 172,
"Pop Goes the Easel" 172,
"Pop Goes the Joker/"Flop Goes the Joker" 172,
Porter, Don 202, 203, 204,
Poseidon Adventure, The 251,
Powell, Richard 63, 64,
Powers, Beverly 101, 104, 107, 108, 189,
Pratt, Judson 69,
Presley, Elvis
    acting ability 13, 19, 21, 23, 25, 95, 96, 111, 121, 132, 138, 141, 149, 151, 167, 172, 199, 203, 247, 248,
    acting ambitions 18, 114, 165,
    alternate futures 237 – 240, 254 – 256,
    attitude towards sex and women 20, 45, 98, 99, 177, 226,
    attitude towards his own films 45, 46, 74, 109, 122, 129, 165, 166, 249,
    choice of films 13, 56, 129, 146, 151, 165, 202, 206, 209, 210, 211, 214, 220, 222, 223, 247, 248, 249, 250, 251,
    choice of music 33, 38, 45, 46, 56, 66, 67, 73, 82, 96, 130, 142, 143, 146, 155, 156, 187, 191, 198, 225, 227, 228, 229, 230, 234, 235, 249, 253,
    co-stars' comments 21, 22, 75, 76, 83, 107, 116, 123, 124, 134, 136, 152, 154, 160, 161, 163, 169, 181, 185, 186, 205, 212,
    the critics 14, 18, 19, 20, 37, 41, 67, 109, 127, 128, 129, 160, 208, 226, 228, 230, 232, 233, 237, 247, 259,
    dating actresses 21, 45, 48, 68, 88, 91 – 100, 123, 146, 153, 162, 177,
    drafted into the army 10, 13, 14, 26, 35 – 47,
    drugs problem 39, 40, 162, 172, 183, 184, 241, 253, 256,
    friends in Hollywood 20, 21, 48, 59, 79, 91 – 100, 105, 127, 146, 171, 187, 190, 199, 202, 254, 256, 258,
    his parents 10, 29, 42, 202, 234,
    karate film project 252, 253,
    musical performances 24, 25, 32, 50, 52, 69, 96, 105, 115, 146, 150, 154, 158, 167, 187, 191, 198, 225, 228, 229, 230, 231, 233, 234, 235,
    on the set 14, 25, 71, 76, 98, 113, 114, 115, 122, 134, 135, 152, 153, 156, 165, 166, 167, 183, 187, 190, 204, 205,
    personal character 19, 20, 35, 38, 42, 67, 73, 98, 99, 107, 123, 136, 145, 146, 177, 183, 184, 191, 205, 212, 224, 225, 229, 230, 240, 241, 256, 257, 258, 260,
    price of fame 21, 22, 34, 57, 98, 99, 145, 146, 154, 162, 172, 183, 184, 212, 226, 232, 233, 237, 256, 257, 258,
    racial issues 77, 78, 79, 83, 197, 198, 205, 215 – 218,
Presley, Gladys 17, 29, 42, 240,
Presley, Vernon 29, 202, 236,
Presley, Vester 236,
Price, Vincent 28, 147, 210, 213,
Priest, Pat 165, 166, 169,
Prime Cut 226,
"The Prince of Darkness Affair" 70,
Prince of Pirates 103,
"The Prisoner of Zalamar Affair" 140,
Prisoners of the Casbah 138,
Private Secretary 204,
Project UFO 125, 211,
Prowse, Juliet 41, 44, 45, 46, 48, 61, 66, 74, 93,
Pryor, Richard 215,

Psycho 66,
Public Enemy, The 200,
Puglia, Frank 72, 77,
Pulp Fiction 189,
Puppet Master 5 161,
"Puppet on a String" 119,
"Put On a Happy Face" 233,
"Put the Blame on Me" 129,

Quantrill's Raiders 130,
Quantum Leap 80, 238, 239, 240,
Queen of Outer Space 130,
"Queenie Wahini's Papaya" 151,
Quillan, Eddie 91,
Quinn Martin productions 212,
Quincy 135, 156,
Quo, Beulah 72, 77,

Raceway 164,
Rafferty, Chips 174, 177, 178,
Rainey, Ford 49, 51,
Rainey, Kathleen 210,
Rally Round the Flag, Boys 53,
Rand, Linda 85,
Randall and Hopkirk (Deceased) 172,
Rat Pack 42, 181,
Rat Pack Confidential 43,
Rat Patrol, The 178,
Raval, Francis 91,
Rawhide 67, 124, 207, 209, 222,
Rawlins, Judith 41,
Raymond, Alex 103,
Raymond, Guy 81, 82,
Raymond, Robin 31, 52, 54,
RCA 26, 36,
Reagan, Maureen 101,
Reagan, Ronald 149,
Real McCoys, The 110,
Rebel, The 21, 48,
Rebel Without a Cause 20, 71,
Red River 38,
Redigo 21,
Redmond, Liam 69,
Redwing, Rodd 49, 51, 207, 209,
Reed, Donna 160,
Reed, Phillip 138,
Reed, Sandy 189,

Reed, Toby 112,
Reese, Tom 49,
Reeves, Richard 55, 119, 127, 138,
Reindel, Carl 189,
"Relax" 81,
Reluctant Astronaut, The 115,
Remington Steele 124, 236,
Renard, David 215,
Renegade 80, 115, 155, 237,
Reno Brothers, The 17, 24,
Republic serials 22, 28, 103, 140, 255,
Return of Captain Nemo 200,
Return of the Ape Man 102,
Return of the Fly 1§30,
"Return to Sender" 48, 72, 73, 79, 81,
"The Revenge of Robin Hood" 178,
Revenge of the Nerds 121, 241,
Rey, Alejandro 85, 88,
Reynolds, Burt 154,
Reynolds, Debbie 124, 136, 147,
Rhodes, Grandon 31,
Rhys-Meyers, Jonathan 242,
Rich, Dick 31,
Rich, John 112, 114, 118, 165, 166,
Rich, Vernon 24,
Richard Boone Show, The 147,
Richard Diamond 220, 222,
Richmond, Ted 81,
Riddle, Sam 180,
Ride the High Country 201,
Ride the Whirlwind 53,
Ride the Wild Surf 160, *194,*
"Riding the Rainbow" 69,
Rifleman, The 181,
Riot in Cell Block Eleven 22, 49,
Riptide 115, 137, 163, 254,
Risk, Linda Sue 210,
Ritchie, Michael 211,
Rivera, Linda 85,
Road Racers 170,
Robards Snr., Jason 52,
Roberts, Roy 69, 70,
Robbins, Harold 37,
Robinson, Edward G. 65, 70,
"Rock-a-Hula Baby" 55, 60,
"Rock and Roll Rookie" 231,
Rock Around the Clock 26, 28, 104,
Rock, Pretty Baby 160,
Rock, Rock, Rock 53,

"Rocked in the Cradle of the Deep" 210,
Rockford Files, The 66, 79, 124, 125, 153, 155, 161, 163, 213,
Rocky 200,
Rodann, Ziva 35,
Roddenberry, Gene 70, 215,
Roeg, Nicolas 250,
Rogers, Linda 129, 135, 136,
Rogues, The 70, 176, 178,
Rolling Stone 229,
Rolling Stones, the 10, 20, 143,
Romain, Yvonne 174, 176, 177,
Roman, Leticia 41,
Romero, Cesar 172,
Rookies, The 252,
Rose, Bobby 17,
Rose, Si 81,
Rosetti and Ryan 221,
Ross, Diana 10,
Ross, Michael 55,
Rossington, Norman 174, 177, 178,
Roth, Gene 41, 46, 110,
Rothman, Stephanie 209,
Rounders, The 201,
Roustabout 78, 105, 108, 111, **112–118**, 114 120, 126, 129, 131, 139, 147, 152, 165, 176, 210, 253,
"Roustabout" 112,
Route 66 53, 62, 65, 68, 76, 83, 124, 147, 162, 192, 221,
Rowan and Martin's Laugh-In 61, 185, 249,
"Rubberneckin'" 215,
Rubinstein, John 210, 213,
Rudley, Herbert 63, 65,
Ruggles, The 163,
"Rule, Britannia" 175,
Rumery, Leonard 210,
Run, Buddy, Run 74,
Russell, Bing 236,
Russell, Jackie 129,
Russell, Kurt 81, 83, 190, 235, 237, 242,
Russo, Joey 138, 139,
Ryan, Dick 24,
Rydell, Bobby 232,
Ryden, Rick 138,

Sabrina 176,
Sabrina the Teenage Witch 161,
Sagal, Boris 119, 120,
Sailor Beware 47,

Saints and Sinners 20, 97,
Salamance, J.R. 52,
San Francisco International Airport 209,
Sanders, Denis 224, 226, 227, 228,
Sanders, Hugh 31, 138,
Sands, Tommy 232,
Santa Clause 3 99,
"Santa Lucia" 91, 96,
Saracen Blade 103,
Sargent, Dick 202, 203,
Sassoon, Vidal 126,
Say One For Me 136,
Scarecrow and Mrs. King 211,
Scared Stiff 26,
Scarface Mob, The 22,
Scatter 99,
Schallert, William 189, 190, 192,
Schilling, Jerry 78, 236, 241, 252,
Schmidlin, Rick 224, 227,
Schneer, Charles 104,
Schuken, Phil 189,
Schwalb, Ben 129, 130, 131,
Schwarzenegger, Arnold 247, 255,
Schweitzer, William 215,
Scooby-Doo (character/franchise) 131, 202, 212, 213,
Scorsese, Martin 228, 250,
Scott, Karen 24,
Scott, Lizbeth 24, 25, 26, 27,
Scott, Randolph 201,
"Scratch My Back" 151,
Seagal, steven 255,
Seinfeld 212,
Sellers, Peter 12, 199,
Sensuous Nurse, The 88,
Sergeant Deadhead 162,
Serpent of the Nile 103
Sessions, Almira 24,
Seven Women 155,
Seven Year Itch, The 76,
Sex Kittens Go to College 53, 117, 125,
Sex Pistols 20,
Seymour, Anne 197, 199,
Shaft 217,
Shaggy D.A., The 125,
Shaggy Dog, The 105,
Shake, Rattle, and Rock 29, 34, 195,
"Shake That Tambourine" 138,
Sharkey's Machine 125,

Shatner, William 153,
Shaughnessy, Mickey 31, 34,
Shaw, Sid 257,
Shawlee, Joan 202, 205,
She 88,
Sheldon, Jerry 17,
Shepard, Jan 35, 39, 151, 152, 154, 156,
Sherman, Harry 52,
Shigeta, James 151, 154, 155,
Shindig 108, 168, 187, 231,
Shooting, The 53,
Shootist, The 201,
"Shoppin' Around" 41,
Shotgun Wedding 62,
"Shout It Out" 145, 150,
Showboat 97, 146,
Shuken, Phil 189, 190,
Shute, Susan 202,
Sidney, George 91, 92, 101, 120, 176, 233,
Siegel, Don 49, 50, 66, 114, 251,
Siegel Film, A 50,
"Signs of the Zodiac" 210,
Sikking, James B. 207 209,
Silencers, The 75, 147,
Silvers, Phil 97, 231,
Simon and Simon 79, 82, 95, 124, 125, 140, 155, 162, 163, 192, 255,
Simpsons, The 172, 208, 221,
Sinatra, Frank 19, 29, 38, 41, 42, 43, 45, 48, 66, 127, 136, 190, 200, 204, 222, 250,
Sinatra, Nancy 83, 123, 132, 141, 189, 190, 191, *259,*
"Sing, You Children" 165,
Sing, You Sinners 37,
"The Singing Idol" 232,
Siren of Bagdad 138,
Six Million Dollar Man, The 82, 83, 107, 187, 200,
Ski Party 107, 162, *195,*
Slagle, Lisa 180,
Slamdance 53,
Slate, Jeremy 41, 44, 46, 72, 76, 135, 149, 161, 184, 185,
Slaughter 75, 218,
Slave Girl 143,
Slaves of Babylon 138,
Slaves of the Cannibal God 88,
Sleeper 144,
"Slicin' Sand" 55, 56,
Sliders 237,

Slifer, Elizabeth 31,
"Slowly But Surely" 129,
Small, Ed 145,
Smile 211,
Smith, Billy 165,
Smith, Myrna 78,
Smith, Patti 10,
Smith, Paul 24
Smith, Roger 9, *99,*
"Smorgasbord" 159,
Snider, Duke 210,
Snoop Sisters, The 213,
"So Close, Yet So Far" 138, 142,
Solomon, Michael 224,
Solow, Herb 224,
Some Came Running 136, 222,
"Somebody Just Walked Over My Grave" 172,
"Something" 235,
Son of Ali Baba 139,
"Song of the Shrimp" 72, 73,
Sonny and Cher 250,
Sons of Katie Elder, The 76,
"Sophia's Wedding" 237,
Sorority Girls and the Creature from Hell 186,
"The Sort Of Do-It-Yourself Dreadful Affair" 97,
Sothern, Ann 204,
Soule, Olan 81, 119,
"Sound Advice" 63,
South Park 64,
Southern Comfort 250,
Southern, Terry 139,
Space Children, The 125,
"The Space Croppers" 110,
Space Master X-7 130,
Spector, Phil 234,
Spectre 70,
Speedway 11, 79, 97, 107, 122, 132, 173, 184, **189—193**, 197, 202, 214, 247, *259,*
"Speedway" 189,
Spelling, Aaron 39, 123, 147, 252, 253, 255,
Spice Girls 20,
Spielberg, Steven 202,
Spillane, Mickey 34,
Spinout 11, 97, 107, 121, 123, 125, 126, 131, 151, **159—164**, 164, 168, 182, 184, 202, 247, 248,
"Spinout" 159, 164,
Splendor in the Grass 147,
"Spock's Brain" 186,
Spook Busters 103, 131,

"The Squire of Gothos" 21,
"Spring Fever" 119, 121,
St. Gerard, Michael 240, 242,
Stagecoach 213,
Staley, Joan 101, 105, 112, 113,
Stallone, Sylvester 247, 255,
Standells, the 250,
Stanley, David 251,
Stanwyck, Barbara 112, 113, 181,
Stapleton, Maureen 233,
Star is Born, A 250,
Star Time Kids 185,
Star Trek 21, 74, 75, 76, 77, 82, 83, 98, 107, 125, 140, 141, 147, 153, 154, 170, 179, 184, 185, 205, 224, 258,
Star Trek: Deep Space Nine 21, 140,
Star Trek – the Next Generation 80,
Star Trek – Voyager 155,
Star Wars 226,
Starlet 75,
Starman 76,
Starr, Ronald 41,
Starsky and Hutch 39, 83, 107, 147, 204, 213, 222, 252,
State Fair 91,
"Stay Away" 197, 198,
Stay Away, Joe 12, 22, 189, **197 – 201**, 201, 214,
"Stay Away Joe" 197,
"Steadfast, Loyal and True" 35,
Steele, Barbara 49,
Steve Allen Show, The 156, 170, 231,
Stevens, Connie 71,
Stevens, Stella 72, 73, 75, 76, 106, 153,
Stewart, Jimmy 135, 251,
Stewart, Maja 138,
Stewart, Paul 35, 39,
Stockwell, Dean 238, 240,
Stoller, Mike 33,
Stone for Danny Fisher, A 37,
Stone, Harold J. 119, 124,
Stone, James 17,
Stone, Oliver 221, 254,
Stone, Robert 101,
"Stop, Look, Listen" 159,
"Stop Where You Are" 151,
Stossel, Ludvig 41,
Strange, Glenn 31,
Strauss, Robert 72, 76, 145, 147, 149,
Streethawk 59,

Streets of San Francisco, The 68, 135, 140, 155, 208, 211,
Streisand, Barbra 250,
Streissguth, Michael 249,
Strock, Herbert 148,
Stroll, Edward 41,
Stu Erwin Show, The 136,
Sturges, Preston 209,
Sturges, Solomon 207, 208, 209,
Sugarfoot 161, 163, 184,
Sullivan, Ed 26, 232,
Summer Love 160,
Sun Records 117, 237, 238,
Superfly 218,
Superman (1940s serials) 102, 103, 110,
Superman (1970s movie) 249,
Support Your local Gunslinger 200,
Support Your Local Sheriff 200,
"Surf's Up! Joker's Under!" 171,
Surfside Six 61, 107, 116, 124, 135, 136, 147, 161, 184, 192, 220,
Survivors, The 205,
"Suspicious Minds" 225, 235, 237,
Sutton, Grady 129, 134, 136, 151, 156,
Sweet Inspiration 78,
Sweet Ride, The 204,
Swenson, Karl 49,
"Swing Down, Sweet Chariot" 210,
Swinger, The 176,
Swingin' Maiden, The 67,
Swingin' Summer 108, 137,
Sword of Ali Baba 135, 154,

Tab Hunter Show, The 116,
"Take a Day Out of Your Life" 35, 38,
Take Her, She's Mine 61, 107, 154,
"Take Me to the Fair" 81,
"The Take Me To Your Leader Affair" 191,
Taking Woodstock 15,
Talbot, Lyle 103,
Talbot, Nita 119, 124,
Tamla Motown 9, 10, 12,
Tammy and the Doctor 185,
Tannen, William 31,
Tarantino, Quentin 189, 191, 220, 237, 254,
Target: the Corruptors 22, 124,
Tarzan (character/franchise) 22,
Tarzan (tv series) 65,

Tarzan and the Valley of Gold 147,
Tashlin, Frank 155,
Taurog, Norman 41, 46, 47, 50, 55, 59, 72, 81, 87, 120, 124, 129, 130, 152, 159, 160, 163, 174, 176, 189, 202, 205, 206,
Taxi 221,
Taylor, Vaughn 31,
Taylor, Wilda 112, 117, 138, 139, 145,
Teague, Anthony 210,
Tedrow, Irene 24, 29,
"Teddy Bear" 24,
"Teenage Crush" 232,
Temple Houston 153,
Ten Commandments, The 21,
Ten Thousand Bedrooms 119,
"Tender Feelings" 101,
Tennessee Ernie Ford 110,
Tenspeed and Brownshoe 254,
Tewkesbury, Peter 197, 210, 211, 214,
Texas Wildcats 102,
"Thanks to the Rolling Sea" 72,
That Darn Cat 34,
That Funny Feeling 124,
That Touch of Mink 125,
"That's Alright, Mama" 225, 240,
"There Ain't Nothin' Like A Song" 189,
"There's a Brand New Day on the Horizon" 112,
"There's Gold in the Mountains" 101,
"There's No Room to Rhumba in a Sports Car" 85,
"There's So Much World to See" 174,
"These Boots were Made for Walking" 191,
They Call Me Mister Tibbs 221,
"They Remind Me Too Much of You" 81,
They Shoot Horses, Don't They? 70,
Thief 53,
Thief of Damascus 138,
Thing, The 236,
Thing from Another World, The 66,
This is Elvis 236,
"This is Living" 69,
"This Is My Heaven" 151,
This Island Earth 127, 214,
Thomas, Gerald 67,
Thomas, Larry 145,
Thompson, Charles P. 210,
Thompson, Linda 236,
Thompson, Mary Agnes 24,
Thorpe, Jerry 33,

Thorpe, Richard 31, 38, 50, 85, 87, 90, 119, 120, 124,
Thorson, Russell 81,
Three Faces of Eve 49,
Three Ring Circus 156,
Three Stooges, The (characters/franchise) 130, 132, 159,
Three Stooges in Orbit, The 130,
Three Tenors, the 147,
Thrill of it All, The 212,
Thumb Tripping 153,
Thunder Alley 161,
Tickle Me 108, 111, *128*, **129—137**, 139, 155, 156, 163, 190, 197, 200, 206,
Tiffin, Pamela 61, 74, 92, 191,
Time 128,
Time Trax 236,
Time Tunnel, The 90, 123, 138, 141, 148, 156, 178, 185, 213,
Tinker, Grant 221,
Tiu, Alexander 72,
Tiu, Elizabeth 72,
Tiu, Ginny 72,
Tiu, Vicky 77, 81, 82, 83,
T.J. Hooker 79, 83, 155, 252, 254,
To Catch a Thief 176,
"Today, Tomorrow, and Forever" 91,
Tom Corbett, Space Cadet 125,
Toma 66,
Tommy 99,
Tompkins, Darlene 55, 61, 85, 87, 90, 106,
"Tonight Is So Right for Love" 41,
Tonight Show, The 149, 170,
Toomey, Regis 215, 219, 222,
"Toot Toot Tootsie, Goodbye" 210,
Top Cat (character/franchise) 121,
Top Cat 172,
Torchy Blaine (character/franchise) 106,
Tormentors, The 148,
Tosches, Nick 43,
Touch of Her Flesh, The 186,
Towering Inferno, The 251,
Train Robbers, The 201,
Trapper John 155,
"Treat Me Nice" 31,
Treen, Mary 72, 77, 85, 90, 151, 156,
Treisault, Ivan 91,
Troupe, Bobby 34,
Trosper, Jay 31,
"Trouble" 35,

Trouble With Girls, The 12, 176, 200, 206, *209*, **210 – 214,**
"The Trouble with Tribbles" 21, 82, 179,
True Grit 53, 126, 201, 248, 251,
Trustman, Susan 197,
Tsu, Irene 136, *150*, 151, 152, 154, 155, 160, 161,
Turner 224, 227,
Turner, Blaine 41,
Turner, Lana 106,
Twelve Angry Men 1225,
Twelve O'Clock High 68, 83, 135, 140, 147, 178, 208,
Twenty Million Miles to Earth 77,
Twilight of Honor 70,
Twilight Zone, The (1950s/'60s series) 34, 61, 62, 65, 70, 71, 82, 124, 125, 127, 141, 146, 147, 149, 161, 176, 178, 179, 192, 200, 212, 213,
Twilight Zone, The (1980s series) 237, 238,
Twilight Zone – the Movie 193,
Twist Around the Clock 104,
Tyler, Judy 31, 33, 34,
Tyler, Walter 85,
Tyler Moore, Mary 215, 218, 219, 220,

Ullman, Ellwood 129, 130, 134,
UNCLE (franchise) 13, 125, 175, 177, 213,
"Uncle Sam Wants You" 237,
Undefeated, The 131,
Undersea Kingdom 28, 103,
United Artists 63, 145, 146, 180,
Universal 119, 149, 156, 169, 212, 215, 218, 219,
Untouchables, The 10, 22, 33, 34, 65, 66, 67, 71, 76, 82, 90, 116, 124, 127, 137, 140, 152, 154, 178, 179, 184, 200, 221, 222,
Up Your Teddy Bear 186,

Valenty, Lily 72,
Vallee, Rudy 202, 203, 204, 205,
Valley of the Dragons 117,
Valley of the Headhunters 103,
Van Doren, Mamie 117,
Van Dyke, Dick 92, 232,
Van Patten, Joyce 210, 212,
Vanders, Warren 197,
Vee, Bobby 185,
Vegas 39, 83, 95, 124, 124, 125, 135, 161, 211, 252,

Vegas 193, 228,
Velez, Lupe 106,
Vellenger, Dirk 143,
Velvet Vampire, The 205,
Verne, Jules 120,
Verone, Gigi 151, 157,
Vice Squad 180,
Vietnam 10, 43, 110, 155, 193,
Village of the Giants 139,
Vincent, Virginia 215,
"Vino, Dinero Y Amore" 85,
Virginian, The 22, 61, 68, 115, 116, 207,
Viva Las Vegas 11, 44, 61, 74, 81, 87, **91 – 100**, 92, 94, 98, 101, 108, 109, 111, 112, 121, 123, 151, 188, 220, 223, 233,
"Viva Las Vegas" 91,
Voodoo Man, The 102,
Voyage to the Bottom of the sea (film) 65, 170,
Voyage to the Bottom of the Sea (tv series) 64, 89, 106, 124, 141, 147, 155, 169, 178, 200, 208, 213, 221,
Voyagers 79,

Wagner, Mike 210,
Wagon Train 62, 67, 107, 115, 116, 127, 162,
Walberg, Garry 207,
Wald, Jerry 52,
"Walking Distance" 70,
"Walking in a Dream" 41,
Wall Street 53,
Wallace, Francis 69, 70,
Walley, Deborah 107, 159, 162, 163, *164*, 185, 257,
Wallis, Hal 13, 24, 26, 27, 29, 31, 35, 38, 41, 46, 47, 55, 56, 57, 59, 61, 69, 72, 74, 75, 76, 85, 87, 93, 100, 112, 118, 119, 129, 146, 151, 152, 153, 156, 165, 166, 180, 182, 188, 201, 206, 208, 231, 247, 248, 251, 252, 258,
"The Walls Have Ears" 72,
Walters, Susan 236,
Walters, Nancy 55, 61,
Wanted – Dead or Alive 39, 77, 124, 220,
The War Wagon 201,
Ward, Burt 45,
Ward, Peggy 129,
Ward, Skip 165, 166, 170, 171,
Warners/Warner Bros. 25, 32, 45, 70, 149, 161, 184, 224, 236, 253,
Warner Bros. cartoons 110, 179,
Warren, Charles Marquis 207,
Warren, Katherine 31,

Wasp Woman, The 148,
Watergate 10,
Waters, John 109,
Watson, Debbie 124, 169,
Wayne, John 1, 29, 76, 131, 135, 155, 201, 204, 208, 248, 249, 251,
Wayne, Sid 164,
Weaver, Tom 134, 147, 148,
Webb, Robert 17,
"The Weird Tailor" 170,
Weire Brothers, the 174, 177,
Weisbart, David 17, 49, 63, 69,
Weisman, Ben 142, 164, 257, 259,
Weismuller, Johnny 103,
Weiss, Allan 55, 72, 76, 85, 90, 112, 118, 151, 165,
Welch, Lester 210,
Welch, Raquel 112, 117, 201,
Welcome Home, Elvis 42, 48, 190,
"Welcome to My World" 235,
Weld, Tuesday 48, 52, 53, 76, 106, 149, 250,
Welker, Frank 210, 212, 214,
"We'll Be Together" 72,
"We're Coming in Loaded" 72,
"We're Gonna Move" 17,
Werewolf 48, 255,
Werle, Barbara 129, 136, 138, 139, 207, 208, 209,
West, Christopher 189,
West, Mae 113, 146,
West, Red 48, 49, 51, 52, 55, 59, 63, 72, 80, 81, 85, 91, 98, 112, 115, 117, 119, 129, 131, 138, 141 151, 157, 159, 160, 180, 187, 190, 199, 202, 203, 238, 249, 253, 254, 255, 256, 258,
West Side Story 66, 185,
West, Sonny 48, 135, 197, 199, 203, 253, 256, 258,
"What a Wonderful Life" 63,
"What'd I Say?" 91,
"What Every Woman Lives For" 145,
What's New, Pussycat? 88,
"Wheels on my Heels" 112,
"When the Saints Go Marching In" 145, 146,
"When You Wore a Tulip" 210,
"Where No Man Has Gone Before" 83,
Where the Boys Are 120,
"The Whiffenpoof Song" 210,
"A Whistling Tune" 69,
White, Dan 31,
"Who Are You? Who Am I?" 189, 191,
"Who Killed Lenore Wingfield?" 110,

"Who Killed Sweet Betsy?" 39,
Who'll Stop the Rain? 53,
"Who Needs Money?" 180,
Who's Got the Action? 124,
Wild at Heart 242,
Wild Bunch, The 208,
Wild Guitar 126,
Wild in the Country 31, 48, 49, 51, **52–54**, 56, 61, 83, 106, 132, 240, 248, 249,
"Wild in the Country" 52, 56,
Wild in the Streets 53,
Wild is the Wind 27,
Wild Wild West, The 34, 48, 59, 61, 62, 64, 65, 82, 106, 116, 135, 137, 141, 148, 155, 161, 178, 184, 192, 204, 205, 221, 254,
Wild, Wild Winter 126, 185,
Wilder, Billy 176,
Willcox, Pete 237,
Williams, Bill 129, 136,
Williams, Edy 151, 157,
Williams, Hank 250,
Williams, John 174, 176,
Williams, Lori 91, 101, 108, 112, 119, 123, 129, 137,
Williams, Robert B. 81, 91,
Williams, Van 161,
Wilson, Dick 197,
Windbell, Morgan 202,
Winkler, Irving 174,
Winslow, Dick 35, 41, 46,
Winston, Helene 174, 210, 214,
Winter-a-Go-Go 126, 136, 153,
Winters, David 123,
Winters, Roland 55, 59, 63, 65,
Witch Who Came From the Sea, The 53,
Without Warning 180,
Witness for the Prosecution 176,
Wives and Lovers 76,
Wizard of Oz, The 140,
"Wolf Call" 119,
Women of the Prehistoric Planet 136, 155, 185,
"The Wonder of You" 225,
Wonder Woman 59, 75, 76, 79, 125, 139, 155, 211, 213,
"Wonderful World" 202,
Wong, Linda 150, 151, 152, 154,
"Won't You Come Home, Bill Bailey?" 151, 155,
Wood, Anita 239,
Wood, Ed 62, 154, 164,
Wood, Lana 126,

Wood, Natalie 20, 32,
Wood, Wilson 31, 81,
Woodbine, Paul 137,
Woods, Donald 101, 104, 106,
"Wooden Heart" 41,
Woodstock 10, 12, 14, 249,
Woodstock (film) 228,
"A World of Our Own" 81,
World Without End 130,
Worlock, Frederick 159, 163,
Wright, Roy C. 41,
Wyles, Caitlin 197,
Wynant, H.M. 81, 82,

Yancy Derringer 135,
Yagher, Jeff 237, 238,
Yankee Doodle Dandy 38,
Yarnall, Celeste 202, 205,
"Yellow Rose of Texas" 91,
"Yoga Is As Yoga Does" 165,
Yogi Bear (character/franchise) 105, 233,
York, Kay 165,
"You Can't Say No in Acapulco" 85,
"You Don't Have to Say You Love Me" 225,

"You Don't Know Me" 180,
"You Gotta Stop" 165,
You Only Live Twice 191,
"You've Lost That Loving Feeling" 225,
"Young and Beautiful" 31,
Young Billy Young 200,
Young Dillinger 123,
"Young Dreams" 35, 38,
Young Frankenstein 144,
Young Lawyers, The 155,
Young Lions, The 53,
Young, Gig 27, 69, 71,
Young, Ned 31,
Young, Skip 24,
Young, Tony 207,
York, Francine 129, 135, 137,
"Your Groovy Self" 189, 191,
"Your Time Hasn't Come Yet, Baby" 189,

Zapped 116,
Zimbalist, Stephanie 236,
Zuckert, Bill 210, 213,
Zugsmith, Albert 117, 135, 193,

currently available from Amazon and/or McFarland

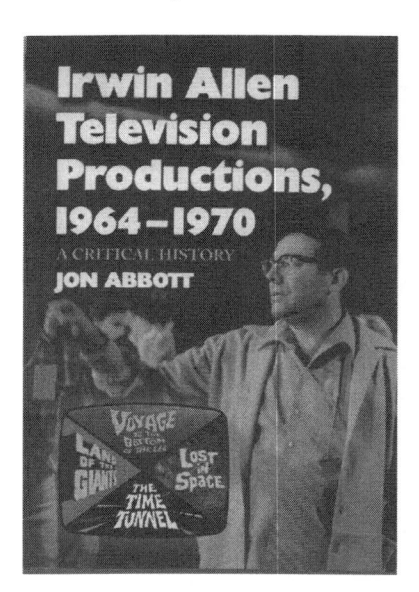

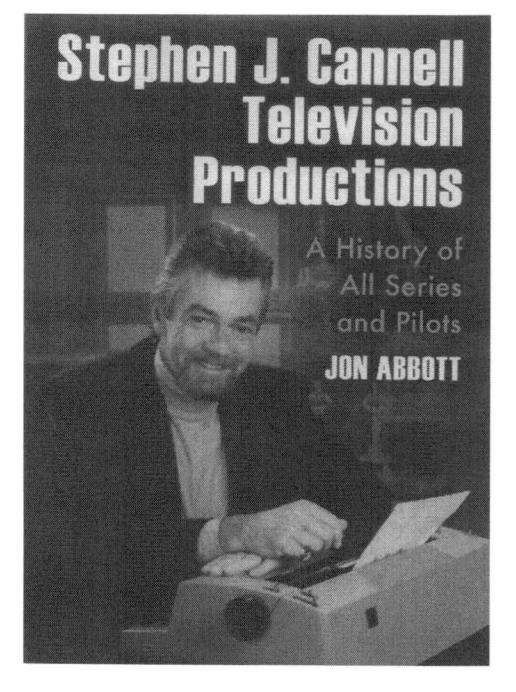

about the author

Jon Abbott has been writing professionally for over thirty years, having started out in 1982 by writing brief previews and reviews for the London listings magazine *City Limits*. For two years he contributed an annual report on the U.S. TV season to the trade paper *Television Weekly* before it was amalgamated with *Broadcast*. Since then, he has written over 400 articles and features for two dozen different trade, specialist, and populist publications, including numerous regular columns and features.

In 1983, he wrote his first article for the British science-fiction and fantasy media magazine *Starburst*, on the cult series *The Prisoner*. This was followed by features on *The Outer Limits, Danger Man, Voyage to the Bottom of the Sea, The Man from UNCLE, V, The Greatest American Hero, Blue Thunder, Knight Rider, Airwolf, Streethawk, Otherworld, ALF, Batman, Battlestar Galactica, The Time Tunnel, Fantastic Journey, Land of the Giants,* and *The Invisible Man*. For the companion title *TV Zone*, he has written about *Misfits of Science, Beauty and the Beast, Planet of the Apes, Fantastic Journey, Quantum Leap,* supernatural anthology shows, *Starman, Man from Atlantis, The Incredible Hulk, Spider-Man, Logan's Run, The Invaders, The Avengers,* and *Hercules--the Legendary Journeys*.

For six years he wrote TV news and individual features for *Video Today* in the popular column *Time-Shift*, which he proposed in 1984 and which became one of the most well-received features in the magazine. These pages included previews of new shows, retrospectives on popular old series, genre pieces, and regular updates on the U.S. TV scene. He wrote individual features on *Night Gallery, Dallas, Dynasty, Soap, The Mary Tyler Moore Show, Hill Street Blues, Mike Hammer,* **Britain's Euston Films, producers Donald Bellisario and Quinn Martin,** *Bilko, V, The Invaders, Cheers, Police Squad, Lou Grant, The A-Team, Crazy Like a Fox, The Equalizer, The Prisoner, The Twilight Zone, Lost in Space, L.A. Law, Moonlighting, Mission: Impossible, Star Trek--the Next Generation, The Time Tunnel,* supernatural anthology shows, the anti-violence-on-TV lobby, and the arrival of satellite TV. He also reviewed video releases. Particularly successful were the occasional TV Index features listing the status of then-current American shows both in the U.S. and the U.K.

Between October 1984 and March 1986 he wrote a regular column of criticism and comment on U.K. scheduling policy for the highly regarded industry journal *Stills*, and from September 1986 he had a number of features on program planning developments in British, American and satellite TV published in *Media Week*. These features covered such issues as the program scheduling strategies of ITV, the birth and growth of Sky Television, a comparison of the original SuperChannel and Sky satellite services, the U.S. TV seasons, video releases of popular television series, merchandising spin-offs from television series, how British broadcasters used imported American programmes in their schedules, the perils of sponsorship and the American experience, television censorship, the merger of satellite broadcasters Sky and BSB, and the purchase of MTM by U.K. broadcaster TVS.

In 1988 he began contributing to *What Satellite* magazine, writing features on such shows as *The Legend of Custer, Hawk, Lost in Space, 21, Jump Street, St. Elsewhere, Murphy Brown, The Flash, Melrose Place, Beverly Hills 90210,* Steven Bochco's *Civil Wars,* Stephen Cannell's *Stingray, The Simpsons, Land of the Giants, Tom and Jerry, Taxi, Cheers, Frasier* and *The Twilight Zone.*

For *The Dark Side,* a horror and sci-fi magazine, he has provided features on *Alien Nation, The Outer Limits, Werewolf, Land of the Giants, Star Trek, Star Trek--the Next Generation, Voyage to the Bottom of the Sea, Lost in Space,* the Stephen King mini-series *It, The Flash,* and *The X-Files.*

For *Video Buyer* he covered the video release of *Star Trek, V, The Avengers, Robin of Sherwood, Doctor Who,* the Marvel Video Comics, '50s sci-fi films, the early *Superman* serials and TV shows, the output of the Hanna-Barbera and Warner Brothers animation studios, *The Outer Limits, The Twilight Zone,* and *Twin Peaks.* For *Video World* he covered the video release of *Lost in Space, Cheers, The Simpsons,* and *Twin Peaks* and wrote their *Satellite Preview* column, which has included features on *Beverly Hills 90210, The New Avengers, Charlie's Angels, MASH, Twin Peaks,* Robin Hood films, *Quantum Leap, Lou Grant, Star Trek--Voyager, Earth 2, The Invaders, Kolchak--the Night Stalker, Planet of the Apes, Alien Nation, Automan, Manimal, Starsky and Hutch, Murder One, The X-Files,* modern westerns, *Space--Above and Beyond, Bewitched, Star Trek: Deep Space Nine, Starman, Strange Luck,* and *Hercules--the Legendary Journeys.*

In November 1989 he was awarded a special commendation for his writing on American TV and satellite TV in *Media Week* from the first *Broadcast Journalist Awards,* sponsored by TV-am.

During 1990 and 1991 he produced the column *Broadcast News,* a monthly collection of strange stories, anecdotes, and comment and criticism on television for *What Video* magazine.

In 1995, he was asked to contribute a monthly TV news column for *Home Entertainment,* and also wrote additional features on the U.S. TV season, the Cartoon Network and TNT, and Bravo's `Weird Worlds' strip. He was also invited to join the writing team of *SFX,* for which he reviewed *Robocop--the series, The X-Files, Sliders, Highlander, and Space: Above and Beyond.* For `Yesterday's Heroes', a regular monthly feature in the early issues of *SFX,* he featured *The Six Million Dollar Man, Wonder Woman, Blue Thunder, The Invisible Man, Randall and Hopkirk (Deceased), UFO, The Time Tunnel, Manimal, Max Headroom, The Man from UNCLE, Voyage to the Bottom of the Sea, Starman, V, Batman, Mission: Impossible, The Incredible Hulk* and *Land of the Giants.* For another then-new publication, *Cult Times,* he wrote about *Earth 2, The Six Million Dollar Man, Kolchak--the Night Stalker,* and *Sliders.*

In 1996, he was invited to write for the SF media magazine *Dreamwatch* and the new publications *Infinity* and *Comedy Review.* For *Comedy Review,* he prepared features and episode listings for the series *Soap* and *MASH.* For *Infinity,* he wrote a monthly *Cult TV* column and contributed articles on *The X-Files, War of the Worlds--the series, Space--Above and Beyond, V, Star Trek: Deep Space Nine, Dark Skies* and *Lois and Clark: New Adventures of Superman.* For *Dreamwatch,* he wrote about *The Green Hornet,* the *Fantasy Worlds of Irwin Allen* documentary, *The X-Files,* sci-fi in *The Simpsons, Fantastic Journey, The Man from Atlantis, Fireball XL-5,* the 1950s *Superman* series, and *The Pretender.* His exclusive reviews of *Millennium* and *Dark Skies* were the first published in the U.K.

Over a five year period between 1997 and 2001, he covered over forty episodes of different vintage sci-fi series for the `Fantasy Flashback' series for *TV Zone,* which featured an individual episode of a classic TV fantasy series examined in detail. Shows covered included *Star Trek, The Outer Limits, The Time Tunnel, Lost in Space, Batman, Voyage to the Bottom of the Sea, Mork and Mindy, Battlestar Galactica, The Greatest American Hero, Once a Hero, The Flash, Land of the Giants, Otherworld, The Man from UNCLE, The Wild Wild West, Airwolf, Kolchak--the Night Stalker, The Invaders, Thunderbirds, Quantum Leap, Mission: Impossible, Bewitched, The Flintstones, The Twilight Zone, Streethawk,* and *I Dream of Jeannie.* He also reviewed third season *Stargate* for *TV Zone,* and later wrote a `Retro TV' column for *TV Zone* covering all aspects of classic TV.

In 2006, American publishers McFarland published his book *Irwin Allen Television Productions 1964-1970,* a detailed critical review of the 1960s sci-fi series *Lost in Space, Voyage to the Bottom of the Sea, The Time Tunnel,* and *Land of the Giants*, and in 2009 *Stephen J. Cannell Television Productions: A History of All Series and Pilots*, a critical study of 22 series from this prolific producer, including *The Rockford Files, The A-Team,* and *Wiseguy*. Also in 2009, the Irwin Allen book was reprinted in softback. Now concentrating solely on 20th century film and TV, he is currently working on further book projects. Forthcoming are *20th Century Time Travel Television and Movies, Cool TV of the 1960s: Three Shows That Changed the World,* and *Strange New World: Sex Films of the 1970s.*

Free Reading

See my lists on the Internet Movie Data Base, all under the pre-fix DISCOVER...

coming in 2015 from the same author

Cool TV of the 1960s: Three Shows that Changed the World

It was perhaps synchronicity, everything in the right place at the right time. After Prohibition, the Depression, WWII, and McCarthyism, mainstream America wanted some fun--in color. The post-war world was ready for a new age for which Elvis and JFK had paved the way. When pop music, the art world, and the fashion world told the rest of the world to lighten up and loosen up, television followed other aspects of popular culture just as enthusiastically as the public did--and the buzzword of 1960s pop culture and media was NEW! NEW! NEW!

The 1960s was an extraordinary time of creativity for television, with over thirty classic shows on the air in the mid-1960s simultaneously. September 1964 had seen the debut of secret agent show *The Man from UNCLE*, which in 1965 soared up the ratings to become an all-media phenomenon. Although its beginning was a little more complicated, *The Man from UNCLE* was conceived quite bluntly as a TV version of James Bond, but with an American and a Russian agent working side by side. It became an entity in its own right when development fell to the enormously creative Sam Rolfe, who single-handedly devised the complicated, multi-faceted organisation that was the United Network Command for Law Enforcement--UNCLE. The end result was the most dynamic, complex, fast-paced, action-packed, exhilarating adventure show of the 20th century; as the first television series to employ the hand-held Arriflex camera, the faddish, youth-orientated shows that preceded it moved at a snail's pace in comparison.

But with the death of President Kennedy, killed while the pilot was filming, the brave new world of detente, youthful hope and co-operation that UNCLE represented had taken a severe blow. As a result, *The Man from UNCLE* became less of a hopeful dream and more of an escapist fantasy in the years that followed. UNCLE wanted global peace too, and worked toward that idealistic shared vision of 1960s youth, but instead of growing its hair long and throwing flowers around, it wore a dinner suit and used smoke bombs and bullets!

But 1966 was to get wilder still. The *Batman* TV series had made its debut in January 1966 as a mid-season replacement that, following dire test screenings, ABC had no great hopes for. This colorful and stylish parody of the popular comic-book character delighted kids and adults alike with its bizarre confrontations between the preposterous cowled boy scout Batman and marvelous performances from familiar Hollywood character actors as the heroes' eccentric adversaries. It became television's second major fad of the 1960s.

The primary legacy of the *Batman* TV show was to give everybody in film and TV permission to go completely loopy, and late '60s film and TV still looks quite bizarre today because of it. Nowhere was this more evident than in the wacky TV series *The Monkees*, a half-hour freestyle sit-com imitating the madcap style of the Beatles feature films. The show was the precursor of the pop video, and the birth of the manufactured boy band, and the on-screen spot gags, parodies, and imaginings of the four leads pre-date series such as *The Simpsons* and *Family Guy* by decades. There had been nothing like these three series before.

Cool TV of the 1960s looks at the origins, development, and influence on surrounding media of *The Man from UNCLE, Batman,* and *The Monkees,* and provides the most detailed study to date of every single episode of all three series, their feature film versions, and spin-off *The Girl from UNCLE*, each one a total original that displays 1960s media styles, fashions and obsessions in all their influential and inspirational glory.

This is the story of the secret agent craze, the super-hero fad, and the first boy band--three media phenomena of the 1960s that still influence pop culture today, productions unique among most television shows of any decade in that their influence spread beyond television to affect all aspects of other media as well--books, film, music, fashion, and advertising.

JON ABBOTT is a freelance writer and pop culture enthusiast with over four hundred articles on TV and film published in over two dozen different magazines, trade, specialist, and populist. He has previously written about the four pulp sci-fi series *Lost in Space, Voyage to the Bottom of the Sea, The Time Tunnel,* and *Land of the Giants* in *Irwin Allen Television Productions 1964-1970* (McFarland, 2006) and the creator of *The Rockford Files* and *The A-Team* in *Stephen J. Cannell Productions: A History of All Series and Pilots* (McFarland, 2009). He lives in Brighton, England.

coming in 2015 from the same author

Strange New World: Sex Films of the 1970s

To look at the world of the past through films can be a sobering insight into how things have changed, but to look at the world of the 20th century through sex films is to witness a world that is almost inexplicable. In no decade is this experience more bizarre than the 1970s, and yet it is less than half a century in the past. Was society really so strange and different only forty years ago?

JON ABBOTT, born in 1956 and a teenager in the 1970s, looks back at the era through over two hundred films exploiting sex and nudity, some of which he loved, and some of which he... liked a little less!

This opinionated and fact-filled history looks at the strange new world that adults of both sexes and all ages and sexual preferences found themselves in during the 1970s and surrounding decades, from the 1950s to the present day. It looks at films from all around the world, including America, Britain, France, Italy, Sweden, Germany, Spain, Czechoslovakia, China, and Japan, at sci-fi, horror, crime thrillers, comedies that weren't funny, and serious-minded films that were hilarious. Some of the best-known masters of sexploitation are well represented--Stanley Long, Greg Smith, Joe Sarno, Russ Meyer, Mac Ahlberg, Jess Franco, Jean Rollin, Tinto Brass--as are some of the sex films' most beautiful and prolific practitioners--Sylvia Kristel, Gloria Guida, Lina Romay, Maria Forsa, Edwige Fenech, Felicity Devonshire, Christina Lindberg, Joelle Coeur... and such mainstream movie names as Jane Fonda, Jenny Agutter, Julie Christie, and Pam Grier.

These films were often not pornography, as we understand the term. But what were they? Who made these films and why, and who were they made for? What did they say then, and what do they tell us now? In some cases, what were we thinking?? But in others, what have we lost?

JON ABBOTT is a freelance writer and pop culture enthusiast with over four hundred articles on TV and film published in over two dozen different magazines, trade, specialist, and populist. He has had two previous books published by McFarland in the U.S., and lives in Brighton, England

Printed in Great Britain
by Amazon.co.uk, Ltd.,
Marston Gate.